BASIC CONVERSATIONAL
ITALIAN

Robert A. Hall Jr.
CORNELL UNIVERSITY

Cecilia M. Bàrtoli
UNIVERSITY OF ROME

HOLT, RINEHART AND WINSTON
New York — Toronto

33395–0113

Printed in the United States of America

INTRODUCTION

It has been the authors' intent, in preparing this book, to provide a text for students of elementary Italian which could be used in accordance with modern audio-lingual methods, but which would at the same time be adaptable to a more traditional approach. For this purpose, the book has been divided into forty conversations, and after each pair of conversations a grammar unit has been provided; in addition, the student's need for reading matter has been met by a series of eight narrative selections based on the material learned to date. A supplement on phonetics and orthography and one on the inflection of substantives and verbs provide brief résumés of these points, and a separate list of irregular verbs presents the forms of all such verbs used in the text.

1. *The Conversations.* Each of these is built around a specific situation reflecting some aspect of Italian life or culture, and introduces characters who are typical of modern Italian youth. The language of the conversations is that which is normal among present-day educated Italians, especially in Rome. The student should learn each conversation by heart; the conversations should be presented in class by the customary audio-lingual techniques, including choral repetition and rapid-fire individual repetition. When the students have learned the conversation, they may take turns in standing up and acting it out before the class, making it as realistic and life-like as possible.

2. *The Exercises* which accompany the conversations are intended to reinforce the learner's knowledge of the material of the dialogues themselves, to help him learn how to vary the material, and to afford a review of previous material. The exercises may be done either in writing or orally; if the latter, the student may prepare them in advance if it is desired, but he should be discouraged from writing them down before class meets and then simply reading them off.

3. *The Grammar Units* embody discussions of such aspects of grammatical structure as are relevant to the understanding and extension of the immediately preceding or immediately following conversations. In general, the illustrations of grammatical points are drawn from sentences the student has already learned. The exposition has been kept as simple as possible, consonant with accuracy and clarity in the presentation; not grammar for its own sake, but grammar to help the learner use the language more accurately and extensively has been our aim. Terminological innovations have been

iii

made only where traditional grammatical analysis is inadequate. The grammatical pattern exercises accompanying each grammar unit may be used as either written or oral exercises; these exercises are of course only small samples of the almost infinite number of variations which could be built up on every point.

4. *The Narrative Passages* may either be assigned beforehand for class use and translation, or may be treated as rapid, unprepared reading for comprehension. In these passages, the style is somewhat closer to formal expository usage than is that of the conversations, but the language of the narrative passages has been kept at approximately the same level of difficulty as that of the surrounding material. In the new vocabulary of the narrative passages, at least half of the words introduced are obvious cognates of related English words and therefore offer the learner no difficulty; and many of the remaining new words are derived from those which the learner already knows.

5. *Review* of the conversations may be given from time to time, especially by having an appropriate number of students act out earlier conversations with extempore variations based on grammatical structures and new vocabulary studied since the dialogue was originally learned.

6. *The Grammatical Supplements* are intended to provide convenient sources of reference, rather than to be the object of study for their own sake. The teacher may of course assign various sections of the supplements for outside study; but it is suggested that, if class or home work is to be based on the grammatical supplements, it be embodied in variation drills (substitution, correlation, transformation, progressive variation, etc.) rather than assigned for rote memorization.

7. *The Vocabularies* provide a listing of all the Italian words used in the text of the conversations and the narrative passages, or introduced separately in the exercises or grammatical units. The English-Italian vocabulary is primarily a reverse index of the Italian-English, and is not intended to function as a complete dictionary for any of the concepts referred to by the English key words.

Many of the illustrations used in the text have been made available through the Italian State Tourist Office (Foto ISTO).

In the preparation of the book, Miss Bàrtoli has provided the Italian conversations and narrative passages, and Mr. Hall the remaining parts of the text.

R. A. H., Jr.

Ithaca, N. Y. and Rome, Italy   C. M. B.

TABLE OF CONTENTS

Conversation Unit 1 *Office of a Publisher in Rome*   3

Conversation Unit 2 *Asking for Directions*   7

Grammar Unit I   12
    1. The Indefinite Article; **2.** The Definite Article; **3.** The Plural of Nouns.

Conversation Unit 3 *Catching a Train*   17

Conversation Unit 4 *Telling Time*   20

Grammar Unit II   24
    4. Combinations of Prepositions + Definite Article; **5.** Present of **èssere**; **6.** Present of **stare**; **7.** Formal and Informal Address.

Conversation Unit 5 *At the Restaurant*   28
       PRIMA LETTURA: *Viaggiando per l'Italia*, p. 32

Conversation Unit 6 *Getting a Room*   36

Grammar Unit III   40
    8. The Partitive; **9.** Present Tense of Verbs (*First Conjugation*); **10.** Present Tense of **avere**; **11.** Present of Modal Auxiliaries.

Conversation Unit 7 *At the Museum*   46

Conversation Unit 8 *At a Newsstand*   50

Grammar Unit IV   54
    12. Adjectives; **13.** Demonstrative Adjectives.

Conversation Unit 9 *The Weather*   60

Conversation Unit 10 *At the Bank*   64
       LETTURA SECONDA: *In un Ristorante all'Aperto*, p. 68

Grammar Unit V   70
    14. Possessive Adjectives; **15.** Present Tense of the Second Conjugation; **16.** Present Tense of the Third Conjugation; **17.** Present Tense of **andare**, **dare**, **dire**, and **fare**.

Conversation Unit 11 *In St. Peter's*   78

Conversation Unit 12 *Buying Clothes*   82

Grammar Unit VI   86
    18. Conjunctive Pronouns—Direct and Indirect Object; **19.** Reflexive Verbs; **20.** Impersonal-Passive Use of Reflexive Verbs; **21. piacere**; **22. conóscere** and **sapere**.

Conversation Unit 13 *In an Espresso Bar*   94

CONVERSATION UNIT 14 *Strolling in Via del Tritone*   97
   Grammar Unit VII   102
      23. Pro-Phrases **ci**, **vi**, **ne**; **24.** Imperatives (First and Second Person); **25.** Subjunctive in Formal Commands (Third Person); **26.** Irregular Noun Plurals.
CONVERSATION UNIT 15 *The Pincio at Sunset*   108
      LETTURA TERZA: *Autunno Romano*, p. 114

CONVERSATION UNIT 16 *How Do You Feel?*   116
   Grammar Unit VIII   120
      27. Comparative and Superlative; **28.** The Past Participle; **29.** The Compound Past; **30.** Present Indicative of **tenere**, **venire**, **uscire**.
CONVERSATION UNIT 17 *Planning a Trip*   127
CONVERSATION UNIT 18 *At San Paolo Fuori Le Mura*   132
   Grammar Unit IX   136
      31. The Future; **32.** Present tense with **da**; **33.** Nouns with Masculine Singular in **-o** and Feminine Plural in **-a**; **34.** Plural of Masculine Nouns in **-a**; **35.** Adverbs in **-mente**.
CONVERSATION UNIT 19 *University Students*   142
CONVERSATION UNIT 20 *Sending a Letter*   146
      LETTURA QUARTA: *Una Gita nei Castelli Romani*, p. 150

   Grammar Unit X   152
      36. Disjunctive Personal Pronouns; **37.** Conjunctive Personal Pronouns—Indirect Object + Direct Object; **38.** Verbs—Imperfect; **39.** Verbs—Agreement of Past Participle in Compound Past with **avere**.
CONVERSATION UNIT 21 *The Roman Forum*   158
CONVERSATION UNIT 22 *Chitchat on the Palatine*   164
   Grammar Unit XI   168
      40. Compound Past of Reflexive Verbs; **41.** The Present Participle; **42.** Progressive Phrases; **43.** Pro-Complements: Combinations with **ne**; **44.** Interrogative and Relative Pronouns.
CONVERSATION UNIT 23 *Buying Tobacco*   174
CONVERSATION UNIT 24 *Planning a Visit*   178
   Grammar Unit XII   182
      45. Verbs: The Conditional; **46.** Negatives; **47.** Definite Article in Generic Meaning; **48.** Diminutive Suffixes; **49.** Apocope.
CONVERSATION UNIT 25 *Roman History*   188
      LETTURA QUINTA: *Un Po' di Storia Romana*, p. 193

CONVERSATION UNIT 26 *On the Telephone*   196

TABLE OF CONTENTS

Grammar Unit XIII 200
    50. The Past Absolute; **51.** Dative of Persons Affected; **52. ecco** +
Pro-Complements.

Conversation Unit 27 *After Christmas Vacation* 206

Conversation Unit 28 *At a Pensione in Perugia* 210

Grammar Unit XIV 214
    53. Verbs: The Subjunctive; **54.** Verbs: Perfect Phrases; **55.** Relative
Pronoun Phrases: **il quale, etc.**

Conversation Unit 29 *Going to a Concert* 220

Conversation Unit 30 *In the Tuscan Hills* 224

           LETTURA SESTA: *Una Vacanza a Porto S. Stèfano,* p. 229

Grammar Unit XV 231
    56. Verbs: The Subjunctive—Automatic Uses; **57.** Ordinal
adjectives; **58.** Collectives on Numerals; **59.** Pre-Vocalic Forms of
Prepositions and Conjunctions.

Conversation Unit 31 *Trains vs. Automobiles* 236

Conversation Unit 32 *In the Dining Car* 240

Grammar Unit XVI 244
    60. Verbs: The Subjunctive—Meaningful Uses; **61.** Term of
Comparison other than Noun or Pronoun; **62.** Prepositions and
Prepositional Phrases; **63.** Elision.

Conversation Unit 33 *At the Beach* 250

Conversation Unit 34 *A Recent Movie* 254

Grammar Unit XVII 258
    64. The Past Subjunctive; **65.** Transformations of Dependent
Clauses; **66.** Pro-Complements in Modal Phrases.

Conversation Unit 35 *Learning a Foreign Language* 264

        LETTURA SETTIMA: *Un Concerto a Castel Sant'Angelo,* p. 268

Conversation Unit 36 *The Italian Elections* 272

Grammar Unit XVIII 276
    67. Verbs; Adjectives in **-ante, -ente**; **68.** Verb + Preposition +
Infinitive; **69.** Verbs: Pro-Complements with Impersonal **si**;
70. Verbs: Future of Probability; **71.** Verbs: Subjunctive with Adjectives Indicating Extremes.

Conversation Unit 37 *At a Café in Via Veneto* 282

Conversation Unit 38 *At Santa Maria Sopra Minerva* 286

Grammar Unit XIX 290
    72. Verbs: Passive Phrases; **73.** Verbs—Causative Phrases;
74. Verbs: **fare** and Impersonal Meteorological Expressions;
75. Exclamations; **76.** Noun-Suffixes: Augmentative and Pejorative.

CONVERSATION UNIT 39 *A Street Accident* 296
CONVERSATION UNIT 40 *Veii and the Etruscans* 300
LETTURA OTTAVA: *Cervèteri*, p. 304

Grammar Unit XX 306
    77. Verbs: Subjunctive with **sembrare**, **parere**, **etc.**; **78.** Verbs:
Past Subjunctive with **come se** or **quasi**; **79.** Further Constructions
with **fare**; **80.** Uses of the Preposition **da**; **81.** Prepositions after
Adjectives.

APPENDICES
    I. Italian Phonetics and Orthography ii
   II. Italian Substantive and Verb Inflection vii
 III. Vocabularies:
      Italian-English xviii
      English-Italian xl

INDEX lxi

Foto Goldman — Rapho-Guillumette

Basic Conversational Italian

Foto Bright — Rapho-Guillumette

Via del Tritone, Roma

Office of a Publisher in Rome

Miss Fulvia Bruni, who has just arrived in the city, meets Mr. Giovanni Dossi, an old friend of her parents.

LA SIGNORINA BRUNI — ¹Buon giorno, signor Dossi.

Il SIGNOR DOSSI — ²Buon giorno, signorina. ³Lei è la signorina Bruni?

LA SIGNORINA BRUNI — ⁴Sì signore, sono Fulvia Bruni.

Il SIGNOR DOSSI — ⁵Si accòmodi, signorina. ⁶Che piacere fare la sua conoscenza! ⁷Come sta?

LA SIGNORINA BRUNI — ⁸Bene, grazie. ⁹E Lei?

Il SIGNOR DOSSI — ¹⁰Non c'è male, grazie.

(Più tardi)

Il SIGNOR DOSSI — ¹¹Ecco una léttera per Lei.

LA SIGNORINA BRUNI — ¹²Davvero? ¹³Per me? ¹⁴Oh! che sorpresa! ¹⁵Molte grazie e arrivederLa.

Il SIGNOR DOSSI — ¹⁶Prego, signorina Bruni. ¹⁷ArrivederLa.

MISS BRUNI — ¹Good morning, Mr. Dossi.

MR. DOSSI — ²Good morning, miss. ³You are Miss Bruni?

MISS BRUNI — ⁴Yes, sir, I am Fulvia Bruni.

MR. DOSSI — ⁵Sit down, miss. ⁶What a pleasure [it is] to make your acquaintance! ⁷How are you?

MISS BRUNI — ⁸Well, thank you. ⁹And you?

MR. DOSSI — ¹⁰Not badly, thank you.

(Later)

MR. DOSSI ¹¹Here's a letter for you.

MISS BRUNI — ¹²Really? ¹³For me? ¹⁴Oh, what a surprise! ¹⁵Many thanks and good-bye.

MR. DOSSI — ¹⁶You're welcome, Miss Bruni. ¹⁷Good-bye.

NOTES

1. **Signore, signorina**. The basic meaning of **signore** is *gentleman*, *lord*; that of **signorina** is *young lady*. **Signorina** is a diminutive based on **signora** *lady;Mrs.*

2. **Signor** for *Mr.* is the form used before a name. When it is not used before a name, its form is **signore**.

3. When speaking to someone with the titles **signor(e), signora, signorina,** no definite article is used; when speaking about someone with these titles, the definite article must be used.

4. **Lei** means both *you* (in formal direct address) and *she*, *her*. In the meaning of *you*, **Lei** and related forms are usually capitalized, even when they come to stand in the middle of a word (as in **arrivederLa,** sentences 15 and 17).

Leggete

Il Messaggero

A sinistra:
Il Colosseo

Foto Henle — Monkmeyer

In basso:
Ponte sul Tévere

Foto Silberstein — Monkmeyer

Esercizi

A. *Dica in italiano* (Say in Italian):

1. Good morning, Mr. Dossi. 2. Good morning, miss. 3. Are you (= you are) Miss Bruni? 4. Yes, sir, I am Fulvia Bruni.
5. Sit down, miss. 6. What a pleasure [it is] to make your aqcuaintance! 7. How are you? 8. Well, thank you. And you? 9. Not bad, thank you.
10. Here is a letter for you. 11. Really? For me? 12. Oh, what a surprise! 13. Many thanks and good-bye. 14. You're welcome, Miss Bruni. Good-bye.

B. *Dia una risposta adatta, in italiano, a ciascuna delle seguenti frasi* (Give a suitable answer in Italian for each of the following sentences):

1. Buon giorno, signore. 2. Buon giorno, signorina. 3. Lei è il signor Dossi? 4. Lei è la signorina Bruni?
5. Come sta? 6. E Lei? 7. Si accómodi, signorina. 8. Ecco una léttera per Lei. 9. Per me?
10. Grazie, signorina. 11. Grazie, signore. 12. ArrivederLa, signore. 13. ArrivederLa, signorina.

C. *Dica in italiano* (Say in Italian):

1. Mi dica buon giorno (*Say* **buon giorno** *to me*). 2. Mi dica arrivederLa. 3. Dica buon giorno a un altro studente (*Say* **buon giorno** *to another student* [*m.*]). 4. Dica buon giorno a un'altra studentessa (*Say* **buon giorno** to another student [*f.*]).
5. Dica arrivederLa a un altro studente. 6. Dica arrivederLa a un'altra studentessa.

D. *Faccia le seguenti domande in italiano* (Ask the following questions in Italian):

1. Mi domandi se sono il signor Dossi (*Ask me if I am Mr. Dossi*). 2. Mi domandi se sono la signorina Bruni. 3. Mi domandi come sto (*Ask me how I am*). 4. Domandi a un altro studente se è il signor Dossi.
5. Domandi a un'altra studentessa se è la signorina Bruni. 6. Domandi a un altro studente come sta (*Ask another student how he is*). 7. Domandi a un'altra studentessa come sta (*Ask another student how she is*).

E. DIALOGUE:

Act out the scene between Fulvia Bruni and Mr. Dossi. Practice doing the scene until you are perfectly at home in both parts.

Asking for Directions

Fulvia Bruni plans to do some sightseeing and shopping, but before starting out she has first to locate the "Firenze" restaurant and the post office.

FULVIA — ¹Buon giorno, signore, scusi ...

UN PASSANTE — ²Buon giorno ...?

FULVIA — ³Mi saprebbe dire dov'è la trattoria Firenze?

IL PASSANTE — ⁴Certamente, signorina, è proprio accanto alla stazione. ⁵Sa dov'è la stazione?

FULVIA — ⁶No, purtroppo non so neppure dov'è la stazione.

FULVIA — ¹Good morning, sir; excuse me ...

A PASSER-BY — ²Good morning ...?

FULVIA — ³Could you tell me where is the "Firenze" restaurant?

THE PASSER-BY — ⁴Certainly, miss; it is right next to the station. ⁵Do you know where the station is?

FULVIA — ⁶No, unfortunately I don't even know where the station is.

Nel centro della città

A SINISTRA
Foto ISTO

A DESTRA
Foto Bright — Rapho-Guillumette

IL PASSANTE — [7]Guardi, la stazione è lì, in quella piazza, a destra. [8]E la trattoria è proprio lì accanto.

FULVIA — [9]Grazie e buon giorno.

IL PASSANTE — [10]Prego, si figuri.

(Nella trattoria)

FULVIA — [11]Scusi, quella è la stazione, vero?

IL CAMERIERE — [12]Sì signorina.

FULVIA — [13]Sa se c'è un tabaccaio dentro la stazione?

IL CAMERIERE — [14]Sì signorina, è a sinistra appena entra.

FULVIA — [15]Grazie mille e scusi ...

IL CAMERIERE — [16]Dica pure ...

FULVIA — [17]C'è anche un ufficio postale?

IL CAMERIERE — [18]No, l'ufficio postale è fuori, ma non è lontano. [19]Guardi, vada sempre dritto e poi sùbito a destra.

FULVIA — [20]Grazie di nuovo.

IL CAMERIERE — [21]Prego e arrivederLa.

THE PASSER-BY — [7]Look; the station is there, in that square, on the right. [8]And the restaurant is right there next to it.

FULVIA — [9]Thank you and good morning.

THE PASSER-BY — [10]You're welcome; don't mention it.

(In the Restaurant)

FULVIA — [11]Excuse me, that's the station, isn't it?

THE WAITER — [12]Yes, miss.

FULVIA — [13]Do you know if there's a tobacconist inside the station?

THE WAITER — [14]Yes, miss, it's on the left just as you go in.

FULVIA — [15]A thousand thanks, and excuse me ...

THE WAITER — [16]Yes, ma'am ...?

FULVIA — [17]Is there a post office too?

THE WAITER — [18]No, the post office is outside, but it is not far away. [19]Look; go straight ahead and then sharply to the right.

FULVIA — [20]Thank you again.

THE WAITER — [21]You're welcome; and good-bye.

NOTES

1. **Vero?** (or **Non è vero?** *Isn't it true?* or **Nevvero?**) is an expression added to the end of a sentence (positive or negative) to get from the hearer an indication of agreement.
2. **Dica** or **dica pure** (literally meaning *say* or *just say*) is a formula widely used to encourage someone who is hesitant to speak.

CONVERSATION UNIT TWO

Il tabaccaio è a
sinistra appena
si entra
Foto ISTO

L' ufficio postale
non è lontano
*Foto Bright — Rapho-
Guillumette*

Esercizi

A. *Dica in italiano:*

1. Good morning, sir; excuse me. Could you tell me where the "Firenze" restaurant is? 2. Certainly, miss. It is right next to the station. 3. Do you know where the station is? 4. No, unfortunately I don't even know where the station is.

5. Look; the station is there, in that square, on the right. 6. And the restaurant is right there next to it. 7. Thank you and good morning. 8. You're welcome; don't mention it. 9. Excuse me, that's the station, isn't it?

10. Yes, miss. 11. Do you know if there's a tobacconist inside the station? 12. Yes, miss, it's on the left just as you go in. 13. A thousand thanks, and excuse me ... 14. Yes, ma'am (*lit.*, just speak)?

15. Is there a post office too? 16. No, the post office is outside; but it is not far away. 17. Look. Go straight ahead and then immediately to the right. 18. Thank you again. 19. You're welcome; and good-bye.

B. *Risponda in italiano a ciascuna delle seguenti domande* (Answer each of the following questions in Italian):

1. Mi saprebbe (*could*) dire dov'è la trattoria Firenze? 2. Sa dov'è la stazione? 3. Sa se c'è un tabaccaio dentro la stazione? 4. C'è anche l'ufficio postale? 5. Lei è la signorina Bruni? 6. Lei è il signor Dossi? 7. Come sta, signorina? 8. Come sta, signore? 9. C'è una léttera per me?

C. *Domandi a un altro studente (a un'altra studentessa):*

1. dov'è la trattoria. 2. dov'è la stazione. 3. dov'è un tabaccaio. 4. dov'è l'ufficio postale.

5. se sa dove c'è una trattoria. 6. se sa dove c'è un tabaccaio. 7. se sa dov'è la stazione. 8. se sa dov'è l'ufficio postale. 9. se c'è un tabaccaio dentro la stazione.

10. se c'è un ufficio postale dentro la stazione. 11. come sta. 12. se c'è una léttera per Lei.

D. *Mi domandi:*

1. dov'è la stazione. 2. dov'è il tabaccaio. 3. dov'è la trattoria. 4. dov'è l'ufficio postale.

5. dove c'è un tabaccaio. 6. se c'è un tabaccaio accanto alla stazione. 7. se c'è un ufficio postale accanto alla stazione. 8. se c'è una trattoria in quella piazza. 9. se c'è un tabaccaio in quella piazza.

10. se so ... (domande 1-9 [*questions* 1-9]).

E. I Numeri.

1. *Conti in italiano da uno a dieci* (Count in Italian from one to ten).

uno (1)	tre (3)	cinque (5)	sette (7)	nove (9)
due (2)	quattro (4)	sei (6)	otto (8)	dieci (10).

2. *Dia i numeri pari da due a dieci* (Give the even numbers from two to ten):

due (2)	quattro (4)	sei (6)	otto (8)	dieci (10)

3. *Dia i nùmeri dìspari da uno a nove* (Give the odd numbers from one to nine):

uno (1)	tre (3)	cinque (5)	sette (7)	nove (9)

F. Conversation:

1. Good morning, miss. 2. Do you know where the restaurant is? 3. Look, there is the restaurant, in that square, on the left. 4. Is the post office in that square, too?
5. No, the post office is on the right. Go straight ahead and then immediately to the right. 6. Thank you very much. 7. You are welcome; don't mention it.

G. Dialogue:

You stop someone and ask for the location of a restaurant (post-office, tobacconist, station).

GRAMMAR UNIT _____ I

1. THE INDEFINITE ARTICLE.

The indefinite article, meaning *a, an*, has the forms:

THE INDEFINITE ARTICLE		
	Masc.	*Fem.*
Before words beginning with a vowel	un	un'
Before words beginning with a *pure* consonant	un	una
Before words beginning with an *impure* consonant	uno	

An "impure" consonant is any of the following: **s** followed by a consonant; **z** ; **ps** and **gn**. A "pure" consonant is any other.

un ufficio	an office	**un'amica**	a friend (*f.*)
un signore	a gentleman	**un'eccezione**	an exception
un treno	a train	**un'òpera**	an opera
uno zio	an uncle	**una léttera**	a letter
uno studente	a student	**una signorina**	a young lady
uno sportello	a ticket-window	**una studentessa**	a student (*f.*)

2. THE DEFINITE ARTICLE.

The definite article, meaning *the*, has the forms:

THE DEFINITE ARTICLE				
	SINGULAR		PLURAL	
	Masc.	*Fem.*	*Masc.*	*Fem.*
Before words beginning with a vowel	l'	l'	gli	le
Before words beginning with a "pure" consonant	il	la	i	le
Before words beginning with an "impure" consonant	lo	la	gli	le

l'orario	*the* time-table	gli orari	*the* timetables
l'ufficio	*the* office	gli uffici	*the* offices
l'autunno	*the* autumn	gli autunni	*the* autumns
il signore	*the* gentleman	i signori	*the* gentlemen
il treno	*the* train	i treni	*the* trains
il pomeriggio	*the* afternoon	i pomeriggi	*the* afternoons

lo zio	*the* uncle	gli zii	*the* uncles
lo studente	*the* student	gli studenti	*the* students
lo sportello	*the* ticket-window	gli sportelli	*the* ticket-windows
l'amica	*the* friend (*f.*)	le amiche	*the* friends (*f.*)
l'eccezione	*the* exception	le eccezioni	*the* exceptions
l'òpera	*the* opera	le òpere	*the* operas
la signorina	*the* young lady	le signorine	*the* young ladies
la sorpresa	*the* surprise	le sorprese	*the* surprises
la studentessa	*the* student (*f.*)	le studentesse	*the* students (*f.*)

The form of the definite article is determined by the sound which begins the immediately following word, not the noun which the article modifies: thus, **uno studente** *a student*, but **un buono studente** *a good student*; **la léttera** *the letter*, but **l'altra léttera** *the other letter*.

🔴 **3.** THE PLURAL OF NOUNS.

The plural of the nouns presented so far follows these patterns:

THE PLURAL OF NOUNS		
GENDER	ENDING IN SINGULAR	ENDING IN PLURAL
Masculine	**-o**	**-i**
Feminine	**-a**	**-e**
Masculine or Feminine	**-e**	**-i**

Most, but not all, Italian nouns belong to one of these three types.

il treno	the train	**i treni**	the trains
l'autunno	the autumn	**gli autunni**	the autumns
lo sportello	the ticket-window	**gli sportelli**	the ticket-windows
la sorpresa	the surprise	**le sorprese**	the surprises
l'amica	the friend (*f.*)	**le amiche**	the friends (*f.*)
l'òpera	the opera	**le òpere**	the operas
il signore	the gentleman	**i signori**	the gentlemen
lo studente	the student	**gli studenti**	the students
l'eccezione	the exception	**le eccezioni**	the exceptions

When a noun ending in **-ca, -ga, -co** or **-go** forms its plural by simply adding **-e** or **-i** with no change in the pronunciation of the "hard" **c** or **g** of the stem, the resultant plural is automatically spelled with **-che, -ghe, -chi** or **ghi** respectively, as in **amica** *friend* (*f. sg.*), **amiche** *friends* (*f. pl.*).

- CINEMA -

Grammatical Exercises

A. *Give the Italian equivalents of the following:*

A	B
(1) ¹a gentleman	¹a young lady
²a student *(m.)*	²an acquaintance
³a tobacconist	³a letter
⁴a post office	⁴a student *(f.)*
⁵a waiter	⁵a question
⁶a train	⁶a restaurant
⁷an uncle	⁷a station
⁸a ticket-window	⁸a square
⁹an autumn	⁹a friend *(f.)*
¹⁰a timetable	¹⁰an exception
¹¹a passer-by	¹¹an opera

GRAMMAR UNIT ONE

(2) ¹the gentleman   ¹the young lady
      ²the student *(m.)*   ²the acquaintance
      ³the tobacconist   ³the letter
      ⁴the post office   ⁴the student *(f.)*
      ⁵the waiter   ⁵the question
      ⁶the train   ⁶the restaurant
      ⁷the uncle   ⁷the station
      ⁸the ticket-window   ⁸the square
      ⁹the autumn   ⁹the friend *(f.)*
      ¹⁰the timetable   ¹⁰the exception
      ¹¹the passer-by   ¹¹the opera

(3) ¹the gentlemen   ¹the young ladies
      ²the students *(m.)*   ²the acquaintances
      ³the tobacconists   ³the letters
      ⁴the post offices   ⁴the students *(f.)*
      ⁵the waiters   ⁵the questions
      ⁶the trains   ⁶the restaurants
      ⁷the uncles   ⁷the stations
      ⁸the ticket-windows   ⁸the squares
      ⁹the autumns   ⁹the friends *(f.)*
      ¹⁰the timetables   ¹⁰the exceptions
      ¹¹the passers-by   ¹¹the operas

B. *Using the combinations formed in Exercise* **A**, *as far as possible, make the following substitutions:*

1. Where is a ...? [*e.g.*, Where is a gentleman? Where is a student? Where is a tobacconist? *etc.*]   2. Where is the ...?   3. Where are the ... -s?   4. Here is a ... .   5. Here is the ... .   6. Here are the ... -s.   7. The ... is there.   8. The ... -s are there.

C. PROGRESSIVE VARIATION. *Give the Italian for:*

¹a tobacconist	⁶a letter	¹¹the passer-by	¹⁶the squares
²the tobacconist	⁷an exception	¹²a passer-by	¹⁷the square
³the tobacconists	⁸the exception	¹³a station	¹⁸a square
⁴the letters	⁹the exceptions	¹⁴the station	¹⁹a tobacconist
⁵the letter	¹⁰the passers-by	¹⁵the stations	²⁰the tobacconist

Roma-Firenze

(Trazione elettrica)

Treni: **1376** accel. 1e2 · **872** (48 ◆, A) accel. 1e2 · **RV** (◆872) rapido 1 cl. accel. · **1850** (◆) accel. 1e2 · **768** (A) diret. · **874** (◆) accel. 1e2 · **1206** (◆) accel. 1e2 · **68** (◆) 1e2

№	Alt. s.m.	Dist. Km	Stazione	1376	872 (48)	RV	1850	768	874	1206	68
4	58	—	■■ Roma Tèrmini ✕ p.	11 15	12 30	13 32	14 42				15 30
5	18	—	Roma Ostiense p.		12 39						
6	40	—	Roma Tuscolana p.		12 45						
7	20	5	■ Roma Tiburtina ℧ 254, 255, 288, 359	11 22	12 54		14 49				
8	27	17	■ Sette Bagni	11 37	13 06		15 03				
9	25	26	■ Monterotondo ✕ (K. 3)-Mentana (K. 6)	11 46	13 15		15 13				
10	31	38	■ Fara Sabina (K.16)-Montelibretti (K.11)	11 57	13 27		15 25				
11	35	49	■ Pòggio Mirteto ✕ (Km. 8)	12 08	13 39		15 36				
12	36	53	Gavignano Sabino		13 44		15 42				
13	41	58	■ Stimigliano (Km. 5) ℧	12 16	13 50		15 48				
14	39	61	■ Collevecchio-Poggio Sommavilla	—			15 53				
15	46	71	Civita Castellana K.9-Magliano ✕ K.6	12 30	14 03		16 04				
16	46	75	■ Gallese Teverina (Km. 4)	12 36	14 07		16 10				
17			a.	12 45	14 15		16 19				
18	52	84	■ Orte ✕ (Km. 4) Civitavecchia 253, Terni ed Ancona 287 p.	13 03			16 56	17 16			
19	68	92	■ Bassano in Teverina (Km. 4)	13 12			17 04				
20	87	97	■ Attigliano-Bomarzo ✕ (Km. 7) a.	13 17			17 09				
21			Viterbo 252 p.	13 18			17 10				
22	89	106	■ Alviano (Km. 4)	13 29			17 19				
23	93	113	■ Castiglione in Teverina (Km. 3)	13 36			17 25				
24	104	118	■ Baschi (Km. 3)-Montecchio (Km. 12)	13 43			17 31				
25	124	126	■ Orvieto ✕ Orvieto C. 947	14 04			17 40				
26	172	136	■ Allerona (Km. 7)-Castel Viscardo (K. 9)	14 18			17 51				
27	239	148	■ Fabro ✕ (Km. 5)-Ficulle (Km. 8)	14 33			18 04				
28	249	158	Città della Pieve (Km. 6)	14 45			18 13				
29			■ Chiusi-Chianciano Terme ✕ (K.11) a.	14 54	014 30		18 20 —				
30	252	165	Siena ed Empoli 221, Chianciano Terme 456 p.		014 31			17 06		18 36	
31	268	177	■ Panicale (Km. 7)-Sanfatucchio					17 18		18 48	
32	267	184	■ Castigliòn del Lago					17 26		18 57	
33			a.					17 36	18 12	19 06	
34	271	194	Terontola ✕ ... Perugia e Foligno 266 p.					18 20	18 14	19 11	
35	256	200	■ Cortona (Km. 6)-Camucia ✕					18 27		19 19	
36	259	211	■ Castigliòn Fiorentino					18 38		19 30	
37	264	217	■ Rigutino Frassineto (Km. 2)					18 45		19 37	
38	260	223	■ Olmo					18 51		19 43	
39	256	229	Arezzo ✕ Sinalunga 671, Pratovecchio a.	◆ AT	15 16			18 56	18 36	19 49	18 04
40			Stia 672, Città di Castello 457 p.	AT	15 17			19 10	18 37	20 04	18 05
41	258	235	■ Indicatore	676				19 17		20 11	
42	255	245	■ Ponticino	accel				19 27		20 21	
43	248	250	■ Laterina (Km. 6)					19 34		20 28	
44	207	255	■ Bùcine	1e2				19 40		20 34	
45	147	263	■ Montevarchi-Terranuova ✕					19 48	19 03	20 43	
46	138	268	■ S. Giovanni Valdarno ✕					19 55	19 10	20 51	
47	126	276	■ Figline Valdarno ℧					20 03		20 59	
48	123	281	■ Incisa					20 09		21 05	
49	121	288	■ Rignano sull'Arno-Reggello					20 18		21 13	
50	112	292	■ S. Ellero-Vallombrosa (Km. 12)					20 23		21 18	
51	91	296	Pontassieve ✕ a.	15 12		16 49		20 30		21 24	
52			Borgo S. Lorenzo, Faenza e Ravenna 274 p.	15 15		16 51		20 42		21 25	
53	80	300	■ Sieci	—		—		20 47		21 30	
54	74	303	■ Compiobbi					20 52		21 35	
55	53	312	Firenze Campo di Marte ✕ a.	15 27		17 02		21 00		21 43	
56			Firenze Rifredi 260 p.	15 28		17 03		21 01		21 44	
57	48	316	■■ Firenze S. M. N. ✕ 213, 215, 218, 269 a.	15 33	16 23	17 08	16 32	21 06	19 48	21 50	19 12

Note di instradamento: *Per Foligno* · *1392 accel. 1e2 — Da Foligno Via Perugia (Vedasi quadro 266)* · *Da Faenza* · *Da Borgo S. Lorenzo*.

In Italy, as elsewhere in Europe, the twenty-four-hour system is used on the railways and in other public situations involving telling time. In this system, the afternoon hours continue the numbering of the morning hours, with thirteen o'clock = one p.m., fourteen o'clock = two p.m., *etc.*, as far as twenty-four o'clock = midnight.

Catching a Train

Miss Bruni inquires about train schedules

LA SIG.NA BRUNI *(all'albergatore)* —
¹Buon giorno.

L'ALBERGATORE — ²Buon giorno, signorina. ³Come sta stamattina?

LA SIG.NA BRUNI — ⁴Bene, grazie, e
Lei?

L'ALBERGATORE — ⁵Non c'è male,
grazie.

LA SIG.NA BRUNI — ⁶Che ore, sono,
per favore?

L'ALBERGATORE — ⁷Sono le dieci e
mezzo. ⁸Parte oggi per Firenze,
signorina?

LA SIG.NA BRUNI —⁹Sì, ma non so
l'orario dei treni.

L'ALBERGATORE — ¹⁰Ecco un orario.
¹¹Ci sono dei treni per Firenze a
tutte le ore.

LA SIG.NA BRUNI — ¹²Vediamo.

L'ALBERGATORE — ¹³Quello che parte
a mezzogiorno e quarantacinque è
molto comodo. ¹⁴E anche quello
delle quattro e venticinque del
pomeriggio. ¹⁵O, per essere esatti,
delle sedici e venticinque.

LA SIG.NA BRUNI — ¹⁶Allora partirò
con quello del pomeriggio, credo.
¹⁷Grazie mille e buon giorno.

L'ALBERGATORE — ¹⁸Prego, signorina,
e arrivederLa.

MISS BRUNI *(to the hotelkeeper)* —
¹Good morning.

THE HOTELKEEPER — ²Good morning, miss. ³How are you this
morning?

MISS BRUNI — ⁴Well, thank you, and
you?

THE HOTELKEEPER — ⁵Not bad,
thanks.

MISS BRUNI — ⁶What time is it,
please?

THE HOTELKEEPER — ⁷It's half past
ten. ⁸Are you leaving for Florence
today, miss?

MISS BRUNI — ⁹Yes, but I don't know
the train schedule [*lit.*, the time-
table of the trains].

THE HOTELKEEPER — ¹⁰Here is a time-
table. ¹¹There are trains for Florence
at all hours.

MISS BRUNI — ¹²Let's see.

THE HOTELKEEPER — ¹³The one
which leaves at twelve forty-five is
very convenient. ¹⁴And also the
four twenty-five in the afternoon
[*lit.*, the one of four twenty-five of
the afternoon]. ¹⁵Or, to be exact,
the sixteen twenty-five.

MISS BRUNI — ¹⁶Then I'll leave on
[*lit.*, with] the afternoon one [*lit.*,
the one of the afternoon], I believe.
¹⁷A thousand thanks, and good
morning.

THE HOTELKEEPER — ¹⁸You're welcome, miss, and good-bye.

Foto Cash — Rapho-Guillumette

Stazione Termini, Roma

Esercizi

A. *Dica in Italiano:*

1. Good morning.   2. Good morning, miss.   3. How are you this morning?
4. Well, thank you, and you?
5. Not badly, thanks.   6. What time is it, please?   7. It's half past ten.
8. Are you leaving for Florence today, miss?   9. Yes, but I don't know the times of the trains.
10. Here is a timetable.   11. There are trains for Florence at all hours.   12. Let's see.   13. The one which leaves at twelve forty-five is very convenient.
14. And also the four twenty-five in the afternoon.
15. Or, to be exact, the sixteen twenty-five.   16. Then I'll leave on the afternoon one, I believe.   17. A thousand thanks, and good-bye.

B. *Risponda in italiano a ciascuna delle seguenti domande:*

1. Come sta stamattina?   2. E Lei?   3. Che ore sono, per favore?   4. Parte oggi per Firenze?
5. Dov'è la stazione?   6. Dov'è il tabaccaio?   7. Dov'è l'ufficio postale?
8. Lei è la signorina Bruni?   9. Lei è il signor Dossi?
10. Lei è l'albergatore?   11. C'è una léttera per me?

C. *Conti in italiano da ùndici a venti* (Count in Italian from eleven to twenty):

ùndici (11)	sédici (16)
dódici (12)	diciassètte (17)
trédici (13)	diciótto (18)
quattórdici (14)	diciannove (19)
quìndici (15)	venti (20)

D. *Conti in italiano da dieci a cento* (Count in Italian from ten to one hundred):

dieci (10)	trenta (30)	cinquanta (50)	settanta (70)	novanta (90)
venti (20)	quaranta (40)	sessanta (60)	ottanta (80)	cento (100)

E. *Dica in italiano i seguenti nùmeri:*

ventuno (21)	ventiquattro (24)	ventisette (27)
ventidue (22)	venticinque (25)	ventotto (28)
ventitré (23)	ventisei (26)	ventinove (29)

F. *Conti in italiano, secondo il modello presentato nel nùmero* **E** (Count in Italian, according to the model presented in number **E**):

1. da trenta a quaranta.   2. da quaranta a cinquanta.   3. da cinquanta a sessanta.   4. da sessanta a settanta.
5. da settanta a ottanta.   6. da ottanta a novanta.   7. da novanta a cento.

G. CONVERSATION:

1. Good morning, Miss. Are you leaving for Florence today?   2. Yes, but I don't know the train schedule [times of the trains].   3. There are trains at all times.   4. Let's see. The midday train (= the train of noon) is very comfortable.
5. What time is it?   6. It is half past ten.   7. Then I'll leave on the midday train.   8. Very well, miss.   9. Thank you, and good day.
10. You're welcome, and good-bye.

H. DIALOGUE:

You stop someone and ask where the station is. You also ask when the train for Florence leaves.

CONVERSATION UNIT ——————— 4

Telling Time

Fulvia has just picked up her ticket from the clerk in the railroad station in Rome.

LA SIG.NA BRUNI — [1]A che ora parte esattamente il treno per Firenze?

MISS BRUNI — [1]At what time, exactly, does the train for Florence leave?

L'IMPIEGATO — [2]Alle sédici e ventisette, signorina.

THE CLERK — [2]At four twenty-seven p.m., miss.

LA SIG.NA BRUNI — [3]Che ora è adesso?

L'IMPIEGATO — [4]È mezzogiorno e un quarto.

LA SIG.NA BRUNI — [5]E a che ora entra il treno in stazione?

L'IMPIEGATO — [6]Oh, non prima delle tre e mezza.

LA SIG.NA BRUNI — [7]C'è ancora molto tempo, allora.

L'IMPIEGATO — [8]Sì signorina.

MISS BRUNI — [3]What time is it now?

THE CLERK — [4]It's a quarter past twelve noon.

MISS BRUNI — [5]And at what time does the train come into the station?

THE CLERK — [6]Oh, not before half-past three.

MISS BRUNI — [7]There's still a lot of time, then.

THE CLERK — [8]Yes, miss.

(The train has just pulled into the station at Florence and Fulvia is met by her cousin, Peter, who is studying at the University.)

FULVIA — [9]Ciao, Pietro.

PIETRO — [10]Buona sera.

FULVIA — [11]Che piacere vederti. [12]Come stai?

PIETRO — [13]Benìssimo, grazie, e tu?

FULVIA — [14]Bene, bene [15]Sei stato veramente gentile a venire alla stazione.

PIETRO — [16]Ma figùrati, è un piacere per me.

FULVIA — [17]Come stanno gli zii?

PIETRO —[18]Stanno benone; e i tuoi genitori?

FULVIA —[19]Anche loro stanno bene. [20]Andiamo a mangiare, ora, ché ho una fame da morire.

FULVIA — [9]Hi, Peter.

PETER — [10]Good evening.

FULVIA — [11]What a pleasure to see you. [12]How are you?

PETER — [13]Very well, thanks, and you?

FULVIA — [14]Fine, fine. [15]You were really kind to come to the station.

PETER — [16]Oh, don't mention it; it's a pleasure for me.

FULVIA — [17]How are my aunt and uncle [*lit.*, the uncles]?

PETER — [18]They're very well indeed; and your parents?

FULVIA — [19]They are well too. [20]Let's go and eat, now, [for] I'm starving [dying of hunger].

NOTES

1. Both **che ora è?** (*lit., what hour is it?*) and **che ore sono?** (*lit., what hours are they?*) are in everyday use for *what time is it?*; both are equally correct and acceptable.

2. The forms of the second person singular (**tu** *you* and related forms) are used in informal, intimate address; members of the same family (including cousins) would normally use **tu** to each other.

3. **Ho una fame da morire** *I'm dying of hunger* means literally *I have a hunger to die [of it]*.

Esercizi

A. *Dica in italiano:*

1. At what time, exactly, does the train for Florence leave? 2. At four twenty-seven, miss. 3. What time is it now? 4. It's a quarter past twelve (noon).
5. And at what time does the train come into the station? 6. Oh, not before half-past three. 7. There's still a lot of time, then. 8. Yes, miss. 9. Hi, Peter.
10. Good evening. 11. What a pleasure to meet you. 12. How are you? 13. Very well, thanks, and you? 14. Very well.
15. You were really kind to come to the station. 16. Oh, don't mention it; it's a pleasure for me. 17. How are my aunt and uncle? 18. They're very well indeed; and your parents? 19. They are well too.
20. Let's go and eat, now, [for] I'm starving (dying of hunger).

B. *Dia una risposta adatta a ciascuna delle seguenti frasi:*

1. A che ora parte il treno per Firenze? 2. Che ora è adesso? 3. A che ora entra il treno in stazione? 4. Come stai?
5. Come stanno gli zii? 6. Come stanno i tuoi genitori?

C. *Dica in italiano:*

1. At what time does the train leave? 2. At what time does Mr. Dossi leave? 3. At what time does Miss Bruni leave? 4. At four twenty-seven.
5. At five thirty-seven. 6. At six thirty-three. 7. At eight forty-nine. 8. At two fifty-one. 9. At seven twenty-eight.
10. It leaves at nine thirty-one. 11. It leaves at eleven sixteen. 12. It leaves at nineteen forty-six. 13. It leaves at sixteen twenty-seven. 14. How are you **(tu)**?
15. How are you **(Lei)**? 16. How are the aunt and uncle (*lit.* the uncles)? 17. How are your parents? 18. How are the students (*m.*) 19. How are the students (*f.*)?
20. How are the young ladies? 21. How are the gentlemen?

D. *Dica in italiano i seguenti numeri:*

17	83	52	33	95	27	19
9	49	90	14	59	72	76
38	7	11	40	88	9	63

E. Conversation:

1. At what time does the train leave?   2. It leaves at ten forty-nine, sir.   3. What time is it now?   4. It's ten twenty-five.
5. When does the train come into the station?   6. At ten thirty.   7. Then there's still a lot of time.

F. Dialogue:

You meet your cousin at the station and each of you inquires after the other's health and after the health of your relatives (aunt and uncle, parents).

Foto Bright — Rapho-Guillumette

4. COMBINATIONS OF PREPOSITIONS + DEFINITE ARTICLE.

When the prepositions **a** *to*, **da** *from*, **di** *of*, **in** *in* and **su** *on*, come immediately before the definite article, they combine with it to form single words which must be used instead of the sequence of preposition plus article. Fused forms exist also for **con** *with* and **per** *for*, but are now rare or obsolete. The resultant fused forms (known in Italian as **preposizioni articolate**) are:

	a	da	di	in	su	con	per
il (m.sg.)	al	dal	de	nel	sul	col	[pel]
lo (m.sg.)	allo	dallo	dello	nello	sullo	[collo]	[pello]
la (f.sg.)	alla	dalla	della	nella	sulla	[colla]	[pella]
l' (m. or f.sg.)	all'	dall'	dell'	nell'	sull'	[coll']	[pell']
i (m.pl.)	ai	dai	dei	nei	sui	coi	[pei]
gli (m.pl.)	agli	dagli	degli	negli	sugli	[cogli]	[pegli]
le (f pl.)	alle	dalle	delle	nelle	sulle	[colle]	[pelle]

COMBINATIONS OF PREPOSITIONS AND THE DEFINITE ARTICLE

Of the forms given in the last two columns, only **col** and **coi** are used to any extent in present-day Italian. The others (here enclosed in brackets) are out of date.

a	to	+ **il vento**	the wind	= **al vento**	to the wind
di	of	+ **la stanza**	the room	= **della stanza**	of the room
di	of	+ **l'àlbero**	the tree	= **dell'àlbero**	of the tree
da	from	+ **lo specchio**	the mirror	= **dallo specchio**	from the mirror
in	in	+ **gli orari**	the timetables	= **negli orari**	in the timetables
su	on	+ **le òpere**	the operas	= **sulle òpere**	on the operas

5. PRESENT OF **èssere** *to be.*

sono	I am	**siamo**	we are
sei	you (*fam.*) are	**siete**	you (*fam., pl.*) are
è	he, she, it is; you (*formal*) are	**sono**	they are; you (*formal, pl.*) are

6. Present of **stare** *to stand; to be (in health)*.

sto	I stand, I am	**stiamo**	we stand, are
stai	you *(fam.)* stand, are	**state**	you *(fam., pl.)* stand, are
sta	he, she, it stands, is; you *(formal)* stand, are	**stanno**	they stand, are; you *(formal pl.)* stand, are

The basic meaning of **stare** is *to stand, be located*. In referring to health, however, **stare** is used and not **èssere** *to be*: e.g., **sto bene** *I am well*.

7. Formal and Informal Address.

Whereas we have in English only one pronoun of direct address, *you*, for speaking to both one person and more than one person, in all social situations, Italian distinguishes between singular and plural, and also between the types of social relationship involved. Persons not well acquainted with each other normally use the pronoun **Lei** *you* *(formal, sg.)* and related forms in speaking or writing to each other. This pronoun is third person singular, and verbs and adjectives agreeing with it (whether it is present in the sentence or simply understood) must also be in the third person singular. The plural corresponding to **Lei** is **Loro** *you* *(formal, pl.)*. All verbs and adjectives referring to **Loro**, must be in the third person plural. Persons who are close friends or relatives use the familiar, less formal second person with each other; in the singular, the pronoun for the second person is **tu,** and in the plural it is **voi.** Thus:

	FAMILIAR AND FORMAL ADDRESS		
	FAMILIAR	FORMAL	TRANSLATION
SING.	**(Tu) sei** gentile.	**(Lei)** è gentile.	*You're nice.*
PLUR.	**(Voi) siete** gentili.	**(Loro) sono** gentili.	
SING.	Come **stai** ?	Come **sta** ?	*How are you?*
PLUR.	Come **state** ?	Come **stanno** ?	
SING.	**Parti** oggi per Firenze ?	**Parte** oggi per Firenze ?	*Are you leaving for*
PLUR.	**Partite** oggi per Firenze ?	**Pàrtono** oggi per Firenze ?	*Florence today?*

It is not necessary to have an expressed subject for every verb. Since the form of the verb itself tells the person and number of the actor, an expressed subject pronoun (*e.g.*, **tu, Lei,** *etc.* in the sentences above) is needed only if it is desired to emphasize the subject.

Grammatical Exercises

A. *Give the Italian equivalents of the following:*

<table>
<tr><td align="center">A</td><td align="center">B</td></tr>
</table>

(1) ¹to the gentleman
    ²to the uncle
    ³to the hotelkeeper

    ⁴to the gentlemen
    ⁵to the uncles
    ⁶to the hotelkeepers

¹to the young lady
²to the student *(f.)*
³to the opera

⁴to the young ladies
⁵to the students *(f.)*
⁶to the operas

(2) ¹from the train
    ²from the ticket-window
    ³from the tree

    ⁴from the trains
    ⁵from the ticket-windows
    ⁶from the trees

¹from the letter
²from the station
³from the hour

⁴from the letters
⁵from the stations
⁶from the hours

(3) ¹of the wind
    ²of the student *(m.)*
    ³of the tree

    ⁴of the winds
    ⁵of the students *(m.)*
    ⁶of the trees

¹of the acquaintance
²of the station
³of the exception

⁴of the acquaintances
⁵of the stations
⁶of the exceptions

(4) ¹in the afternoon
    ²in the pleasure
    ³in the mirror

    ⁴in the afternoons
    ⁵in the pleasures
    ⁶in the mirrors

¹in the square
²in the room
³in the hour

⁴in the squares
⁵in the rooms
⁶in the hours

(5) ¹on the pleasure
    ²on the student *(m.)*
    ³on the timetable

    ⁴on the pleasures
    ⁵on the students *(m.)*
    ⁶on the timetables

¹on the letter
²on the exception
³on the opera

⁴on the letters
⁵on the exceptions
⁶on the operas

B. *Say or write in Italian:*

1. I am Fulvia Bruni.
2. You *(2nd sg.)* are Fulvia Bruni.
3. You *(3rd sg.)* are Fulvia Bruni
4. She is Fulvia Bruni.
5. I am Roberto Williams.
6. You *(2nd sg.)* are Roberto Williams.
7. You *(3rd sg.)* are Roberto Williams.
8. We are Fulvia Bruni and Roberto Williams.
9. You *(2nd pl.)* are Fulvia Bruni and Roberto Williams.
10. You *(3rd pl.)* are Fulvia Bruni and Roberto Williams.
11. They are Fulvia Bruni and Roberto Williams.
12. I am well.
13. You *(2nd sg.)* are well.
14. You *(3rd sg.)* are well.
15. He is well.
16. She is well.
17. We are well.
18. You *(2nd pl.)* are well.
19. You *(3rd pl.)* are well.
20. They are well.

C. Substitution. *Give the Italian for:*

(1) ¹The train leaves.
²The train leaves from Florence.
³The train leaves from the station.
⁴The train leaves from the square.
⁵The train leaves at three o'clock.
⁶The train leaves at noon.
⁷The train leaves at a quarter past twelve noon.
⁸The train leaves at half past twelve noon.
⁹The train leaves at seven thirty-eight.
¹⁰The train leaves at sixteen twenty-one.

(2) ¹The restaurant is in the square.
²The restaurant is in the station.
³The restaurant is in Florence.
⁴The restaurant is to the right.
⁵The restaurant is the the left.
⁶The restaurant is there next to it.

(3) ¹The waiter is in the restaurant.
²The waiter is in the postoffice.
³The waiter is in the square.
⁴The waiter is in the station.
⁵The waiter is at the ticket-window.
⁶The waiter is at the opera.

D. Progressive Variation. *Give the Italian for:*

¹You *(2nd sg.)* are Fulvia Bruni.
²You *(3rd sg.)* are Miss Bruni.
³You *(3rd sg.)* are Mr. Dossi.
⁴The hotelkeeper is Mr. Dossi.
⁵The hotelkeeper is at the ticket-window.
⁶The tobacconist is at the ticket-window.
⁷The tobacconist is in the square.
⁸The station is in the square.
⁹The train is in the station.
¹⁰The train leaves from the station.
¹¹The train leaves at five forty-seven.
¹²Miss Bruni leaves at five forty-seven.
¹³Miss Bruni leaves from the square.
¹⁴The student *(f.)* leaves from the square.
¹⁵The student *(f.)* leaves from the station.
¹⁶You *(3rd sg.)* leave from the station.
¹⁷You *(3rd sg.)* are in the station.
¹⁸You *(2nd sg.)* are in the station.
¹⁹You *(2nd sg.)* are Fulvia Bruni.

At the Restaurant

Fulvia is tired and hungry after the trip from Rome.

PIETRO — [1]Ecco un ristorante; entriamo?

FULVIA — [2]C'è una tàvola lìbera qui. [3]Possiamo mangiare all'aperto. [4]Tu hai fame?

PIETRO — [5]Sediàmoci qui, va bene? [6]Cameriere? [7]Il menù, per favore.

IL CAMERIERE — [8]Ecco signore, vògliono dell'antipasto?

PIETRO — [9]No, grazie; *(a Fulvia)* tu ne vuoi?

FULVIA — [10]No, grazie; vorrei una bistecca ai ferri e dell'insalata verde.

PIETRO — [11]Ed io una cotoletta alla milanese con patate e fagiolini.

IL CAMERIERE — [12]Come vuole le patate: fritte, arrosto o puré di patate?

PIETRO — [13]Fritte, e del vino rosso.

IL CAMERIERE — [14]Lei vuole del vino bianco o rosso, signorina?

FULVIA — [15]Vorrei dell'acqua minerale, per favore.

IL CAMERIERE — [16]Cosa vògliono per fine pasto?

FULVIA — [17]Io vorrei della frutta. [18]Cosa hanno?

PETER — [1]Here's a restaurant; shall we go in?

FULVIA — [2]There's a table free here. [3]We can eat in the open air. [4]Are *you* hungry?

PETER — [5]Let's sit down here, O.K.? [6]Waiter! [7]The menu, please.

THE WAITER [8]Here it is, sir; would you like some hors d'œuvres?

PETER — [9]No, thank you; do *you (to Fulvia)* want any?

FULVIA — [10]No, thanks; I'd like a grilled steak and some lettuce [*lit.,* green] salad.

PETER — [11]And I [would like] a breaded veal cutlet with potatoes and string beans.

THE WAITER — [12]How do you want the potatoes: fried, roasted, or mashed [potatoes]?

PETER — [13]Fried, and some red wine.

THE WAITER — [14]Do you want white or red wine, miss?

FULVIA — [15]I'd like mineral water, please.

THE WAITER — [16]What do you wish for dessert?

FULVIA — [17]I'd like some fruit. [18]What have you got?

Panorama di Firenze

IL CAMERIERE — ¹⁹Uva, pesche, pere, banane.

THE WAITER — ¹⁹Grapes, peaches, pears, bananas.

FULVIA — ²⁰Mi porti dell'uva.

FULVIA — ²⁰Bring me some grapes.

PIETRO ²¹E a me del formaggio .

PETER — ²¹And [to] me, some cheese.

IL CAMERIERE — ²²Desìderano anche del caffè?

THE WAITER — ²²Do you wish coffee too?

PIETRO — ²³Sì, due caffè, per favore.
(Più tardi:)

PETER — ²³Yes, two coffees, please.
(Later:)

PIETRO — ²⁴Cameriere? Il conto, per favore.

PETER — ²⁴Waiter? The bill, please.

IL CAMERIERE — ²⁵Sùbito, signore.

THE WAITER — ²⁵Immediately, sir.

NOTES

1. The form **entriamo,** although translated here *Shall we go in?* means literally *Do we go in?* Likewise, **vuole,** here translated *Would you like?* means literally *Do you* (3rd sg., **Lei)** *want?*, and **vògliono** means literally *Do you* (3rd pl., **Loro)** *want?*
2. **Antipasto (hors d'oeuvres)** is a selection of such highly-seasoned foods as tuna fish, olives, artichokes, sausages, thin slices of ham, cheese, fennel, *etc.*, served at the beginning of a meal.

Esercizi

A. *Dica in Italiano:*

1. Here is a restaurant: shall we go in?   2. There's a table free here.   3. We can eat in the open air.   4. Are *you* hungry?
5. Let's sit down here, O.K.?   6. Waiter!   7. The menu, please.   8. Here it is, sir; would you like some hors d'œuvres?   9. No, thank you; do you want any?
10. No, thanks; I'd like a grilled steak and some green salad.   11. And I, (would like) a breaded veal cutlet with potatoes and string beans.   12. How do you want the potatoes: fried, roasted, or mashed [potatoes]?   13. Fried, and some red wine.   14. And do you want white or red wine, miss?
15. I'd like mineral water, please.   16. What do you wish for dessert?   17. I'd like some fruit.   18. What do you have?   19. Grapes, peaches, pears, bananas.
20. Bring me some grapes.   21. And [to] me, some cheese.   22. Do you wish coffee too?   23. Yes, two coffees, please.   24. Waiter! The bill, please.
25. Immediately, sir.

CONVERSATION UNIT FIVE

B. *Risponda in italiano alle seguenti domande:*

1. Entriamo nel ristorante? 2. Possiamo mangiare all'aperto? 3. Hai fame?
4. Vuole dell'antipasto?
5. Vuole una bistecca ai ferri? 6. Vuole delle patate? 7. Come vuole le
patate? 8. Vuole vino bianco o rosso? 9. Cosa vuole per fine pasto?
10. Cosa hanno? 11. Vuole uva, pesche, pere o banane? 12. Desìdera del
caffè?

C. *Dica a un altro studente o a un'altra studentessa:*

1. che è mezzogiorno e mezzo. 2. che ha una fame da morire. 3. che vuole
dell'antipasto. 4. che vuole una cotoletta alla milanese.
5. che vuole delle patate arrosto. 6. che vuole del vino bianco. 7. che
vuole delle pere. 8. che vuole il conto.

D. *Domandi a un altro studente o a un'altra studentessa:*

1. che ore sono. 2. se ha fame. 3. se vuol mangiare. 4. dove c'è un ristorante.
5. se desidera dell'insalata verde. 6. come vuole le patate. 7. se desidera
del vino bianco o rosso. 8. cosa vuole per fine pasto. 9. se vuole delle
pesche.
10. se vuole del formaggio.

E. CONVERSATION:

1. I'm starving (dying of hunger). Here's a restaurant. Shall we go in? We can
eat in the open air. Let's sit down.
2. Waiter! Yes, sir. Bring me the menu, please. Here is the menu, sir. Do you
wish some hors d'œuvres? Yes, thank you.
3. And do you wish a breaded veal cutlet? No, thank you. I'd like a grilled
steak. With some lettuce [green] salad?
4. No, thank you; with mashed potatoes and string beans. White wine or
red? Bring me some mineral water, please.
5. And for dessert? I don't know. What do you have. We have fruit and
cheese. Bring me some cheese. And coffee? Not now, thanks; later.
6. Waiter! The bill, please. Immediately, sir.

F. DIALOGUE:

Act out a scene in a restaurant, one or two people deciding to enter, order-
ing a meal, and later asking for the bill.

Piazza e basilica di San Pietro
A DESTRA: Foro Romano

Viaggiando[1] per l'Italia

(Conversations 1-5)

Fulvia Bruni é una gióvane[2] studentessa di Storia dell'Arte all'università di Roma. Decide di viaggiare un po'[3] per l'Italia prima dell'inizio[4] della scuola.[5]

Appena[6] arrivata a Roma va a conoscere un amico dei suoi genitori. Il dottor Dossi è un signore molto gentile e le dà[7] tutte le informazioni per familiarizzarsi[8] con la città. Fulvia passa così i primi[9] giorni nella capitale; visita i musei e i monumenti più[10] importanti di Roma, mangia in vari e diversi ristoranti, esplora la città a piedi.

[1]**viaggiando** traveling; **viaggiare** to travel.
[2]**gióvane** young.
[3]**un po'** a little.
[4]**l'inizio** *(m.)* the beginning.
[5]**la scuola** the school.
[6]**appena** scarcely; just as soon as.
[7]**dà** gives.
[8]**familiarizzarsi** to be come familiar, get acquainted.
[9]**primo** first.
[10]**più** more; **i più importanti** the most important.

Foto ISTO

¹¹**incontrare** to meet.
¹²**divertente** amusing.
¹³**lui** he, him.
¹⁴**figurativo** representational.
¹⁵**préndere** to take.
¹⁶**la cena** the dinner *(evening meal)*.
¹⁷**fa** makes; *[here]* gets (**fare il biglietto** to get one's ticket).
¹⁸**in anticipo** in advance.
¹⁹**il binàrio** the track.
²⁰**ferroviàrio** of the railroad.
²¹**mentre** while.
²²**trovare** to find.
²³**facilmente** easily.
²⁴**il posto** the place.
²⁵**vicino** near.
²⁶**il finestrino** the window *(in a train or bus)*.
²⁷**léggere** to read.
²⁸**insieme** together.
²⁹**vanno** they go.
³⁰**già** yes indeed; of course.

Alla fine della settimana decide di partire per Firenze, e incontrare[11] là suo cugino Pietro. Firenze è la città ideale per uno che si interessa di storia dell'arte ed è molto più divertente[12] visitarla in due.

Pietro è americano e studia medicina, ma anche lui[13] adora le arti figurative.[14]

Così Fulvia prende[15] il treno del pomeriggio e arriva a Firenze all'ora della cena.[16] Fulvia fa[17] il biglietto in antìcipo[18] ed arriva ai binari[19] ferroviari[20] proprio mentre[21] il treno entra in stazione. Trova[22] facilmente[23] un posto[24] còmodo vicino[25] al finestrino[26] e comincia a léggere.[27] Alla stazione di Firenze Pietro viene a prénderla e insieme[28] vanno[29] in un ristorante. Sono già le nove e i due cugini non hanno ancora mangiato. "Ma già,"[30] commenta Pietro, "in Italia non si

Foto ISTO

A sinistra:
  Ponte Vecchio
  e Palazzo Vecchio,
  Firenze

A destra:
  "Primavera"
  di Botticelli,
  Museo degli Uffizi,
  Firenze

Foto Alinari

riesce[31] mai[32] a cenare[33] prima delle otto, otto
e mezzo." Màngiano all'aperto e òrdinano[34]
una buona e sostanziosa[35] cena.

Dopo cena Fulvia è stanca[36] e va in albergo.
Ha la stanza nùmero ventidue; è una bella
stanza che dà[37] sull'Arno.

La mattina seguente sùbito dopo colazione
i due cugini vanno al museo degli Uffizi. Ci
vanno a piedi perché[38] non è lontano dall'-
albergo. Pietro rimane[39] incantato[40] dallo
splendore dei quadri degli Uffizi. A completare il piacere del suo soggiorno[41] a Firenze
Pietro si ferma[42] spesso[43] a fare lunghe conver-
sazioni con "l'uomo[44] della strada", come
giornalai, tabaccai e così via.[45]

[31]**si riesce** one succeeds.
[32]**mai** never.
[33]**cenare** to dine.
[34]**ordinare** to order.
[35]**sostanzioso** substantial.
[36]**stanco** tired.
[37]**dà su** looks out on.
[38]**perché** because.
[39]**rimanere** to remain, be.
[40]**incantato** enchanted.
[41]**il soggiorno** the sojourn, stay.
[42]**fermarsi** to stop.
[43]**spesso** often.
[44]**l'uomo** *(m.)* the man.
[45]**e così via** and so forth.

Foto Bright — Rapho-Guillumette

CONVERSATION UNIT _____ 6

Getting a Room

After dinner together, Peter drops Fulvia off at her hotel.

LA SIG.NA BRUNI — [1]Ho la prenotazione per una stanza sìngola con bagno.

L'ALBERGATORE — [2]Come si chiama, signorina?

LA SIG.NA BRUNI — [3]Mi chiamo Fulvia Bruni.

L'ALBERGATORE — [4]Sì, èccola. [5]Purtroppo, però, non è con bagno. [6]C'è solo la doccia e il gabinetto.

LA SIG.NA BRUNI — [7]Non importa, va bene così. [8]Quanto costa al giorno?

L'ALBERGATORE — [9]Duemila ottocento lire al giorno.

LA SIG.NA BRUNI — [10]Devo pagare in antìcipo?

L'ALBERGATORE — [11]Non importa, può pagare quando lascia l'albergo. [12]Quando parte da Firenze?

MISS BRUNI — [1]I have a reservation for a single room with bath.

THE HOTELKEEPER — [2]What is your name, miss?

MISS BRUNI — [3]My name is Fulvia Bruni.

THE HOTELKEEPER — [4]Yes, here it is. [5]Unfortunately, however, it is not with bath. [6]There's only the shower and the toilet.

MISS BRUNI — [7]It doesn't matter; it's all right that way. [8]How much does it cost per day?

THE HOTELKEEPER — [9]Two thousand eight hundred lire per day.

MISS BRUNI — [10]Do I have to pay in advance?

THE HOTELKEEPER — [11]It doesn't matter; you can pay when you leave the hotel. [12]When are you departing from Florence?

LA SIG.NA BRUNI — ¹³Tra una settimana circa. ¹⁴L'università comincia la settimana pròssima. ¹⁵Mio cugino ed io dobbiamo èssere a Roma per lunedì. ¹⁶Così credo che partiremo sàbato o doménica.

L'ALBERGATORE — ¹⁷Suo cugino è quel signore americano?

LA SIG.NA BRUNI — ¹⁸Sì, è venuto in Italia a studiare.

L'ALBERGATORE — ¹⁹Cosa studia?

LA SIG.NA BRUNI — ²⁰Medicina.

L'ALBERGATORE — ²¹E Lei cosa studia?

LA SIG.NA BRUNI — ²²Io? Storia dell'arte.

L'ALBERGATORE — ²³Che bravi! ²⁴Ma ecco la chiave della stanza, signorina: nùmero ventidue. ²⁵Il cameriere Le porterà su la valigia tra un momento.

LA SIG.NA BRUNI — ²⁶Grazie mille e buona notte.

L'ALBERGATORE — ²⁷Buona notte, signorina.

MISS BRUNI — ¹³In a week, approximately. ¹⁴The university starts next week. ¹⁵My cousin and I have to be at Rome for Monday. ¹⁶So, I think that we shall leave Saturday or Sunday.

THE HOTELKEEPER — ¹⁷Your cousin is that American gentleman?

MISS BRUNI — ¹⁸Yes, he has come to Italy to study.

THE HOTELKEEPER — ¹⁹What is he studying?

MISS BRUNI — ²⁰Medicine.

THE HOTELKEEPER — ²¹And what do you study?

MISS BRUNI — ²²I? History of art.

THE HOTELKEEPER — ²³Excellent! ²⁴But here is the key of the room, miss: number twenty-two. ²⁵The bell-boy will carry up your suitcase in a minute.

MISS BRUNI — ²⁶Thank you very much [*lit.,* a thousand thanks and] good night.

THE HOTELKEEPER — ²⁷Good night, miss.

NOTES

1. Terms for *toilet*. The normal, everyday word for *toilet* is **gabinetto**. Some persons consider this term insufficiently elegant, and use the French word **la toilette** (*pron.* **twalèt**) instead. The word **cesso** is universally regarded as coarse and vulgar.

2. **Che bravi!** literally *How excellent!* This exclamation, since it refers to Miss Bruni and her cousin, is in the masculine plural. If it referred to two or more women, it would be feminine plural (**Che brave!**); if it referred to one man, masculine singular (**Che bravo!**); if to one woman, feminine singular (**Che brava!**).

3. **Il cameriere** means not only *the waiter*, but (as can be seen by its derivation from **camera** *room*), *the room servant, the bellboy*. In small hotels, waiter and bellboy are often the same man.

Sua cugina ha la
stanza numero
ventidue

*Foto Bright —
Rapho-Guillumette*

Esercizi

A. *Dica in italiano :*

1. I have a reservation for a single room with bath.   2. What is your name, miss?   3. My name is Fulvia Bruni.   4. Yes, here it is.

5. Unfortunately, however, it is not with bath.   6. There's only the shower and the toilet.   7. It doesn't matter; it's all right that way.   8. How much does it cost per day?   9. Two thousand eight hundred lire per day.

10. Do I have to pay in advance?   11. It doesn't matter; you can pay when you leave the hotel.   12. When are you departing from Florence?   13. In a week, approximately.   14. The university starts next week.

15. My cousin and I have to be at Rome for Monday.   16. So, I think that we shall leave Saturday or Sunday.   17. Your cousin is that American gentleman?   18. Yes, he has come to Italy to study.   19. What is he studying?

20. Medicine.   21. And what do you study?   22. I? History of art.   23. Excellent!   24. But here is the key of the room, miss; number twenty-two.

25. The bellboy will carry up your suitcase in a minute.   26. A thousand thanks and good night, miss.

B. *Risponda in italiano alle seguenti domande:*

1. Ha la prenotazione per una stanza?   2. Come si chiama?   3. Come vuole la stanza?   4. Quanto costa al giorno?

5. Devo pagare in antìcipo?   6. Quando parte da Firenze?   7. Quando comincia l'Università?   8. Quando dobbiamo èssere a Roma?   9. Cosa studia Lei?

10. Cosa studia suo cugino?   11. Che ore sono?   12. Dove possiamo mangiare?

CONVERSATION UNIT SIX

C. *Dica a un altro studente o a un'altra studentessa:*

1. che ha la prenotazione per una stanza.   2. che Lei è Fulvia Bruni (Roberto Williams).   3. che studia medicina.   4. che ha una fame da morire.
5. che non sa dove c'è un buon ristorante.   6. che sta bene.   7. che vuole una stanza con doccia.   8. che vuole il conto.

D. *Domandi a un altro studente o a un'altra studentessa:*

1. se vuole una stanza con bagno.   2. come si chiama.   3. se studia storia dell'arte.   4. se c'è un ristorante dentro la stazione.
5. se il cameriere è americano.   6. dov'è l'ufficio postale.   7. a che ora il treno entra in stazione.   8. a che ora il treno parte.   9. se vuole antipasto.

E. *Ripeta i nomi dei giorni della settimana* (Repeat the names of the days of the week):

Monday	Tuesday	Wednesday	Thursday	Friday	Saturday	Sunday
lunedì	**martedì**	**mercoledì**	**giovedì**	**venerdì**	**sàbato**	**doménica**

(Note that, in Italian, the names of the days of the week are not spelled with capital letters. All are masculine, except for **doménica** which is feminine.)

F. *Risponda alle seguenti domande, dando* [giving] *il giorno della settimana e l'ora esatta:*

1. Quando parte per Roma?   2. Quando vuol mangiare?   3. Quando entra il treno in stazione?   4. Quando studia medicina?
5. Quando studia storia dell'arte?   6. Quando va all'ufficio postale?   7. Quando dobbiamo èssere a Firenze?

G. Dialogues:

1. I am Giorgio Dossi. Have you a reservation, sir? Yes, I have a reservation for a room with bath. Here it is ; two thousand lire per day. Very good.
2. Have you a room with bath? No, sir, but we have a room with shower and toilet. How much does it cost per day? Two thousand eight hundred lire per day. Must I pay in advance? No, you can pay when you leave the hotel. Very well. Bellboy! Carry the gentleman's suitcase to number thirty-six.
3. When does the university begin? It begins next Wednesday. Have you come to Italy to study? Yes. What are you studying? I'm studying history of art. Ah, excellent!

⬤ **8.** THE PARTITIVE.

An Italian noun, singular or plural, may be preceded by the combination of **di** + the definite article in the meaning of *some* or *any*:

Vògliono **dell'**antipasto?   Would you like *some* hors d'œuvres?

AND SIMILARLY

Del vino rosso.	*Some* red wine.
Dell'acqua minerale.	*Some* mineral water.
Della frutta.	*Some* fruit.
Dell'uva.	*Some* grapes.
Del caffè.	*Some* coffee.
Dello zùcchero.	*Some* sugar.
Delle patate.	*Some* potatoes.
Delle chiavi.	*Some* keys.
Degli albergatori.	*Some* hotelkeepers.

In the negative, normally no partitive is used:

Non voglio antipasto.	I don't want [any] hors d'œuvres.
Non abbiamo frutta.	We haven't got [any] fruit.
Non ci sono patate.	There aren't any potatoes.

⬤ **9.** PRESENT TENSE OF VERBS *(First Conjugation)*.

Most Italian verbs belong to the first conjugation, with the infinitive in **-are**: **portare** *to carry*, **lasciare** *to leave*, **mangiare** *to eat*.

PRESENT TENSE—REGULAR VERBS—FIRST CONJUGATION			
portare *to carry* **port-**			
porto	I carry	port**iamo**	we carry
porti	you (**tu**) carry	portate	you (**voi**) carry
porta	he, she, it carries; you (**Lei**) carry	pòrtano	they carry; you (**Loro**) carry

III

Similarly with **chiamare** *to call*, **desiderare** *to desire*, **domandare** *to ask*, **entrare** *to go in*, **guardare** *to look*, **scusare** *to excuse*, *etc*.

With verbs whose stem ends in **-i-** (whether pronounced or simply a graphic device to indicate the "soft" pronunciation of a preceding **c, g** or **sc**), the **-i-** of the endings **-i** (*2 nd sg.*) and **-iamo** (*1 st pl.*) is automatically absorbed in the **-i-** of the verb root:

lasciare   *to leave*
lasc-

lascio	I leave	**lasciamo**	we leave
lasci	you (**tu**) leave	**lasciate**	you (**voi**) leave
lascia	he, she, it leaves; you (**Lei**) leave	**làsciano**	they leave; you (**Loro**) leave

With verbs whose root ends in a "hard" **c** or **g**, the graphic indication of these sounds automatically changes to **ch** or **gh**, respectively, before an ending beginning with **-i-**, as in **pagare** *to pay*:

pagare   *to pay*
pag-

pago	I pay	pa**gh**iamo	we pay
pa**gh**i	you (**tu**) pay	pagate	you (**voi**) pay
paga	he, she, it pays; you (**Lei**) pay	pàgano	they pay; you (**Loro**) pay

⚫ 10. PRESENT TENSE OF **avere** *to have*.

avere   *to have*

ho	I have	**abbiamo**	we have
hai	you (**tu**) have	**avete**	you (**voi**) have
ha	he, she, it has; you (**Lei**) have	**hanno**	they have; you (**Loro**) have

The three persons of the singular and the third person plural of this verb are normally written with silent **h-**. Some persons prefer to omit the **h-**, but in this case a grave accent mark is written over the verb forms: **ò, ài, à, ànno**, thus distinguishing them from their homonyms **o** *or*, **ai** *to the*, **a** *to* and **anno** *year*, respectively.

11. PRESENT OF MODAL AUXILIARIES.

The verbs **dovere** *to have to*, **potere** *to be able to* and **volere** *to wish, want (to)* are known as MODAL AUXILIARIES. They have the following forms in the present:

dovere *to have to*

devo	I have to	**dobbiamo**	we have to
devi	you (**tu**) have to	**dovete**	you (**voi**) have to
deve	he, she, it has to; you (**Lei**) have to	**dévono** *or* **débbono**	they have to; you (**Loro**) have to

Used independently, **dovere** means *to owe, e.g.,* **Mi devi cento lire.** *You owe me a hundred lire.*

potere *to be able to*

posso	I am able	**possiamo**	we are able
puoi	you (**tu**) are able	**potete**	you (**voi**) are able
può	he, she, it is able; you (**Lei**) are able	**pòssono**	they are able; you (**Loro**) are able

volere *to wish, want (to)*

voglio	I want	**vogliamo**	we want
vuoi	you (**tu**) want	**volete**	you (**voi**) want
vuole	he, she, it wants; you (**Lei**) want	**vògliono**	they want; you (**Loro**) want

When another verb is dependent on one of these verbs, the dependent verb is in the infinitive, with no intervening preposition: *e.g.*, **devo partire** *I have to depart*; **può mangiare** *she is able to eat, she can eat*; **non vogliamo lasciare questo albergo** *we don't want to leave this hotel.*

Grammatical Exercises

A. SUBSTITUTIONS. *Say or write in Italian:*

(1) ¹I have some acquaintances.
²I have some letters.
³I have some potatoes.
⁴I have some keys.
⁵I have some timetables.
⁶I have some uncles.
⁷I have some restaurants.

⁸I have some hors d'œuvres.
⁹I have some cheese.
¹⁰I have some wine.
¹¹I have some [green] lettuce.
¹²I have some grapes.
¹³I have some water.

(2) ¹We have no acquaintances.
²We have no letters.
³We have no potatoes.
⁴We have no keys.
⁵We have no timetables.
⁶We have no uncles.
⁷We have no restaurants.

⁸We have no hors d'œuvres.
⁹We have no cheese.
¹⁰We have no wine.
¹¹We have no [green] lettuce.
¹²We have no grapes.
¹³We have no water.

(3) ¹I call.
²I desire.
³I ask.
⁴I enter.
⁵I look.

⁶I leave.
⁷I pay.
⁸I carry.
⁹I excuse.
¹⁰I study.

(4) ¹You (tu) call.
²You desire.
³You ask.
⁴You enter.
⁵You look.

⁶You leave.
⁷You pay.
⁸You carry.
⁹You excuse.
¹⁰You study.

(5) ¹He calls.
²He desires.
³He asks.
⁴He enters.
⁵He looks.

⁶He leaves.
⁷He pays.
⁸He carries.
⁹He excuses.
¹⁰He studies.

(6) ¹You (Lei) call.
²You desire.
³You ask.
⁴You enter.
⁵You look.

⁶You leave.
⁷You pay.
⁸You carry.
⁹You excuse.
¹⁰You study.

(7) ¹We call.
²We desire.
³We ask.
⁴We enter.
⁵We look.

⁶We leave.
⁷We pay.
⁸We carry.
⁹We excuse.
¹⁰We study.

(8) ¹You (voi) call.
²You desire.
³You ask.
⁴You enter.
⁵You look.

⁶You leave.
⁷You pay.
⁸You carry.
⁹You excuse.
¹⁰You study.

(9) ¹They call.
⁵They desire.
³They ask.
⁴They enter.
⁵They look.

⁶They leave.
⁷They pay.
⁸They carry.
⁹They excuse.
¹⁰They study.

(10) ¹You **(Loro)** call.
²You desire.
³You ask.
⁴You enter.
⁵You look.

⁶You leave.
⁷You pay.
⁸You carry.
⁹You excuse.
¹⁰You study.

(11) ¹I have to eat.
²I can eat.
³I want to eat.

(12) ¹You **(tu)** have to eat.
²You can eat.
³You want to eat.

(13) ¹She has to ask.
²She can ask.
³She wants to ask.

(14) ¹You **(Lei)** have to look.
²You can look.
³You want to look.

(15) ¹We have to depart.
²We can depart.
³We want to depart.

(16) ¹You **(voi)** have to pay.
²You can pay.
³You want to pay.

(17) ¹They have to carry.
²They can carry.
³They want to carry.

(18) ¹You **(Loro)** have to study.
²You can study.
³You want to study.

B. PROGRESSIVE VARIATION. *Say or write in Italian:*

(1) ¹I eat some fruit.
²I eat some bananas.
³We eat some bananas.
⁴We don't eat any bananas.
⁵We don't eat any potatoes.
⁶We don't want any potatoes.
⁷They don't want any potatoes.
⁸They want some potatoes.
⁹They want to eat some potatoes.
¹⁰I want to eat some potatoes.
¹¹I want to eat some fruit.
¹²I want some fruit.
¹³I eat some fruit.

(2) ¹They have a suitcase.
²They have some suitcases.
³They have no suitcases.
⁴They have no string beans.
⁵They don't want any string beans.
⁶They want some string beans.
⁷He wants some string beans.
⁸He wants some hors d'œuvres.
⁹He doesn't want any hors d'œuvres.
¹⁰He doesn't want any lettuce.
¹¹He doesn't eat lettuce.
¹²He eats lettuce.
¹³They eat lettuce.
¹⁴They have lettuce.
¹⁵They have a suitcase.

(3) ¹You (**tu**) want white wine.
²You (**voi**) want white wine.
³You (**voi**) don't want white wine.
⁴You (**voi**) don't want a grilled steak.
⁵You (**voi**) want a grilled steak.
⁶You (**Loro**) want a grilled steak.
⁷You (**Loro**) want to eat a grilled steak.
⁸You (**Loro**) want to leave the hotel.
⁹You (**Lui**) want to leave the hotel.
¹⁰You (**Lei**) want white wine.
¹¹You (**tu**) want white wine.

(4) ¹We have to depart.
²We want to depart.
³You (**voi**) want to depart.
⁴You (**voi**) can depart.
⁵They can depart.
⁶They have to depart.
⁷He has to depart.
⁸He can depart.
⁹I can depart.
¹⁰I want to depart.
¹¹You (**tu**) want to depart.
¹²You (**tu**) have to depart.
¹³We have to depart.

(5) ¹The student *(m.)* has to study.
²The students *(m.)* have to study.
³The students *(f.)* have to study.
⁴The students *(f.)* want to study.
⁵The students *(f.)* don't want to study.
⁶The students *(m.)* don't want to study.
⁷The students *(m.)* can't study.
⁸The students *(m.)* can study.
⁹The student *(m.)* can study.
¹⁰The student *(m.)* wants to study.
¹¹The student *(m.)* has to study.

At the Museum

Fulvia is talking with Peter on the phone about plans for the day.

FULVIA — [1]Vuoi andare agli Uffizi stamattina?

PIETRO — [2]Ottima idea. [3]Dove sono?

FULVIA — [4]Non sono lontani da qui. [5]Sono in Piazza della Signorìa, propio accanto al Palazzo Vecchio.

PIETRO — [6]Possiamo andarci a piedi, allora.

FULVIA — [7]Certamente. [8]A che ora vuoi andare?

PIETRO — [9]Sùbito dopo colazione, va bene?

FULVIA — [10]Che ore sono?

PIETRO — [11]Sono le otto e mezzo.

(Più tardi:)
PIETRO *(all'impiegato del museo)* — [12]Due biglietti, per favore.

L'IMPIEGATO — [13]Ecco, signore.

PIETRO — [14]Quanto cóstano?

L'IMPIEGATO — [15]Duecento lire ciascuno.

PIETRO — [16]Ecco quattrocento lire.

FULVIA — [17]Dov'è l'entrata?

L'IMPIEGATO — [18]È lì a sinistra, signorina.

FULVIA — [19]Grazie.

PIETRO — [20]Questi quadri sono davvero meravigliosi.

FULVIA –- [1]Do you want to go to the Uffizi [Gallery] this morning?

PETER — [2]An excellent idea. [3]Where is it?

FULVIA –- [4]It's not far from here. [5]It's in Piazza della Signoria, right next to the Palazzo Vecchio.

PETER — [6]We can go there on foot, then.

FULVIA — [7]Certainly. [8]At what time do you want to go?

PETER — [9]Right after breakfast, O.K.?

FULVIA — [10]What time is it?

PETER — [11]It's half-past eight.

(Later:)
PETER *(to the museum employee)* — [12]Two tickets, please.

THE EMPLOYEE — [13]Here they are, sir.

PETER — [14]How much do they cost?

THE EMPLOYEE — [15]Two hundred lire each.

PETER — [16]Here are four hundred lire.

FULVIA — [17]Where is the entrance?

THE EMPLOYEE — [18]It's there on the left, miss.

FULVIA — [19]Thank you.

PETER — [20]These pictures are really marvellous.

FULVIA — [21]Hai ragione, e si prova un piacere sempre nuovo ogni volta che si ritorna.

FULVIA — [21]You're right, and you get new pleasure from them every time you return [one feels an ever new pleasure every time one returns].

PIETRO — [22]Dobbiamo tornare allora prima di partire.

PETER — [22]We must come back, then, before we leave [leaving].

FULVIA — [23]Senza dubbio.

FULVIA — [23]Without fail [without doubt].

NOTES

1. The noun **Uffizi** (literally meaning *Offices*) is masculine plural, and hence the verb in sentences 3, 4 and 5 is plural to refer to **Uffizi**. The official name of the Uffizi Gallery in Florence is **la galleria degli Uffizi.**

2. The **Piazza della Signoria** is the chief square in the old part of Florence, where the reformer Savonarola was executed and burned in 1498. Its chief landmark is the *Old Palace* (**Palazzo Vecchio**), with its tall tower.

Nel Museo degli Uffizi

Foto Deller — Monkmeyer

Foto Gendreau

Nella Piazza della Signoria

Esercizi

A. *Dica in Italiano:*

1. Do you want to go to the Uffizi this morning? 2. An excellent idea. 3. Where is it? 4. It's not far from here.

5. It's in the Piazza della Signoria, right next to the Palazzo Vecchio. 6. We can go there on foot, then. 7. Certainly. 8. At what time do you want to go? 9. Right after breakfast, O.K.?

10. What time is it? 11. It's half-past eight. 12. Two tickets, please. 13. Here they are, sir. 14. How much do they cost?

15. Two hundred lire each. 16. Here are four hundred lire. 17. Where is the entrance? 18. It's there on the left, miss. 19. Thank you.

20. These pictures are really marvelous. 21. You're right, and one feels an ever new pleasure every time one returns. 22. We must come back, then, before leaving. 23. Without doubt.

B. *Risponda in italiano alle seguenti domande:*

1. Vuoi andare agli Uffizi stamattina? 2. Dove sono gli Uffizi? 3. Possiamo andarci a piedi? 4. A che ora vuoi andarci?

5. Che ore sono? 6. Quanto cóstano i biglietti? 7. Dov'è l'entrata? 8. Sono meravigliosi questi quadri? 9. Dobbiamo tornare prima di partire?

C. *Dica a un altro studente o a un'altra studentessa:*

1. che vuole andare agli Uffizi.   2. che è un'ottima idea.   3. che può andarci a piedi.   4. che ci vuol andare dopo colazione.
5. che desìdera due biglietti.   6. che ha ragione.   7. che deve tornare prima di partire.

D. *Domandi a un altro studente o a un'altra studentessa:*

1. se vuol andare agli Uffizi.   2. dove sono gli Uffizi.   3. se si può andarci a piedi.   4. a che ora vuol andare.
5. se ha due biglietti.   6. se ha quattrocento lire.   7. se Lei ha ragione.   8. se vuol tornare.

E. *Ripeta i nùmeri da cento a mille:*

cento (100)   duecento (200)   trecento (300)   novecento (900)   mille (1,000)

F. *Ripeta i nùmeri da duemila a diecimila:*

duemila (2,000) tremila (3,000) quattromila (4,000) diecimila (10,000)

G. *Dica in italiano i seguenti nùmeri:*

700	3000	275	900	717	5700
1200	3400	1800	1349	4538	18
600	87	1534	94	8000	4067

H. *Dica in italiano:*

1. Where do you want to go this morning? To the Uffizi. Can we go there on foot?   Yes, it's next to the Palazzo Vecchio. All right.
2. What time is it? It's nine-thirty. I'd like four tickets. A hundred lire each, sir. Four hundred lire, then. Yes, sir. Here are five hundred lire. Thank you, sir; here are four tickets, and here are a hundred lire.
3. These pictures are marvelous. You are right. We must return. When can we return? At three o'clock.

J. DIALOGUE:

You are in a museum with a friend. You admire the pictures and find them marvelous. You ask what time it is. It is six o'clock. You decide to go and eat. You ask the employee where there is a restaurant. He says there is a restaurant in the Piazza della Signoria. You thank him and leave.

At a Newsstand

Fulvia and Peter leave the Uffizi Gallery and stop to buy a newspaper.

PIETRO — [1]Vorrei comprare un giornale.

PETER — [1]I'd like to buy a newspaper.

FULVIA — [2]Guarda, c'è un giornalaio là.

FULVIA — [2]Look, there's a newsdealer over there.

(Dal giornalaio)

(At the newsdealer's)

PIETRO — [3]Scusi, hanno dei giornali americani?

PETER — [3]Excuse me, have you any American newspapers?

GIORNALAIO — [4]Mi dispiace, signore, ma non ne abbiamo. [5]Lei è americano, vero?

NEWSDEALER — [4]I'm sorry, sir, but we haven't any. [5]You are American, aren't you?

PIETRO — [6]Sì, sono americano.

PETER — [6]Yes, I'm American.

GIORNALAIO — [7]Parla benìssimo l'italiano, però.

NEWSDEALER — [7]You speak Italian very well, however.

PIETRO — [8]Con una buonissima pronuncia americana, vuol dire.

PETER — [8]With a very good American pronunciation, you mean.

GIORNALAIO — [9]Oh no. [10]Certo non ha la pronuncia fiorentina, ma parla molto bene.

NEWSDEALER — [9]Oh, no. [10]Certainly you haven't got a Florentine pronunciation, but you speak very well.

PIETRO — [11]Grazie. [12]Mi dia *Il Messaggero*, per favore.

PETER — [11]Thank you. [12]Give me *Il Messaggero*, please.

GIORNALAIO — [13]Ecco, signore.

NEWSDEALER — [13]Here it is, sir.

PIETRO — [14]Quant'è?

PETER — [14]How much is it?

GIORNALAIO — [15]Venticinque lire, signore.

NEWSDEALER — [15]Twenty-five lire, sir.

PIETRO — [16]Ecco cento lire.

PETER — [16]Here are a hundred lire.

GIORNALAIO — [17]Venticinque ... cinquanta ... ecco settantacinque lire di resto.

NEWSDEALER — [17]Twenty-five ... fifty ... here are seventy-five lire change.

PIETRO — [18]Vende anche cartoline?

PETER — [18]Do you sell postcards too?

GIORNALAIO — [19]No, mi dispiace, signore. [20]Per le cartoline deve andare da un tabaccaio.

NEWSDEALER — [19]No, I'm sorry, sir. [20]For postcards you have to go to a tobacconist's.

CORRIERE

Foto Bright — Rapho-Guillumette

PIETRO — ²¹E dov'è il tabaccaio?

GIORNALAIO — ²²Guardi, è lì in quella piazza, a destra.

PIETRO — ²³Grazie mille per l'informazione.

GIORNALAIO — ²⁴Ma prego, si figuri.

PETER — ²¹And where is the tobacconist?

NEWSDEALER — ²²Look, it's there in that square, on the right.

PETER — ²³A thousand thanks for the information.

NEWSDEALER — ²⁴Oh, you're welcome, don't mention it.

NOTES

1. *Il Messaggero* (literally *The Messenger*) is a daily newspaper published in Rome, but widely read all over Italy.
2. Postcards (and also postage stamps) are normally sold in tobacco shops in Italy.

ELLA SERA

Foto Bright — Rapho-Guillumette

Un giornalaio italiano

Esercizi

A. *Dica in italiano:*

1. I'd like to buy a newspaper.　2. Look, there's a newsdealer over there. 3. Excuse me, have you any American newspapers?　4. I'm sorry, sir, but we haven't got any.

5. You are American, aren't you?　6. Yes, I'm American.　7. You speak Italian very well, however.　8. With a very good American pronunciation, you mean.　9. Oh, no.

10. Certainly you haven't got a Florentine pronunciation, but you speak very well.　11. Thank you.　12. Give me *Il Messaggero*, please.　13. Here it is, sir.　14. How much is it?

15. Twenty-five lire, sir.　16. Here are a hundred lire.　17. Twenty-five ... fifty ... here are seventy-five lire change.　18. Do you sell postcards too? 19. No, I'm sorry, sir.

20. For postcards you have to go to the tobacconist's.　21. And where is the tobacconist?　22. Look, it's there in that square, on the right.　23. A thousand thanks for the information.　24. Oh, you're welcome, don't mention it.

B. *Risponda in italiano alle seguenti domande:*

1. Vuol comprare un giornale? 2. Dov'è un giornalaio? 3. Ha dei giornali americani? 4. Ha "Il Messaggero"?
5. È americano Lei? 6. È italiano Lei? 7. Sono americani Loro? 8. Sono italiani Loro? 9. Parlo bene l'italiano?
10. Quanto costa il giornale? 11. Vende anche cartoline? 12. Dove posso avere delle cartoline? 13. Dov'è un tabaccaio?

C. *Dica a un altro studente o a un'altra studentessa:*

1. che vuol comprare un giornale. 2. che non sa dov'è un giornalaio. 3. che è americano. 4. che non vende cartoline.
5. che deve andare da un tabaccaio. 6. che c'è un tabaccaio nella piazza a destra. 7. che il giornale costa venti lire. 8. che ha una buona pronuncia americana.

D. *Domandi a un altro studente o a un'altra studentessa:*

1. se vuol comprare un giornale. 2. se c'è un giornalaio in questa piazza. 3. se ha dei giornali americani. 4. se ha *Il Messaggero.*
5. quanto costa il giornale americano.* 6. quanto costa *Il Messaggero.* 7. se ha delle cartoline. 8. quanto costa una cartolina. 9. dov'è un tabaccaio.
10. dov'è la stazione. 11. dov'è un ristorante.

E. CONVERSATIONS:

1. Do you want to buy a newspaper? Yes, I'd like to buy a newspaper. Where is a newsdealer? Here's a newsdealer. Do you have American newspapers. How much do they cost? Seventy-five lire, sir. Here are five hundred lire. And here are four hundred twenty-five lire change, sir.
2. Have you any postcards? Yes, miss, we have postcards. How much does a postcard cost? Thirty lire, miss. Give me three postcards, please. Yes, miss; ninety lire. Here are a hundred lire. And here are ten lire.
3. Do you speak Italian well? No, I speak with an American pronunication. Oh, no, you speak very well. Certainly I don't have a Florentine pronunciation. But you speak well, however. Thank you. Don't mention it.

F. DIALOGUE:

You go to a newsdealer's and buy a newspaper, giving him a hundred lire and getting change for thirty lire; then you go to a tobacconist's and buy one or more postcards.

---

* *In Italia, un giornale americano costa generalmente da sessanta a cento lire.*

12. ADJECTIVES.

Almost all Italian adjectives fall into one of two classes: those with masculine in **-o** and feminine in **-a** in the singular, with masculine plural in **-i** and feminine plural in **-e**; and those with singular (both masculine and feminine) in **-e** and plural (both genders) in **-i**.

	PLURAL OF ADJECTIVES			
M. SG.	M. PL.	F. SG.	F. PL.	*Translation*
americano	americani	americana	americane	*American*
certo	certi	certa	certe	*certain*
ferroviàrio	ferroviari	ferroviària	ferroviàrie	*of the railroad*
molto	molti	molta	molte	*much, many*
òttimo	òttimi	òttima	òttime	*excellent*

PLURAL OF ADJECTIVES IN **-e**		
M. AND F. SG.	M. AND F. PL.	*Translation*
divertente	divertenti	*amusing*
gióvane	gióvani	*young*
ideale	ideali	*ideal*
importante	importanti	*important*
milanese	milanesi	*Milanese*

IV

Certain adjectives, used only in the masculine singular, have special forms when they precede the noun they modify.

BEFORE VOWEL	buon		grande		Sant'		bello
BEFORE PURE CONSONANT	buon	*good*	gran	*big*	San	*St.*	bel *beautiful*
BEFORE IMPURE CONSONANT	buono		grande		Santo		bello

buon giorno	*good* day	**Sant'** Andrea	*St.* Andrew
un **buon** albergatore	a *good* hotelkeeper	**San** Biagio	*St.* Blasius
un **buono** studente	a *good* student	**Santo** Stèfano	*St.* Stephen
un **grande** albergo	a *big* hotel	un **bell'**àlbero	a *beautiful* tree
un **gran** dubbio	a *big* doubt	un **bel** giorno	a *beautiful* day
un **grande** spècchio	a *big* mirror	un **bello** scherzo	a *fine* joke

Of these adjectives, only **bello** *fine, beautiful* has special forms for use in the plural: **begli** before vowel or *impure* consonant, **bei** before *pure* consonant. These special forms, likewise, are used only when the adjective precedes a noun it modifies:

begli alberghi	*beautiful* hotels
begli sposi	*fine* bridegrooms (or married couple) (*sg.* **sposo**)
bei musei	*fine* museums

The special forms of **bello** *beautiful* parallel the forms of the definite article. Those of **buono** *good* parallel the indefinite article.

La Stampa

solo conoscerebbe signorina o scopo matrimonio. Scrivere: à Stampa 8455 — Torino ».

UENNE operaia serie inten- serebbe 40enne anche vedovo iccola serietà buona posizione. mi. Scrivere: Pubblicità Stam — Torino ». A91416

UENNE seria, graziosa, requi- moglie, distinta, fine educa- dente località marina, spose- 5enne anche vedovo, sani prin- lmente elevato, posizione si- ere: Pubblicità Stampa A92189 ».

IE, alto, distinto, bella pre- ro professionista, agiato, cor- be scopo matrimonio signo- alta, distinta, pari condizione. A91616

IE buon impiego spo

uona laureata semp... trimonio considerevole sposerebbe ade- guatamente massimo 45enne. Trattano parenti. Scrivere: Pubblicità A91084

DISTINTO ricco 46enne giovanile, leale, simpatico, sposerebbe veramente bella, educata, affettuosa. Indicare requisiti, nominativo Riservatezza assoluta. Scri- vere: Pubblicità Torino ». A90850

GENITORI sposano figlia 29enne signo- rina carina preferibile vedovo con bam- bino. Scrivere: Pubblicità Stampa — Torino ». A92416

GIOVANE 31enne 1,65 impiego sicuro conoscerebbe scopo matrimonio signorina seria e affettuosa pari condizioni. Scrive- re: Pubblicità Stampa — Torino ».

GIOVANILISSIMA signorina canavesana 39enne benestante, impiegata industria, colta, affettuosa, attiva, doti casalinghe, disposta trasferirsi, collaborare, spose- rebbe preferibilmente settentrionale, se- rio, colto, posizione sicura, senza im- portanza lieve imperfezione fisica. Scrive- Pubblicità St...

TRENTUNENNE, principi morali cepibili, buona posizione, conoscerebbe signorina scopo matrimonio. Scrivere: — Torino ».

VEDOVA distintissima bella ricca spose- rebbe vedovo pari condizioni 60-65enne. Scrivere: Pubblicità Torino ». A91704

VEDOVA 40enne benestante distintissima giovanile affettuosa conoscerebbe persona seria adeguata scopo matrimonio. Cesti- nansi anonimi. Scrivere: — Torino ». A92054

VEDOVA 40enne piemontese alta robusta benestante relazionerebbe scopo matrimo- nio con distinto alto pari condizioni. Scrivere: Torino ». A92003

VEDOVA 48enne distinta, attività in pro- prio, relazionerebbe scopo matrimonio con industriale benestante, vedovo senza figli. Scrivere: Pubblicità — Torino ». A90346

An adjective must agree in gender and number with the noun it modifies, whether the adjective accompanies the noun or is a predicate adjective with **èssere** *to be* and similar verbs (*e.g.* **divenire** or **diventare** *to become*). When acting as modifiers in a noun phrase, most adjectives normally follow the noun they modify. Certain adjectives, however (*e.g.* **buono** *good*, **cattivo** *bad*, **bello** *beautiful*, **brutto** *ugly*, **gióvane** *young*, **vecchio** *old*, **stesso** *same*) normally precede their noun. Thus:

una pronuncia **fiorentina**	a *Florentine* pronunciation
una stanza **còmoda**	a *comfortable* room
un'òpera **importante**	an *important* opera
un vento **forte**	a *strong* wind

BUT

un **bell'**albergo	a *fine* hotel
una **bella** piazza	a *beautiful* square
una **brutta** cartolina	an *ugly* postcard
un **gióvane** studente	a *young* student
un **vecchio** amico	an *old* friend
la **stessa** trattoria	the *same* restaurant

● 13. DEMONSTRATIVE ADJECTIVES.

Demonstrative adjectives include **questo** *this* and **quello** *that*. These adjectives normally precede the noun they modify. The forms **questo** (*m.sg.*) and **questa** (*f.sg.*) may become **quest'** before a vowel, but not necessarily. The adjective **quello** has special masculine forms parallel to those of **bello: quell'** before a vowel and **quel** before a pure consonant in the singular, **quegli** before a vowel or impure consonant and **quei** before a pure consonant.

quest'àlbero (*or* **questo** àlbero)	*this* tree
quest'òpera (*or* **questa** ôpera)	*this* opera
quell'albergo	*that* hotel
quel nùmero	*that* number
quello sbaglio	*that* mistake
quegli alberghi	*those* hotels
quegli sbagli	*those* mistakes
quei nùmeri	*those* numbers

GRAMMAR UNIT FOUR

Grammar Exercises

A. SUBSTITUTIONS. *Say or write in Italian:*

	A	B
(1)	¹an Italian hotelkeeper	¹some Italian hotelkeepers
	²an Italian autumn	²some Italian autumns
	³ an Italian waiter	³some Italian waiters
	⁴an Italian cheese	⁴some Italian cheeses
	⁵an Italian gentleman	⁵some Italian gentlemen
	⁶an Italian train	⁶some Italian trains
	¹an Italian friend *(f.)*	¹some Italian friends *(f.)*
	²an Italian beefsteak	²some Italian beefsteaks
	³an Italian dinner	³some Italian dinners
	⁴an Italian peach	⁴some Italian peaches
	⁵an Italian suitcase	⁵some Italian suitcases
	⁶an Italian station	⁶some Italian stations
(2)	¹the American newspaper	¹the American newspapers
	²the amusing newspaper	²the amusing newspapers
	³the Florentine newspaper	³the Florentine newspapers
	⁴the ideal newspaper	⁴the ideal newspapers
	⁵the Italian newspaper	⁵the Italian newspapers
	⁶the free newspaper	⁶the free newspapers
	⁷the important newspaper	⁷the important newspapers
(3)	¹a good wine	¹some good wines
	²a Florentine wine	²some Florentine wines
	³a fine wine	²some fine wines
	⁴a white wine	⁴some white wines
	⁵that wine	⁵those wines
	⁶this wine	⁶these wines
(4)	¹that newspaper	¹those newspapers
	²that art	²those arts
	³that autumn	³those autumns
	⁴that dinner	⁴those dinners
	⁵that joke	⁵those jokes
(5)	¹that good newspaper	¹those good newspapers
	²that same newspaper	²those same newspapers
	³that good breakfast	³those good breakfasts
	⁴that same breakfast	⁴those same breakfasts

B. PROGRESSIVE VARIATION. *Say or write in Italian:*

(1) ¹the next week
²the next autumn
³the Italian autumn
⁴the Italian autumns
⁵the Italian museums
⁶the fine museums
⁷the fine (handsome) students *(m.)*
⁸the beautiful students *(f.)*
⁹the Milanese students *(f.)*
¹⁰the Milanese student *(f.)*
¹¹the Milanese pronunciation
¹²the good pronunciation
¹³the good picture
¹⁴the American picture
¹⁵the American pictures
¹⁶the next pictures
¹⁷the next picture
¹⁸the next week

(2) ¹an excellent newsdealer
²some excellent newsdealers
³some important newsdealers
⁴some important tobacconists
⁵that important tobacconist
⁶that important student
⁷this important student
⁸this young student
⁹these young students
¹⁰those young students
¹¹those American students
¹²those American hotelkeepers
¹³that American hotelkeeper
¹⁴that excellent hotelkeeper
¹⁵an excellent hotelkeeper
¹⁶an excellent newsdealer

(3) ¹of the representational *(figurative)* arts
²to the representational arts
³to the fine arts
⁴in the fine arts
⁵in the fine pictures
⁶on the fine pictures
⁷on the amusing pictures
⁸on the amusing picture
⁹from the amusing picture
¹⁰from the amusing conversation
¹¹with the amusing conversation
¹²with the good conversation
¹³with the good waiter
¹⁴of the good waiter
¹⁵of the good art
¹⁶of the representational art
¹⁷of the representational arts

C. *Translate into Italian:*

1. The lettuce is good.   2. She wants to familiarize herself with the city.   3. This mirror is good.   4. I'd like a single room.
5. The station is very big.   6. In the big palace there are many pictures.   7. We have to eat in the restaurant of the hotel.   8. They are studying medicine in an Italian university.   9. Let's go to the museum of the Uffizi this afternoon.
10. These bananas are excellent.

The Weather

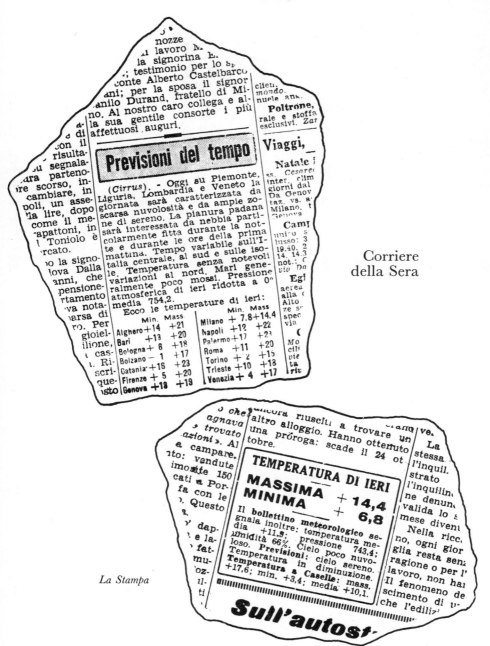

nozze
...l lavoro M.
la signorina E.
; testimonio per lo s...
conte Alberto Castelbarco
...ni; per la sposa il signor
...anilo Durand, fratello di Mi-
no. Al nostro caro collega e alla sua gentile consorte i più
affettuosi auguri.

Previsioni del tempo

(Cirrus). - Oggi su Piemonte,
Liguria, Lombardia e Veneto la
giornata sarà caratterizzata da
scarsa nuvolosità e da ample zo-
ne di sereno. La pianura padana
sarà interessata da nebbia particolarmente fitta durante la notte e durante le ore della prima
mattina. Tempo variabile sull'I-
talia centrale, al sud e sulle iso-
le. Temperatura senza notevoli
variazioni al nord. Mari generalmente poco mossi. Pressione
atmosferica di ieri ridotta a 0°
media 754,2.
Ecco le temperature di ieri:

	Min.	Mass		Min.	Mass
Alghero	+14	+21	Milano	+ 7.8	+14.4
Bari	+13	+20	Napoli	+12	+22
Bologna	+ 6	+18	Palermo	+17	+23
Bolzano	− 1	+17	Roma	+11	+20
Catania	+16	+23	Torino	+ 7	+15
Firenze	+ 5	+20	Trieste	+10	+18
Genova	+13	+19	Venezia	+ 4	+17

clien.
mondo
nucle an.
Poltrone,
rale e stoffa
esclusivi. Zar

Viaggi,
Natale i
ss. Cesare
inter. clim
giorni dal
Da Genov
taz. vs. a
Milano. t
Genova

Camp
unico s
lusso: 3
19.40. 2
14. 14.3
not.: C
via Do

Egi
aerea
alla (
Alto
ze s'
spec
via

Mo
cili
vie
ta
rit

Corriere
della Sera

...o che...ancora riusciti a trovare un
...agnava...altro alloggio. Hanno ottenuto
... trovato una proroga: scade il 24 ot
...azioni». Al tobre.
...campare.
...to: vendute
...imo..te 150
...cati a Por-
...fa con le
... Questo

TEMPERATURA DI IERI

MASSIMA	+ **14,4**
MINIMA	+ **6,8**

Il **bollettino meteorologico** se-
gnala inoltre: temperatura media +11.9; pressione 743,4;
umidità 66%. Cielo poco nuvoloso. **Previsioni:** cielo sereno.
Temperatura in diminuzione.
Temperatura a Caselle: mass.
+17,6; min. +3,4; media +10,1.

Sull'autost-

La
stessa
l'inquil.
strato
l'inquilin
ne denun
valida lo s
mese divent
Nella ricc.
no, ogni gior
glia resta sen
ragione o per l'
lavoro, non ha
Il fenomeno de
scimento di v
che l'edili...

La Stampa

Foto ISTO

Città Universitaria, Roma

It's a fine October morning as Peter leaves his pensione *for the University.*

(Pietro parla con la portiera)

PORTIERA — ¹Buon giorno, signorino. ²Bella giornata oggi, vero?

PIETRO — ³Sì, ma fa freddo per ottobre.

PORTIERA — ⁴Fa fresco perché ha piovuto tutta la settimana. ⁵Ma il sole è ancora caldo.

PIETRO — ⁶Piove spesso in autunno qui a Roma?

PORTIERA — ⁷Generalmente in settembre e ottobre fa bello, ma piove molto in novembre e dicembre.

(Peter talks with the door keeper's wife)

DOORKEEPER'S WIFE — ¹Good morning, young sir. ²[A] fine day today, isn't it?

PETER — ³Yes, but it's cold for October.

DOORKEEPER'S WIFE — ⁴It's cool because it has rained all week. ⁵But the sun is still hot.

PETER — ⁶Does it often rain in autumn here in Rome?

DOORKEEPER'S WIFE — ⁷Generally, in September and October the weather is fine, but it rains a lot in November and December.

CONVERSATION UNIT NINE

PIETRO — ⁸D'inverno névica?

PORTIERA — ⁹Oh no, quasi mai. ¹⁰A volte, però, fa molto freddo. ¹¹Specialmente quando tira vento ed è sereno.

PIETRO — ¹²Io vivo nello Stato del Massachusetts. ¹³Da noi névica molto, a volte persino in primavera.

PORTIERA — ¹⁴Davvero? ¹⁵Qui la primavera è la stagione più bella e allegra. ¹⁶I prati e gli àlberi sono pieni di fiori e di foglie. ¹⁷L'estate è calda, ma ogni tanto ci sono dei temporali violenti che rinfréscano l'aria.

PIETRO — ¹⁸Sì, ma scommetto che voi non avete nulla come il nostro autunno. ¹⁹Le foglie divéntano di mille colori.

PORTIERA — ²⁰Dev'èssere molto bello! ²¹Ma devo andare ora; arrivederLa.

PIETRO — ²²Buon giorno.

PETER — ⁸Does it snow in winter?

DOORKEEPER'S WIFE — ⁹Oh no, almost never. ¹⁰At times, however, it's very cold. ¹¹Especially when the wind is blowing and it's clear.

PETER — ¹²I live in the State of Massachusetts. ¹³Where we are (with us), it snows a lot, at times even in spring.

DOORKEEPER'S WIFE — ¹⁴Really? ¹⁵Here the spring is the most beautiful and cheerful season. ¹⁶The fields and trees are full of flowers and leaves. ¹⁷The summer is hot, but every so often there are violent storms which cool off the air.

PETER — ¹⁸Yes, but I bet that *you* don't have anything like our autumn. ¹⁹The leaves become [of] a thousand colors.

DOORKEEPER'S WIFE — ²⁰It must be very beautiful! ²¹But I have to go now; good-bye.

PETER — ²²Good-bye. (Good morning).

NOTES

1. The **portiera** (*f.*) and **portiere** (*m.*) are the doorkeepers in Italian apartment houses. They normally live in an apartment opening off the main street entrance of the building and act as overseers, janitor and janitress. The **portiere** is usually a handyman, making small repairs, taking in large packages for the tenants, *etc.* The **portiera** often acts as a practical nurse, *e.g.,* in giving injections. The Italian institution of the **portiere** corresponds closely to the French custom of having a **concierge** for an apartment house.
2. **Signorino,** literally *little gentleman* or *young sir*, is the masculine equivalent of **signorina,** and is often used, especially by **portieri, portiere** and maids, in addressing young men in their late teens or early twenties.
3. **Giorno** refers to the day as a unit time; **giornata,** to the whole length of the day, to its state or condition (*e.g.* with regard to weather), or to what is accomplished during a day.

Foto ISTO

Primavera a Roma. Trinità dei Monti

Esercizi

A. *Dica in Italiano:*

1. Good morning, young sir.   2. A fine day today, isn't it?   3. Yes, but it's cold for October.   4. It's cool because it has rained all week.

5. But the sun is still hot.   6. Does it often rain in autumn here in Rome? 7. Generally, in September and October the weather is fine, but it rains a lot in November and December.   8. Does it snow in winter?   9. Oh no, almost never.

10. At times, however, it's very cold.   11. Especially when the wind is blowing and it's clear.   12. I live in the State of Massachusetts.   13. Where we are (with us), it snows a lot, at times even in spring.   14. Really?

15. Here the spring is the most beautiful and cheerful season.   16. The fields and trees are full of flowers and leaves.   17. The summer is hot, but every so often there are violent storms which cool off the air.   18. Yes, but I bet that you don't have anything like our autumn.   19. The leaves become (of) a thousand colors.   20. It must be very beautiful.

B. *Risponda in italiano alle seguenti domande:*

1. Fa bello oggi?   2. È caldo il sole?   3. Piove spesso qui?   4. Névica molto a Roma?
5. Fa fresco ora?   6. È sereno adesso?   7. È bella la primavera?   8. È calda l'estate?   9. Fa caldo oggi?
10. Come divéntano le foglie in autunno?

C. *Domandi a un altro studente o a un'altra studentessa:*

1. se névica ora.   2. se fa freddo nello Stato del Massachusetts.   3. se fa caldo d'inverno.   4. di che cosa sono pieni i prati e gli àlberi in primavera.
5. se piove quando fa bello.   6. come divéntano le foglie in autunno.   7. che cosa fanno i temporali.   8. se tira vento oggi.   9. se piove qui in ottobre.
10. se la giornata è bella.

D. *Ripeta i nomi dei mesi* (Repeat the names of the months):

gennaio	*January*	maggio	*May*	settembre	*September*
febbraio	*February*	giugno	*June*	ottobre	*October*
marzo	*March*	luglio	*July*	novembre	*November*
aprile	*April*	agosto	*August*	dicembre	*December*

Note that the names of the months are all masculine, and in Italian are always written with a small, not a capital, letter.

E. *Dica o scriva in italiano:*

1. It's hot for February.   2. It often snows here in the winter.   3. It's cold when the wind is blowing.   4. At times it rains a lot, even in spring.
5. The spring isn't a beautiful season here.   6. In the state of New York, the summer is the most cheerful season.   7. There are't any storms.   8. The flowers are of a thousand colors.   9. It is very clear.
10. It hasn't rained this week.

F. CONVERSATIONS:

1. You discuss the weather in Rome (as described in this unit) as compared with that in your home town.
2. You talk about the different months of the year and what kind of weather there is in each.

Foto Bright — Rapho-Guillumette

Nel banco

CONVERSATION UNIT——————IO

At the Bank

Peter, who will be spending the year in Florence, decides it's time to open a bank account.

L'IMPIEGATO — ¹Buon giorno, signore. ²Posso servirLa?

PIETRO — ³Buon giorno. ⁴Vorrei depositare del denaro.

L'IMPIEGATO — ⁵Ha del denaro lìquidó o in assegni?

PIETRO — ⁶Ho degli assegni viaggiatori.

L'IMPIEGATO — ⁷Vuole aprire un conto corrente o un libretto di risparmio?

PIETRO — ⁸Non so. ⁹Forse potrei depositare seicento dòllari, cioè trecentosettantacinquemila lire in un conto corrente, e centocinquantamila lire in un libretto di risparmio.

THE CLERK — ¹Good morning, sir. ²Can I help (serve) you?

PETER — ³Good morning. ⁴I'd like to deposit some money.

THE CLERK — ⁵Do you have money in cash or in checks?

PETER — ⁶I have travellers' cheques.

THE CLERK — ⁷Do you want to open a checking account or a savings account (booklet)?

PETER — ⁸I don't know. ⁹Perhaps I might deposit six hundred dollars, that is three hundred seventy-five thousand lire in a checking account, and a hundred and fifty thousand lire in a savings account (booklet).

64

L'Impiegato — ¹⁰Bene, vuole un libretto al portatore o un libretto personale?

Pietro — ¹¹Che differenza c'è?

L'Impiegato — ¹²Nel libretto personale c'è il Suo nome e solamente Lei può ritirare il denaro.

Pietro — ¹³Me lo faccia personale.

L'Impiegato — ¹⁴Deve depositarmi la firma e darmi il passaporto per l'identificazione. ¹⁵Riempia questa distinta di versamento e firmi qui. ¹⁶Per il depòsito, si accòmodi alla cassa.

Pietro — ¹⁷Ecco fatto, grazie.

(Dal Cassiere)

Pietro — ¹⁸Ecco gli assegni firmati.

Cassiere — ¹⁹Grazie, signore; ecco la ricevuta di pagamento.

Pietro — ²⁰Può cambiarmi diecimila lire in biglietti da mille e da cinquecento?

Cassiere — ²¹Certamente, signore; ecco a Lei.

The Clerk — ¹⁰Very well; do you want a booklet [made out] to the bearer or a personal booklet?

Peter — ¹¹What difference is there?

The Clerk — ¹²In the personal booklet there is your name and only you can withdraw the money.

Peter — ¹³Make it personal for me.

The Clerk — ¹⁴You have to file (deposit) your signature *with* me and give me your passport for identification. ¹⁵Fill out this deposit slip and sign here. ¹⁶For the deposit, please go to the cashier's window.

Peter — ¹⁷Here it is; thank you.

(At the Cashier's)

Peter — ¹⁸Here are the signed cheques.

Cashier — ¹⁹Thank you, sir; here is the receipt for the payment.

Peter — ²⁰Can you change ten thousand lire for me into one-thousand and five-hundred lire notes?

Cashier — ²¹Certainly, sir; here you are (it is for you).

NOTES

1. The official term for *traveller's cheques* is **assegni viaggiatori** (*sg.* **assegno viaggiatori**), literally *cheques [for] travellers*; but the English term is widely used in Italian banks.

2. The **cassa** is the cashier's office, desk or window in an Italian bank or store, where the customer pays in the money for his deposit or his purchase, or where (in the bank) he receives the money he is drawing out.

3. Italian monetary units (1962) are in the form of bank notes for 10,000 lire (approximatively $16.00); 5,000 lire ($8.00); 1,000 lire ($1.60); 500 lire ($0.80). The coinage includes silver coins worth 500 lire. and alloy coins for 100, 50, 20, 10, 5, 2 lire and 1 lira. In writing out sums in lire, the abbrevations L, £, or Lit. are frequently used; *e.g.,* L. 12.000 **dodicimila lire.**

Foto Bright —
Rapho-Guillumette

Esercizi

A. *Dica in italiano:*

1. Good morning, sir. 2. May I help you? 3. Good morning. 4. I'd like to deposit some money.

5. Do you have money in cash or in cheques? 6. I have travellers' cheques. 7. Do you want to open a checking account or a savings account (booklet)? 8. I don't know. 9. Perhaps I might deposit six hundred dollars, that is three hundred seventy-five thousand lire in a checking account, and a hundred and fifty thousand lire in a savings account (booklet).

10. Very well; do you want a booklet made out to the bearer, or a personal booklet? 11. What difference is there? 12. In the personal booklet there is your name and only you can withdraw the money. 13. Make it personal for me. 14. You have to file (deposit) your signature with me, and give me your passport for identification.

15. Fill out this deposit slip and sign here. 16. For the deposit, please go to the cashier's window. 17. Here it is; thank you. 18. Here are the signed checks. 19. Thank you, sir; here is the receipt for the payment.

CONVERSATION UNIT TEN

20. Can you change ten thousand lire for me into one-thousand and five-hundred lire notes?   21. Certainly, sir; here you are (it is for you).

B. *Risponda in italiano alle seguenti domande:*

1. Posso servirLa?   2. Vuol depositare del denaro?   3. Quanti dòllari vuol cambiare in lire?   4. Ha del denaro lìquido o in assegni?
5. Vuol aprire un conto corrente o un libretto di risparmio?   6. Vuole un libretto personale o un libretto al portatore?   7. Che differenza c'è tra un libretto personale e un libretto al portatore?   8. Ha il passaporto?   9. Dov'è la ricevuta di pagamento.
10. Può cambiarmi cinquemila lire in biglietti da mille?

C. *Dica a un altro studente o a un'altra studentessa:*

1. che vuol depositare del denaro.   2. che ha degli assegni viaggiatori.   3. che può depositare seicento dòllari.   4. che non sa che differenza ç'è tra un libretto al portatore e un libretto personale.
5. che deve riempire la distinta di versamento.   6. che deve firmare.   7. che deve accomodarsi alla cassa.   8. che vuol cambiare cinquecento dòllari in lire.

D. *Domandi a un altro studente o a un'altra studentessa:*

1. se può servirlo (servirla).   2. che cosa vuol depositare.   3. che tipo (*type*) di conto vuol aprire.   4. che tipo di libretto di risparmio desìdera.
5. che differenza c'è tra i due tipi di libretto.   6. dove sono gli assegni.   7. dov'è la cassa.   8. dov'è la ricevuta di pagamento.   9. se può cambiare ventimila lire in biglietti più pìccoli.

E. *Dica o scriva in italiano:*

1. How can I help you, sir?   2. I have to deposit some travellers' cheques.   3. We want to open a checking account.   4. You (**Lei**) can deposit four hundred dollars.
5. I'd like a booklet made out to the bearer.   6. Can you give me a personal booklet?   7. I'm withdrawing the money today.   8. They are filing (depositing) their (the) signatures.   9. I can't change a ten-thousand lire note.
10. We are signing the cheques.

F. CONVERSATIONS:

1. You talk with a bank clerk about opening accounts; he tells you what kind of accounts there are, and you decide which you want.
2. You deposit some money with the bank cashier, and get him to change some five- or ten-thousand lire notes.

LETTURA SECONDA

In un Ristorante all'Aperto

(Conversations 6-10)

[1] **di lusso**   de luxe.
[2] **piacévole**   pleasant.
[3] **pulito**   clean.
[4] **si sièdono**   they sit down.
[5] **la lista**   the list.
[6] **il piatto**   the dish.
[7] **elencato**   listed (**elencare**   to list).
[8] **per di più**   moreover.
[9] **la calligrafia**   the handwriting (calligraphy).

Fulvia e Pietro cénano in un ristorante vicino alla stazione. Non è un ristorante di lusso[1] ma è piacévole[2] e pulito.[3] Si sièdono[4] ad una tàvola all'aperto perché è più fresco fuori. Il cameriere porta la lista[5] (il menù). Pietro non sa cosa préndere perché non conosce i nomi dei piatti[6] elencati[7] nella lista. Per di più,[8] la calligrafia[9] italiana è così diversa da quella americana!

Pietro òrdina saltimbocca alla romana[10] che sono una specialità[11] del posto, contorno[12] di zucchine[13] e purée di patate e vino rosso: del chianti.[14] Fulvia invece[15] òrdina pesce[16] con fagiolini e insalata di pomodori,[17] e naturalmente vino bianco. Pietro vuole del burro[18] con il pane,[19] ma in Italia nessuno[20] mangia pane e burro durante[21] i pasti.

— Cosa màngiano, pane solo? — domanda Pietro stupito.[22]

— Sì, certo — gli[23] spiega[24] Fulvia — ma se proprio vuoi del burro puoi chièderlo[25] al cameriere.

Alla fine del pasto Pietro òrdina due espressi,[26] paga il conto e lascia[27] il resto di mancia[28] al cameriere.

Dopo cena Fulvia e Pietro vanno a piedi fino[29] all'albergo perché non è lontano. Si férmano un istante[30] in un chiosco[31] di giornali, ma l'istante diventa dieci minuti; infatti[32] il giornalaio è un tipo[33] buffo[34] e cordiale.[35] Comincia una lunga conversazione sul tempo, sugli Stati Uniti,[36] sull'educazione,[37] eccètera[38] eccètera. Fa molte domande[39] a Pietro e da buon cavaliere[40] fa dei complimenti[41] a Fulvia; le[42] dice che è una ragazza[43] carina[44] e intelligente.

Pietro compra infine[45] un giornale. I due cugini salùtano[46] il giornalaio e vanno per i fatti[47] loro.[48]

[10]**saltimbocca alla Romana** *a rolled-up slice of veal with various piquant sauces.*
[11]**la specialità** the specialty.
[12]**il contorno** *the vegetables accompanying a meat dish.*
[13]**la zucchina** the squash.
[14]**Chianti** *an Italian red wine.*
[15]**invece** instead, on the other hand.
[16]**il pesce** the fish.
[17]**il pomodoro** (*pl.* **i pomodori** *or* **i pomidoro**) the tomato.
[18]**il burro** the butter.
[19]**il pane** the bread.
[20]**nessuno** nobody.
[21]**durante** during.
[22]**stupito** amazed (**stupire** to amaze).
[23]**gli** to him.
[24]**spiegare** to explain.
[25]**chièderlo** to ask for it (**chièdere** to ask, request).
[26]**l'espresso** *(m.)* espresso coffee.
[27]**lasciare** to leave.
[28]**la mancia** the tip; **di mancia** as a tip.
[29]**fino a** as far as.
[30]**l'istante** *(m.)* the instant.
[31]**il chiosco** the kiosk, stand.
[32]**infatti** in fact.
[33]**il tipo** the type, character, fellow.
[34]**buffo** funny.
[35]**cordiale** cordial.
[36]**gli Stati Uniti** the United States.
[37]**l'educazione** *(f.)* the education.
[38]**eccètera** etcetera.
[39]**la domanda** the question (**fare una domanda** to ask a question).
[40]**il cavaliere** the knight, gentleman (**da buon cavaliere** like a courteous gentleman).
[41]**il complimiento** the compliment.
[42]**le** to her.
[43]**la ragazza** the girl.
[44]**carino** nice.
[45]**infine** finally.
[46]**salutare** to greet, say good-bye to.
[47]**il fatto** the fact, deed, activity.
[48]**loro** their (**vanno per i fatti loro** they go on about their business).

GRAMMAR UNIT ———————————— V

● 14. POSSESSIVE ADJECTIVES.

Italian has the following possessive adjectives:

	POSSESSIVE ADJECTIVES			
M. SG.	F. SG.	M. PL.	F. PL.	TRANSLATION
mio	mia	miei	mie	*my*
tuo (*2nd sg.*)	tua	tuoi	tue	*your*
suo	sua	suoi	sue	*his, her, its*
Suo (*3rd sg., formal*)	Sua	Suoi	Sue	*your*
nostro	nostra	nostri	nostre	*our*
vostro (*2nd pl.*)	vostra	vostri	vostre	*your*

The possessives **mio, tuo** and **suo (Suo)** have the iregular masculine plural forms **miei, tuoi** and **suoi (Suoi)**, respectively. All of these adjectives agree in gender and number with whatever noun they modify.

il **mio** denaro	*my* money
la **tua** cartolina	*your* postcard
il **suo** giornale	*her* newspaper
la **sua** pronuncia	*his* pronunciation
i **Suoi** alberghi	*your* hotels
le **nostre** scuole	*our* schools
i **vostri** vini	*your* wines

The possessive **suo** means *his, her* and *its*, i.e., it tells the hearer or reader nothing about the sex of the possessor involved.

There is no corresponding possessive adjective for *their* (third person plural possessive). The place of such an adjective is taken by the possessive pronoun **loro** *of them*, which since it is a pronoun, is not declined like an adjective, but remains invariable regardless of the gender and number of the noun it modifies. The same form (usually capitalized in writing, **Loro**) is used for *your* (formal, *3rd pl.*).

il **loro** posto	*their* place
la **loro** stanza	*their* room
i **loro** posti	*their* places
le **loro** stanze	*their* rooms
il **Loro** posto *etc.*	*your* (*3rd pl.*) place

When these possessive forms (the possessive adjectives and **loro**) modify a noun, they normally precede it, and are themselves preceded by the definite article, or by an indefinite article, a demonstrative or indefinite adjective, or a numeral:

la **mia** cartolina	*my* postcard
una **mia** cartolina	*a* postcard *of mine*
questa **mia** cartolina	*this* postcard *of mine*
tre **mie** cartoline	*three* postcards *of mine*
i **miei** ristoranti	*my* restaurants
alcune **mie** idee	*some* ideas *of mine*

A possessive follows its noun only to indicate emphasis: *e.g.*, **un'idea mia,** *an idea of mine.*

If the noun modified by the possessive adjective is one of a small group of terms indicating family relationship, and if the noun is in the singular without any other modifiers, and has no suffixes (diminutive, *etc.*) added to it, the definite article is omitted and only the possessive adjective + the noun are left. This principle holds true only for possessive adjectives. The possessive pronoun **loro** does not behave in this way.

mio zio	*my* uncle		**i miei** zii	*my* uncles
tua cugina	*your* cousin	BUT	la **tua** cugina americana	*your* American cousin
nostro fratello	*our* brother		il **nostro** fratellino	*our* little brother
suo padre	*his* father		il **loro** padre	*their* father

The kinship terms with which the definite article, before a possessive adjective, is cancelled out in this way include :

cognata	sister-in-law	**nipote** (*f.*)	niece, granddaughter
cognato	brother-in-law	**nipote** (*m.*)	nephew, grandson
cugina (*f.*)	cousin	**nonna**	grandmother
cugino (*m.*)	cousin	**nonno**	grandfather
figlia	daughter	**nuora**	daughter-in-law
figlio	son	**padre**	father
fratello	brother	**sorella**	sister
gènero	son-in-law	**suòcera**	mother-in-law
madre	mother	**suòcero**	father-in-law
marito	husband	**zia**	aunt
moglie	wife	**zio**	uncle

15. PRESENT TENSE OF THE SECOND CONJUGATION.

The verbs of the second conjugation have their infinitive in **-ire**, *e.g.*, **aprire** *to open*, **partire** *to depart*, **capire** *to understand*. Some verbs of this conjugation add all the endings of the present to the root without any intervening suffix; others, however, insert **-isc-** in the singular and in the third person plural.

PRESENT TENSE—REGULAR VERBS—SECOND CONJUGATION			
partire *to depart* **part-**		**capire** *to understand* **cap-**	
parto	I depart	capisco	I understand
parti	you (*fam.*) depart	capisci	you (*fam.*) understand
parte	he, she, it departs; you (*formal*) depart	capisce	he, she, it understands; you (*formal*) understand
partiamo	we depart	capiamo	we understand
partite	you (*fam.pl.*) depart	capite	you (*fam.pl.*) understand
pàrtono	they depart; you (*formal pl.*) depart	capiscono	they understand; you (*formal pl.*) understand

The following, among others, are also conjugated like **partire**: **aprire** *to open*; **coprire** *to cover*; **dormire** *to sleep*; **mentire** *to lie (tell a falsehood); and **sentire** *to feel, hear*

 16. PRESENT TENSE OF THE THIRD CONJUGATION.

In the third conjugation are included verbs having their infinitive in **-ere**, *e.g.*, **véndere** *to sell*, **vedere** *to see*, *etc.* Using **préndere** *to take* as an example:

PRESENT TENSE—REGULAR VERBS—THIRD CONJUGATION			
préndere to take **prend-**			
prendo	I take	prendiamo	we take
prendi	you (*fam.*) take	prendete	you (*fam. pl.*) take
prende	he, she, it takes; you (*formal*) take	préndono	they take; you (*formal pl.*) take

◆ « Dottore — dice una voce affannata al telefono — mio marito si crede un cavallo. Che devo fare? ». « Vostro marito è un fantino, ci scommetto » ribatte il dottore. « Esattamente ». « Allora — continua il medico — si tratta semplicemente di un caso di deformazione professionale. Comunque venite al più presto da me ». « D'accordo, dottore. Lo sello e arrivo di galoppo ».

◆ Uno psichiatra incontra nella hall di un grande albergo della Costa Azzurra uno dei suoi clienti che era afflitto da cleptomania. « Caro amico — gli dice — come va? Completamente guarito, nevvero? ». « Oh, sì, dottore, grazie — replica l'altro. — Prima rubavo qualsiasi cosa: adesso, grazie alle vostre cure, non prendo che oggetti di grande valore ».

Dal "Settimo Giorno", 9.10.62

● **17.** PRESENT TENSE OF **andare** *to go,* **dare** *to give,* **dire** *to say,* and **fare** *to do.*

andare	*to go*	**dare**	*to give*
vado	I go	**do**	I give
vai	you (*fam.*) go	**dai**	you (*fam.*) give
va	he, she, it goes; you (*formal*), go	**dà**	he, she, it gives; you (*formal*) give
andiamo	we go	**diamo**	we give
andate	you (*fam. pl.*) go	**date**	you (*fam. pl.*) give
vanno	they go; you (*formal pl.*) go	**dànno**	they give; you (*formal pl.*) give

dire	*to say*	**fare**	*to do*
dico	I say	**faccio**	I do
dici	you (*fam.*) say	**fai**	you, (*fam.*) do
dice	he, she, it says; you, (*formal*) say	**fa**	he, she, it does; you (*formal*) do
diciamo	we say	**facciamo**	we do
dite	you (*fam. pl.*) say	**fate**	you (*fam. pl.*) do
dicono	they say; you (*formal pl.*) say	**fanno**	they do; you (*formal pl.*) do

Grammatical Exercises

A. SUBSTITUTIONS. *Say or write in Italian:*

<table>
<tr><td align="center">A</td><td align="center">B</td></tr>
</table>

(1) [1]my booklet
    [2]your *(fam.)* booklet
    [3]his booklet
    [4]your *(formal)* booklet

[1]our booklet
[2]your *(fam. pl.)* booklet
[3]their booklet
[4]your *(formal pl.)* booklet

(2) [1]my pronunciation
    [2]your *(fam.)* pronunciation
    [3]her pronunciation
    [4]your *(formal)* pronunciation

[1]our pronunciation
[2]your *(fam. pl.)* pronunciation
[3]their pronunciation
[4]your *(formal pl.)* pronunciation

(3) [1]my feet
    [2]your *(fam.)* feet
    [3]its feet
    [4]your *(formal)* feet

[1]our feet
[2]your *(fam. pl.)* feet
[3]their feet
[4]your *(formal pl.)* feet

(4) [1]my tables
    [2]your *(fam.)* tables
    [3]his tables
    [4]your *(formal)* tables

[1]our tables
[2]your *(fam. pl.)* tables
[3]their tables
[4]your *(formal pl.)* tables

(5) [1]my medicine
    [2]my train

[1]my medicines
[2]my trains

(6) [1]your *(fam.)* wine
    [2]your *(fam.)* breaded veal cutlet

[1]your *(fam. sg.)* wines
[2]your *(fam. sg.)* breaded veal cutlets

(7) [1]his check
    [2]his acquaintance

[1]his checks
[2]his acquaintances

(8) [1]your *(formal)* tree
    [2]your *(formal)* banana

[1]your *(formal sg.)* trees
[2]your *(formal sg.)* bananas

(9) [1]our newspaper
    [2]our beefsteak

[1]our newspapers
[2]our beefsteaks

(10) [1]your *(fam. pl.)* name
    [2]your *(fam. pl.)* salad

[1]your *(fam. pl.)* names
[2]your *(fam. pl.)* salads

A	B
(11) ¹their meal	¹their meals
²their potato	²their potatoes
(12) ¹your *(formal pl.)* bill	¹your *(formal pl.)* bills
²your *(formal pl.)* suitcase	²your *(formal pl.)* suitcases
(13) ¹my brother	¹my brothers
²my sister	²my sisters
(14) ¹your *(fam.)* uncle	¹your *(fam. sg.)* uncles
²your *(fam.)* aunt	²your *(fam. sg.)* aunts
(15) ¹her husband	¹her husbands
²his wife	²his wives
(16) ¹our father	¹our fathers
²our mother	²our mothers
(17) ¹your *(fam. pl.)* son	¹your *(fam. pl.)* sons
²your *(fam. pl.)* daughter	²your *(fam. pl.)* daughters
(18) ¹their cousin *(m.)*	¹their cousins *(m.)*
²their cousin *(f.)*	²their cousins *(f.)*
(19) ¹your *(formal)* son-in-law	¹your *(formal sg.)* sons-in-law
²your *(formal)* daughters-in-law	²your *(formal sg.)* daughter-in-laws
(20) ¹your *(formal pl.)* son	¹your *(formal pl.)* sons
²your *(formal pl.)* daughter	²your *(formal pl.)* daughters
(21) ¹my son-in-law	¹their son-in-law
²my young son-in-law	²their young son-in-law
³my Italian son-in-law	³their Italian son-in-law
(22) ¹her husband	¹your *(formal sg.)* husband
²her handsome husband	²your *(formal sg.)* handsome husband
³her American husband	³your *(formal sg.)* American husband

B. Progressive Variation.

(1) ¹my son
   ²my sons
   ³my flowers
   ⁴her flowers
   ⁵her salads
   ⁶her salad
   ⁷her grandfather
   ⁸her American grandfather
   ⁹her American grandfathers
   ¹⁰our American grandfathers
   ¹¹our grandfathers
   ¹²our grandfather
   ¹³my grandfather
   ¹⁴my son

(2) ¹their booklet
   ²their sister
   ³your *(fam. pl.)* sister
   ⁴your sisters
   ⁵your rooms
   ⁶his rooms
   ⁷his room
   ⁸my room
   ⁹my number
   ¹⁰my numbers
   ¹¹your *(formal pl.)* numbers
   ¹²your *(formal pl.)* receipts
   ¹³your *(formal pl.)* receipt
   ¹⁴your *(formal pl.)* booklet
   ¹⁵their booklet.

(3) ¹I hear
   ²you *(formal sg.)* hear
   ³you take
   ⁴we take
   ⁵we go
   ⁶they go
   ⁷they say
   ⁸she says
   ⁹she does
   ¹⁰you *(fam. pl.)* do
   ¹¹you *(fam. pl.)* understand
   ¹²he understands
   ¹³he hears
   ¹⁴I hear

(4) ¹you *(formal pl.)* go
   ²it goes
   ³it gives
   ⁴we give
   ⁵we understand
   ⁶they understand
   ⁷they do
   ⁸you *(fam. sg.)* do
   ⁹you *(fam. sg.)* see
   ¹⁰I see
   ¹¹I say
   ¹²he says
   ¹³he goes
   ¹⁴you *(formal pl.)* go

C. *Say or write in Italian:*

1. Three cousins (*m.*) of mine are going to Florence. 2. Where are my travellers' cheques? 3. I'm opening a checking account with eight hundred dollars. 4. In the summer our fields and our trees are very beautiful.
5. Your (*formal sg.*) pronunciation is very good. 6. Your (*fam. sg.*) idea is excellent. 7. We're going on foot to the museum. 8. He says that it's nine thirty. 9. What are you doing?
10. What do you hear? I don't hear anything.

Foto Gendreau

CONVERSATION UNIT —————— II

In St. Peter's

Peter and Fulvia discuss the various ways of going to St. Peter's.

FULVIA — ¹Che si fa oggi?

PIETRO — ²Non so. ³È una bella giornata. ⁴Possiamo andare a San Pietro, se vuoi.

FULVIA — ⁵Òttima idea. ⁶Ricòrdati di portare la màcchina fotogràfica.

PIETRO — ⁷Non temere, quella è la prima cosa. ⁸A propòsito, come ci si va da qui?

FULVIA — ⁹Possiamo préndere l'àutobus, il fìlobus, il tram, un tassì, o perfino una carrozza.

PIETRO — ¹⁰Mezzi non ne màncano di sicuro! ¹¹Resta ora da decìdere qual'è il mezzo migliore.

FULVIA — ¹What do we do today?

PETER — ²I don't know. ³It's a beautiful day. ⁴We can go to St. Peter's if you want.

FULVIA — ⁵An excellent idea. ⁶Remember to bring the camera.

PETER — ⁷Don't worry (be afraid), that's the first thing [I'll think of]. ⁸By the way, how do you (does one) go there from here?

FULVIA — ⁹We can take the bus, the trolley-bus, the street-car, a taxi, or even a carriage.

PETER — ¹⁰Means [of transportation] certainly aren't lacking! ¹¹The only thing left now is (it remains now) to decide which is the best means.

FULVIA — ¹²Io scarterei la carrozza e il tassì perché cóstano cari. ¹³Il tram ci mette troppo.

PIETRO — ¹⁴Prendiamo il filobus, va bene?

FULVIA — ¹⁵Il nùmero sessantadue si ferma proprio dietro il colonnato di San Pietro. ¹⁶E il biglietto costa solo venticinque lire.

(A San Pietro)

PIETRO — ¹⁷Com'è imponente! ¹⁸Però, con tutte le cartoline e fotografie che ho viste, mi sembra di conoscerlo già.

FULVIA — ¹⁹Devi amméttere, però, che è una grande òpera d'arte.

PIETRO — ²⁰Sì, è la più grande chiesa dell'età barocca.

FULVIA — ²¹A me, mi piace di più delle cattedrali gòtiche.

FULVIA — ¹²I'd eliminate the carriage and the taxi because they cost a lot. ¹³The street-car takes too much [time].

PETER — ¹⁴Let's take the trolley-bus, O.K.?

FULVIA — ¹⁵Number sixty-two stops right behind the colonnade of St. Peter's. ¹⁶And the ticket costs only twenty-five lire.

(At St. Peter's)

PETER — ¹⁷How imposing it is! ¹⁸However, with all the postcards and photographs that I've seen, it seems to me that I know it already.

FULVIA — ¹⁹You have to admit, however, that it is a great work of art.

PETER — ²⁰Yes, it's the greatest church of the baroque age.

FULVIA — ²¹As for me, I like it better (to me, it is more pleasing) than the Gothic cathedrals.

NOTES

1. **Un mezzo** *a means* is the over-all term for any kind of city transportation. **Mezzi non ne màncano** means literally *Means, there are not lacking of them.*
2. **Il tram ci mette troppo,** literally *the streetcar puts in too much [time] on it.*
3. **Mi piace meglio,** literally *to me it pleases better.*

Foto Alinari

Esercizi

A. *Domandi a un altro studente o a un'altra studentessa:*

1. Che tempo fa? 2. Dove possiamo andare? 3. Che cosa devo portare? 4. Come si va a San Pietro da qui? 5. Che cosa possiamo préndere? 6. Che cosa resta ora da decìdere? 7. Perché non prendiamo una carrozza o un tassì? 8. Perché non prendiamo il tram? 9. Che fìlobus prendiamo? 10. Dove si ferma il fìlobus? 11. Quanto costa il biglietto? 12. Com'è San Pietro? 13. Conosce già San Pietro? 14. Le sembra di conóscere già San Pietro? 15. San Pietro è una grande òpera d'arte? 16. San Pietro è una chiesa barocca? 17. Le piace San Pietro meglio delle cattedrali gòtiche?

B. *Risponda alle seguenti domande:*

1. Che si fa oggi? 2. Possiamo andare a San Pietro? 3. Non vuol andare a San Pietro? 4. Se no, perché no? 5. Che cosa deve ricordarsi di portare? 6. Qual'è la prima cosa da portare a San Pietro. 7. Come ci si va? 8. Quali mezzi possiamo préndere? 9. Qual'è il mezzo migliore? 10. Perché Fulvia vuole scartare la carrozza e il tassì? 11. Quanto tempo ci mette il tram? 12. Qual'è il nùmero del fìlobus che dobbiamo prendere? 13. Quanto costa? 14. Le piace San Pietro? 15. Ha visto delle fotografie o delle cartoline di San Pietro? 16. Le piace l'arte barocca? 17. San Pietro è una cattedrale gòtica?

C. *Dica in Italiano:*

1. The day is beautiful. 2. What are Fulvia and Peter doing today? 3. They can go to St. Peter's, if they wish. 4. Peter brings the camera. 5. That is the first thing that he wants to do. 6. He asks how one goes to St. Peter's. 7. Fulvia says that there are many means [of transportation]. 8. There is no lack of means. 9. They have to decide which is the best means.

10. The carriage and the taxi cost a lot. 11. The streetcar is pleasant, but it takes (= puts in on it) an hour. 12. The trolley-bus goes as far as the colonnade. 13. It costs twenty-five lire. 14. St. Peter's is an imposing church.

15. We have seen many photographs of that church. 16. It is a great work of baroque art. 17. Fulvia likes it more (to Fulvia, it is more pleasing) than the Gothic churches.

Foto ISTO

Altare Papale e Statua di San Pietro

D. REVIEW OF NUMERALS. *Say or write in Italian:*

1. This postcard costs twenty lire.   2. The ticket costs thirty-five lire.   3. These cameras cost fifty thousand lire each.   4. We have to pay three hundred lire.
5. I'd like to deposit two hundred and fifty dollars.   6. My room costs two thousand seven hundred lire per day.   7. Can you change a five-thousand lire note?   8. Here is a travellers' cheque for a hundred dollars.   9. They are withdrawing fifteen thousand lire.
10. He signs a cheque for three thousand five hundred dollars.

E. CONVERSATIONS:

1. You decide that you wish to go to St. Peter's (or the Uffizi or the Palazzo Vecchio) and discuss the means of transportation for getting there, with their relative advantages and disadavantages.
2. You are at St. Peter's and discuss its attractions and its quality as a monument of baroque art.

CONVERSATION UNIT_____12

Buying Clothes

Anna persuades Fulvia to go shopping with her.

(Per la strada)

FULVIA — ¹Ciao, Anna, come stai?

ANNA — ²Non c'è male, e tu?

FULVIA — ³Bene, grazie. ⁴Dove vai?

ANNA — ⁵Vado in centro a fare delle spese. ⁶Accompàgnami.

FULVIA — ⁷Volentieri. ⁸Anch'io devo comprare qualcosa.

(Alla commessa)

FULVIA — ⁹Questo completo di giacca e gonna è veramente bellissimo. ¹⁰Quanto costa?

COMMESSA — ¹¹Trentacinquemila lire, signorina, ma è pura lana. ¹²Ne abbiamo anche di più econòmici.

ANNA — ¹³E questa camicetta bianca di cotone, quanto costa?

COMMESSA — ¹⁴Oh, quella è veramente a buon mercato, costa solamente mille settecento perché è in liquidazione. ¹⁵Viene anche in altri colori: giallo, azzurro, rosso e verde.

ANNA — ¹⁶Hanno anche dei fazzoletti?

(On the street)

FULVIA — ¹Hi, Anna, how are you?

ANNA — ²Not bad, and you?

FULVIA — ³Well, thanks. ⁴Where are you going?

ANNA — ⁵I'm going downtown to do some shopping. ⁶Come along with me.

FULVIA — ⁷Gladly. ⁸I have to buy something too.

(To the saleswoman)

FULVIA — ⁹This suit [consisting] of jacket and skirt is really very beautiful. ¹⁰How much does it cost?

SALESWOMAN — ¹¹Thirty-five thousand lire, miss, but it's pure wool. ¹² We have some [that are cheaper,] too.

ANNA — ¹³And this white cotton blouse, how much does it cost?

SALESWOMAN — ¹⁴Oh, that's really cheap, it costs only seventeen hundred because it's on sale. ¹⁵It also comes in other colors: yellow, blue, red and green.

ANNA — ¹⁶Do you have handkerchiefs too?

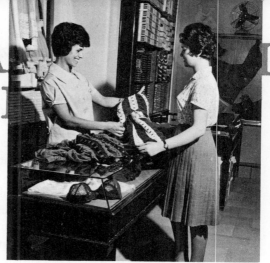

Foto Bright —
Rapho-Guillumette

COMMESSA — [17]Sì, li può trovare in quel reparto lì a destra.

FULVIA — [18]Hanno anche cravatte e calzini da uomo?

COMMESSA — [19]No, signorina, per questi artìcoli dévono andare in un negozio di abbigliamento maschile.

FULVIA — [20]Grazie mille.

(Ad un'altra commessa)

ANNA — [21]Vorrei sei fazzoletti di lino.

COMMESSA — [22]Le piàcciono questi?

ANNA — [23]Cosa dici, Fulvia? [24]Sono carini, vero?

FULVIA — [25]Molto, cómprali senz'altro.

COMMESSA — [26]Ecco a Lei, signorina. [27]Si accòmodi alla cassa e grazie.

SALESWOMAN — [17]Yes, you can find them in that department there to the right.

FULVIA — [18]Have you also got men's ties and socks?

SALESWOMAN — [19]No, miss, for these articles you have to go to a men's clothing store.

FULVIA — [20]Many (a thousand) thanks.

(To another saleswoman)

ANNA — [21]I'd like six linen handkerchiefs.

SALESWOMAN — [22]Do you like these?

ANNA — [23]What do you say, Fulvia? [24]They're nice, aren't they?

FULVIA — [25]Very; buy them right away.

SALESWOMAN — [26]Here, you are, miss. [27]Please go to the cashier's, and thank you.

NOTES

1. **Cravatte e calzini da uomo,** literally *ties and socks suitable for* [a] *man.*

2. **Le piàcciono questi?** literally *To-you are-pleasing these* (= *Are these pleasing to you?*).

CONVERSATION UNIT TWELVE

Esercizi

A. *Risponda in italiano alle seguenti domande:*

1. Come sta Anna? 2. Come sta Fulvia? 3. Dove va Anna? 4. A fare che cosa?
5. Che cosa dice Anna a Fulvia? 6. Che cosa risponde Fulvia? 7. Che cosa dice Fulvia del completo di giacca e gonna? 8. Quanto costa il completo? 9. Perché?
10. La commessa ne ha anche di più economici? 11. La camicetta di cotone quanto costa? 12. Perché? 13. In quanti colori viene la camicetta? 14. Fulvia e Anna dove pòssono trovare dei fazzoletti?
15. Dove devono andare per comprare cravatte e calzini da uomo? 16. Quanti fazzoletti desìdera Anna? 17. Le piàcciono i fazzoletti? 18. Che cosa dice Fulvia? 19. Dove dévono andare per pagare?

B. *Domandi a un altro studente (o a un'altra studentessa):*

1. dove va. 2. che cosa vuol fare. 3. di accompagnarLa (*to go along with you*). 4. che cosa vuol comprare.
5. quanto costa una giacca. 6. quanto costa una gonna. 7. perché costa tanto (*so much*). 8. se ha una giacca più econòmica. 9. se ha una gonna più econòmica.
10. quanto costa una camicetta di cotone. 11. se ha delle camicette a buon mercato. 12. perché le camicette sono a buon mercato. 13. se le camicette vèngono in altri colori. 14. se ha delle camicette gialle (rosse; azzurre; verdi).
15. dove può trovare dei fazzoletti. 16. se ha anche cravatte da uomo. 17. dove può comprare dei calzini da uomo. 18. se ha dei fazzoletti di lino. 19. quanto cóstano i fazzoletti. 20. dove deve andare per pagare.

C. *Dica o scriva in italiano:*

1. Hi, Peter, where are you going? 2. I'm going downtown. 3. Do you want to come with (= *to accompany*) me? 4. Do you want to buy something too?
5. I have to buy some ties. 6. Where can we buy some men's socks? 7. You can't buy socks in this store. 8. You have to go (= *in*) a men's clothing store. 9. All right, let's buy something for our girls.
10. Here is a blue blouse. 11. It's really cheap, because it's on sale. 12. How much do these blouses cost? 13. They cost only two thousand two hundred lire each. 14. I don't want to pay two thousand for a blouse.

15. I'm buying a handkerchief for my girl.   16. It only costs three hundred lire.   17. Yes, but it's not of linen.   18. It doesn't matter; she doesn't know (**non sa**) the difference.

D. REVIEW OF SECOND CONJUGATION VERBS. *Say or write in Italian:*

1. She departs.   2. We depart.   3. I depart.   4. You (**tu**) open.
5. He opens.   6. They open.   7. You (**voi**) feel.   8. We feel.   9. I feel.
10. They sleep.   11. I sleep.   12. You (**Lei**) sleep.   13. I understand.   14. We understand.
15. They understand.

E. CONVERSATION:

1. You meet a friend on the street and try to persuade him (her) to go downtown with you. (*Vary the conversation by making the effort unsuccessful as well as successful, with reasons for not going downtown.*)
2. Two or more of you are in a store, and talk with the salesperson, deciding what to get in the way of men's or women's clothing. The salesperson finally asks the customers to go to the cashier's desk and thanks them.

🌑 18. CONJUNCTIVE PRONOUNS—DIRECT AND INDIRECT OBJECT.

Italian has a special series of pronouns for use only in conjunction with verbs and hence called *conjunctive* pronouns. These pronouns follow infinitive, participle and imperative forms, and are written together with them. The conjunctive elements precede all other verb forms and are written separately. In the first and second persons, the conjunctive pronouns have the meaning of both direct and indirect objects. In the third person, however, there are separate forms for these two objects.

CONJUNCTIVE PRONOUNS—DIRECT AND INDIRECT OBJECT			
		SINGULAR	PLURAL
1. —		**mi** me; to me	**ci** us; to us
2. (*fam.iliar*)		**ti** you; to you	**vi** you; to you
3. direct object	*m.*	**lo** him; it	**li** them
	f.	**la** her; it	**le** them
3. indirect object	*m.*	**gli** to him; to it	
	f.	**le** to her; to it	

In the third person, the masculine object pronouns take the place of any noun whose grammatical gender is masculine, and the feminine pronouns replace any noun of feminine grammatical gender:

Vedo **la cattedrale.**	I see *the cathedral.*	> **La** vedo.	I see *it.*
Vedo **l'albergo.**	I see *the hotel.*	> **Lo** vedo.	I see *it.*
Vedo **le cattedrali.**	I see *the cathedrals.*	> **Le** vedo.	I see *them.*
Vedo **gli alberghi.**	I see *the hotels.*	> **Li** vedo.	I see *them.*

AND FURTHER

Mi vede.	He sees *me.*	**Ci** vede.	He sees *us.*
Ti vede.	He sees *you* (*fam. sg.*).	**Vi** vede.	He sees *you* (*fam. pl.*)
Mi dà l'assegno.	He gives (to) *me* the cheque.	**Ci** dà l'assegno.	He gives [to] *me* the cheque.

Ti dà l'assegno. He gives (to) *you* (*fam. sg.*) the cheque.

Gli dà l'assegno. He gives (to) *him* the cheque.

Le dà l'assegno. He gives (to) *her* the cheque.

Vi dà l'assegno. He gives (to) *you* (*fam. pl.*) the cheque.

If any doubt arises in your mind as to whether a given pronoun should be in the direct or indirect object form in Italian, try expanding the corresponding English sentence by placing *to* or *for* before the pronoun involved. If you can expand *him* into *to him* or *for him*, etc., then it is a dative (indirect object) in English, and should have an indirect object form of the pronoun in Italian (**gli** *etc.*).

For the polite (**Lei**) form of address, in the third person singular, Italian uses **La** as the direct object and **Le** as the indirect object, whether speaking to a man or to a woman. In the plural, **Li** is used as the direct object in speaking to a group of men or a mixed group, and **Le** in speaking to a group of women. (For the absence of a plural indirect object conjunctive pronoun in the third person, see below.)

La vedo. I see *you* (*formal sg., m. or f.*).

Le dò l'assegno. I give [to] *you* (*formal sg., m. or f.*) the cheque.

Li vedo. I see *you* (*formal, m. pl.*).

Le vedo. I see *you* (*formal, f. pl.*).

Italian has no third person plural indirect object conjunctive pronoun forms meaning *to them*. The lack of such forms is made up for by the use of **loro** *to them* (in formal plural direct address, **Loro** *to you*. Since **loro** is not a conjunctive pronoun, it never precedes the verb as to conjunctive elements:

Dò **loro** l'assegno. I give [to] *them* the check.

Dò **Loro** l'assegno. I give [to] *you* (*formal pl.*) the check.

In modern Italian, **gli** (*m.*) and **le** (*f.*) are coming to be used more and more for the plural as well as the singular indirect object: *e.g.*, **Gli dò l'assegno** *I give [to] them the cheque*. Although purists frown on this usage, it is already widespread.

🔴 19. Reflexive Verbs.

Reflexive verbs, or those whose object refers back to their subject (*e.g.*, *I see myself.*, *He gives* [*to*] *himself a pat on the back.*), in English take a special type of object pronoun ending in -*self*, -*selves*. In Italian, the ordinary object pronoun is used in the first and second persons. For the third person Italian uses the special reflexive pronoun **si** *him-, her-, itself*; *to him-, her-, itself*; *themselves*; *to themselves* for both direct and indirect object meaning, and for both singular and plural.

THE REFLEXIVE VERB WITH DIRECT OBJECT MEANING			
vedere to see **ved-**			
	SINGULAR		PLURAL
mi vedo	I see *myself*	**ci** vediamo	we see *ourselves*
ti vedi	you (*fam.*) see *yourself*	**vi** vedete	you (*fam.*) see *yourselves*
si vede	he sees *himself*; she sees *herself*; it sees *itself*; you (*formal*) see *yourself*	**si** védono	they see *themselves*; you (*formal*) see *yourselves*

THE REFLEXIVE VERB WITH INDIRECT OBJECT MEANING	
comprare *to buy* **compr-**	
SINGULAR	PLURAL
mi compro un fazzoletto *I buy* [*for*] *myself* a handkerchief	**ci compriamo** dei fazzoletti *we buy* [*for*] *ourselves* some handkerchiefs
ti compri un fazzoletto *you* (*fam.*) *buy* [*for*] *yourself* a handkerchief	**vi comprate** dei fazzoletti *you buy* [*for*] *yourselves* some handkerchiefs
si compra un fazzoletto *he* (*she*) *buys* [*for*] *himself* (*herself*), *you* (*formal*) *buy* [*for*] *yourself* a handkerchief	**si cómprano** dei fazzoletti *they buy* [*for*] *themselves, you* (*formal*) *buy for yourselves* some handkerchiefs

In many instances, an Italian reflexive verb corresponds to an English verb which is not reflexive: *e.g.*, **chiamarsi** *to be called* [*lit., to call oneself*]; **accomodarsi** *to go, to sit down* [*lit., to accommodate oneself*]; **fermarsi** *to stop* [*lit., to stop oneself*]; **interessarsi** *to interest oneself*; **ricordarsi** *to remember* [*lit., to remember oneself*].

20. IMPERSONAL-PASSIVE USE OF REFLEXIVE VERBS.

The third person of Italian reflexive verbs is used to indicate an indefinite actor, equivalent to English *one* (as in *one goes, one writes, etc.*). With intransitive verbs, this construction is always in the third person singular:

Come **si va** a San Pietro?	How *does one go* to St. Peter's?
In Italia non **si riesce** mai a cenare prima delle otto.	In Italy *one* never *succeeds* in dining before eight o'clock.

With transitive verbs, however, the noun which in English would be the object is the subject in Italian. It normally follows the verb, but the verb agrees with it in number:

Si prova un piacere sempre nuovo.	*One experiences* an ever new *pleasure* (*lit.*, an ever new pleasure experiences itself).
Si pròvano dei piaceri sempre nuovi.	*One experiences* ever new *pleasures* (*lit.*, ever new pleasures experience themselves).
Qui si vende pasta asciutta.	Here *macaroni is sold* (*lit.*, sells itself).
Qui si véndono francobolli.	Here *stamps are sold* (*lit.*, sell themselves).

 21. Piacere *to be pleasing*.

This verb, meaning *to give pleasure, be pleasing*, takes an indirect object. It has forms for all three persons, singular and plural.

piacere *to give pleasure* piac-			
piaccio	I give pleasure	piacciamo	we give pleasure
piaci	you (*fam.*) give pleasure	piacete	you (*fam. pl.*) pleasure
piace	he, she, it gives pleasure; you (*formal*) give pleasure	piàcciono	they give pleasure; you (*formal pl.*) give pleasure

It often occurs in sentences which would be translated using the English verb *like*, but Italian **piacere** never has the meaning of *to like*. Its use is quite different from that of English *to like*, as can be seen from these examples:

Mi piace San Pietro.	*I like* St. Peter's (*lit.*, to-me is-pleasing *St. Peter's*).
Piace loro la mia idea?	*Do they like* my idea (*lit.*, is-pleasing *to-them my idea*)?
Le piàcciono queste?	*Do you like* these (*lit.*, to-you are pleasing *these*)?
Non ci piàcciono questi fazzoletti.	*We don't like* these handkerchiefs (*lit.*, not to-us are-pleasing these handkerchiefs).

"Mi piàcciono i prati e gli àlberi d'Italia"

In an English sentence referring to *liking*, the person who does the liking is denoted by the subject, and what he likes is the direct object of the verb *to like*. In Italian, on the other hand, what is liked is the subject of **piacere**, and the person who does the liking is referred to by an indirect object. **Piacere** can, on occasion, be used in the first or second person, but always with the meaning *give pleasure to, be liked by*: *e.g.*, **Piaccio agli italiani.** *The Italians like me* (*lit.*, I am pleasing to the Italians).

GRAMMAR UNIT SIX

⬤ 22. Conóscere and **sapere** *to know.*

These two verbs have the following paradigms in the present:

conóscere *to know*		sapere *to know*	
conosco	conosciamo	so	sappiamo
conosci	conoscete	sai	sapete
conosce	conóscono	sa	sanno

The difference in meaning between the two is quite important, and refers to the direction of knowledge. **Conóscere** denotes knowledge from the outside in, whereas **sapere** means to know from the inside out. Thus **conóscere** will refer to superficial knowledge, acquaintanceship, *etc.*, and **sapere** to thorough knowledge. When speaking of *knowing* persons, always use **conóscere**.

Grammatical Exercises

A. SUBSTITUTIONS. *Say or write in Italian:*

(1) ¹He sees me.
²He sees you *(fam. sg.).*
³He sees him.
⁴He sees her.
⁵He sees you *(formal sg.).*
⁶He sees us.

⁷He sees you *(fam. pl.).*
⁸He sees them *(m.).*
⁹He sees them *(f.).*
¹⁰He sees you *(formal pl. m.).*
¹¹He sees you *(formal pl. f.).*

Repeat this exercise with as many other verbs, in different persons and numbers, as makes sense.

(2) ¹He buys [for] me a handkerchief.
²He buys [for] you *(fam. sg.)* a handkerchief.
³He buys [for] him a handkerchief.
⁴He buys [for] her a handkerchief.
⁵He buys [for] you *(formal sg.)* a handkerchief.

⁶He buys [for] us some handkerchiefs.
⁷He buys [for] you *(fam. pl.)* a handkerchief.
⁸He buys [for] them a handkerchief.
⁹He buys [for] you *(formal pl.)* a handkerchief.

Repeat this exercise with as many other verbs as makes sense.

(3) ¹I sit down (= I accommodate myself).
²You *(fam. sg.)* sit down.
³He sits down.
⁴You *(formal sg.)* sit down.

⁵We sit down.
⁶You *(fam. pl.)* sit down.
⁷They sit down.
⁸You *(formal pl.)* sit down.

(4) ¹I like this Gothic cathedral.
²I like these Gothic cathedrals.
³We like this Gothic cathedral.
⁴We like these Gothic cathedrals.
⁵You *(fam. sg.)* like this Gothic cathedral.
⁶You *(fam. sg.)* like these Gothic cathedrals.
⁷You *(fam. pl.)* like this Gothic cathedral.
⁸You *(fam. pl.)* like these Gothic cathedrals.
⁹He likes this Gothic cathedral.
¹⁰He likes these Gothic cathedrals.
¹¹She likes this Gothic cathedral.
¹²She likes these Gothic cathedrals.
¹³You *(formal sg.)* like this Gothic cathedral.
¹⁴You *(formal sg.)* like these Gothic cathedrals.
¹⁵They like this Gothic cathedral.
¹⁶They like these Gothic cathedrals.
¹⁷You *(formal pl.)* like this Gothic cathedral.
¹⁸You *(formal pl.)* like these Gothic cathedrals.

(5) ¹I find the handkerchief.
²I find it.
³I find the handkerchiefs.
⁴I find them.
⁵I find the necktie.
⁶I find it.
⁷I find the neckties.
⁸I find them.

(6) ¹We give the cheque to our brother.
²We give it to our brother.
³We give the cheque to him.
⁴We give the cheque to our brothers.
⁵We give them to our brothers.
⁶We give the cheque to them.
⁷We give the cheque to our sister.
⁸We give it to our sister.
⁹We give the cheque to her.
¹⁰We give the cheque to our sisters.
¹¹We give them to our sisters.
¹²We give the cheque to them.
¹³We give the receipt to our brother.

(Continue exercise using the word for "receipt" instead of the word for "cheque" throughout).

(7) ¹We sell the camera.
²The camera is for sale (= one sells the camera).
³We sell the cameras.
⁴The cameras are for sale.
⁵I'm going to St. Peter's.
⁶One is going to St. Peter's.

GRAMMAR UNIT SIX

B. PROGRESSIVE VARIATION. *Say or write in Italian:*

(1)
¹We buy the camera.
²We buy [for] ourselves the camera.
³We buy [for] ourselves the cameras.
⁴We buy the cameras.
⁵We buy them.
⁶We give them.
⁷We give the neckties.
⁸We give [to] him the neckties.
⁹We give [to] him the necktie.
¹⁰We give [to] him the newspaper.
¹¹We give [to] her the newspaper.
¹²We give [to] our aunt the newspaper.
¹³We give it to our aunt.
¹⁴We buy it for our aunt.
¹⁵We buy the camera for our aunt.
¹⁶We buy the camera.

(2)
¹My name is Giovanni.
²His name is Giovanni.
³Her name is Giovanna.
⁴Her name is Teresa.
⁵Their names are Teresa and Giovanni.
⁶Our names are Teresa and Giovanni.
⁷Our names are Caterina and Marco.
⁸Your *(fam. pl.)* names are Caterina and Marco.
⁹Your *(fam. sg.)* name is Caterina.
¹⁰My name is Caterina.
¹¹My name is Giovanni.

(3)
¹She likes that baroque cathedral.
²She doesn't like that baroque cathedral.
³I don't like that baroque cathedral.
⁴I don't like those baroque cathedrals.
⁵I don't like those Gothic cathedrals.
⁶I don't like those Gothic churches.
⁷I like those Gothic churches.
⁸I like that Gothic church.
⁹We like that Gothic church.
¹⁰Do we like that Gothic church?
¹¹Why do we like that Gothic church?
¹²Why do you *(formal sg.)* like that Gothic church?
¹³Why don't you *(formal sg.)* like that Gothic church?
¹⁴Why don't you *(formal pl.)* like that Gothic church?
¹⁵Don't you *(formal pl.)* like that Gothic church?
¹⁶Don't you *(formal pl.)* like that baroque church?
¹⁷Do you *(formal pl.)* like that baroque church?
¹⁸Does she like that baroque church?
¹⁹Does she like that baroque cathedral?
²⁰She likes that baroque cathedral.

C. *Say or write in Italian:*

1. The carriages stop right here, next to the station. 2. Do you know St Peter's? Yes, we already know it. 3. Which means [of transportation] do we have to take? 4. The taxi costs a lot, but the tram and the trolley-bus take too much time.

5. Are you remembering to bring the cameras? Yes, I'm bringing them. 6. Is your *(formal sg.)* name Giorgio? No, my name is Filippo. 7. We're going along with (= accompanying) Pierina; she's going downtown to do some shopping. 8. That blouse and that skirt, how much do they cost? 9. Where can I find some men's socks? You *(formal sg.)* find them in that department there on the left.

10. Do you *(fam. pl.)* like this necktie? No, we don't like it.

In an Espresso Bar

Peter and Anna go in an espresso bar for refreshments.

PIETRO — [1]Sono stanco e ho una sete tremenda. [2]Perché non andiamo a préndere qualcosa?

ANNA — [3]Òttima idea. [4]Io voglio un gelato.

(Al Bar)

PIETRO — [5]Lo prendiamo al tàvolo o al banco?

ANNA — [6]O no, sediàmoci a quel tàvolo lì fuori.

PIETRO (al cameriere) — [7]Cameriere! [8]Che gelati hanno?

CAMERIERE — [9]Coppe, granite, torte e semifreddi.

ANNA — [10]Io vorrei una coppa di fràgola e limone con panna.

PIETRO — [11]Limone e panna! [12]Che gusti! [13]Limone e panna sono due sapori che proprio non vanno insieme.

ANNA — [14]Va bene, me la porti senza limone, allora. [15]E vorrei anche un'aranciata.

CAMERIERE — [16]E per Lei, signore?

PIETRO — [17]Per me, una birra e delle olive.

CAMERIERE — [18]Mi dispiace, signore, ma le olive le serviamo solo con gli aperitivi.

PETER — [1]I'm tired and I'm awfully thirsty (I have a tremendous thirst). [2]Why don't we go and get (take) something?

ANNA — [3]An excellent idea. [4]I want an ice-cream.

(At the Bar)

PETER — [5]Shall we take it at the table or at the counter?

ANNA — [6]Oh, no, let's sit down at that table out there.

PETER (to the waiter) — [7]Waiter! [8]What kinds of ice-cream (what ice-creams) do you have?

WAITER — [9]Sundaes, ices, tarts and frozen custards.

ANNA — [10]I'd like a strawberry and lemon sundae with whipped cream.

PETER — [11]Lemon and whipped cream! [12]What tastes! [13]Lemon and whipped cream are two flavors that really don't go together.

ANNA — [14]All right, bring it to me without lemon, then. [15]And I'd like an orangeade, too.

WAITER — [16]And for you, sir?

PETER — [17]For me, a beer and some olives.

WAITER — [18]I'm sorry, sir, but we serve olives only with apéritifs.

Caffè Espresso

Pietro — [19]Un espresso, allora, e una pizzetta napoletana, calda.

Anna — [20]Capisci tutto, quando si parla in italiano?

Pietro — [21]No, a volte non capisco, specialmente se pàrlano molto in fretta.

Peter — [19]An espresso coffee, then, and a little Neapolitan pizza, hot.

Anna — [20]Do you understand everything, when people talk in Italian?

Peter — [21]No, at times I don't understand, especially if they speak very fast (very much in a hurry).

NOTES

1. **Al tàvolo, al banco.** In Italian espresso bars, the customer can take his food either seated at a table (inside or, in warm weather, outside), or standing at the counter behind which the drinks and food are prepared. Prices are higher (usually, about 30% to 50% more) for items served **al tàvolo,** in addition to which the customer normally leaves a tip.
2. **Una pizzetta napoletana** is a small Neapolitan pizza for one person.

Esercizi

A. *Risponda in italiano alle seguenti domande:*

1. Come si sente Pietro? 2. Dove vuol andare? 3. Che cosa vuol fare? 4. Anna che cosa pensa di questa idea? 5. Che cosa vuole Anna? 6. Dove si accòmodano (si sièdono) Pietro e Anna? 7. Pietro che cosa domanda al cameriere? 8. Che tipi di gelati hanno nel bar? 9. Che cosa prende Anna? 10. Che obiezione (*objection*) fa Pietro? 11. Pietro che cosa domanda dapprima (*at first*)? 12. Che cosa gli risponde il cameriere? 13. Infine che cosa prende Pietro? 14. Pietro capisce tutto quando si parla in italiano? 15. Perché no?

B. *Dica a un altro studente o a un'altra studentessa:*

1. che Lei ha sete. 2. che è stanco (stanca). 3. che vuol andare a préndere qualcosa. 4. che vuol sedersi al tàvolo. 5. che desidera una granita al caffè. 6. che Le piace il sapore del caffè. 7. che capisce tutto quando si parla in italiano. 8. che non capisce se si parla troppo in fretta.

C. *Domandi a un altro studente o a un'altra studentessa:*

1. se è stanco (stanca). 2. se ha sete. 3. se vuol préndere qualcosa. 4. che cosa vuole. 5. se vuol prénderlo al banco. 6. se desidera un semifreddo. 7. se il limone e la panna vanno bene insieme. 8. se serve le olive con la birra. 9. di portarLe un caffè espresso.

D. REVISIONE DEI VERBI IN -IRE. *Dica o scriva in italiano:*

1. I understand. 2. You (*fam. sg.*) understand. 3. She understands. 4. You (*formal, sg.*) understand. 5. We understand. 6. You (*fam. pl.*) understand. 7. They understand. 8. You (*formal, pl.*) understand.

E. CONVERSATION:

1. You and a friend decide you are tired and thirsty, see an espresso bar, and decide to go there. You discuss whether you want to take your ice-cream (coffee, *etc.*) at the counter or at a table.
2. You and a friend ask the waiter what they have in the way of ice-cream, coffee, beer, pizza, etc., and order. Then you call the waiter, ask for the bill, and pay him, leaving a tip. (An **espresso**, at the counter, is from 35 to 50 lire, and at a table is from 60 to 100 lire; an ice-cream is from 50 to 100 lire at the counter, and from 80 to 150 or 200 at a table; a beer, around 70 (100) lire; a **pizzetta**, around 100 (150).)

CONVERSATION UNIT————14

Strolling in Via del Tritone

Fulvia and Anna window-shop along the Via del Tritone.

FULVIA — ¹Ci sono veramente dei bei negozi in questa via.

ANNA — ²Ci si compra bene qui. ³Ma se vuoi vedere delle belle vetrine devi andare in Via Sistina.

FULVIA — ⁴Dov'è Via Sistina?

FULVIA — ¹There are really some beautiful shops in this street.

ANNA — ²You can shop (buy) well here. ³But if you want to see beautiful shopwindows, you should go to Via Sistina.

FULVIA — ⁴Where's Via Sistina?

Foto Bright — Rapho-Guillumette

Via Sistina

ANNA — ⁵Oh, non è affatto lontano. ⁶È la prima strada a destra all'inizio della salita.

FULVIA — ⁷Anna, guarda che borse magnifiche ci sono qui.

ANNA — ⁸E guarda quella valigia di pelle bianca. ⁹Non è una meraviglia?

FULVIA — ¹⁰Dévono costare un occhio della testa.

ANNA — ¹¹Ci puoi giurare. ¹²Però credo che gli artìcoli in pelle come guanti, scarpe eccètera, in Italia cóstano molto meno che in altri paesi. ¹³In Inghilterra, per esempio, hanno dei prezzi proibitivi; sono carìssimi.

FULVIA — ¹⁴Che cìnema è quello?

ANNA — ¹⁵È lo Splendore. ¹⁶È un cìnema di prima visione.

FULVIA — ¹⁷Che film dànno oggi?

ANNA — ¹⁸Un film americano. ¹⁹Una commedia, credo, ma niente di speciale.

FULVIA — ²⁰Sono già le cinque. ²¹Facciamo presto, altrimenti faremo tardi all'appuntamento con Pietro e il suo amico.

ANNA — ⁵Oh, it's not at all far. ⁶It's the first street on the right at the beginning of the rise.

FULVIA — ⁷Anna, look what magnificent purses there are here.

ANNA — ⁸And look at that suitcase of white leather. ⁹Isn't it a marvel?

FULVIA — ¹⁰They must be dreadfully expensive (they must cost an eye of the head).

ANNA — ¹¹You can be sure of that (you can swear on it). ¹²However, I believe that leather articles like gloves, shoes, etc., cost much less in Italy than in other countries. ¹³In England, for example, they have prohibitive prices; they are very expensive.

FULVIA — ¹⁴What movie-house is that?

ANNA — ¹⁵It's the Splendor. ¹⁶ It's a first-run house (a movie-house of first vision).

FULVIA — ¹⁷What movie are they giving today?

ANNA — ¹⁸An American film. ¹⁹A comedy, I think, but nothing special.

FULVIA — ²⁰It's already five o'clock. ²¹Let's hurry up (let's make quick), otherwise we'll be (we'll make) late for the date with Peter and his friend.

NOTES

1. The **Via del Tritone,** one of Rome's main traffic arteries, is an important shopping street. The **Via Sistina** is less heavily traveled, but has the most elegant and expensive shops in Rome.
2. The English word *film* is used for movies; the Italian word **pellìcola** *film* refers to the film itself, *e.g.*, which one puts in a camera.

Esercizi

A. *Risponda in italiano alle seguenti domande:*

1. Che cosa pensa Fulvia dei negozi in Via del Tritone? 2. Come ci si compra in Via del Tritone? 3. Dove si deve andare per vedere dei negozi veramenti bèlli (delle vetrine veramente belle)? 4. Dov'è Via Sistina? 5. Che cosa vede Fulvia nella vetrina? 6. Che cosa vede Anna? 7. Quanto còstano? [Fra L. 50.000 e L. 100.000] 8. Quanto còstano questi stessi artìcoli in altri paesi? 9. Che cìnema védono Fulvia e Anna? 10. Che tipo di film dànno in quel cìnema? 11. Che ore sono? 12. Dove dévono andare Anna e Fulvia?

B. *Domandi a un altro studente (o a un'altra studentessa):*

1. dove ci sono dei bei negozi. 2. dove si compra bene. 3. dove si pòssono vedere delle belle vetrine. 4. che cosa c'è nelle vetrine. 5. quanto còstano le valigie in Italia. 6. quanto còstano i guanti in Inghilterra. 7. quanto còstano le scarpe negli Stati Uniti. 8. se i prezzi americani sono proibitivi. 9. che tipo di cìnema è lo Splendore. 10. che film si dà oggi. 11. se ha appuntamento con degli amici o delle amiche.

C. *Dica a un altro studente (o a un'altra studentessa):*

1. che vuol vedere un bel negozio. 2. che desìdera sapere dov'è Via Sistina. 3. di guardare le borse e le valigie nella vetrina. 4. che crede che còstano meno che in altri paesi. 5. che dévono far presto. 6. che non vògliono far tardi all'appuntamento con le Loro amiche.

D. *Dica o scriva in italiano:*

1. These shops are really beautiful. 2. I like beautiful shops. 3. Where are there fine shop windows? 4. This shop window isn't very beautiful. 5. Via Caccini is the first street on the left at the beginning of the rise. 6. This suitcase is magnificent. 7. These shoes are magnificent. 8. That purse is a marvel. 9. St. Peter's is a magnificent baroque church. 10. These gloves are dreadfully expensive. 11. We're giving an Italian comedy today. 12. However, it's nothing special. 13. Is it two o'clock already? 14. I have a date with my boyfriend. 15. I don't want to be late for the date.

E. REVISIONE DEI NUMERI E DELLE ORE (Review of numbers and time). *Dica o scriva in italiano:*

1. What time is it? 2. It's one o'clock. 3. It's six o'clock. 4. It's half-past nine.
5. It's fifteen thirty-eight. 6. It's one and three quarters. 7. It's a quarter of four. 8. It's twenty-one o'clock. 9. It's nine eighteen.

F. CONVERSATION:

1. Two or more of you stroll along Via Sistina, admire and name the various objects you see in the shop windows, and talk about their prices.
2. You and a friend converse about the movie-house(s) you see and what films they are showing.
3. You have a date with a friend, and make excuses for having to hurry, because you don't want to be late for the date.

23. Pro-Phrases: **ci, vi, ne.**

In Italian, certain elements of the sentence act as replacements for phrases introduced by certain prepositions. A phrase introduced by a preposition referring to place where or place to which, may be replaced by either **ci** or (somewhat more literary and formal) **vi**. (These forms **ci** and **vi**, acting as pro-phrases and virtually interchangeable, must not be confused with the personal pronoun forms **ci** [*to*] *us* and **vi** [*to*] *you*, which are not interchangeable.) Similarly, a phrase introduced either by **di** *of* (either by itself or as part of the partitive construction, *Sec.* **8**) or by **da** *from*, may be replaced by **ne**.

Vado **a San Pietro.**	I'm going *to St. Peter's.*
Ci vado.	I'm going *there.*
Come si va **a San Pietro?**	How does one go *to St. Peter's?*
Come **ci** si va?	How does one go *there?*
Possiamo andare **agli Uffizi.**	We can go *to the Uffizi.*
Possiamo andar**ci.**	We can go *there.*
Il filobus si ferma **dietro il colonnato.**	The trolley-bus stops *behind the colonnade.*
Il filobus **vi** si ferma.	The trolley-bus stops *there.*
Penso **al giornale.**	I'm thiking *of the newspaper.*
Ci penso.	I'm thinking *of it.*
Parliamo **dell'articolo.**	We're talking *about the article.*
Ne parliamo.	We're talking *about it.*
Abbiamo **delle sigarette.**	We have *cigarettes.*
Ne abbiamo.	We have *some.*
Il tram parte **dalla stazione.**	The street car leaves from *the station.*
Il tram **ne** parte.	The street car leaves from *there.*

The English equivalent of **ci** or **vi** and of **ne** is likely to vary according to the meaning of the particular phrase involved. Thus, **ci** and **vi** will usually mean *there*, but occasionally *on it* or *of it* (e.g., with **giurarci** *to swear on it* or **pensarci** *to think of it* = *to direct one's thoughts towards it*); and **ne** may mean *some, of it, about it,* or *from there*, depending on the meaning of the preposition **di** or **da** in the particular construction involved.

Like the conjunctive personal pronouns (*Sec.* **18**), the elements **ci, vi** and **ne** are used only together with verbs. Since they replace certain types of phrases, they are known as *pro-phrases*. The conjunctive personal pronouns and the pro-phrases all act as replacements for various types of verbal complements. They are, therefore, known collectively as *pro-complements*. With infinitives, participles and imperatives (*cf. Sec.* **24**), the pro-complements are suffixed to the verb forms and written together with them. With other verb forms, the pro-complements precede and are written separately:

andar**ci**	to go *there*		**Ci** vado.	I go *there*.
mangiàndo**ne**	eating *some*		**Ne** màngiano.	They eat *some*.
vedùto**lo**	having seen *him*	BUT	**Lo** vede.	He sees *him*.
prénd**ili**	take *them!*		**Li** prendi.	You (*fam. sg.*) take *them*.
non prénder**li**	don't take *them!*		**Non** li prendi.	You don't take *them*.

-- **Oggi mi è andata male: ne ho preso uno solo!**

"La palestra dei lettori", *Corriere dei piccoli, 9.23.62*

24. IMPERATIVES (FIRST AND SECOND PERSON).

For giving orders in the first person plural (*let's*) and in the second person plural (*you, familiar*), Italian uses the same forms as those of the present, except for **avere** *to have* and **essere** *to be*. As pointed out in Section **23**, the pro-complements are attached to these forms, when they are used as imperatives:

| **andiamo** | *we go; let's go* | + **ci** | *there* | > **andiàmoci** | *let's go there!* |
| **prendete** | *you take; take!* | + **ne** | *some* | > **prendétene** | *take some!* |

For **avere**, there is the special form **abbiate** in the second person plural of the imperative, and for **èssere**, the special form **siate**.

Abbiate pazienza!   *Have (fam. pl.) patience!*   **Siate** buoni!   *Be (fam. pl.) good!*

In the second person singular, the verbs of the first conjugation have an imperative form ending in -**a**. Those of the other regular conjugations use the same form as that of the present. The verbs **avere**, **èssere** and **andare** *to go*, **dare** *to give*, **fare** *to do, make* and **stare** *to stand, be located* also have special second person singular imperative forms.

mangia	eat!			**mangi**	you eat
abbi	have!			**hai**	you have
sii	be!			**sei**	you are
va[+]	go!	BUT		**vai**	you go
da[+]	give!			**dai**	you give
fa[+]	do! make!			**fai**	you do, you make
sta[+]	stand!			**stai**	you stand

After the forms marked with [+], the initial consonant sound of any immediately following word in the same phrase is doubled. This doubling is written out when a pro-complement is suffixed: thus:

da[+]	*give!*	+ **mi**	*(to) me*	> **dammi**	*give me!*
fa[+]	*do!*	+ **lo**	*it*	> **fallo**	*do it!*
sta[+]	*stand!*	+ **ci**	*there*	> **stacci**	*stand there!*

In the negative, the normal imperative forms are used in the plural, but in the second person singular, as soon as the sentence is made negative, the imperative form is automatically replaced by the corresponding infinitive, while all the other elements of the sentence remain unchanged:

non *not* + **andiamo** *let's go* > **non andiamo** *let's not go.*
non *not* + **fàtelo** *do it! (fam. pl.)* > **non fàtelo** *don't do it!*

BUT

non *not* + **giura** *swear! (fam. sg.)* > **non giurare** *don't swear!*
non *not* + **abbi paùra** *have fear (= be afraid)!* > **non aver paùra** *don't be afraid!*
non *not* + **màngiane** *eat some!* > **non mangiarne** *don't eat any!*

25. SUBJUNCTIVE IN FORMAL COMMANDS (THIRD PERSON).

When addressing someone in the third person formal mode of address, either singular (**Lei**) or plural (**Loro**), Italian does not use the imperative, but instead uses the third person singular or plural, as the case may be, of the subjunctive. For the first conjugation, these forms end in **-i** (*sg.*) and in **-ino** (*pl.*). For regular verbs of the second and third conjugations, they end in **-a** and **-ano**, respectively. Certain verbs, as shown below, have irregular subjunctives. Thus:

			FORMAL SINGULAR (Lei)		FORMAL PLURAL (Loro)	
SUBJUNCTIVE IN FORMAL COMMANDS *(Third Person)*						
REGULAR VERBS						
		INFINITIVE				
1st CONJ.	**portare**	to bring	porti!	*bring!*	pòrtino!	*bring!*
2nd CONJ.	**dormire**	to sleep	dorma!	*sleep!*	dòrmano!	*sleep!*
	capire	to understand	capisca!	*understand!*	capiscano!	*understand!*
3rd CONJ.	**vedere**	to see	veda!	*see!*	védano!	*see!*
IRREGULAR VERBS						
1st CONJ.	**andare**	to go	vada!	*go!*	vàdano!	*go!*
	dare	to give	dia!	*give!*	dìano!	*give!*
	fare	to do	faccia!	*do!, make!*	fàcciano!	*do!, make!*
2nd CONJ.	**dire**	to say	dica!	*say!*	dìcano!	*say!*
3rd CONJ.	**avere**	to have	abbia!	*have!*	abbiano!	*have!*
	èssere	to be	sia!	*be!*	sìano!	*be!*
	sapere	to know	sappia!	*know!*	sàppiano!	*know!*

With the subjunctive used in formal commands, the pro-complements are not suffixed as with the imperative, but precede and are written separately: *e.g.*, **mi porti** *bring me!* **lo védano** *see it!* **ne màngino** *eat some!* **non lo fàcciano** *don't do it!*, etc. Reflexive conjunctive pronouns are treated just like any others, in combination with both imperatives and formal command subjunctives: **accòmodati** *sit down!* (*fam. sg.*), **accomodàtevi** *sit down!* (*fam. pl.*), but **si accòmodi** *sit down!* (*formal sg.*) and **si accòmodino** *sit down!* (*formal pl.*).

26. IRREGULAR NOUN PLURALS.

The following nouns have irregularities in the relation between their singular and plural:

SINGULAR		PLURAL	
uomo	man	**uòmini**	men
bue	ox	**buoi**	oxen
dio	god	**dei**	gods

Before the plural form **dei** *gods*, the form **gli** of the definite article is used, not **i**: **gli dei** *the gods*, **degli dei** *of the gods, etc.*

The noun **moglie** *wife* has the plural **mogli** *wives*, which is not a true irregularity, since it involves only the automatic replacement of **gli** (before **e**) by **gl** (before **i**) in the representation of the palatal l sound (*cf.* Appendix **I**, p. v). Certain classes of nouns are invariable, *i.e.*, do not change in the plural: all nouns ending in a stressed vowel (*e.g.*, **la città** *the city, pl.* **le città** *the cities*); all nouns ending in a consonant (*e.g.*, **il tram** *the streetcar, pl.* **i tram** *the streetcars*); and all abbreviations (*e.g.*, **il cìnema** *the movie-house* [for **il cinematògrafo** *the cinematograph*], *pl.* **i cìnema** *the movie-houses*).

Grammatical Exercises

A. SUBSTITUTIONS.

(1) *Say or write in Italian:*

A	B
[1]I'm going to Florence.	[1]I'm going there.
[2]You *(fam. sg.)* are going to Florence.	[2]You're going there.
[3]He's going to Florence.	[3]He's going there.
[4]You *(formal sg.)* are going to Florence.	[4]You're going there.
[5]We're going to Florence.	[5]We're going there.
[6]You *(fam. pl.)* are going to Florence.	[6]You're going there.
[7]They are going to Florence.	[7]They're going there.
[8]You *(formal pl.)* are going to Florence.	[8]You're going there.

Repeat this exercise with the expressions:

[1]arrivare a Roma *to arrive at Rome* → arrivarci *to arrive there*

[2]cenare nel ristorante *to dine in the restaurant* → cenarci *to dine there*

[3]dormire nell'albergo *to sleep in the hotel* → dormirvi *to sleep there*

[4]incontrare un amico alla stazione *to meet a friend at the station* → incontrarvi un amico *to meet a friend there*

[5]méttere un quadro nel museo *to put a picture in the museum* → méttervi un quadro *to put a picture there*

(2) *Say or write in Italian:*

A	B
¹I'm eating some bread.	¹I'm eating some.
²You *(fam. sg.)* are eating some bread.	²You're eating some.
³She's eating some bread.	³She's eating some.
⁴You *(formal sg.)* are eating some bread.	⁴You're eating some.
⁵We're eating some bread.	⁵We're eating some.
⁶You *(fam. pl.)* are eating some bread.	⁶You're eating some.
⁷They're eating some bread.	⁷They're eating some.
⁸You *(formal pl.)* are eating some bread.	⁸You're eating some.

Repeat this exercise with the expressions:

¹chièdere del denaro *to ask for some money* → chièderne *to ask for some*
²compare dei fazzoletti *to buy some handkerchiefs* → comprarne *to buy some*
³elencare dei nomi *to list some names* → elencarne *to list some*
⁴firmare degli assegni *to sign some checks* → firmarne *to sign some*
⁵parlare dei monumenti *to talk about the monuments* → parlarne *to talk about them*
⁶partire da Roma *to depart from Rome* → partirne *to depart from there*
⁷portare dei gelati *to bring some ice-cream* → portarne *to bring some*
⁸vedere delle chiese *to see some churches* → vederne *to see some*

(3) *Go through the exercise of Nos. 1 and 2, making all the sentences negative.*

(4) *Say or write in Italian (familiar, sg. and pl.):*

¹Let's be good! Be good!
²Let's eat! Eat!
³Let's bring! Bring!
⁴Let's sleep! Sleep!

⁵Let's depart! Depart!
⁶Let's take! Take!
⁷Let's see! See!

(5) ¹Let's not be good! Don't be good!
²Let's not eat! Don't eat!
³Let's not bring! Don't bring!
⁴Let's not sleep! Don't sleep!

⁵Let's not depart! Don't depart!
⁶Let's not take! Don't take!
⁷Let's not see! Don't see!

(6) Be good; *(formal, sg. and pl.). Give the command (formal, sg. and pl.) for orders in numbers 4 and 5.*

(7) *Say or write in Italian:*

¹the man; the men
²the ox; the oxen
³the god; the gods
⁴the city; the cities
⁵the bus; the buses

⁶the trolley-bus; the trolley buses
⁷the street car; the street cars
⁸the coffee; the coffees
⁹the tea; the teas
¹⁰the film; the films

B. PROGRESSIVE VARIATION. *Say or write in Italian:*

(1) ¹I'm buying some jackets.
²I'm buying some.
³Buy some! *(fam. pl.)*
⁴Buy it!
⁵Don't buy it!
⁶Don't look at it!
⁷Look at it!

⁸Let's look at it!
⁹We're looking at it.
¹⁰You *(formal pl.)* are looking at it.
¹¹You *(formal pl.)* are buying it.
¹²You *(formal pl.)* are buying some jackets.
¹³I'm buying some jackets.

(2) ¹We're dining in the station.
²We're dining there.
³Let's dine there!
⁴Dine there! *(fam. sg.)*
⁵Don't dine there! *(fam. sg.)*
⁶Don't remain there! *(fam. sg.)*
⁷Don't remain there! *(fam. pl.)*

⁸Remain there! *(fam. pl.)*
⁹Remain in the store!
¹⁰We're remaining in the store.
¹¹We're remaining there.
¹²We're dining there.
¹³We're dining in the station.

(3) ¹You see yourselves *(fam. pl.)*
²See yourselves! *(fam.)*
³See yourself! *(fam. sg.)*
⁴Stop yourself! *(fam. sg.)*
⁵Don't stop yourself! *(fam. sg.)*
⁶Let's not stop ourselves!
⁷Don't stop yourselves! *(formal)*

⁸Don't stop yourself! *(formal)*
⁹You *(formal sg.)* aren't stopping yourself.
¹⁰You *(formal sg.)* don't see yourself.
¹¹You don't see yourselves *(formal pl.)*
¹²You don't see yourselves *(fam. pl.)*

C. *Dica o scriva in italiano:*

1. Does the trolley-bus leave from the station? Yes, it leaves from there.   2. Have you any blouses or any jackets? No, we haven't any.   3. We're eating beefsteaks; we eat some every Sunday.   4. Have (fam. sg.) patience and don't sign the cheques.

5. Sit down (formal pl.) and look at these pictures of oxen.   6. See yourself (formal) in the mirror.   7. I want some ice cream; why doesn't the waiter bring some?   8. Where's the museum? We have to meet our cousins there.

9. These men are strong, you can be sure of it [= you can swear to it].

10. From where do the trolley-buses depart? I don't see any.

The Pincio at Sunset

Foto Bright — Rapho-Guillumette

Fulvia and Anna meet Paul and his friend and see the sunset from the terrace of the Pincio Garden.

FULVIA — ¹Eccoli là, seduti comodamente su quella panchina.

ANNA — ²Chi sono quei bambini che giòcano con loro?

FULVIA — ³Mah, non so. ⁴Forse li hanno incontrati qui. ⁵Quello è Paolo, l'amico di Pietro; studia legge.

PIETRO — ⁶Salve, in ritardo come al sòlito, eh?

FULVIA — ⁷Solo di cinque minuti.

FULVIA — ¹There they are, seated comfortably on that bench.

ANNA — ²Who are those children who are playing with them?

FULVIA — ³Oh, I don't know. ⁴Perhaps they have met them here. ⁵That fellow is Paul, Peter's friend; he's studying law.

PETER — ⁶Hello, late as usual, eh?

FULVIA — ⁷Only by five minutes.

Foto Bright —
Rapho-Guillumette

CONVERSATION UNIT FIFTEEN

PÀOLO — 8Buona sera, come stanno?

ANNA — 9Bene, grazie, e Lei?

FULVIA — 10Diàmoci del tu, d'accordo? 11È molto più sémplice.

PIETRO — 12Muoviàmoci, se vogliamo vedere il tramonto dalla terrazza del Pincio.

ANNA — 13Da quanto tempo sei in Italia, Pietro?

PIETRO — 14Dalla fine dell'estate, esattamente da un mese e mezzo.

FULVIA — 15Sapete che è la prima volta che vedo Roma da questa terrazza?

PÀOLO — 16Davvero? 17Vergogna! 18Per me il Pincio è uno dei giardini più belli di Roma.

ANNA — 19Sì, ma io lo preferisco in primavera, con gli àlberi in fiore.

PIETRO — 20Come si dice in italiano "quando le foglie divèntano gialle?"

PÀOLO — 21Vuoi dire "ingiallìscono"?

PIETRO — 22Esattamente. 23Grazie, Pàolo.

PAUL — 8Good evening, how are you?

ANNA — 9Well, thanks, and you?

FULVIA — 10Let's call each other *tu*; all right? 11It's much simpler.

PETER — 12Let's move, if we want to see the sunset from the terrace of the Pincio.

ANNA — 13How long (For how long) have you been in Italy, Peter?

PETER — 14Since the end of the summer, exactly for (since) a month and a half.

FULVIA — 15Do you know that this is the first time that I've seen Rome from this terrace?

PAUL — 16Really? 17Shame [on you]! 18For me, the Pincio is one of the most beautiful gardens in Rome.

ANNA — 19Yes, but I prefer it in spring, with the trees in flower.

PETER — 20How do you say in Italian "when the leaves become yellow?"

PAUL — 21Do you mean "they turn yellow"?

PETER — 22Exactly. 23Thanks, Paul.

NOTES

1. **Mah** is an emphatic form of **ma** *but*, often accompanied by a shrug of the shoulders.

2. **Salve**, like **ciao**, is a greeting given among friends who would use **tu** to each other.

3. **Diàmoci del tu** *let's call each other* **tu** (literally *let's give of the* **tu** *to each other*). Passage from the formal mode of address with **Lei** to the familiar *tu* is a sign of absence of social barriers. Young people, especially, will use **tu** among themselves to avoid the stiffness and reserve which **Lei** connotes.

4. The **Pincio** is a hill to the northwest of the central part of Rome; from a terrace above the **Piazza del Pòpolo,** one has a view westward across the Tiber to St. Peter's and the Vatican.

Ristorante nel Pincio

Esercizi

A. *Risponda in italiano alle seguenti domande basate* (based) *sul testo* (text):

1. Chi sta seduti su una panchina?   2. Chi sono i bambini?   3. Che cosa studia Pàolo?   4. Fulvia e Anna arrìvano in tempo?
5. Che cosa propone [*proposes*] Fulvia?   6. Perché suggerisce (*suggests*) di darsi del tu?   7. Perché dice Pietro "Muoviàmoci"?   8. Da dove vògliono vedere il tramonto?   9. Da quanto tempo è Pietro in Italia?
10. Quante volte Fulvia ha visto Roma da quella terrazza?   11. Che cosa dice Pàolo del Pincio?   12. Quando lo preferisce Anna?   13. Quando sono in fiore gli àlberi?   14. Che cosa vuol dire "ingiallire"?

B. *Domandi a un altro studente o a un'altra studentessa:*

1. se ha incontrato qui i bambini.   2. che cosa studia Pàolo.   3. che cosa studia Pietro.   4. che cosa studia Fulvia.
5. da quanto tempo è in Italia.   6. se è la prima volta che vede Roma.   7. in che stagione preferisce gli àlberi.   8. in che stagione ingialliscono le foglie.

C. *Dica a un altro studente (o a un'altra studentessa):*

1. che Lei vede il Suo amico seduto su una panchina.   2. che i Suoi amici sono in ritardo.   3. che Lei li ha incontrati qui.   4. che è in Italia da cinque mesi.

5. che questa è la prima volta che vede Roma.   6. che per Lei il Pincio è il giardino più bello di Roma.   7. che Lei preferisce l'autunno, perché le foglie divèntano gialle.

D. Review of Imperatives.

a. *Say or write the following in the second person singular (familiar, tu) imperative:*
1. Accompany!   2. Accompany me!   3. Bring!   4. Bring it!
5. Begin!   6. Begin them!   7. Swear!   8. Swear to it!   9. Deposit!
10. Deposit some!

b. *Say or write in the second person plural* (familiar, **voi**) *imperative:*
1. Sign!   2. Sign them (*m.*)!   3. Enter!   4. Enter there!
5. Explore!   6. Explore it (*i.e.*, the city)!   7. Look!   8. Look at us!   9. Call!
10. Call us!

c. *Say or write in the first person plural imperative:* 1. Let's order!   2. Let's order some!   3. Let's pay!   4. Let's pay it [*the bill*]!
5. Let's serve!   6. Let's serve them!   7. Let's return!   8. Let's return there!
9. Let's depart!
10. Let's depart from thence!

d. *Put the imperatives of sections* (**a**), (**b**) *and* (**c**) *into the negative.*

E. Translate into Italian:

1. The children are seated on a bench.   2. We are playing with them.   3. Why are you late as usual?   4. They are calling each other **tu**.
5. We have to move ourselves.   6. The sunset seen from the Pincio is very beautiful.   7. We like this terrace.   8. We prefer it in summer, when it's hot.   9. The autumn is the season when the leaves turn yellow.
10. I've been in Rome for two months.

F. Conversation:

1. You meet your friend, who is playing with some children. You ask him who they are, and he introduces them by name. He has met them here. Then you say good-bye to him and to them.
2. A group of Americans and Italians are on the Pincio, looking out westward. They point out St. Peter's, the Piazza del Pòpolo and the Tiber (**il Tévere**), and comment on the view.
3. You discuss your preferences as to the seasons in view of the kind of weather that prevails in each, the state of the trees, flowers and leaves, *etc.*

Autunno Romano

(Conversations 11-15)

¹**coperto** covered.
²**morto** dead.
³**la tonalità** the tonality.
⁴**arancio** orange.
⁵**marrone** brown.
⁶**dorato** gilded, golden.
⁷**scuro** dark.
⁸**la passeggiata** the walk; **fare una passeggiata** to take a walk.
⁹**camminare** to walk.
¹⁰**appena** [*here*] scarcely, barely.
¹¹**tièpido** tepid, lukewarm.
¹²**limpido** limpid, clear.
¹³**il cristallo** the crystal.
¹⁴**il cielo** the sky, the heaven.
¹⁵**intenso** intense.

L'autunno è già arrivato. Le foglie sugli àlberi sono tutte ingiallite, le strade sono coperte¹ di foglie morte.²

I colori dell'autunno a Roma sono di una sola tonalità:³ giallo, arancio,⁴ marrone⁵ dorato,⁶ marrone più scuro.⁷

Pietro va spesso a fare delle passeggiate⁸ per i giardini di Roma; gli piace molto camminare,⁹ specialmente quando non piove e il sole è appena¹⁰ tièpido.¹¹ In queste giornate l'aria è cosi limpida¹² che sembra fatta di cristallo,¹³ e il cielo¹⁴ è generalmente di un azzurro intenso.¹⁵

IN ALTO: Via Appia. *Foto* ISTO

Un giorno Anna e Pietro, dopo le lezioni[16] all'università, vanno a fare una passeggiata. Pietro non è per natura[17] un sentimentale,[18] ma l'autunno romano[19] così bello e malincònico[20] gli fa venire [21] la nostalgia[22] per casa.[23]

Parla ad Anna dell'autunno nel Massachusetts, dell'estate di San Martino,[24] l'equivalente dell'*Indian Summer* in Amèrica: le descrive[25] gli àlberi le cùi[26] foglie càmbiano in mille colori, lo splendore di panorami[27] multicolori,[28] il gioco[29] di luce[30] ed ombra[31] tra[32] le foglie.

Anna rimane incantata alla descrizione[33] di Pietro e spera[34] di visitare questi luoghi[35] così belli.

Pietro ha con sé[36] la màcchina fotogràfica e insieme ad[37] Anna prende delle fotografìe. Ci sono sempre cose interessanti[38] e nuove da fotografare:[39] monumenti, chiese, gruppi[40] di bambini che giòcano nei giardini pùbblici[41] al ritorno[42] dalla scuola, vecchie signore[43] che, sedute sulle panchine, pàrlano tra loro.

[16]**la lezione** the lesson; the lecture.
[17]**la natura** the nature.
[18]**sentimentale** sentimental; *as noun,* sentimentalist.
[19]**romano** Roman.
[20]**malincónico** melancholy.
[21]**venire** to come.
[22]**la nostalgia** the nostalgia, homesickness, yearning.
[23]**la casa** the house, home.
[24]**San Martino** St. Martin; **l'estate di San Martino,** *literally* St. Martin's summer.
[25]**descrivere** to describe.
[26]**cùi** of whom, whose; **le cui foglie** whose leaves.
[27]**il panorama** the panorama.
[28]**multicolore** multicolored, many-colored
[29]**il gioco** the play, the game.
[30]**la luce** the light.
[31]**l'ombra** *(f.)* the shadow.
[32]**tra** between, among.
[33]**la descrizione** the description.
[34]**sperare** to hope.
[35]**il luogo** the place.
[36]**sé** himself (herself, itself).
[37]**insieme a(d)** together with.
[38]**interessante** interesting.
[39]**fotografare** to photograph.
[40]**il gruppo** the group.
[41]**pùbblico** public.
[42]**il ritorno** the return.
[43]**la signora** the lady.

IN ALTO: Foro Romano. *Foto* ISTO

How Do You Feel?

Fulvia warns Peter to take care of his cold before it becomes a serious matter.

FULVIA — [1]Come ti senti oggi?

PIETRO — [2]Così così. [3]Ho ancora un tremendo raffreddore.

FULVIA — [4]Ti fa male la testa, la gola?

PIETRO — [5]Un po'. [6]Credo di avere anche un po' di febbre. [7]Ieri sono uscito con la pioggia. [8]Non avevo né l'ombrello né l'impermeàbile, e mi sono preso un malanno.

FULVIA — [9]Chiama un mèdico.

PIETRO — [10]Oh, ma non è niente di grave.

FULVIA — [11]Sì, ma se ti trascuri può diventare una cosa seria.

PIETRO — [12]Sta tranquilla, non si muore per un raffreddore.

FULVIA — [13]Fa come ti pare. [14]Poi, però, non ti lamentare se non stai bene.

PIETRO — [15]Tu piuttosto dimmi come vanno i tuoi malanni?

FULVIA — [16]Oh, il mio mal di stòmaco è completamente passato. [17]Era solo un po' d'indigestione. [18]Domani ho un appuntamento con il dentista per farmi otturare un dente.

PIETRO — [19]Vedi, tu sei più malata di me. [20]Riguàrdati, non ti strapazzare!

FULVIA — [1]How do you feel today?

PETER — [2]So-so. [3]I still have a terrific cold.

FULVIA — [4]Does your head [or] your throat hurt?

PETER —- [5]A little. [6]I think I have a little fever too. [7]Yesterday I went out in (with) the rain. [8]I didn't have either my umbrella or my raincoat, and I got sick.

FULVIA —- [9]Call a doctor.

PETER — [10]Oh, but it's nothing serious.

FULVIA — [11]Yes, but if you neglect yourself, it might become a serious matter.

PETER — [12]Don't worry, people don't die on account of a cold.

FULVIA — [13]Do as you like. [14]Afterwards, though, don't complain if you're not well.

PETER — [15]You, now (rather), tell me how are your troubles coming?

FULVIA — [16]Oh, my stomach ache is completely gone. [17]It was only a bit of indigestion. [18]Tomorrow I have an appointment with the dentist to have a tooth filled.

PETER — [19]See, you're sicker than me (I am). [20]Take care of yourself, [and] don't overwork!

Fulvia — ²¹Certo, préndimi in giro, spiritoso!	Fulvia — ²¹That's right, make fun of me, wise guy!
Pietro — ²²Non te la préndere, scherzavo.	Peter — ²²Don't get mad, I was joking.

NOTES

1. **Sentirsi** *to feel* (with regard to health) is reflexive.
2. **Far male** *to hurt* (said of body parts) takes the dative showing who is hurt.
3. **Sta tranquilla** *don't worry*, literally *be tranquil, calm*.
4. **Fa come ti pare** *do as you like*, literally *do as it seems* [best] *to you*.
5. **Préndere in giro** is *to make fun of* (someone).
6. **Préndersela**, *to get angry, start a quarrel*.

Irregular verbs: **uscire** *to go out*: present **esco, esci, esce, usciamo, uscite, èscono**; subjunctive command forms (**Lei**) **esca**, (**Loro**) **èscano**.

Una Giornata di pioggia a Firenze

Foto Henle — Monkmeyer

Esercizi

A. *Risponda in italiano alle seguenti domande basate sul testo:*

1. Come si sente Pietro?   2. Perché?   3. Gli fa male la testa?   4. Gli fa male la gola?
5. Pietro ha un po' di febbre?   6. Quando è uscito Pietro?   7. Sotto quali condizioni?   8. Che cosa aveva con sé?   9. Che cosa si è preso Pietro?
10. Che cosa gli dice Fulvia di fare?   11. Pietro vuol farlo, o no?   12. Perché?
13. Che cosa può diventare il raffreddore?   14. Si muore per un raffreddore?
15. Se Pietro si trascura, può lamentarsi se poi non sta bene?   16. Come vanno i malanni di Fulvia?   17. Quando deve andare dal dentista?   18. Per fare che cosa?   19. Dei due, chi è più malato—Fulvia o Pietro?
20. Che cosa dice Pietro a Fulvia di fare?   21. Che cosa dice Fulvia a Pietro?
22. Come risponde (*answer*) Pietro a Fulvia?

B. *Dica a un altro studente (a un'altra studentessa):*

1. che Lei non si sente bene.   2. che ha un tremendo raffreddore.   3. che Le fa male la testa.   4. che Le fa male la gola.
5. che Le fa male lo stòmaco.   6. che Le fa male un dente.   7. che ha un po' di febbre.   8. che ha una febbre tremenda.   9. che Lei vuol chiamare un mèdico.
10. che è passato il suo mal di testa.   11. che è passato il suo mal di stòmaco.   12. che è passata la sua indigestione.   13. che deve farsi otturare un dente.   14. che Lei è più malato (malata) dello studente (della studentessa) con cùi parla.
15. che Lei si riguarda.   16. che Lei non si strapazza.   17. che Lei non prende in giro l'altro studente (l'altra studentessa).   18. che Lei non se la prende con l'altro (l'altra).

C. *Domandi a un altro studente (a un'altra studentessa):*

1. se si sente male.   2. se ha un raffreddore.   3. se gli fa male la testa (la gola, lo stòmaco, un dente).   4. se ha un po' di febbre.
5. se ha l'ombrello.   6. se ha l'impermeàbile.   7. se si è preso un malanno.   8. se vuol chiamare un mèdico. 9. se è qualcosa di grave.
10. se si trascura.   11. se si riguarda.   12. se si strapazza.   13. se il suo raffreddore può diventare una cosa seria.   14. se si lamenta.
15. se ha un appuntamento con il dentista.   16. se La prende in giro.   17. se se la prende con Lei.   18. se vuol èssere spiritoso.

D. Review of Formal (Singular) Direct Address. *Say or write in Italian the following sentences, using the formal singular (**Lei**) mode of address:*

1. How do you feel today? 2. Have you a cold? 3. Does your head hurt? 4. Have you a little fever?
5. Call a doctor! 6. If you neglect yourself, it can become a serious matter. 7. Be calm. 8. Do as it seems [best] to you. 9. Don't complain if you're not well.
10. *You* tell me, how are your troubles coming? 11. Is your toothache gone? 12. Have you an appointment with the dentist? 13. You are sicker than I am (*me*). 14. Take care of yourself!
15. Don't overwork (yourself)! 16. Make fun of me! 17. Don't get mad!

E. *Dica o scriva in italiano:*

1. I feel so-so. 2. My head hurts. 3. We haven't either the umbrella or the raincoat. 4. We're calling a doctor.
5. We're not neglecting ourselves. 6. We're calm. 7. We are doing as we like (as seems best) [to us]. 8. Are they complaining? 9. It's only a little indigestion.
10. He is filling the tooth. 11. I'm not making fun of you. 12. We're not wise guys. 13. She's getting mad.

F. Conversation:

1. Two or more of you ask after each other's health and tell what troubles you have.
2. Two or more of you kid each other about how you are overworking yourselves and are sick as a result.

GRAMMAR UNIT ———————— VIII

🌑 27. COMPARATIVE AND SUPERLATIVE.

In English, the comparative of an adjective can be formed either with the suffix *-er* (*heavier*, *wiser*) or with the adverb *more* (*more heavy*, *more wise*); the negative comparative, with the adverb *less* (*less heavy*, *less wise*). In Italian, there is only one way of forming the comparative: making a phrase with the adverb **più** *more* or the adverb **meno** *less* preceding the adjective.

Sei **più malata** di me.	You're *sicker* than me.
Questa valigia è **più cara** di quella	This suitcase is *more expensive* than that one.
Roma è **più bella** di Firenze.	Rome is *more beautiful* than Florence.
Sei **meno malata** di me.	You're *less sick* than me.
Questa valigia è **meno cara** di quella.	This suitcase is *less expensive* than that one.
Roma è **meno bella** di Firenze.	Rome is *less beautiful* than Florence.

The comparative of adverbs is formed in the same way:

più esattamente	*more exactly*
più certamente	*more certainly*
meno intensamente	*less intensely*
meno bene	*less well*

There are four irregular comparatives in regular use at present: **migliore** *better* (*adj.*) and **meglio** *better* (*adv.*); and **peggiore** *worse* (*adj.*) and **peggio** *worse* (*adv.*).

Questo museo è **migliore** di quello.	This museum is *better* than that one.
Questo museo è **peggiore** di quello.	This museum is *worse* than that one.
Mi piace **meglio** delle cattedrali gotiche.	I like it *better* than the Gothic cathedrals.
Giorgio parla **peggio** di te.	George talks *worse* than you.

Two other irregular comparatives, *maggiore* and *minore*, were formerly used for *greater* and *lesser*, respectively, but now mean principally *elder* and *younger*.

English superlatives are normally formed either with the suffix *-est* (*heaviest*, *wisest*) or with the adverb *most* modifying an adjective or adverb (*most heavy*, *most wise*; *most heavily*, *most wisely*). Similarly, our negative superlatives are formed with the adverb *least* (*least heavy*, *least wise*; *least heavily*, *least wisely*). Italian superlatives, however, are formed with the definite article + the adverbs **più** *more* or **meno** *less*. If the superlative formation is on an adjective, the definite article of course agrees in gender and number with the adjective. If it is on an adverb, the definite article is always in the masculine singular.

Questa è **la stagione più bella e allegra.**	This is *the most beautiful and cheerful* season.
Il Pincio è uno **dei** giardini **più belli** di Roma.	The Pincio is one *of the most beautiful gardens* in Rome.
San Pietro è **la più grande** chiesa dell'età barocca.	St. Peter's is *the greatest* church of the Baroque age.
Giovanni è **il** ragazzo **meno intelligente** del gruppo.	John is *the least intelligent* boy of the group.
il più allegramente	*the most cheerfully*

The superlative corresponding to the four irregular comparatives **migliore, meglio, peggiore** and **peggio** is formed by preceding them by the definite article as with the other superlatives.

Questo è **il migliore** albergo della città.	This is *the best* hotel in the city.
Questo è **il peggiore** albergo della città.	This is *the worst* hotel in the city.
il meglio possìbile	*the best* (in the best way) possible

The element introduced by *than* in English and by **di** or **che** in Italian, after a comparative, is known as the "term of comparison". In Italian the term of comparison is introduced by **di,** if it is a noun or pronoun (or adjective used as a noun), but by **che** if it is some other part of speech or a phrase:

Sei più malata **di** me.	You're sicker *than* me.
Mi piace **di** più delle cattedrali gotiche.	I like it better *than* the Gothic cathedrals.

BUT

È meglio dare **che** ricevere.	It is better to give *than* to receive.
Cóstano molto meno **che** in altri paesi.	They cost much less *than* in other countries.

In English, the extent of a superlative is normally indicated by a phrase introduced by *in*: e.g., *the best teacher in the city, the least interesting church in Rome.* In Italian such a phrase is normally introduced by the preposition **di,** *of.*

il migliore albergo **della** città	the best hotel *in* (*lit., of*) the city
la più grande chiesa **dell'**età barocca	the greatest church *of the* Baroque age

28. THE PAST PARTICIPLE.

The past participle of regular verbs is formed by adding **-ato** to the root of first conjugation verbs, **-ito** and **-uto** to the root of second and third conjugation verbs respectively.

		THE PAST PARTICIPLE		
	INFINITIVE		PAST PARTICIPLE	
1ST CONJUGATION	arrivare	*to arrive*	arrivato	*arrived*
	incontrare	*to meet*	incontrato	*met*
	passare	*to pass*	passato	*passed*
	portare	*to bring*	portato	*brought*
	tornare	*to return*	tornato	*returned*
2ND CONJUGATION	capire	*to understand*	capito	*understood*
	preferire	*to prefer*	preferito	*preferred*
	uscire	*to go out*	uscito	*gone out*
3RD CONJUGATION	sedere	*to seat*	seduto	*seated*
	vedere	*to see*	veduto	*seen*

Some verbs (mostly those of the third conjugation in **-ere**) have irregular past participles. To date you have had the following verbs whose past participles are irregular:

aprire	to open	**aperto**	opened, open
coprire	to cover	**coperto**	covered
dire	to say	**detto**	said
chièdere	to ask, request	**chiesto**	asked, requested
èssere	to be	**stato**	been
fare	to do	**fatto**	done
méttere	to put	**messo**	put
morire	to die	**morto**	dead
piacere	to give pleasure	**piaciuto**	given pleasure
parere	to seem	**parso**	seemed
préndere	to take	**preso**	taken
rimanere	to remain	**rimasto**	remained
scomméttere	to bet	**scommesso**	betted
vedere	to see	**visto** *or* **veduto**	seen
venire	to come	**venuto**	come
vivere	to live	**vissuto**	lived

🖤 29. The Compound Past.

The compound past, often known in Italian as the **passato pròssimo** or *near past*, is formed with an auxiliary verb + the past participle. For certain verbs the auxiliary is always **èssere**. These verbs are always intransitive (*i.e.*, do not take a direct object) and refer to change of position or condition. Of the verbs which you have had to date, the following take **èssere** as their regular auxiliary:

andare	to go	piacere	to give pleasure
arrivare	to arrive	restare	to remain
costare	to cost	rimanere	to remain
diventare	to become	ritornare	to return
èssere	to be	sembrare	to seem
mancare	to fail, be lacking	stare	to stand, be located
morire	to die	tornare	to return
parere	to seem	uscire	to go out
partire	to depart	venire	to come
passare	to pass	vìvere	to live

Most verbs, including all transitive verbs (*i.e.*, those taking a non-reflexive, direct object), take **avere** as their auxiliary.

Ho comprato una giacca.	*I have bought* a jacket.
Abbiamo camminato fino a San Pietro.	*We have walked* as far as St. Peter's.
Ha incontrato la sua amica.	*She has met* her friend.
Avete cenato bene?	*Have you dined* well?
Non **hanno potuto** trovare un albergo.	*They haven't been able* to find a hotel.

BUT

Sono tornato a Roma.	*I (m.) have gone back* to Rome.
Sono tornata a Roma.	*I (f.) have gone back* to Rome.
È morto.	*He has died.*
È morta.	*She has died.*
Dove **siete andati**?	Where *did you (m.pl.) go?*
Dove **siete andate**?	Where *did you (f.pl.) go?*
Siamo arrivati alle cinque.	*We (m.) arrived* at five o'clock.
Dove **sono rimaste**?	Where *have they (f.) remained?*

In compound past phrases formed with **èssere**, the past participle agrees in gender with the subject. In compound pasts formed with **avere**, the past participle does not agree with the subject.

● 30. PRESENT INDICATIVE OF tenere, venire, uscire.

The present tense forms of **tenere** *to hold* and **venire** *to come* rhyme except in the second person plural.

tenere	*to hold*	**venire**	*to come*
tengo	I hold	**vengo**	I come
tieni	you (*fam. sg.*) hold	**vieni**	you (*fam. sg.*) come
tiene	he, she, it holds; you (*formal sg.*) hold	**viene**	he, she, it comes; you (*formal sg.*) come
tenga	hold (*formal sg.*)	**venga**	come (*formal sg.*)
teniamo	we hold	**veniamo**	we come
tenete	you (*fam. pl.*) hold	**venite**	you (*fam. pl.*) come
tèngono	they hold; you (*formal pl.*) hold	**vèngono**	they come; you (*formal pl.*) come
tèngano	hold (*formal pl.*)	**vèngano**	come (*formal pl.*)

In the present indicative and in the present subjunctive of **uscire** *to go out*, the vowel **u** changes to **e** whenever the stress falls on the root.

	uscire	*to go out*		
esco	I go out	**usciamo**	we go out
esci	you (*fam. sg.*) go out	**uscite**	you (*fam. pl.*) go out
esce	he, she, it goes out; you (*formal sg.*) go out	**èscono**	they go out; you (*formal pl.*) go out
esca	go out (*formal sg.*)	**èscano**	go out (*formal pl*)

Grammatical Exercises

A. SUBSTITUTIONS.

(1) ¹An intense pleasure.
²A more intense pleasure.
³The most intense pleasure.
⁴A less intense pleasure.
⁵The least intense pleasure.

⁶More intensely.
⁷Most intensely.
⁸Less intensely.
⁹Least intensely.

(2) ¹A good description.
²A better description.
³The best description.
⁴A worse description.
⁵The worst description.

⁶He talks well.
⁷He talks better.
⁸He talks badly.
⁹He talks worse.

(3) ¹A more beautiful girl.
²A more cheerful girl.
³A sicker girl.
⁴A dearer girl.

⁵A stronger girl.
⁶A more interesting girl.
⁷A more sentimental girl.

(4) The most beautiful girl ... (etc., as in A 3)
(5) A less beautiful girl ... (etc.)
(6) The least beautiful girl ... (etc.)
(7) Some more beautiful girls ... (etc.)
(8) The most beautiful girls ... (etc.)
(9) Some less beautiful girls ... (etc.)
(10) The least beautiful girls ... (etc.)

(11) ¹I bring; I have brought.
²We see; we have seen.
³They buy; they have bought.
⁴You (**tu**) sign; you have signed.
⁵She understands; she has understood.

⁶You (**voi**) say; you have said.
⁷You (**Lei**) ask; you have asked.
⁸We bet; we have betted.
⁹You (**Loro**) do; you have done.

(12) ¹They pass. They have passed.
²You (**tu**) are. You have been.
³I return. I have returned.
⁴You (**Lei**) depart. You have departed.
⁵He becomes. He has become.

⁶We go out. We have gone out.
⁷You (**voi**) come. You have come.
⁸She dies. She has died.
⁹You (**Loro**) live. You have lived.

(13) ¹We come. We hold. We go out.
²They hold. They come. They go out.
³You (**Lei**) go out. You come. You hold.
⁴You (**tu**) come. You go out. You hold.
⁵He goes out. He holds. He comes.
⁶You (**Loro**) hold. You go out. You come.

⁷She comes. She holds. She goes out.
⁸You (**voi**) hold. You go out. You come.
⁹Come (**voi**)! Go out! Hold!
¹⁰Go out (**Lei**)! Hold! Come!
¹¹Hold (**tu**)! Come! Go out!
¹²Let's come! Let's hold! Let's go out!
¹³Go out (**Loro**)! Hold! Come!

B. PROGRESSIVE VARIATION.

(1) ¹A big church.
²A bigger church.
³Some bigger churches.
⁴Some more beautiful churches.
⁵Some more beautiful girls.
⁶The most beautiful girls.
⁷The tiredest girls.
⁸The least tired girls.
⁹The least tired students (f.).

¹⁰A less tired student (f.).
¹¹A less cheerful student (f.).
¹²A cheerful student (f.).
¹³A young student (f.).
¹⁴A less young student (f.).
¹⁵A less interesting student (f.).
¹⁶A less interesting church (f.).
¹⁷An interesting church.
¹⁸A big church.

(2) ¹Some expensive socks.
²Some more expensive socks.
³The most expensive socks.
⁴The least expensive socks.
⁵Some less expensive socks.
⁶Some less expensive newspapers.
⁷A less expensive newspaper.
⁸A less expensive skirt.
⁹A more expensive skirt.
¹⁰A cheaper skirt.
¹¹The cheapest skirt.
¹²The cheapest price.

¹³The most prohibitive price.
¹⁴The most prohibitive prices.
¹⁵The least prohibitive prices.
¹⁶A less prohibitive price.
¹⁷A less good price.
¹⁸A better price.
¹⁹Some better prices.
²⁰Some better socks.
²¹Some worse socks.
²²Some less expensive socks.
²³Some expensive socks.

(3) ¹I'm going out.
²I've gone out.
³I've arrived.
⁴They have arrived.
⁵They have eaten.
⁶She has eaten.
⁷She eats.
⁸She plays.
⁹You (**voi**) play.
¹⁰You (**voi**) have played.
¹¹You (**voi**) have come.
¹²Come (**voi**)!
¹³Carry (**voi**)!
¹⁴Carry (**Loro**)!

¹⁵Hold (**Loro**)!
¹⁶You (**Loro**) have held.
¹⁷You (**Loro**) have gone.
¹⁸We have gone.
¹⁹We have bought.
²⁰Let's buy!
²¹Let's return!
²²Return (**tu**)!
²³You (**tu**) return.
²⁴You (**tu**) have returned.
²⁵I have returned.
²⁶I have gone out.
²⁷I'm going out.

C. Translate into Italian:

1. Have you (**Loro**) any peaches better than these?   2. Where did you (**tu**) buy those newspapers?   3. Where has she put her purse?   4. Who is more tired than I?
5. They are the most interesting girls in Rome.   6. Strawberry and lemon are the best flavors.   7. They (*f.*) have departed for Florence.   8. Why haven't you (**Lei**) called the best doctor in the city?   9. Peter and Anna are going out together this morning.
10. How does one go from St. Peter's to the station?

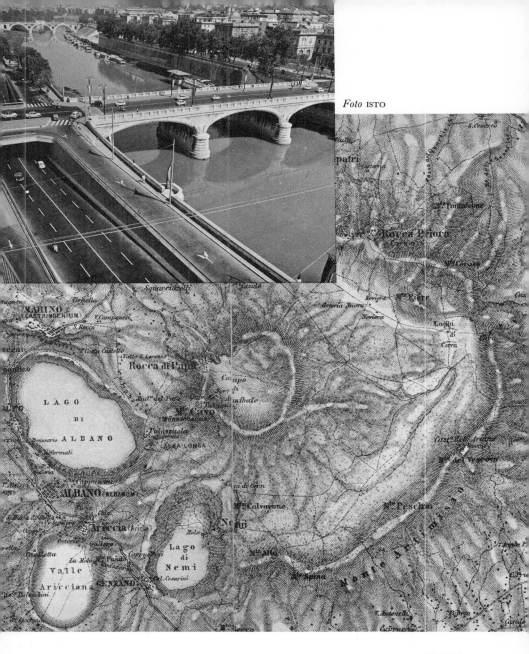

CONVERSATION UNIT———————17

Planning a Trip

I Castelli Romani

Foto Henle — Monkmeyer

Paul and his friends are going on a picnic excursion to the grape festival at Marino.

PÀOLO — ¹Pensavo di andare a fare una gita. ²Spero che voi due verrete.

PIETRO — ³Dove andrete?

FULVIA — ⁴Quando sarà? ⁵Chi verrà?

PÀOLO — ⁶Doménica pròssima ci sarà la sagra dell'uva a Marino. ⁷Potremo fare il giro dei Castelli e nel pomeriggio fermarci a Marino. ⁸Che ve ne pare?

PIETRO — ⁹Magnìfico, ma come ci andremo?

PÀOLO — ¹⁰Ho telefonato ad Enrico e Teodora. ¹¹Hanno detto che verranno volentieri. ¹²Loro hanno la màcchina.

PIETRO — ¹³Lo hai detto ai gemelli?

PÀOLO — ¹⁴I gemelli non pòssono venire, ma Stèfano e Maria Dolores verranno con la Seicento. ¹⁵Con la mia Lambretta e due automòbili siamo a posto per il trasporto.

FULVIA — ¹⁶Compreremo da mangiare per la strada o dobbiamo portarci dei panini imbottiti?

PAUL — ¹I was thinking of going to make an excursion (of going on an excursion). ²I hope that you two will come.

PETER — ³Where will you go?

FULVIA — ⁴When will it be? ⁵Who will come?

PAUL — ⁶Next Sunday there will be the grape festival at Marino. ⁷We can [*lit.*, we'll be able to] take the trip around the Alban Hills and in the afternoon stop at Marino. ⁸What do you think of it?

PETER — ⁹Magnificent, but how will we go there?

PAUL — ¹⁰I've telephoned [to] Henry and Theodora. ¹¹They've said that they'll come gladly. ¹²They have a car.

PETER — ¹³Did you tell the twins?

PAUL — ¹⁴The twins can't come, but Stephen and Mary Dolores will come with the "600". ¹⁵With my Lambretta and two cars we're all set as far as transportation is concerned.

FULVIA — ¹⁶Shall we buy [something] to eat along the way or are we to bring sandwiches for ourselves?

PIETRO — ¹⁷Portiàmoci dei panini. ¹⁸È più divertente e anche più sémplice.

FULVIA — ¹⁹Bene, io penso al pane e companàtico: formaggio, prosciutto, uova, salame. ²⁰Tu, Pàolo, pensa al vino e alle bìbite. ²¹Di' aTeodora ed Enrico di pensare alla frutta e a Maria Dolores e Stèfano di provvedere ai tovagliuoli, forchette, coltelli, cucchiai eccetera. ²²D'accordo?

PETER — ¹⁷Let's bring sandwiches ¹⁸It's more fun and also simpler.

FULVIA — ¹⁹Very well, I'll see to the bread and fixin's: cheese, ham, eggs, salame. ²⁰You, Paul, see to the wine and the drinks. ²¹Tell Theodora and Henry to see to the fruit, and Maria Dolores and Stephen to take care of the napkins, forks, knives, spoons, etcetera. ²²O.K.?

NOTES

1. A **sagra** is a local festival, in popular style, often (though not always) with religious overtones.
2. **I Castelli Romani** are the Alban Hills, to the southeast of Rome.
3. **Marino** is a town southeast of Rome, in the Alban Hills.
4. **Che ve ne pare,** literally *What does it seem to you about it?*
5. **La Seicento,** a type of small automobile.
6. **La Lambretta,** a type of motor-scooter.
7. **Panini imbottiti,** literally *stuffed rolls,* a term widely used instead of the English word *sandwich.*
8. **Il companàtico** is anything which is eaten along with bread.
9. **pensare a,** literally *to think of* = *to take thought for.*

IRREGULAR FORMS

l'uovo   *the egg (m.),* plural **le uova** *the eggs (f.)*
parere   *to appear;* present indicative; **paio, pari, pare, paiamo, parete, pàiono;** subjunctive command forms (**Lei**) **paia,** (**Loro**) **pàiano.**

Esercizi

A. *Risponda in italiano alle seguenti domande:*

1. Chi pensa di andare a fare una gita? 2. Dove pensa di andare? 3. Con chi parla? 4. Quante persone (*persons*) ci saranno in tutto? 5. Che cosa vògliono vedere a Marino? 6. Dov'è Marino? 7. Che cosa pensa Pietro dell'idea di Pàolo. 8. Che cosa domanda? 9. A chi ha telefonato Pàolo? 10. Che cosa hanno detto? 11. Che cosa hanno loro? 12. Chi non puó venire? 13. Chi verrà con una Seicento? 14. Quanti veìcoli (*vehicles*) ci saranno in tutto? 15. Che cosa decìdono di fare per il mangiare? 16. Che cosa si deve portare? 17. Perché? 18. Chi penserà al pane e companàtico? 19. Che cosa vuol dire "companàtico"? 20. A che cosa penserà Pàolo? 21. A che cosa dévono pensare Teodora ed Enrico? 22. A che cosa dévono pensare Maria Dolores e Stèfano?

B. *Dica a un altro studente (a un'altra studentessa):*

1. che pensava di fare una gita. 2. che spera che l'altra persona verrà. 3. che potrete fare il giro dei Castelli. 4. che ci andrete in automòbile. 5. che verrete volentieri. 6. che Lei l'ha detto ai gemelli. 7. che l'avete detto ai gemelli. 8. che comprerà da mangiare. 9. che porterà dei panini. 10. che penserete al pane e companàtico. 11. che provvederete ai tovagliuoli ecc.

C. *Domandi a un altro studente (a un'altra studentessa):*

1. se andrà a fare una gita. 2. se farà una gita. 3. se verrà. 4. dove andrà. 5. quando ci andrà. 6. se potrà fermarsi a Marino. 7. che cosa ne pensa. 8. come ci andrà. 9. se verrà volentieri. 10. se ha la màcchina. 11. se ha lo scooter. 12. se sarà a posto per il trasporto. 13. se porterà dei panini. 14. se comprerà del formaggio. 15. se penserà alla frutta.

D. REVISIONE DEI PRO-COMPLEMENTI **ci, vi.** *Dica o scriva in italiano:*

1. We'll go to Marino; we'll go there. 2. The fork is on the table; the fork is on it. 3. They'll come to the grape festival; they'll come to it. 4. We've been at St. Peter's; we've been there.

Foto Telefoto —
Monkmeyer

Supermercato romano

5. The twins can come to the Alban Hills; the twins can come there.   6. I'll see to (= think to) the fixin's; I'll see to them.   7. I could deposit some money in the bank; I could deposit some money there.   8. She's going downtown; she's going there.   9. She has gone downtown; she has gone there.

10. Are you in Rome?; are you there?

E. *Dica o scriva in italiano:*

1. We shall take [*lit.* make] a trip.   2. We hope that they'll come.   3. They'll be able to accompany us.   4. Stephen will come and will bring Maria Dolores.

5. I'll bring ham and eggs.   6. We will be all set for transportation.   7. We'll go there by [*lit.* in] automobile.   8. What will they buy?   9. Henry will buy a Lambretta.

10. There will be the grape festival next Wednesday.

F. Conversation:

1 You talk of your friends, discussing who will be able to go with you on an excursion and who will not, and who has what means of transportation.

2 You plan a picnic, discussing the various foods that are needed and who is to bring what.

Fulvia explains the history of a very ancient church.

PIETRO — ¹Questa chiesa è un misto di moderno e di antico.

FULVIA — ²San Pàolo ha tutta una storia. ³La prima chiesa fu construita in questo luogo al tempo di Costantino.

PIETRO — ⁴C'era una ragione speciale da commemorare?

FULVIA — ⁵Naturalmente, la decapitazione dell'apòstolo San Pàolo.

PIETRO — ⁶E poi cosa accadde?

FULVIA — ⁷La chiesa originària subì delle modificazioni nei sècoli seguenti. ⁸Divenne sempre più bella e perfetta. ⁹Nel mille ottocento ventitré, però, fu quasi totalmente distrutta da un incèndio.

PIETRO — ¹⁰Che peccato!

FULVIA — ¹¹La restaurazione della basìlica iniziò immediatamente. ¹²Ma, come vedi, lo stile contrasta molto con la struttura antica.

PETER — ¹This church is a mixture of modern and (of) old.

FULVIA — ²St. Paul's has a whole history. ³The first church was built in this place in the time of Constantine.

PETER — ⁴Was there a special reason to commemorate?

FULVIA — ⁵Naturally, the beheading of the apostle St. Paul.

PETER — ⁶And then what happened?

FULVIA —⁷The original church underwent modifications in the following centuries. ⁸It became ever more beautiful and perfect. ⁹In 1823, however, it was almost wholly destroyed by a fire.

PETER — ¹⁰What a shame!

FULVIA — ¹¹The restoration of the basilica began immediately. ¹²But, as you see, the style contrasts very much with the old structure.

Foto ISTO

At
San Paolo
Fuori Le Mura

A SINISTRA: Interiore.
L'Altare Maggiore
A DESTRA: Portico
della chièsa

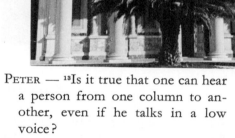

Foto ISTO

PIETRO — ¹³È vero che si può sentire una persona da una colonna all'altra, anche se parla a bassa voce?

FULVIA — ¹⁴Questo non lo so. ¹⁵Proviamo.

PIETRO — ¹⁶Mi senti?

FULVIA — ¹⁷Io non sento niente. ¹⁸Forse c'è troppa gente.

PIETRO — ¹⁹Andiamo a vedere le tre fontane.

FULVIA — ²⁰Sì, sono proprio qui vicino.

PETER — ¹³Is it true that one can hear a person from one column to another, even if he talks in a low voice?

FULVIA — ¹⁴This I don't know. ¹⁵Let's try.

PETER — ¹⁶Do you hear me?

FULVIA — ¹⁷*I* don't hear anything. ¹⁸Perhaps there are too many people.

PETER — ¹⁹Let's go to see the three fountains.

FULVIA — ²⁰Yes, they're right near here.

NOTES

1. **San Pàolo Fuori le Mura** (*St. Paul Outside the Walls*) is one of the most ancient churches of Rome, located near the banks of the Tiber to the south of the city. As its name implies, it is outside the circuit of the Aurelian Walls.

2. **Constantine the Great** (*ca.* 288-337 A.D.), the Roman emperor under whom Christianity become the official religion of Rome.

3. **la gente** *people* is a singular noun. Its plural **le genti** means *the peoples, the races.*

Foto ISTO

IRREGULAR FORMS

accade   *it happened*, past absolute of **accadere** *to happen*.
divenne   *it became*, past absolute of **divenire** *to become*, conjugated like **venire**
            to come.
fu   *it was*, past absolute of **èssere** *to be*.
costruire   *to construct* and **subire** *to undergo* are conjugated like **finire**.

Esercizi

A. *Risponda in italiano alle seguenti domande:*

1 Dove sono Pietro e Fulvia? 2. Come è la basìlica di San Pàolo fuori le
Mura? 3. Quando vi fu costruita la prima chiesa? 4. Che ragione
speciale c'era da commemorare?

5. Chi fu San Pàolo? 6. Che cosa accadde alla chiesa originaria? 7. Quali
modificazioni subì la basìlica? 8. Che cosa accadde nel mille ottocento
ventitré? 9. Quando iniziò la restaurazione della basìlica?

10. Come è lo stile della basìlica nuova? 11. Perché Pietro parla a bassa
voce? 12. Che cosa sente Fulvia? 13. Che cosa vanno a vedere? 14.
Dove sono le tre fontane?

B. *Domandi a un altro studente (a un'altra studentessa):*

1. se conosce la basìlica di San Pàolo. 2. se San Pàolo è una chiesa completamente antica. 3. se San Pàolo è una chiesa completamente nuova. 4. se trova questa chiesa bella o perfetta.
5. se può sentirLa quando Lei parla a bassa voce. 6. se c'è troppa gente. 7. se verrà a vedere le fontane.

C. *Dica a un altro studente (a un'altra studentessa):*

1. che lui (lei) diviene sempre più bello (bella). 2. che Lei vuol costruire una chiesa. 3. a quale santo Lei vuol dedicare (*dedicate*) la chiesa che costruirà.
4. quali chiese spera di vedere quando andrà a Roma.
5. che stile preferisce. 6. che trova il barocco migliore del gòtico (o viceversa). 7. che differenza c'è tra la struttura antica e quella nuova.

D. Revisione del Pro-Complemento **ne**. *Dica o scriva in italiano:*

1. We're talking about St. Paul's Outside the Walls; we're talking about it.
2. Rome has many churches; Rome has many of them. 3. Has he brought any cheese?; has he brought any? 4. The basilica was destroyed by the fire; it was destroyed by it.
5. These churches have many columns; these churches have many of them.
6. We have come from St. Peter's; we have come from there. 7. You are eating too much ham; you are eating too much of it. 8. The style of the basilica is beautiful; the style of it is beautiful. 9. They are departing from the basilica; they are departing from there.
10. You (**Loro**) have bought too many skirts; you have bought too many of them.

E. *Dica o scriva in italiano:*

1. This basilica commemorates the beheading of St. Paul. 2. It has become continually more beautiful. 3. However, a fire almost wholly destroyed it. 4. This was a great shame.
5. Are you (**Loro**) talking in a low voice? 6. Are there a lot of people here?
7. What do you (**voi**) hear? 8. What happened in 1664. 9. Let's take a trip around the Alban Hills.
10. The old structure was more beautiful and perfect than the new.

F. Conversations:

1. You tell your friends the story of the basilica of St. Paul Outside the Walls.
2. Two or more friends visit a church, test its acoustics, and speak about its history.

GRAMMAR UNIT ——————————IX

⬤ 31. The Future.

The future of all verbs is formed by adding the following endings: 1st sg. **-o**, 2nd sg. **-ai**, 3rd sg. **-à**; 1st pl. **-emo**, 2nd pl. **-ete**, 3rd pl. **-anno** to a stem which for almost all verbs is the same as the infinitive minus its final **-e**, except that in the first conjugation the **-a-** of the infinitive is changed to **-e-**.

FIRST CONJUGATION	SECOND CONJUGATION	THIRD CONJUGATION
portare *to bring* **porter-**	dormire *to sleep* **dormir-**	véndere *to sell* **vender-**
porterò *I shall bring,* porterai *etc.* porterà porteremo porterete porteranno	dormirò *I shall sleep,* dormirai *etc.* dormirà dormiremo dormirete dormiranno	venderò *I shall sell,* venderai *etc.* venderà venderemo venderete venderanno

With verbs of the first conjugation whose root ends in **-c-** or **-g-** (*e.g.,* **pagare** *to pay*), the "hard" consonant sound remains the same in the future stem, and the spelling automatically changes to **-ch-** or **-gh-** respectively: *e.g.,* **pagherò** *I shall pay.* Similarly, verbs whose roots end in **-ci-, -gi-** or **-sci-** (e.g. **cominciare** *to begin*, **mangiare** *to eat* or **lasciare** *to leave*), indicating a "soft" consonant sound, the letter **i** is omitted in the spelling of the future: *e.g.,* **comincerò** *I shall begin*, **mangerò** *I shall eat*, **lascerò** *I shall leave.*

A number of verbs, especially of the third conjugation, have special future stems, either with the loss of the characteristic vowel of the stem, or with other peculiarities. Of the verbs you have had to date, the following have irregular future stems:

Fontana delle Naiadi

Photo Enit-Roma

VERBS WITH IRREGULAR FUTURE STEMS

accadere	to happen:	**accadrà**	*it will happen*
andare	to go:	**andrò**	*I shall go*
avere	to have:	**avrò**	*I shall have*
divenire	to become:	**diverrò**	*I shall become*
dovere	to owe:	**dovrò**	*I shall owe*
èssere	to be:	**sarò**	*I shall be*
morire	to die:	**morrò**	*I shall die*
parere	to appear:	**parrò**	*I shall appear*
potere	to be able:	**potrò**	*I shall be able*
provvedere	to provide:	**provvedrò**	*I shall provide*
sapere	to know:	**saprò**	*I shall know*
tenere	to hold:	**terrò**	*I shall hold*
vedere	to see:	**vedrò**	*I shall see*
venire	to come:	**verrò**	*I shall come*
volere	to wish:	**vorrò**	*I shall wish*

32. PRESENT TENSE WITH **da** *since.*

In English, the present perfect (*I have been*, *etc.*) refers to an action lasting up to and including or affecting the present time; hence, in indicating an action which has gone on for a given time and which is still going on, we use the present perfect: *e.g.*, *I have been here for six weeks.* In Italian, the compound past (*e.g.* **sono stato**) refers only to an action over and done with in the past. To refer to an action still going on, one must use the present, and the time since when the action has been going on is indicated by **da** *since.*

Sono qui **da** sei mesi.	I have been (*lit.*, am.) here *for* (*lit.*, since) six months.
Da quanto tempo sei in Italia?	*For* (*lit.* since) how much time have you been (*lit.*, are you) in Italy?
Mangia **da** ore e ore.	He has been eating (*lit.*, he is eating) *for* (*lit.*, since) hours and hours.

33. NOUNS WITH MASCULINE SINGULAR IN **-o** AND FEMININE PLURAL IN **-a**.

A certain number of nouns ending in **-o** in the masculine singular have a plural in **-a**, which is feminine.

l'uo**vo**	the egg	le uo**va**	the eggs
il muro	the wall	le mura	the walls (*of a city*)
il braccio	the arm	le braccia	the arms
il ginòcchio	the knee	le ginòcchia	the knees
il labbro	the lip	le labbra	the lips
il lenzuolo	the sheet	le lenzuola	the sheets (*when counted by pairs*)

Many of these nouns refer to parts of the body which come in pairs. Many of them also have normal masculine plurals with transferred or special meanings: *e.g.*, **i muri** the walls [of a house]; **i lenzuoli** *the sheets* [not counted by pairs].

34. PLURAL OF MASCULINE NOUNS IN **-a**.

Masculine nouns ending in **-a-** have their plural in **-i-**. The masculine gender remains unchanged:

il programma	the program	i programmi	the programs
il telegramma	the telegram	i telegrammi	the telegrams
il dentista	the dentist	i dentisti	the dentists
l'artista	the artist	gli artisti	the artists
il fonema	the phoneme	i fonemi	the phonemes

35. Adverbs in -mente.

An adverb in **-mente**, corresponding to an English adverb in -*ly* can be formed of virtually any adjective. The Italian suffix **-mente** is normally added to the feminine form of adjectives in **-o -a**. With adjectives in -e, which have no distinction between feminine and masculine, it is added to the form in **-e**, except that the final vowel of the adjective is dropped when the adjective ends in **-le** or **-re** preceded by a vowel.

certo	certain	cert**amente**	certainly
còmodo	comfortable	comod**amente**	comfortably
complet**o**	complete	complet**amente**	completely
esatto	exact	esatt**amente**	exactly
cordia**le**	cordial	cordia**lmente**	cordially
gener**ale**	general	genera**lmente**	generally
insistente	insistent	insistent**emente**	insistently
regola**re**	regular	regola**rmente**	regularly

Exception: The adverb of **altro** *other* is **altrimenti** *otherwise*.

Grammatical Exercises

A. Substitutions.

(1) ¹We shall eat tomorrow.
²We shall sleep tomorrow.
³We shall talk tomorrow.

⁴We shall depart tomorrow.
⁵We shall study tomorrow.
⁶We shall pay tomorrow.

(2) ¹She will buy the jacket.
²She will sell the jacket.
³She will see the jacket.

⁴She will want the jacket.
⁵She will have the jacket.
⁶She will hold the jacket.

(3) ¹They will depart for Marino.
²They will go to Marino.
³They will be at Marino.

⁴They will come from Marino.
⁵They will return from Marino.
⁶They will remain at Marino.

(4) ¹You (**tu**) will eat in the restaurant.
²You will dine in the restaurant.
³You will be in the restaurant.

⁴You will come into the restaurant.
⁵You will enter into the restaurant.
⁶You will pay in the restaurant.

(5) ¹I shall walk as far as St. Peter's.
²I shall come to St. Peter's.
³I shall go to St. Peter's.
⁴I shall stay at St. Peter's.
⁵I shall live at St. Peter's.
⁶I shall die at St. Peter's.

(6) ¹You (**voi**) will find it.
²You will be able to find it.
³You will want to find it.
⁴You will have to find it.
⁵You will decide it.
⁶You will eliminate it.

B. Progressive Variation.

(1) ¹You (**Lei**) will see me.
²You (**Lei**) will want to see me.
³You (**Loro**) will want to see me.
⁴You (**Loro**) will want to see them.
⁵We shall want to see them.
⁶We shall see them.
⁷We shall see you (**voi**).
⁸I shall see you (**voi**).
⁹He will see you (**voi**).
¹⁰He will see you (**tu**).
¹¹They will see you (**tu**).
¹²They will see me.
¹³You (**voi**) will see me.
¹⁴You (**tu**) will see me.
¹⁵You (**Lei**) will see me.

(2) ¹We shall look.
²They will look.
³They will die.
⁴She will die.
⁵She will speak.
⁶I shall speak.
⁷I shall know.
⁸You (**Lei**) will know.
⁹You (**Lei**) will come.
¹⁰You (**voi**) will come.
¹¹You (**voi**) will appear.
¹²You (**tu**) will appear.
¹³You (**tu**) will look.
¹⁴We shall look.

(3) ¹They will stop [themselves].
²She will stop [herself].
³She will see herself.
⁴We shall see ourselves.
⁵We shall interest ourselves.
⁶You (**Loro**) will interest yourselves.
⁷You (**Loro**) will accommodate yourselves.
⁸I shall accommodate myself.
⁹I shall complain.
¹⁰You (**tu**) will complain.
¹¹You (**tu**) will be called [call yourself]
Giovanni.
¹²You (**Lei**) will be called [call yourself]
Giovanni.
¹³You (**Lei**) will stop [yourself.]
¹⁴They will stop [themselves].

(4) ¹He's eating now.
  ²He has been eating for an hour.
  ³He has been walking for an hour.
  ⁴He will walk for (per) an hour.
  ⁵I shall walk for an hour.
  ⁶I've been walking for an hour.
  ⁷I'm walking now.
  ⁸He's walking now.

  ⁹He's talking now.
  ¹⁰He's been talking for a year.
  ¹¹They've been talking for a year.
  ¹²They'll talk for an hour.
  ¹³They talk for hours and hours.
  ¹⁴They're talking now.
  ¹⁵They're eating now.
  ¹⁶He's eating now.

(5) ¹the wall.
  ²the walls [of the city].
  ³the dentists.
  ⁴the dentist.
  ⁵the lip.
  ⁶the lips.

  ⁷the artists.
  ⁸the artist.
  ⁹the sheet
  ¹⁰the sheets [by pairs].
  ¹¹the sheets [not by pairs].
  ¹²the programs.

  ¹³the program.
  ¹⁴the arm.
  ¹⁵the arms.
  ¹⁶the walls [of the house].
  ¹⁷the wall.

(6) ¹certain.
  ²certainly.
  ³only (adv.).
  ⁴only (adj.).
  ⁵good.
  ⁶well.
  ⁷regularly.

  ⁸regular.
  ⁹pure.
  ¹⁰purely.
  ¹¹exactly.
  ¹²exact.
  ¹³strong.
  ¹⁴strongly.

  ¹⁵otherwise.
  ¹⁶other.
  ¹⁷complete.
  ¹⁸completely.
  ¹⁹totally.
  ²⁰total.
  ²¹certain.

C. Dica o scriva in italiano:

1. We shall take the trolley-bus and we shall go to St. Peter's.   2. They will have to go to a men's clothing store.   3. She won't like the handkerchiefs [to her will not be pleasing the handkerchiefs].   4. You (voi) will dine in the open air.
5. Peter will order two espressi.   6. The cashier will be able to change the bank note.   7. There will be a beautiful sun.   8. Dr. Dossi will give the letter to Fulvia.   9. Pietro will want to buy a newspaper.
10. He will buy it.

CONVERSATION UNIT————19

University Students

Stephen is unhappy over having to repeat the oral exam in chemistry.

TEODORA — ¹Le lezioni sono cominciate da un mese, e ancora non ho aperto libro.

ENRICO — ²Brava, poi all'ùltimo momento piangi perché non sai niente.

TEODORA — ³Guarda chi sta venendo! ⁴Ciao, Stèfano, come stai?

STÈFANO — ⁵Benìssimo, e voi?

ENRICO — ⁶Dove ti sei cacciato? ⁷Sono sècoli che non ti fai vivo.

STÈFANO — ⁸Sono stato occupato con gli esami.

TEODORA — ⁹Esami? ¹⁰Di quest'època?

THEODORA — ¹Classes have been going for a month, and I still haven't cracked a book.

HENRY — ²Bravo, and then at the last minute you'll cry because you don't know anything.

THEODORA — ³Look who's coming ⁴Hi, Steve, how are you?

STEPHEN — ⁵Very well, and you?

HENRY — ⁶Where have you been hiding? ⁷You haven't been around for ages.

STEPHEN — ⁸I've been busy with exams.

THEODORA — ⁹Exams? ¹⁰At this time of year?

142

STÈFANO — ¹¹Mia cara, ricòrdati che io non sono una matrìcola come te. ¹²La sessione di ottobre dura spesso fino a metà novembre.

TEODORA — ¹³Scusa, non volevo offènderti.

ENRICO — ¹⁴Come sono andati gli esami?

STÈFANO — ¹⁵Così così; sono arrivato all'interrogazione stanco morto. ¹⁶Fìsica è andata benone. ¹⁷Ho preso ventotto. ¹⁸A Chìmica invece mi sono ritirato, altrimenti mi bocciàvano.

TEODORA — ¹⁹Pazienza, non te la préndere.

STÈFANO — ²⁰Sì, lo so. ²¹Lo ripeterò a febbraio.

STEPHEN — ¹¹My dear girl, remember that *I'm* not a freshman like you. ¹²The October exam period often lasts until the middle of November.

THEODORA — ¹³Excuse me, I didn't mean to offend you.

HENRY — ¹⁴How did the exams go?

STEPHEN — ¹⁵So-so. I arrived at the oral exam dead tired. ¹⁶Physics went very well. ¹⁷I got twenty-eight. ¹⁸In chemistry, on the other hand, I withdrew, otherwise they would have flunked me.

THEODORA — ¹⁹Never mind, don't get upset about it.

STEPHEN — ²⁰Yes, I know. ²¹I'll repeat it in February.

NOTES

1. **Sono cominciate da un mese,** literally *They have been begun since a month.*
2. **Brava,** here feminine singular because spoken to a girl. When said to someone, **bravo** *fine, excellent, splendid,* varies with the number and gender of the person(s) spoken to.
3. Sentence 7, literally *It's centuries that you are not making yourself alive.* **Farsi vivo** = *to show signs of life, to come around, etc.*
4. The examination system in Italian universities involves three examination periods (**sessioni** *sessions*) every year: one at the end of the academic year, in June (often lasting into July), and two others, in October and February. All examinations are oral (hence the reference in sentence 15 to the *interrogation*). The highest possible mark is thirty (hence 28 would equal our "A").
5. **Pazienza!** (literally *patience!*) is an extremely widespread exclamation in Italy in any frustrating situation.

Dopo
gli
esami
Foto Adsum

IRREGULAR FORMS

offèndere: past participle **offeso**.
piàngere: past participle **pianto**.

Studenti di scambio,
Genova

Foto Aigner — Monkmeyer

Esercizi

A. *Risponda alle seguenti domande basate sul testo:*

1. Da quando sono cominciate le lezioni?   2. Ha studiato molto Teodora?
3. Che cosa accadrà all'ùltimo momento se Teodora non studierà?   4. Chi
viene e comincia a parlare con Enrico e Teodora?
5. Dov'è stato? 6. Chi è matrìcola?   7. In che stagione deve aver luogo
[*take place*] questa conversazione?   8. Fino a quando dura la sessione di
ottobre?   9. Come si è sentito Stèfano quando è arrivato all'interrogazione?
10. Come gli è andato l'esame di fìsica?   11. Perché si è ritirato dall'esame di
chìmica?   12. Quando ripeterà l'esame di chimica?

B. *Domandi a un altro studente (a un'altra studentessa):*

1. se sono cominciate le lezioni, e da quando.   2. se ha studiato.   3. se piangerà all'ùltimo momento.   4. dove si è cacciato.
5. perché non si è fatto vivo.   6. se è stato occupato con gli esami.   7. se è
una matrìcola.   8. in che stagione hanno luogo le sessioni.   9. come sono
andati gli esami.
10. se è stanco morto.   11. se si è ritirato da un esame.   12. quali esami ha
dato (*taken*). 13. quanti punti (*points*) ha preso.   14. se è stato bocciato.
15. se ripeterà degli esami, e quando.

C. *Dica a un altro studente (a un'altra studentessa) :*

1. che non piangerà all'ùltimo momento.   2. che ha studiato molto in questi ùltimi mesi. 3. che è stato occupato con gli esami. 4. che non voleva offèn- derlo.
5. che gli esami sono andati benone.   6. che non è stato bocciato.   7. che ripeterà gli esami a febbraio.

D. REVISIONE DEL FUTURO. *Dica o scriva in italiano:*

1. I'm opening the book; I'll open the book; I'll open it.   2. The exam period lasts until November; the exam period will last until November. 3. You (**Lei**) are around (= make yourself alive); you will be around. 4. You (**voi**) are freshmen; you will be freshmen.
5. The examinations are going well; the examinations will go well.   6. We get (= take) twenty-five; we shall get twenty-five.   7. He flunks me; he will flunk me.   8. I arrive dead tired; I shall arrive dead tired.   9. They repeat the examination; they will repeat the examination; they will repeat it.
10. I withdraw [myself]; I will withdraw.

E. *Dica o scriva in italiano:*

1. Where did you buy this book?   2. Why hasn't she opened [a] book?   3. They always cry at the last minute.   4. Look (**voi**), Peter and Fulvia are coming.
5. Where have you (**Lei**) been hiding?   6. Why haven't you (**Lei**) been around?   7. Have you (**Lei**) been busy with exams?   8. Is she a freshman? 9. Until when does the June session last?
10. All my exams went very well.

F. CONVERSATIONS:

1. Two or more of you talk about how many books you have, where you bought them (downtown), and whether you have looked at them.
2. Two or more persons talk about the examinations they have taken and the grades they have received.

Sending a Letter

Peter learns about postal rates from a tobacconist.

(Dal tabaccaio)

PIETRO — ¹Vorrei spedire questa léttera.

TABACCAIO — ²Dove, signore?

PIETRO — ³Negli Stati Uniti. ⁴E ne ho un'altra per la Francia.

TABACCAIO — ⁵Un francobollo per gli Stati Uniti costa centoventi lire. ⁶Per la Francia invece il prezzo è come per l'Italia, trenta lire.

PIETRO — ⁷Centoventi lire per via aérea, immàgino.

TABACCAIO — ⁸Certamente, signore. ⁹Per via mare costa solo settanta lire. ¹⁰Ma non Glielo consiglio. ¹¹Ci mette tre o quattro settimane

PIETRO — ¹²Mi dica una cosa. ¹³Perché il prezzo dei francobolli nelle cartoline vària? ¹⁴A volte còstano venti lire e a volte dieci.

TABACCAIO — ¹⁵Dipende da quante parole ci scrive. ¹⁶Se mette solo i saluti Le costa meno che se la scrive tutta.

PIETRO — ¹⁷Ah, capisco ora. ¹⁸Mi dia tre francobolli da centotrenta e due da trenta, per favore.

TABACCAIO — ¹⁹Ecco, signore. ²⁰Desìdera altro?

(At the tobacconist's)

PETER — ¹I'd like to send this letter.

TOBACCONIST — ²Where, sir?

PETER — ³To the United States. ⁴And I have another one to (for) France.

TOBACCONIST — ⁵A stamp for the United States costs 120 lire. ⁶For France, on the other hand, the price is the same as for Italy, 30 lire.

PETER — ⁷A hundred and twenty lire by air mail, I imagine.

TOBACCONIST — ⁸Certainly, sir. ⁹By regular (ocean) mail it costs only 70 lire. ¹⁰But I don't advise it. ¹¹It takes three or four weeks.

PETER — ¹²Tell me something. ¹³Why does the price of stamps on postcards vary? ¹⁴Sometimes they cost 20 lire and sometimes 10.

TOBACCONIST — ¹⁵It depends on how many words you write on it. ¹⁶If you put only greetings it costs you less than if you write more (it all).

PETER — ¹⁷Ah, I understand now. ¹⁸Give me three 130 [lire] stamps and two 30's, please.

TOBACCONIST — ¹⁹Here you are, sir. ²⁰Do you wish anything else?

Foto Aigner — Monkmeyer

PIETRO — ²¹Sì, mi pesi questa léttera, per favore. ²²Ci vuole un francobollo dóppio?

TABACCAIO — ²³Mi dispiace, signore, ma non posso servirLa. ²⁴La mia bilancia non funziona.

PETER — ²¹Yes, weigh this letter for me, please. ²²Does it need two stamps (a double stamp)?

TOBACCONIST — ²³I'm sorry, sir, but I can't help (serve) you. ²⁴My scales aren't working.

NOTES

1. **Per via aèrea,** literally *by aerial way*; **per via mare,** *by way [of the] sea.*
2. **Non Glielo consiglio,** literally *I don't advise it to you.*
3. **Tre francobolli da centotrenta,** literally *three stamps to the value of 130.*

IRREGULAR FORMS

spedire	*to send:* conjugated like **finire** (II-*isc*)
dipéndere	*to depend:* past participle **dipeso.**
scrivere	*to write:* past participle **scritto**

Esercizi

A. *Risponda in italiano alle seguenti domande basate sul testo:*

1. Che cosa vuol spedire Pietro?   2. Dove deve andare per comprare dei francobolli?   3. Dove vanno le léttere?   4. Quanto cóstano le léttere per gli Stati Uniti?
5. Per via aèrea o per via mare?   6. Quanto cóstano le léttere per l'Italia e la Francia?   7. Quanto ci mette una léttera per arrivare negli Stati Uniti per via mare?   8. Perché il prezzo dei francobolli nelle cartoline varia?   9. Quanto cóstano le cartoline in Italia?
10. Il tabaccaio può servire Pietro, pesàndogli la léttera (*weighing the letter for him*)?   11. Perché no?

B. *Dica a un altro studente (a un'altra studentessa):*

1. che vuol spedire una léttera negli Stati Uniti.   2. che ne ha un'altra per la Francia.   3. che immàgina che costerà centotrenta lire.   4. che non gli (le) consiglia di spedire la léttera per via mare.
5. che spedirà una cartolina ai Suoi genitori.   6. che desìdera cinque francobolli da trenta lire.   7. di pesarLe una léttera.

C. *Domandi a un altro studente (a un'altra studentessa):*

1. quanto cóstano le léttere per gli Stati Uniti.   2. dove vuol spedire la sua léttera.   3. se Le consiglia di spedirla per via aèrea.   4. di dirLe una cosa.
5. perché i francobolli per le cartoline cóstano a volte venti e a volte dieci lire.   6. di darLe sette francobolli da settanta lire.   7. se ci vuole un francobollo dóppio.   8. se funziona la sua bilancia.

D. Revisione del Passato Pròssimo dei Verbi Coniugati con **èssere**. *Dica o scriva in italiano:*

1. We're going; we have gone.   2. She arrives; she has arrived.   3. You (**voi**) are coming; you have come.   4. They (*f.*) are dying; they have died.
5. I'm departing; I have departed.   6. You (**Lei**) go out; you have gone out.   7. We are; we have been.   8. You (**Loro**) remain; you have remained.   9. I seem; I have seemed.
10. You (**tu**) pass; you have passed.

E. *Dica o scriva in italiano:*

1. I'm sending three letters.   2. Where are you (**Lei**) sending them?   3. This one goes to the United States.   4. And we have another one for Italy.
5. How much do they cost?   6. Three letters for Italy will cost you (**Lei**) ninety lire.   7. The price of the stamps varies often.   8. I've put only greetings on this postcard.   9. This, on the other hand, I've written wholly (all).
10. Weigh (**Loro**) these letters for me, please.   11. I'll weigh them for you gladly.   12. My scales are functioning very well.

F. CONVERSATIONS:

1. At a tobacconist's, you inquire about the price of stamps for various types of mail (letters, postcards with only greetings, postcards entirely filled), for various countries (U.S., France, Italy), and by air mail or regular mail, in different combinations.
2. You discuss the relative advantages of air mail and regular mail.

Foto Gary Wagner

LETTURA QUARTA

Una Gita nei Castelli Romani

(Conversations 16-20)

¹**bisognare** to be necessary.
²**approfittare** to profit.
³**insistere** to insist.
⁴**la vacanza** the vacation.
⁵**l'occasione** *(f.)* the opportunity.
⁶**il riposo** the rest.
⁷**i preparativi** *(pl.)* the preparations.
⁸**farsi** to become.
⁹**febbrile** feverish.
¹⁰**l'organizzatrice** *(f.)* the organizer *(m.,* **l'organizzatore***).*
¹¹**aiutare** to help.
¹²**il da farsi** what is to be done.
¹³**il ragazzo** the boy.
¹⁴**la' tenda** the tent.
¹⁵**il sacco** the sack; **il sacco a pelo** the sleeping-bag.
¹⁶**scòmodo** uncomfortable.
¹⁷**il rischio** the risk.
¹⁸**il raffreddore** the cold; **prèndersi un raffreddore** to catch a cold.
¹⁹**qualche** some.
²⁰**per di più** moreover.
²¹**loro** they, them.
²²**cucinare** to cook.
²³**lavare** to wash.
²⁴**finalmente** finally.
²⁵**l'accordo** *(m.)* the agreement.
²⁶**il lavoro** the work.
²⁷**salvare** to save.
²⁸**la capra** the goat.
²⁹**il càvolo** the cabbage; **salvare capre e càvoli** to eat one's cake and have it too.
³⁰**risparmiare** to save.
³¹**la spesa** the expense.
³²**non avranno da lamentarsi** they won't have any reason to complain.

Un gruppo di amici dell'università decìdono di fare una gita nei Castelli Romani. Bisogna¹ approfittare² degli ùltimi giorni di bel tempo, insiste³ Pàolo. L'ùltimo sàbato del mese è vacanza;⁴ è una magnìfica occasione⁵ per préndersi due giorni di riposo.⁶

I preparativi⁷ si fanno⁸ febbrili.⁹ Fulvia è un'organizzatrice¹⁰ perfetta e aiuta¹¹ Pàolo a decìdere sul da farsi.¹² I ragazzi¹³ vògliono dormire fuori con la tenda¹⁴ e i sacchi a pelo.¹⁵ Alle ragazze l'idea non piace: fa freddo, si sta scòmodi,¹⁶ se piove c'è il rìschio¹⁷ di préndersi un raffreddore¹⁸ o qualche¹⁹ altro malanno. Per di più,²⁰ son loro²¹ che dévono pensare a cucinare²² e a lavare²³ i piatti.

Finalmente²⁴ si arriva ad un accordo:²⁵ dormiranno fuori, ma i ragazzi si dévono impegnare ad aiutare le ragazze con il lavoro.²⁶ (Si sàlvano²⁷ così capre²⁸ e càvoli.²⁹) Si rispàrmia³⁰ sulla spesa³¹ dell'albergo e le ragazze non avranno da lamentarsi.³²

C'è il problema[33] del trasporto; per fortuna[34] due dei ragazzi hanno la màcchina e Pàolo ha la Lambretta, per cùi[35] non c'è troppo[36] da preoccuparsi.[37]

Ognuno[38] è incaricato[39] di procurare[40] parte[41] del necessàrio:[42] tovaglioli, forchette, coltelli, cucchiai. Il cibo[43] si comprerà sul luogo; sarà più fresco[44] e più econòmico.

All'ùltimo momento, però, i gemelli telèfonano che non pòssono andare alla gita. I gemelli sono i due fratelli Angelo e Osvaldo Falerta, ma tutti li chiàmano i gemelli perché si somìgliano[45] come due gocce[46] d'acqua, anche se uno è biondo[47] e l'altro è bruno.[48] Sono due ragazzi simpàtici[49] e molto divertenti.

La comitiva[50] parte la mattina[51] prestìssimo; tutti sono allegri e gioviali[52] anche se si son dovuti alzare[53] di buon'ora.[54] Tutti diménticano i propri[55] pensieri:[56] addio[57] lezioni, esami, stùdio;[58] oggi ci si diverte![59]

[33]**il problema** the problem.
[34]**la fortuna** the *(good)* fortune; **per fortuna** fortunately.
[35]**cùi** which; **per cùi** for which reason.
[36]**troppo** too much.
[37]**preoccuparsi** to worry.
[38]**ognuno** everyone.
[39]**incaricare** to charge, entrust.
[40]**procurare** to procure, get.
[41]**la parte** the part.
[42]**necessàrio** necessary; **il necessàrio** what is needed.
[43]**il cibo** the food.
[44]**fresco** fresh.
[45]**somigliare (a ...)** to resemble.
[46]**la goccia** the drop.
[47]**biondo** blond.
[48]**bruno** dark, brunet(te).
[49]**simpàtico** likeable.
[50]**la comitiva** the party.
[51]**la mattina** the morning; [*here*] in the morning.
[52]**gioviale** jovial.
[53]**alzare** to raise; **alzarsi** to get up; **si son dovuti alzare** they have had to get up.
[54]**di buon'ora** early.
[55]**proprio** one's own.
[56]**il pensiero** the thought.
[57]**addio** good-bye (*to ...*).
[58]**lo stùdio** study.
[59]**divertirsi** to amuse oneself, have a good time; **ci si diverte** one amuses oneself.

Foto ISTO

GRAMMAR UNIT —————— X

🔵 **36.** DISJUNCTIVE PERSONAL PRONOUNS.

In addition to the conjunctive object pronouns (**mi** *me*, *etc.*), Italian has a series of personal pronouns which can be used separately or *disjoined* from verbs, and hence are called *disjunctive* pronouns. In the singular, there are separate forms for subject and object pronouns, but not in the plural:

DISJUNCTIVE PERSONAL PRONOUNS					
SINGULAR				PLURAL	
Subject		*Object*		*Subject and Object*	
io	I	me	me	noi	we, us
tu	you (*fam. sg.*)	te	you (*fam. sg.*)	voi	you (*fam. pl.*)
(egli	he)	lùi	he, him ⎞	loro	they, them
(ella	she)	lei	she, her ⎠		
(Ella	you)	Lei	you (*formal sg.*)	Loro	you (*formal pl.*)

The disjunctive subject pronouns are only used when emphasis is desired; otherwise, the ending of the verb alone is sufficient to indicate the person and number of the actor. The disjunctive object pronouns are used in two principal ways: as emphatic objects of verbs and as objects of prepositions. In addition, the third person singular disjunctive object pronouns are nowadays normally used as subjects as well, in place of the literary and archaic subject forms **egli**, **ella** and **Ella**.

Io voglio un gelato.	*I* want an ice-cream.
Cosa vuoi **tu?**	What do *you* want?
Questo lo faremo **noi.**	*We*'ll do this.
Che cosa ne pensa **Lei?**	What do *you* think about it?
Vedo **lùi,** ma non **lei.**	I see *him*, but not *her*.
Io non sono una matrìcola **come te.**	*I*'m not a freshman *like you*.
No ci sono léttere **per me?**	Aren't there any letters *for me?*
Ecco **a Lei.**	Here [it is] *for you*.

37. CONJUNCTIVE PERSONAL PRONOUNS—INDIRECT OBJECT + DIRECT OBJECT.

The conjunctive pronoun and other pro-complement forms may occur not only singly, but in combinations of two. When a pro-complement ending in -i (*e.g.*, **mi, ti** *etc.*) stands before another pro-complement beginning in l- or n-, the -i is automatically replaced by -e. In such a position, both **gli** and **le** become **glie-**, which is written as one word together with the following pro-complement. In such combinations, an indirect object always precedes the direct object, with resultant combinations of the following type:

mi ti	you (*fam. sg.*) to me		**mi vi**	you (*fam. pl.*) to me
me lo	him, it to me		**me li**	them (*m.*) to me
me la	her, it to me		**me le**	them (*f.*) to me
me La	you (*formal sg.*) to me		**me Li**	you (*formal pl. m.*) to me
			me Le	you (*formal pl. f.*) to me

te lo	him, it to you		**te li**	them (*m.*) to you
te la	her, it to you		**te le**	them (*f.*) to you

ci ti	you (*fam. sg.*) to us		**ci vi**	you (*fam. pl.*) to us
ce lo	him, it to us		**ce li**	them (*m.*) to us
ce la	her, it to us		**ce le**	them (*f.*) to us
ce La	you (*formal sg.*) to us		**ce Li**	you (*formal pl. m.*) to us
			ce Le	you (*formal pl. f.*) to us

ve lo	him, it to you		**ve li**	them (*m.*) to you
ve la	her, it to you		**ve le**	them (*f.*) to you

glielo	him, it to him *or* her
gliela	her, it to him *or* her

Glielo	him, it to you (*formal sg.*)
Gliela	her, it to you (*formal sg.*)

se lo	him, it to himself, herself, itself, themselves
se la	her, it to himself, herself, itself, themselves
se li	them (*m.*) to himself, herself, itself, themselves
se le	them (*f.*) to himself, herself, itself, themselves

Since there is no indirect object form for the third person plural in the conjunctive pronoun series, no combination of this type is possible for the meanings *him, her, it to them* or *him, her, it to you (formal pl.*).

Mi ti ha presentato.	He has presented, introduced *you to me.*
Ve li dànno.	They are giving *them to you.*
Ce le véndono.	They sell *them (f. pl.) to us.*
Non **glielo** ha mostrato.	He hasn't shown *it to him (her).*

BUT

Non **lo** ha mostrato **loro**.	He hasn't shown *it to them.*

 38. Verbs—Imperfect.

Italian has not one, but two simple past tenses, corresponding to such English forms as *I ate, I did,* etc. The tense known as the *imperfect* is regular for all verbs except **èssere**. All regular imperfects end in **-vo, -vi, -va, -vamo, -vate, -vano** added to the root + characteristic vowel of the verb. Thus, for the three regular conjugations and **èssere** :

Imperfect Indicative

mangiare *to eat* **mangia-**	**dormire** *to sleep* **dormi-**	**préndere** *to take* **prende-**	**èssere** *to be*
mangiavo *I was eating, I used to eat.*	dormivo *I was sleeping, I used to sleep*	prendevo *I was taking, I used to take*	ero *I was being, I used to be*
mangiavi	dormivi	prendevi	eri
mangiava	dormiva	prendeva	era
mangiavamo	dormivamo	prendevamo	eravamo
mangiavate	dormivate	prendevate	eravate
mangiàvano	dormìvano	prendévano	èrano

The roots of the verbs **fare** *to do* and **dire** *to say* are **fac-** and **dic-**, respectively, so that their imperfects are **facevo** *I used to do,* etc., and **dicevo** *I used to say,* etc,

The meaning of the imperfect is "action in the past not limited to a specific, clearly identifiable point or period of time". Hence it refers to such kinds of action as the *habitual* "I used to eat, I was in the habit of eating"; *background of another action* "I was eating"; or *repetitive* "I ate (e.g., every noon)". It is not possible to predict on the basis of the English form, whether the imperfect or some other kind of past is to be used in Italian. The choice will depend on the situation to be described and the meaning to be conveyed.

Mangiavamo pesce ogni giorno.	*We used to eat* fish every day.
Ero stanco quando **tornai** da Firenze.	*I was tired* when *I came back* from Florence
Dormivamo spesso fino a mezzogiorno.	*We would* often *sleep* until noon.

39. Verbs—Agreement of Past Participle in Compound Past with **avere**.

In a compound past tense formed with the auxiliary **avere** (cf. Grammar Unit **VIII**, *Sec.* **29**), the past participle must agree with the direct object only when the direct object is one of the conjunctive object pronouns **lo, li, la, le**. In other instances, the past participle may agree with the direct object (*e.g.*, a first or second person conjunctive pronoun, a preceding relative pronoun, or a noun object) or it may remain invariable in the masculine singular, as the speaker prefers. In modern usage, there is a strong trend towards keeping the past participle invariable.

Lo ha comprato.	He has bought it (*m. sg.*).
L'ha comprata.	He has bought it (*f. sg.*).
Li ha comprati.	He has bought them (*m. pl.*).
Le ha comprate.	He has bought them (*f. pl.*).

BUT

Mi ha visto (*or* **vista**).	He has seen me (*f.*).
La camicia che ha comprato (*or* **comprata**).	The shirt which he has bought.
Ho comprato (*or* **comprate**) **tre camicie.**	I have bought three shirts.

Grammatical Exercises

A. Substitutions.

(1) *Use first the conjunctive (unstressed) and then the disjunctive (stressed, emphatic) object pronouns in the following sentences:*

(a)
1 He sees me.
2 He sees you (*fam. sg.*).
3 He sees him.
4 He sees her.
5 He sees you (*formal sg.*).
6 He sees us.
7 He sees you (*fam. pl.*).
8 He sees them (*m.*).
9 He sees them (*f.*).
10 He sees you (*formal pl. m.*).
11 He sees you (*formal pl. f.*).

(b)
1 He writes to me.
2 He writes to you (*fam. sg.*).
3 He writes to him.
4 He writes to her.
5 He writes to you (*formal sg.*).
6 He writes to us.
7 He writes to you (*fam. pl.*).
8 He writes to them.
9 He writes to you (*formal pl.*).

(2) *Give the following verb forms first without any subject pronouns and then with an emphatic disjunctive subject pronoun:*

1 I go.
2 You (*fam. sg.*) cook.
3 He writes.
4 She eats.
5 We sleep.
6 You (*fam. pl*) sell.
7 They buy.

(3) *Give the Italian for the following combinations of preposition + object pronoun:*

¹with me.

²for you *(fam. sg.)*.

³to him.

⁴from her.

⁵with us.

⁶for you *(fam. pl.)*.

⁷to them.

(4) *Give the following sequences of verb forms:*

¹I eat; I have eaten; I was eating; I will eat.

²we cry; we have cried; we were crying; we will cry.

³he repeats; he has repeated; he was repeating; he will repeat.

⁴she arrives; she has arrived; she was arriving; she will arrive.

⁵they request; they have requested; they were requesting; they will request.

⁶you *(fam. sg.)* are; you have been; you used to be; you will be.

⁷you *(fam. pl.)* do; you have done; you used to do; you will do.

⁸you *(formal sg.)* talk; you have talked; you used to talk; you will talk.

⁹you *(formal pl.)* hear; you have heard; you used to hear; you will hear.

(5) *Give the following sequences of conjunctive object pronouns, in connection with verbs:*

(a) ¹He gives it to me.

²He gives it to us.

³He gives it to you *(fam. sg.)*.

⁴He gives it to you *(fam. pl.)*.

⁵He gives it to him *(her)*.

⁶He gives it to you *(formal sg.)*.

⁷He gives it to them.

(b) ¹He was writing it *(= the letter)* to them.

²He was writing it to him (her).

³He was writing it to you *(formal sg.)*.

⁴He was writing it to you *(fam. pl.)*.

⁵He was writing it to you *(fam. sg.)*.

⁷He was writing it to us.

⁷He was writing it to me.

(c) *Do the exercises of 5.a and 5.b, with the form for* it *replaced by the form for* them *(m.): e.g.,* He gives them to me; he gives them to us; *etc.*

(d) *As in 5.c, but with the form for* them *(f.) .e.g.,* He gives them to me; he gives them to us; *etc.*

B. PROGRESSIVE VARIATION. *Say or write in Italian:*

(1) ¹She gives me the fork.

²She was giving me the fork.

³She was giving it to me.

⁴She has given it to me.

⁵She has given them *(f.)* to me.

⁶She will give them *(f.)* to me.

⁷She will give them *(f.)* to us.

⁸She will give us the forks.

⁹They will give us the forks.

¹⁰They will give them *(f.)* to us.

¹¹They will give them *(f.)* to me.

¹²They have given them *(f.)* to me.

¹³They have given them *(m.)* to me.

¹⁴They have given me the forks.

¹⁵They give me the forks.

¹⁶They give me the fork.

¹⁷She gives me the fork.

(2) ¹We repeat it *(m.)* to her.
²We repeat it to him.
³They repeat it to him.
⁴They were repeating it to him.
⁵They have repeated it to him.
⁶They have repeated it *(f.)* to him.
⁷They have repeated the question to him.
⁸They have repeated the question to me.
⁹They have repeated it *(f.)* to me.
¹⁰They have repeated it *(f.)* to you *(fam. sg.)*.
¹¹They have repeated it *(m.)* to you.
¹²They will repeat it *(m.)* to you.
¹³They repeat it *(m.)* to you.
¹⁴We repeat it *(m.)* to you.
¹⁵We repeat it *(m.)* to her.

(3) *Use unemphatic conjunctive object pronouns and omit subject pronouns unless the corresponding English forms are italicized:*

¹She's departing from Rome.
²*She's* departing from Rome.
³*She's* departing from there.
⁴*He's* departing from there.
⁵*He's* going there.
⁶*He* will go there.
⁷He will go there.
⁸We shall go there.
⁹*We* shall go there.
¹⁰*We* shall eat there.
¹¹*We* shall eat the Milanese cutlet.
¹²We'll eat the Milanese cutlet.
¹³You *(fam. pl.)* will eat the Milanese cutlet.
¹⁴*You (fam. pl.)* will eat the Milanese cutlet.
¹⁵*You* will eat it.
¹⁶You will eat it.
¹⁷You will eat some.
¹⁸*You* will eat some.
¹⁹*You* will depart from there.
²⁰*You* are departing from there.
²¹*You* are departing from Rome.
²²You're departing from Rome.
²³She's departing from Rome.

C. *Say or write in Italian:*

1. Why are you weeping for her? 2. She hasn't opened a book for six months. 3. The February exam period used to last until the middle of March. 4. In history of art they used to flunk all the students.

5. Stamps for the United States used to cost a hundred and twenty lire. 6. Have you sent the letters? Yes, we've sent them. 7. Are there any letters for me? No, there are none [of them] for you *(fam. sg.)*. 8. I have given them *(i.e.,* the letters) to you *(fam. pl.)*. 9. He has accompanied us *(fem.)* downtown.

10. Give *(fam. pl.)* it to me, please.

The Roman Forum

Fulvia and her friends visit the Forum—the center of ancient Rome.

PIETRO — ¹Finalmente ci avviciniamo al Foro. ²Prima di venire in Italia, il mio più grande sogno era di visitare il Foro. ³Ed ora èccomi qua.

ANNA — ⁴Perché proprio il Foro e non qualche altra cosa?

PIETRO — ⁵Non so. ⁶Forse peŗché il mio professore di latino era un grande entusiasta della civiltà romana. ⁷E noi logicamente ne abbiamo subito l'influenza.

FULVIA — ⁸Quale professore era? ⁹Quello che seguitava a parlarvi in latino?

PIETRO — ¹⁰Sì, proprio lui, era veramente un uomo in gamba. ¹¹Poveretto, è morto l'anno scorso.

ANNA — ¹²Quella lì a destra è la colonna traiana. ¹³Sapete la leggenda dell'imperatore Traiano?

FULVIA — ¹⁴Vediamo, se mi ricordo bene Dante ne parla nella *Divina Commèdia*.

ANNA — ¹⁵Sì, Traiano è l'imperatore che fu risuscitato per un istante da Papa Gregorio Magno. ¹⁶Fu così battezzato e la sua ànima potè salire in cielo.

FULVIA — ¹⁷Questo posto incute tale rispetto che non oso neppure parlare.

PETER — ¹Finally we are nearing the Forum. ²Before coming to Italy, my greatest dream was to visit the Forum. ³And now here I am.

ANNA — ⁴Why just the Forum and not some other thing?

PETER — ⁵I don't know. ⁶Perhaps because my Latin professor was a great enthusiast for Roman civilization. ⁷And we, naturally, fell under his influence.

FULVIA — ⁸Which professor was it? ⁹The one who kept on talking to you in Latin?

PETER — ¹⁰Yes, that's the one, he was really a very smart man. ¹¹Poor fellow, he died last year

ANNA — ¹²That over there on the right is the column of Trajan. ¹³Do you know the legend of the emperor Trajan?

FULVIA — ¹⁴Let's see, if I remember rightly Dante talks of it in the *Divine Comedy*.

ANNA — ¹⁵Yes, Trajan is the emperor who was revived for an instant by Pope Gregory the Great.¹⁶Thus he was baptized and his soul was able to go up to heaven.

FULVIA — ¹⁷This place commands such respect that I don't even dare to speak.

PIETRO — [18]Cosa sono quelle tre colonne laggiù?

PETER — [18]What are those three columns down there?

ANNA — [19]Sono ciò che rimane del tempio di Vespasiano. [20]O per lo meno si attribuìscono ad esso.

ANNA — [19]They are what remains of the temple of Vespasian. [20]Or at least they are attributed to him.

FULVIA — [21]Quella laggiù è la chiesa dove si è sposato tuo fratello?

FULVIA — [21]That over there is the church where your brother got married?

ANNA — [22]Sì, è Santa Francesca Romana.

ANNA — [22]Yes, it is Santa Francesca Romana.

PIETRO — [23]Mamma mia, tu sai tutto, sei meglio di un cicerone.

PETER — [23]Golly, you know everything, you're better than a guide.

NOTES

1. **poveretto,** literally *poor little one*; varies in gender and number according to the person referred to.
2. **Dante Alighieri** (1265-1321), considered Italy's greatest poet; author of the *Divine Comedy*, a long religious poem.
3. **Traiano,** in English, Trajan (53-117 A.D.), one of the greatest of Roman emperors. According to pious legend, the story of his justice towards a poor widow so moved Pope Gregory the Great that the latter prayed to God that Trajan might be restored to life for an instant, converted to Christianity, baptized and admitted to heaven.
4. **Pope Gregory the Great** (ca. 540-604), one of the greatest mediaeval popes.
5. **Vespasian** (9-79 A.D.), Roman emperor.
6. **Santa Francesca Romana** (1384-1440), a fifteenth-century Roman nun and founder of a religious order.
7. **mamma mia,** literally *mother of mine!*

Arco di Sèttimo Severo

Foto ISTO

Foro Romano e
Chièsa di
Santa
Francesca
Romana

Foto ISTO

VERB FORMS

attribuire   *to attribute*, II-*isc*
salire   *to go up;* present **salgo, sali, sale, saliamo, salite, sàlgono**; present
subjunctive (for commands) 3. sg. **salga**, 3. pl. **sàlgano**. In compound
past, auxilary **èssere**.

Esercizi

A. *Risponda in italiano alle seguenti domande:*

1. A quale posto si avvicìnano Pietro, Anna e Fulvia?   2. Qual'era il più
grande sogno di Pietro prima di venire in Italia?   3. Perché voleva visitare
proprio il Foro?   4. Di chi aveva subito l'influenza?
5. Perché?   6. In quale lingua (*language*) il professore parlava ai suoi studenti?   7. Quando era morto quel professore?   8. Chi costruì la colonna
traiana?   9. Quale grande poeta (*poet*) italiano parla della leggenda di
Traiano, e dove?
10. Da chi fu risuscitato Traiano?   11. Che cosa potè fare la sua ànima?   12.
Perché?   13. A chi si attribuìscono le tre colonne?   14. Chi si era sposato
nella chiesa di Santa Francesca Romana?   15. Che cosa fa un cicerone?

B. *Domandi a un altro studente (a un'altra studentessa):*

1. dov'è il Foro. 2. qual'è il suo più grande sogno. 3. se è un grande entusiasta della civiltà romana o italiana. 4. se il suo professore gli parla in latino o in italiano.
5. se è morto il suo professore di latino. 6. se sa la leggenda dell'imperatore Traiano. 7. chi era Traiano. 8. se le tre colonne laggiù fanno parte di un tempio. 9. a quale tempio si attribuìscono.
10. dov'è la chiesa di Santa Francesca Romana. 11. dove si è sposato suo fratello.

C. *Dica a un altro studente (o a un'altra studentessa):*

1. che Lei si avvicina al Foro. 2. che ha subìto l'influenza del Suo professore di latino. 3. che lui seguitava a parlarLe in latino. 4. che Lei è qui.
5. che Lei sa la leggenda di Traiano. 6. che Suo fratello si è sposato nella chiesa di San Pàolo. 7. che Sua sorella si è sposata nella chiesa di Santa Francesca. 8. Racconti (*tell*) la leggenda di Traiano.

D. REVISIONE DELL'IMPERFETTO (Review of the Imperfect). *Dica o scriva in italiano:*

1. We were continuing. 2. He was dying. 3. They were baptizing. 4. You (**tu**) were speaking.
5. I used to be. 6. You (**voi**) were visiting. 7. She used to write. 8. We were bringing. 9. You (**Loro**) used to eat.
10. I was looking. 11. You (**Lei**) used to return. 12. We were coming.

E. *Dica o scriva in italiano:*

1. This column is attributed to the temple of Trajan. 2. I'm not going up on the Palatine. 3. We used to visit the Forum in our dreams. 4. Those men are really smart.
5. Why do you (**Lei**) attribute that idea to me? 6. Poor woman, she died last week. 7. Are you (**voi**) enthusiasts of Italian civilization? 8. Has Dante spoken of it? 9. Go up (**Loro**) with him!
10. In which church was the emperor Trajan baptized?

F. CONVERSATIONS:

1. Two or more of you are enthusiasts of Roman and Italian civilization, and talk of what interests you most.
2. One student takes the role of guide and shows the others around a famous place (St. Paul, the Forum, *etc.*)

Foto Bright — Rapho-Guillumette

Vista del Palatino — Basilica di Massenzio

Chitchat on the Palatine

Anna, Fulvia, Paul and Peter are talking on the Palatine, the hill between the Forum and the river Tiber on the site where the Roman emperors built their palaces.

PIETRO — ¹Chi è quel ragazzo che hai appena salutato?

ANNA — ²È quello di cui ti parlavo ieri.

PIETRO — ³Chi? ⁴Non mi ricordo affatto.

ANNA — ⁵Ma sì, quello il cui padre è andato al polo Nord in una spedizione, e per cui ho lavorato l'estate scorsa.

PÀOLO — ⁶"Per cui"... "di cui" ... " della quale "... volete smétterla di pettegolare voi due! ⁷Non siamo mica venuti al Palatino per sapere vita, morte e miràcoli di tutta la gente che conosciamo.

FULVIA — ⁸Pàolo ha ragione, muovétevi!

PIETRO — ⁹Oh, smettétela con quell'aria di persone serie!

ANNA — ¹⁰Non fate i pedanti. ¹¹Voi non sapete godervi la vita. ¹²È così bello starsene seduti qui a chiacchierare. ¹³A propòsito, Pàolo, dimmi chi era quella ragazza bionda a cui hai fatto l'occhiolino?

PÀOLO — ¹⁴Quale ragazza? Stai scherzando? ¹⁵Ti pare che io sia il tipo da fare l'occhiolino alle ragazze?

ANNA — ¹⁶Oh no, per carità, pòvero innocente!

PETER — ¹Who is that fellow whom you just greeted?

ANNA — ²He's the one about whom I was telling you yesterday.

PETER — ³Who? ⁴I don't remember at all.

ANNA — ⁵Oh yes, the one whose father went to the North Pole in an expedition, and for whom I worked last summer.

PAUL — ⁶"For whom" ... "of whom" ... "of which" ... will you stop gossiping, you two! ⁷We certainly didn't come to the Palatine to learn about (to know) the life, death and miracles of all the people we know.

FULVIA — ⁸Paul's right, get a move on!

PETER — ⁹Oh, don't be so serious (stop it with that manner of serious persons)!

ANNA — ¹⁰Don't act like pedants. ¹¹You don't know how to enjoy life. ¹²It's so nice to sit here chatting. ¹³By the way, Paul, tell me, who was that blonde girl you were making eyes at?

PAUL — ¹⁴What girl? Are you joking? ¹⁵Do you think that I'm the kind who make eyes at girls?

ANNA — ¹⁶Oh no, good heavens, poor innocent fellow!

Foto ISTO

FULVIA — [17]Ehi, calmàtevi. [18]Parlate sottovoce. [19]Non siamo mica al mercato!

PIETRO — [20]Bene, facciàmola finita. [21]Voi andate ad istruirvi alle rovine romane. [22]Noi rimaniamo qui a non far nulla. [23]Ci rincontreremo tra un'oretta, d'accordo?

FULVIA — [17]Hey, calm down. [18]Talk in a low voice. [19]We're not at the market!

PETER — [20]All right, let's stop it. [21]*You* go and improve your minds at the Roman ruins. [22]*We*'ll stay here doing nothing. [23]We'll meet again in an hour or so, O.K.?

NOTES

1. **Muovétevi,** literally *move yourselves!*
2. **Stàrsene seduti,** literally *to stay seated.*
3. **Facciàmola finita,** literally *let's make it finished!*
4. **Istruirvi,** *to instruct yourselves.*
5. **Un'oretta,** literally *a little hour.*

VERBS

istruire   *to instruct;* II-*isc*
muòvere past participle **mosso.**
sméttere *to cease, stop;* past participle **smesso**

Esercizi

A. *Risponda in italiano alle seguenti domande:*

1. Dove sono Anna e i suoi amici?   2. Di che cosa pàrlano?   3. Che cosa domanda Pietro ad Anna?   4. Che cosa risponde Anna?   5. Si ricorda Pietro del ragazzo?   6. Che cosa ha fatto il padre del ragazzo?   7. Che cosa ha fatto Anna per il padre del ragazzo?   8. Che cosa dévono sméttere di fare Anna e Pàolo?   9. Per quale ragione sono venuti al Palatino?   10. Che cosa dice Fulvia ad Anna e Pietro?   11. Che cosa domanda Anna a Pietro?   12. Pietro è il tipo da fare l'occhiolino alle ragazze?   13. Che cosa dice Fulvia agli altri?   14. Che cosa decìdono di fare?   15. Fra quanto tempo si rincontreranno?

B. *Domandi a un altro studente (a un'altra studentessa):*

1. chi è il ragazzo (la ragazza) che ha salutato.   2. se si ricorda del ragazzo (della ragazza) che ha salutato.   3. per chi ha lavorato l'estate scorsa.   4. se gli (le) piace pettegolare.   5. per fare che cosa va al Palatino (al museo ecc.).   6. se si dà l'aria di una persona seria.   7. se fa il pedante.   8. se sa godersi la vita.   9. se fa l'occhiolino alle ragazze (ai ragazzi).   10. se vuol calmarsi.   11. se vuol parlare sottovoce.   12. se si parla sottovoce al mercato.   13. se rimarrà a non far nulla.   14. tra quanto tempo si rincontreranno.

C. *Dica a un altro studente (a un'altra studentessa):*

1. che Lei gli (le) parlava ieri del ragazzo che ha salutato.   2. che Lei fa l'occhiolino solamente ai ragazzi belli (alle ragazze belle).   3. che Suo padre è andato al polo Nord in una spedizione.   4. di smétterla di pettegolare.   5. che Lei non vuol sapere vita, morte e miràcoli di tutta la gente che conosce.   6. che Lei non fa il pedante.   7. che Lei sa godersi la vita.   8. che Le piace starsene seduto a chiacchierare.   9. che Le piàcciono le ragazze bionde (i ragazzi biondi).   10. che Lei andrà ad istruirsi alle rovine romane.

D. Revisione dei Pronomi Oggetti. *Dica o scriva in italiano:*

1. He shows me a girl; he shows her to me.   2. I enjoy life for myself; I enjoy it for myself.   3. We're giving ourselves airs; we're giving them to ourselves.   4. They were telling us the truth; they were telling it to us.

5. You (**tu**) have sent him the letters; you have sent them to him. 6. She sells you (*fam. sg.*) a stamp; she sells it to you. 7. You (**Loro**) will write them a postcard; you will write it to them.

E. *Dica o scriva in italiano:*

1. I have seen her, but I haven't greeted her. 2. Don't (**tu**) move (yourself)!
3. We have stopped talking. 4. How many miracles did St. Peter perform?
5. A really serious person doesn't jabber. 6. They aren't calming themselves.
7. She is instructing us. 8. Let's meet again in two hours. 9. I certainly haven't gone to the North Pole.
10. I like to gossip and to make eyes at the girls.

F. CONVERSATIONS:

1. You tease each other about the boys that the girls have been saying hello to and/or the girls that the boys have been making eyes at.
2. Two or more of you converse about what one does when one visits the Roman Forum and the Palatine.

● 40. COMPOUND PAST OF REFLEXIVE VERBS.
When a reflexive conjunctive object pronoun (direct or indirect) is present in a compound past phrase, the auxiliary **avere** is automatically replaced by **èssere**, and the past participle always agrees in gender and number with the reflexive object pronoun. Thus:

Mio fratello **si è sposato.**	My brother *got married* [*lit.,* married himself].
Mia sorella **si è sposata.**	My sister *got married.*
I miei fratelli **si sono sposati.**	My brothers *got married.*
Le mie sorelle **si sono sposate.**	My sisters *got married.*
Mio fratello **si è comprato** un'automòbile.	My brother *bought himself* [*lit.,* for himself] an automobile.
Mia sorella **si è comprata** un'automòbile.	My sister *bought herself* an automobile.
I miei fratelli **si sono comprati** un'automòbile.	My brothers *bought themselves* an automobile.
Le mie sorelle **si sono comprate** un'automòbile.	My sisters *bought themselves* an automobile.

● 41. THE PRESENT PARTICIPLE.
The present participle is formed, in the first conjugation, by adding **-ando** to the verb root, and in the other conjugations by adding **-endo**.

THE PRESENT PARTICIPLE				
		INFINITIVE		PRESENT PARTICIPLE
1ST CONJUGATION	comprare mangiare parlare scherzare	*to buy* *to eat* *to speak* *to joke*	comprando mangiando parlando scherzando	*buying* *eating* *speaking* *joking*
2ND CONJUGATION	attribuire dormire	*to attribute* *to sleep*	attribuendo dormendo	*attributing* *sleeping*
3RD CONJUGATION	fare véndere	*to do* *to sell*	facendo vendendo	*doing* *selling*

The present participle of **èssere** *to be* is **essendo** *being*; of **dire** *to say*, **dicendo** *saying.*

With the present participles, any pro-complement or combination of pro-complements is suffixed to and written together with the participle as a single word (*cf.* Grammar Unit **VII**, *Sec.* 23): *e.g.,* **parlàndone** *talking about it*; **mangiàndolo** *eating it*; **dormèndovi** *sleeping in it*; **vendèndogli** *selling to him*; etc.

42. PROGRESSIVE PHRASES

Progressive phrases are formed with the verb **stare** *to be in the act of* + a present participle.

Stai scherzando?	*Are you joking?*
Sto comprando una màcchina.	*I'm buying* an automobile.
Stava dormendo.	*He was sleeping.*
Che cosa **state facendo?**	What *are you doing?*
Stiamo parlando con il professore.	*We are talking* with the teacher.

As contrasted with English progressive phrases consisting of *be* + verb form in *-ing*, these Italian progressive phrases lay rather more emphasis on the continuing nature of whatever is being done, and hence have the meaning of *to be in the act of ... -ing*. They are thus comparable to French phrases formed with **être en train de ...**, or Spanish phrases consisting of **estar** + present participle.

When a pro-complement or combination of pro-complements accompanies a progressive phrase, it may occur either suffixed to the present participle (*cf.* above, *Sec.* **41**), or preceding the verb **stare** and written separately from it.

La sto comprando *or* **Sto** compràndo**la**.	I'm buying it.
Ne stava parlando *or* **Stava** parlàndo**ne**.	He was talking about it.
Ci sta dormendo *or* **Sta** dormèndo**ci**.	He's sleeping in it.

43. PRO-COMPLEMENTS: COMBINATIONS WITH NE.

When the pro-phrase **ne** (*cf.* Grammar Unit **VII**, Section 23) is present in a combination with another pro-complement, **ne** is the first of the two if the other pro-complement is one of the third person direct object pronouns **lo, la, li, le**. Direct or indirect object pronouns of other persons (including the third person reflexive pronoun) and the pro-phrases **ci** or **vi** precede **ne**, with the automatic changes set forth in Grammar Unit **X**, Section **37**.

Ne lo ringrazio.	I thank *him* for (*lit.*, of) *it.*
Ne la ringrazio.	I thank *her* for *it.*
Ne la ringrazio.	I thank *you* (*formal sg.*) for *it.*
Ne li ringrazio.	I thank *them* (*m.*) for *it.*
Ne le ringrazio.	I thank *them* (*f.*) for *it.*
Ne Li ringrazio.	I thank *you* (*formal pl.*, *m.*) for *it.*
Ne Le ringrazio.	I thank *you* (*formal pl.*, *f.*) for *it.*

Me **ne** hanno parlato.	They've spoken *to me about it.*
Non **te ne** ha dato?	Hasn't he given *you* any *of it?*
Non vògliono dà**rcene**.	They don't want to give *us any.*
Gliene abbiamo spiegato la ragione.	We've explained the reason for *it to him (to her).*
Se ne sono ricordati.	*They* have remembered *it.*

Certain expressions have a reflexive pronoun + **ne** built into them as part of their structure, *e.g.*, andà**rsene** *to go away* or stà**rsene** *to remain*:

Ce **ne** andiamo.	We're *going away.*
Se **ne** sono andate.	They (*f.*) *have gone away.*
È così bello stà**rsene** seduti.	It's so nice *to remain* seated.
Se **ne** stava solo.	He *was remaining* alone.

● **44.** INTERROGATIVE AND RELATIVE PRONOUNS.

In asking questions, the pronoun **che**? *what*? refers to things and non-human beings, and **chi**? *who*? *whom*? to humans, parallel to English usage. Instead of **che**?, the more easy-going (**che**) **cosa**? *what*? is very widely used.

Che vuoi *or* **Che cosa** vuoi *or* **Cosa** vuoi?	*What* do you want?
Che è questo *or* **Che cos**'è questo *or* **Cos**'è questo?	*What*'s this?
Guarda **che cosa** ho comprato *or* Guarda **cosa** ho comprato.	Look *what* I've bought.
Chi è venuto?	*Who* has come?
Chi vedo?	*Whom* do I see?
Con **chi** vai al cìnema?	With *whom* are you going to the movies?

When introducing relative clauses, however, the form **chi** is not used. **Che** serves as subject and direct object, referring both to people and things. Its place is taken automatically by **cùi** after prepositions. **Cùi** can also be used as an independent form, not preceded by a preposition, in dative (*to whom, to which*) and in possessive meanings (*whose, of whom, of which*).

il professore **che seguitava a parlarvi in Latino**	the teacher *who kept on talking to you in Latin*
l'automòbile **che ho comprato**	the automobile *which I have bought*
ciò **che rimane del tempio di Vespasiano**	that *which remains of the temple of Vespasian*
le scarpe **che mi sono comprato**	the shoes *which I have bought for myself*
il signore **per cùi ho lavorato l'estate scorsa**	the gentleman *for whom I worked last summer*
quella ragazza bionda **a cùi hai fatto l'occhiolino**	that blonde girl *at whom you made eyes*

gli àlberi, **le cùi foglie càmbiano in mille colori**	the trees, *whose leaves change into a thousand colors*
il ragazzo, **il cùi padre é andato al Polo Nord**	the fellow, *whose father went to the North Pole*
l'americano **cùi ho venduto delle cartoline**	the American *to whom I sold some postcards*

The form **cùi**, when used in possessive meaning (*whose, of whom, of which*), fits into the same pattern of definite article + possessive element + noun that we have already observed with possessive adjectives (*cf.* Grammar Unit: **IV**, *Sec.* 12): **le cùi foglie** *whose leaves*, parallel to **le sue foglie** *its leaves*.

Grammatical Exercises

A. SUBSTITUTIONS.

1. *Transform each of the following reflexive expressions into the corresponding compound past, first in the masculine and then in the feminine.* Example: **mi sposo** I get married > **mi sono sposato, mi sono sposata** I have gotten married.

¹ci vediamo	*we see ourselves*	⁹si compra	*he buys for himself*
²ti siedi	*you sit down*	¹⁰mi muovo	*I move myself*
³si méttono	*they put themselves*	¹¹si accòmodano	*you (formal pl.) seat yourselves*
⁴mi diverto	*I amuse myself*		
⁵si ferma	*he stops himself*	¹²ci vendiamo	*we sell to each other*
⁶vi guardate	*you look at yourselves*	¹³ti avvicini	*you approach*
⁷si lamenta	*you (formal sg.) complain*	¹⁴vi parlate	*you talk to each other*
⁸si védono	*you (formal pl.) see yourselves*	¹⁵si costruisce	*he builds for himself*
		¹⁶si strapazza	*you (formal sg.) overwork yourself*

2. *Transform each of the following present tense forms into a progressive phrase, on the model of* **leggo** I read > **sto leggendo** I am in the act of reading.

¹cucina	*she is cooking*	⁹parto	*I depart*
²trascurate	*you are neglecting*	¹⁰véndono	*you (formal pl.) sell*
³spieghiamo	*we are explaining*	¹¹prende	*he takes*
⁴esplórano	*you (formal pl.) are exploring*	¹²dormite	*you sleep*
		¹³sàlgono	*they go up*
⁵gioco	*I am playing*	¹⁴decidi	*you decide*
⁶studia	*you (formal sg.) are studying*	¹⁵facciamo	*we do*
⁷màngiano	*they are eating*	¹⁶dice	*you (formal sg.) say*
⁸porti	*you are bringing*		

3. *In each of the following sentences, replace the phrase introduced by the preposition* **di** *or* **da**, *by* **ne** *on the model of* **gli do dei libri** I give him some books > **gliene do** I give him some.

¹Mi vende **delle cartoline.**	He sells me *some post-cards.*
²Mostra loro **delle rovine.**	He shows them *some ruins.*
³Si compra **del pane.**	He buys himself *some bread.*
⁴Vi pòrtano **dei giornali.**	They bring you *some newspapers.*
⁵Ci dà **dei panini.**	She gives us *some sandwiches.*
⁶Le hanno mostrato **dei guanti.**	They have shown her *some gloves.*
⁷Ti compreranno **dello zùcchero.**	They will buy you *some sugar.*
⁸Gli portàvano **dei quadri.**	They used to bring him *pictures.*
⁹Le dò **della medicina.**	I'm giving you *some medicine.*

4. *In each of the following sentences, replace the indirect object by the appropriate conjunctive pronoun, and the phrase introduced by* **di** *or* **da,** *by* **ne**: *e.g.,* **Hanno venduto delle case al professore.** They sold the professor some houses. > **Gliene hanno venduto.** They sold him some.

¹Fa **dei complimenti alla ragazza.**	He pays *the girl compliments.*
²Porterà **dei gelati a sua zia.**	He brings *some ice-cream to his aunt.*
³Spediva **delle cartoline a me.**	He used to send *me post-cards.*
⁴Mostra **dei quadri ai suoi amici.**	He shows *pictures to his friends.*
⁵Vendo **della frutta a Lei.**	I sell *fruit to you.*
⁶Ha portato **dei giornali a te.**	He has brought *newspapers to you.*
⁷Daremo **dei calzini a lui.**	We shall give *him some socks.*
⁸Ha spedito **delle léttere a noi.**	He has sent *us some letters.*
⁹Farete **dei complimenti a lei?**	Will you pay *her any compliments?*
¹⁰Non portava **dei giornali a voi.**	He didn't bring *you any newspapers.*

B. PROGRESSIVE VARIATION. *Say or write in Italian:*

(1) ¹Whom do you *(formal sg.)* see?
²What do you see?
³What do you eat?
⁴Why do you eat?
⁵Why do you depart?
⁶When do you depart?
⁷When do you arrive?
⁸When do they arrive?
⁹Where do they arrive?
¹⁰Where do they amuse themselves?
¹¹Why do they amuse themselves?
¹²Why do we amuse ourselves?
¹³When do we amuse ourselves?
¹⁴When do we write?
¹⁵What do we write?
¹⁶What do we see?
¹⁷Whom do you *(formal sg.)* see?

(2) ¹Are you *(fam. pl.)* in the act of joking?
²Are you *(formal pl.)* in the act of joking?
³Are you in the act of reading?
⁴Do you read?
⁵Do you gossip?
⁶Does she gossip?
⁷Is she in the act of gossiping?
⁸Is she in the act of jabbering?
⁹Are we in the act of jabbering?
¹⁰Have we jabbered?
¹¹Have we departed?
¹²Have you *(fam. sg.)* departed?
¹³Have you *(fam. sg.)* gone away?

¹⁴Were you *(fam. sg.)* going away?   ¹⁷Are they in the act of joking?
¹⁵Are they going away?   ¹⁸Are you *(fam.pl.)* in the act of joking?
¹⁶Are they in the act of going away?

(3)   ¹I'm sending the letter to my father.
²I'm sending the letter to him.
³I'm sending it to him.
⁴We're sending it to him.
⁵We're sending them [the letters] to him.
⁶We're sending them to her.
⁷We're sending the letters to her.
⁸We're sending the letters to our aunt.
⁹They've sent the letters to our aunt.

¹⁰They've sent the books to our aunt.
¹¹They've sent the books to the teacher.
¹²They've sent them to the teacher.
¹³They've sent them to him.
¹⁴I've sent them to him.
¹⁵I've sent it to him.
¹⁶I'm sending it to him.
¹⁷I'm sending it to my father.
¹⁸I'm sending the letter to my father.

(4)   ¹They're bringing me some newspapers.
²They're bringing me some.
³They're selling me some.
⁴They're selling you *(formal sg.)* some.
⁵They're selling some to *you.*
⁶They're selling some bread to *you.*
⁷I'm selling some bread to *you.*
⁸I'm selling some sandwiches to *you.*
⁹I'm selling some sandwiches to *him.*

¹⁰I'm selling him some sandwiches.
¹¹I'm selling him some.
¹²I'm selling you *(fam. pl.)* some.
¹³He's selling you some.
¹⁴He's selling me some.
¹⁵He's bringing me some.
¹⁶He's bringing me some newspapers.
¹⁷They're bringing me some newspapers.

(5)   ¹I thank the hotelkeeper for the newspaper.
²I thank the hotelkeeper for it.
³I thank him for it.
⁴I thank her for it.
⁵We thank her for it.
⁶We thank her for the supper.
⁷They thank her for the supper.
⁸They thank us for the supper.

⁹They thank us for it.
¹⁰They thank you *(fam. sg.)* for it.
¹¹They thank you for the newspaper.
¹²They thank *you* for the newspaper.
¹³I thank *you* for the newspaper.
¹⁴I thank *him* for the newspaper.
¹⁵I thank the hotelkeeper for the newspaper.

C. *Say or write in Italian:*

1. Why don't you (**Lei**) stop jabbering?   2. Why has she gone away?   3. Do you *(f. fam. sg.)* like to remain seated here?   4. Are they making eyes at the girls?

5. I'm enjoying life.   6. They *(f.)* have neared the museum of the Uffizi.   7. When did she die?   8. Why hasn't she gotten married?   9. He knows the Forum better than the guides.

10. To whom is this temple attributed?

Foto Bright — Rapho-Guillumette

CONVERSATION UNIT

——23——

Buying Tobacco

The tobacconist advises Peter to smoke a pipe.

PIETRO — ¹Hanno delle sigarette americane?

TABACCAIO — ²Mi dispiace, signore, ma non ne abbiamo. ³Dovrebbe andare in uno dei tabaccai al centro. ⁴Abbiamo del tabacco americano, però, se ne vuole.

PIETRO — ⁵Non fumo la pipa. ⁶Un tempo la fumavo, ma non mi soddisfa come le sigarette.

TABACCAIO — ⁷Le sigarette, però, sono più dannose alla salute della pipa, lo sa?

PETER — ¹Have you any American cigarettes?

TOBACCONIST — ²I'm sorry, sir, but we haven't got any. ³You would have to go to one of the tobacconists downtown. ⁴We have American tobacco, however, if you want some.

PETER — ⁵I don't smoke a pipe. ⁶Once upon a time I used to smoke one, but it doesn't satisfy me like cigarettes.

TOBACCONIST — ⁷Cigarettes, however, are more harmful to health than a pipe, do you realize?

PIETRO — ⁸Sì, lo so. ⁹Ma cosa vuole? ¹⁰Fumare è uno di quei vizi che è difficile tògliersi.

TABACCAIO — ¹¹Ha ragione, signore. ¹²E da una parte sono contento che sia così. ¹³Altrimenti andrei in fallimento con il mio negozio.

PIETRO — ¹⁴Che sigarette ci sono non troppo forti?

TABACCAIO — ¹⁵Tutte quelle con il filtro, signore. ¹⁶Io Le consiglierei le *Granfiltro*. ¹⁷Sono veramente molto aromàtiche e leggère. ¹⁸Vuole anche dei cerini?

PIETRO — ¹⁹Ah, già, dimenticavo che in Italia bisogna comprarli, i fiammìferi. ²⁰Anche essi sono monopolio di Stato. ²¹Ho sentito che le sigarette èstere cóstano molto care.

TABACCAIO — ²²Altroché! ²³Un pacchetto di americane costa quattrocentocinquanta lire. ²⁴Sono le tasse che il governo ci mette sopra per protèggere la véndita del tabacco nazionale.

PETER — ⁸Yes, I know. ⁹But what do you expect? ¹⁰Smoking is one of those vices that it's hard to get rid of.

TOBACCONIST — ¹¹You're right, sir. ¹²And from one point of view I'm glad it's that way. ¹³Otherwise I'd go into bankruptcy (with my business).

PETER — ¹⁴What cigarettes are there [that are] not too strong?

TOBACCONIST — ¹⁵All those with filters, sir. ¹⁶I would advise the *Granfiltro* for you. ¹⁷They are really very aromatic and light. ¹⁸Do you also want wax matches?

PETER — ¹⁹Oh, yes, I forgot that in Italy it's necessary to buy matches. ²⁰They too are a State monopoly. ²¹I've heard that foreign cigarettes are very expensive.

TOBACCONIST — ²²They certainly are! ²³A package of American [cigarettes] costs 450 lire. ²⁴It's the taxes that the government imposes on them to protect the sale of domestic (national) tobacco.

NOTES

1. **Non fumo la pipa,** literally *I don't smoke the pipe.*
2. **Lo sa?,** literally *You know it?*
3. **Da una parte,** literally *on one side.*
4. **Tògliersi,** literally *to take away from oneself.*
5. **Altroché!** is an expression used to indicate vigorous agreement with whatever has just been said.

VERB FORMS

protèggere	*to protect:* past participle **protetto**
soddisfare	*to satisfy:* like **fare**
tògliere	*to take away:* present **tolgo, togli, toglie, togliamo, togliete, tòlgono**; subjunctive command forms **tolga** *3rd sg.*, **tòlgano** *3rd pl.*; past participle **tolto**.

Esercizi

A. *Risponda in italiano alle seguenti domande basate sul testo:*

1. Il tabaccaio ha delle sigarette americane? 2. Ha del tabacco americano?
3. Dove dovrebbe andare Pietro per avere delle sigarette americane?
4. Pietro fuma la pipa?
5. La fumava un tempo? 6. Perché ha smesso di fumarla? 7. Le sigarette sono dannose alla salute? 8. Sono più dannose della pipa? 9. Fumare è un vizio?
10. È difficile tògliersi i vizi? 11. Il tabaccaio è contento che sia difficile tògliersi l'abitùdine (*the habit*) di fumare? 12. Altrimenti che cosa gli accadrebbe? 13. Quali sigarette consiglia il tabaccaio a Pietro? 14. Perché?
15. Pietro vuole anche dei cerini? 16. In Italia, sono monopolio di stato i cerini? 17. Cóstano care in Italia le sigarette èstere? 18. Quanto costa un pacchetto di americane in Italia? 19. Perché?

B. *Domandi a un altro studente (a un'altra studentessa):*

1. se fuma. 2. se vuole delle sigarette americane. 3. se fuma la pipa. 4. se preferisce le sigarette alla pipa, o viceversa.
5. se crede che le sigarette siano dannose alla salute. 6. se crede che la pipa sia dannosa alla salute. 7. se trova difficile tògliersi l'abitùdine di fumare. 8. se preferisce le sigarette forti. 9. quali sigarette non sono troppo forti.
10. se in Amèrica le sigarette e i fiammìferi sono monopolio di Stato. 11. se in Amèrica le sigarette cóstano care. 12. se cóstano care in Italia, e perché.

C. *Dica a un altro studente (a un'altra studentessa):*

1. che non ha sigarette americane. 2. che troverà delle sigarette americane in uno dei tabaccai al centro. 3. che Lei e i suoi amici non fùmano la pipa. 4. che non tròvano difficile sméttere di fumare.
5. che non vògliono andare in fallimento. 6. che gli (le) consìgliano delle sigarette aromàtiche e leggère. 7. che non hanno cerini. 8. che in Italia deve comprarsi i fiammìferi. 9. che in Italia il tabacco e i fiammìferi sono monopolio di Stato.
10. che Loro hanno sentito che cóstano molto cari in Italia.

D. REVISIONE DEI PRO-COMPLEMENTI. *Dica o scriva in italiano:*

1. Will you show me some American cigarettes? Will you show me some?
2. They are bringing her some wax matches. They are bringing her some.
3. We advise the *Granfiltro* cigarettes for you. We advise them for you.
4. It's hard to rid oneself of those vices. It's hard to rid oneself of them (*lit.*, to take them from oneself).
5. Do you (**Lei**) desire any matches? Do you desire any?   6. Sell (**Loro**) us some Italian tobacco, please. Sell us some, please.

E. *Dica o scriva in italiano:*

1. The newsdealer has gone into bankruptcy.   2. Does the pipe satisfy you (*fam. sg.*)?   3. Are your cousins (*f.*) happy?   4. Which cigarettes would you (**Lei**) advise for us?
5. Are the restaurants a state monopoly in Italy?   6. No, but the government puts many taxes on them.   7. Who know why the government puts taxes on everything ?   8. Is it necessary to protect the sale of national to-baccos?   9. Are Italian tobaccos better than foreign tobaccos, or viceversa?
10. How much does a package of Italian cigarettes cost?   11. A package costs two hundred lire.

F. CONVERSATIONS.

1. Get a discussion going on whether tobacco-smoking is harmful or not.
2. One person acts the part of a customer, and another that of a tobacconist, and the two enact a scene of purchasing cigarettes or pipe tobacco, and matches, in a tobacconist's shop.

"Cantoria" di Luca della Robbia

CONVERSATION UNIT———————24

Planning a Visit

Peter balks at going to a vocal concert.

FULVIA — ¹Il dottor Dossi e sua moglie ci hanno invitati per il tè domani pomeriggio. ²Sei lìbero nel dopopranzo?

PIETRO — ³Ci devo proprio venire?

FULVIA — ⁴Nessuno ti òbbliga, ma ti assicuro che i Dossi sono veramente simpàtici. ⁵Ti divertirai.

PIETRO — ⁶Come li hai conosciuti?

FULVIA — ¹Dr. Dossi and his wife have invited us to tea tomorrow afternoon. ²Are you free in the "dopopranzo"?

PETER — ³Do I absolutely have to go there?

FULVIA — ⁴No one is forcing you, but I assure you that the Dossis are really pleasant. ⁵You'll have a good time.

PETER — ⁶How did you become acquainted with them?

FULVIA — 7Lui lavorava con mio padre quando era a Bologna. 8Anche lui è avvocato, ma non fa più la professione lìbera. 9Adesso lavora per una società di assicurazioni.

PIETRO — 10A che ora dobbiamo andarci?

FULVIA — 11Oh, quando ci pare... 12non so ... 13direi verso le quattro, quattro e mezzo, va bene? 14Hanno una figlia di sédici anni e un ragazzo di trédici. 15Sono dei ragazzi veramente intelligenti. 16Lei studia canto ed ha una bellìssima voce.

PIETRO — 17Avremo un concerto vocale gratis, allora!

FULVIA — 18Niente di più fàcile. 19Però, devo amméttere che malgrado tutto non si dà affatto delle arie.

PIETRO — 20Tanto meglio! 21Immàgino che avrà il fìsico robusto e tondetto di una prima donna.

FULVIA — 22Niente affatto, è snellìssima.

FULVIA — 7He used to work with my father when he was in Bologna. 8He's a lawyer too, but he's not on his own any more. 9Now he works for an insurance company.

PETER — 10At what time are we supposed to go there?

FULVIA — 11Oh, when we feel like it... 12I don't know... 13I'd say around four or four-thirty, O.K.? 14They have a sixteen-year-old daughter and a boy of thirteen. 15They're really intelligent kids. 16She is studying singing and has a very beautiful voice.

PETER — 17We'll get a free vocal concert, then!

FULVIA — 18Nothing easier. 19However, I must admit that in spite of everything she doesn't put on airs.

PETER — 20So much the better! 21I imagine that she'll have the robust and roundish figure of an opera star.

FULVIA — 22Not at all; she's quite slender.

NOTES

1. The **dopopranzo**, or after-lunch period, is the time from approximately two-thirty or three to four or five p.m., when most Italian families either take a siesta, rest, or exchange visits.
2. **far la professione libera**, literally *to exercise the free profession.*
3. **quando ci pare**, literally *when it seems* [*desirable*] *to us.*
4. **darsi delle arie**, literally *to give oneself airs.*

VERB FORMS

amméttere *to admit:* past participle **ammesso.**

Esercizi

A. *Risponda in italiano alle seguenti domande basate sul testo:*

1. Chi ha invitato Fulvia e Pietro per il tè?   2. Pietro è obbligato a venire?
3. Chi lo òbbliga?   4. Come ha conosciuto i Dossi Fulvia?
5. Che cosa fa il padre di Fulvia?   6. Il dottor Dossi fa ancora la professione
lìbera?   7. Per chi lavora?   8. A che ora dévono andare Fulvia e Pietro?
9. Quanti ragazzi hanno i Dossi?
10. Di che età?   11. Sono intelligenti?   12. Che cosa studia la figlia? 13. Che
cosa teme Pietro?   14. La signorina Dossi si dà delle arie?
15. Come è la signorina Dossi?

B. *Domandi a un altro studente (a un'altra studentessa):*

1. se è libero nel dopopranzo.   2. se vuol venire a prendere il tè nel dopopranzo.   3. se i suoi amici sono simpàtici.   4. come ha conosciuto i suoi
amici.
5. se suo padre è avvocato.   6. se fa la professione lìbera.   7. per chi lavora.
8. a che ora si deve prendere il tè.   9. quanti figli hanno i suoi amici.
10. se sono intelligenti.   11. che cosa stùdiano.   12. se i suoi amici si dànno
delle arie.

C. *Dica a un altro studente (a un'altra studentessa):*

1. che i Suoi amici L'hanno invitato per il tè.   2. che Lei ci deve proprio
andare.   3. che non si divertirà.   4. che i figli dei suoi amici non sono
molto intelligenti.
5. che dovrà sentire un concerto vocale gratis.   6. che la figlia dei Suoi
amici si dà delle arie.   7. che la figlia dei Suoi amici ha un fìsico troppo
robusto.   8. che quella ragazza non è affatto snella.

D. Revìsione dei Tempi "progressivi" con **stare.** *Dica o scriva in
italiano:*

1. I work; I am (in the act of) working.   2. They invite us; they are (in the
act of) inviting us.   3. No one obliges you; no one is (in the act of) oblig-
ing you.   4. We play; we are (in the act of) playing.
5. You (**tu**) amuse yourself; you are (in the act of) amusing yourself.   6.
She used to see it; she was (in the act of) seeing it.   7. We used to call; we
were (in the act of) calling.   8. You (**voi**) write; you are (in the act of)
writing.   9. They were coming; they were (in the act of) coming.
10. Why do you (**Lei**) photograph us?; why are you (in the act of) photo-
graphing us.

Bologna: Le torri degli
Asinelli e Garisenda
(The first, 320 ft. high,
was built in 1109;
the second, 163 ft. high,
was built in 1110)

Foto ISTO

E. *Dica o scriva in italiano:*

1. We invite you (*fam. sg.*) for coffee.   2. Is she a likeable person?
3. How long has she been working for that insurance company?   4. He has assured her that we are very likeable.
5. Why do you (**voi**) give yourselves airs?   6. Is your sister studying singing?
7. No, she studies history of art.   8. Their father is a lawyer.   9. He has been on his own for years and years.
10. I work only when I please.

F. CONVERSATIONS:

1. At a tea party: one person is the hostess and offers tea to the others, asking also if they want sugar or milk (**latte,** *m.*); the hostess and guests chat about their friends and what they are doing.
2. Two or more of you discuss your friends' children and what they are studying.

⬤ 45. VERBS: THE CONDITIONAL.

This tense, for all verbs without exception, is formed, on the same stem as the future. In the place of the future endings, the conditional tense has the following endings:

-ei	1st	**-emmo**
-esti	2nd	**-este**
-ebbe	3rd	**-èbbero**

Note that the first person plural of the conditional has two **m**'s in its ending, whereas the corresponding future from has only one: *e. g.*, **faremmo** *we should do vs.* **faremo** *we shall do.* Examples in context:

Io scarterei la carrozza e il tassì.	I *would eliminate* the carriage and the taxi.
Che cosa **mangeresti?**	What *would you* (**tu**) *eat?*
Dovrebbe andare in un tabaccaio del centro.	You (**Lei**) *would have* to go into a tabacco shop downtown.
Ma dove **dormiremmo?**	But where *would we sleep?*
Come ci **andreste?**	How *would you* (**voi**) *go* there?
Cosa **vorrèbero** vedere?	What *would they* (*or* you, **Loro**) *like* to see?

Sample verbs in the conditional:

telefonare *to telephone*
telefoner-

telefoner**ei**	I would telephone	telefoner**emmo**	we would telephone
telefoner**esti**	you (**tu**) would telephone	telefoner**este**	you (**voi**) would telephone
telefoner**ebbe**	he, she, would telephone; you (**Lei**) would telephone	telefoner**èbbero**	they would telephone; you (**Loro**) would telephone

préndere *to take, get*
prender-

prender**ei**	I would take	prender**emmo**	we would take
prender**esti**	you (**tu**) would take	prender**este**	you (**voi**) would take
prender**ebbe**	he, she, it would take; you (**Lei**) would take	prender**èbbero**	they would take; you (**Loro**) would take

volere   to want, wish

vorrei	I would want	vorremmo	we would want
vorresti	you (**tu**) would want	vorreste	you (**voi**) would want
vorrebbe	he, she, it would want; you (**Lei**) would want	vorrèbbero	they would want; you (**Loro**) would want

🔵 46. NEGATIVES.

In a normal Italian negative sentence, if the negative element precedes the verb, no further negative is needed; but if such a negative element as **nessuno** *no one, nobody,* **niente** or **nulla** *nothing,* **mai** *never, etc,* follows the verb, then the verb must be preceded by a further negative element, normally **non**. Normally, a negative element preceding the verb is emphatic. The order **non** ... (verb) ... negative element is normal and unemphatic.

EMPHATIC

Nessuno è venuto. *No one* came.
Mai ho fatto una cosa sìmile. *Never* have I done such a thing.
Mica siamo venuti al Palatino. We *certainly* didn't come to the Palatine. [Use of **mica** in this position is markedly colloquial.]

NON-EMPHATIC

Non è venuto **nessuno**. *No one* came.
Non ho **mai** fatto una cosa sìmile. I've *never* done such a thing.
Non siamo **mica** venuti al Palatino. We *certainly* did not come to the Palatine.

The double negative in the unemphatic type of sentence shown here does not result in a positive meaning.

🔵 47. DEFINITE ARTICLE IN GENERIC MEANING.

In English, we normally use a noun alone, without definite article, when referring to something considered in general: *e.g., I don't like dogs* (i.e., dogs in general); *Italian women* (taken as a general phenomenon) *are beautiful.* Used in this manner, Italian nouns (singular or plural) are generally preceded by the definite article:

Non mi piàcciono **i cani**.
Le donne italiane sono belle.
Ti pare che io sia **il tipo** da fare l'occhiolino alle ragazze?
Voi non sapete godervi **la vita**.
Le sigarette sono più dannose alla salute della pipa.

I don't like *dogs.*
Italian women are beautiful.
Do you think that I'm *the kind* to make eyes at girls?
You don't know how to enjoy *life.*
Cigarettes are more harmful to health than a pipe.

48. DIMINUTIVE SUFFIXES.

Italian has a number of suffixes which are added to noun and adjective stems to convey various modifications in meaning. Among the most widespread are two, **-etto** and **-ino,** which give a diminutive shade of meaning, *i.e.* make a noun or adjective mean *little* ..., *somewhat* ..., **-ish.** Both of these suffixes have the regular masculine and feminine endings, singular and plural, in **-o -a -i -e.** The suffix **-ino** normally has a favorable meaning: *dear little* ..., *likeable little* ...

un'ora	an hour	**un'oretta**	a *little* hour
una casa	a house	**una casetta**	a *little* house
difficile	difficult	**difficiletto**	*sort of* difficult
tondo	round	**tondetto**	*roundish*
un fratello	brother	**un fratellino**	*little* brother
un treno	train	**un trenino**	a *little* train; a *toy* train
caro	dear	**carino**	*nice, attractive, pretty*
bravo	fine	**bravino**	*rather good*

◆ **49. APOCOPE.**

The omission of the final vowel of a word, before another word beginning with a consonant, is termed *apocope* (a Greek word meaning "cutting off"). This process is called *apocopation* and takes place only within a closely-knit phrase. It is obligatory only when a pro-complement is added to an infinitive: *e.g.*, **vedere** *to see* + **lo** *it* > **vederlo** *to see it*; **mangiare** *to eat some.* In other instances, apocopation in modern usage takes place only after singular forms ending in **-le** or **-re,** in the masculine, or after an infinitive, and before a *pure* consonant or group of consonants. Its use is optional, and indicates a greater unity of thought within the phrase.

un **tal** gioco   *such* a game (*or* un **tale** gioco)
il **Mar** Nero   the *Black* Sea (*but* un **mare** nero a *black* sea)
far sapere   to *make* known (but **fare** presto *to do* quickly, hurry)

Other types of apocopation are now out of date and archaic or poetical: *e.g.*, **O ciel**! (instead of **O cielo**! *Oh heaven!*).

Grammatical Exercises

A. SUBSTITUTIONS.

1. *Transform each future given here into the corresponding conditional of the same person and number, on the model of* **andrò** I'll go > **andrei** I'd go:

¹porteremo	*we'll carry*	¹¹capiranno	*you'll understand*
²dormirete	*you'll sleep*	¹²ti sentirai	*you'll feel*
³verranno	*they'll come*	¹³si accomoderà	*he'll sit down*
⁴farò	*I'll do*	¹⁴verrete	*you'll come*
⁵rimarrai	*you'll remain*	¹⁵comprerò	*I'll buy*
⁶venderà	*she'll sell*	¹⁶leggerà	*you'll read*
⁷lavorerete	*you'll work*	¹⁷apriranno	*they'll open*
⁸tornerò	*I'll return*	¹⁸boccerò	*I'll flunk [someone]*
⁹dovrà	*you'll have to*	¹⁹potranno	*you'll be able*
¹⁰firmeremo	*we'll sign*	²⁰importerà	*it will be important*

2. *Make as many combinations as will make sense, of the following verbs and negative subjects, in the ordinary non-emphatic sentence-type with double negative (e.g.)* **lo fa** *does it* + **nessuno** *nobody* > **non lo fa nessuno** *nobody does it*):

¹arriva	*arrives*		¹nessuno	*no one*
²parte	*departs*	+	²niente	*nothing*
³va	*goes*		³nulla	*nothing*
⁴viene	*comes*			

3. *As in Exercise A, 2, make as many combinations as possible, in the non-emphatic sentence-type with double negative, of the following verbs and negative objects:*

¹conosco	*I know*		¹nessuno	*no one*
²hai trovato	*you've found*	+	²niente	*nothing*
³scartiamo	*we eliminate*		³nulla	*nothing*
⁴védono	*they see*			

4. *As in Exercise A, 2., form as many negative sentences as possible with the following verbs and negative adverbs:*

¹camminiamo	*we walk*		¹affatto	*at all*
²funziona	*it functions*	+	²mai	*never*
³si muove	*it moves*		³mica	*never*
⁴torneranno	*they'll return*			

5. *Form diminutives in* **-etto** **(-etta -etti -ette)**, *in both singular and plural, with the following*:

[1]albergo	*hotel*	[7]cugina	*cousin*
[2]bambino	*child*	[8]giardino	*garden*
[3]borsa	*purse*	[9]lavoro	*work*
[4]capra	*goat*	[10]libro	*book*
[5]chiesa	*church*	[11]màcchina	*machine*
[6]cosa	*thing*	[12]òpera	*opera*

6. *As in Exercise A, 5, form diminutives in* **-ino -ina (-ini -ine)**, *in both singular and plural, with:*

[1]appartamento	*apartment*	[7]cravatta	*tie*
[2]avvocato	*lawyer*	[8]fazzoletto	*handkerchief*
[3]biglietto	*ticket*	[9]formaggio	*cheese*
[4]bistecca	*steak*	[10]giornale	*newspaper*
[5]carrozza	*carriage*	[11]mamma	*mother*
[6]coltello	*knife*	[12]momento	*moment*

B. PROGRESSIVE VARIATION. *Say or write in Italian:*

(1)
[1]To visit.
[2]They'd visit.
[3]They'll visit.
[4]They'll work.
[5]She'll work.
[6]She'll write.
[7]She'd write.
[8]We'd write.
[9]We'd sleep.
[10]You (**tu**) would sleep.
[11]You were sleeping.
[12]You were reading.

[13]You (**voi**) were reading.
[14]You (**voi**) would read.
[15]I'd read.
[16]I'd understand.
[17]I wouldn't understand.
[18]I don't understand.
[19]You (**Lei**) don't understand.
[20]You understand.
[21]You'd understand.
[22]You'd visit.
[23]To visit.

(2)
[1]I would take.
[2]I wouldn't take.
[3]I wouldn't take anything.
[4]We wouldn't take anything.
[5]We wouldn't read anything.
[6]She wouldn't read anything.
[7]She hasn't read anything.
[8]She hasn't eaten anything.
[9]She hasn't eaten.

[10]She doesn't eat.
[11]She eats.
[12]She never eats.
[13]You (**Loro**) never eat.
[14]You never walk.
[15]You would never walk.
[16]You would never take.
[17]You would take.
[18]I would take.

(3)
¹I like this church.
²I like churches.
³We like churches.
⁴We don't like churches.
⁵We don't like museums.
⁶We don't like those museums.
⁷She doesn't like those museums.
⁸She doesn't like that museum.
⁹She doesn't like fish.
¹⁰She doesn't like that fish.
¹¹You (**Loro**) don't like that fish.
¹²You don't like that beefsteak.
¹³You don't like beefsteaks.
¹⁴You don't like churches.
¹⁵I don't like churches.
¹⁶I like churches.
¹⁷I like this church.

C. *Say or write in Italian:*

1. Why would you (**Lei**) continue to work? 2. To whom would they write?
3. When would we depart? 4. Why would no one see us?
5. Haven't you (**tu**) seen anyone? 6. Is fruit harmful to health? 7. We have found a pretty little apartment. 8. Our little sister is coming tomorrow.
9. Here is a little church.
10. I'd return in an hour or so.

Roman History

Fulvia gives Peter a mock examination patterned on the oral examinations customary in Italian schools.

FULVIA — ¹Sono tre mesi che sei in Italia ora. ²Hai visitato quasi tutti i più importanti monumenti dell'antichità. ³Vediamo quanto ti è ritornato in mente della storia romana.

FULVIA — ¹(It's three months that) you've been in Italy for three months now. ²You've visited almost all the most important monuments of antiquity. ³Let's see how much of Roman history has come back to your mind.

PIETRO — ⁴È un esame che mi vuoi fare?

PETER — ⁴Do you want to give me an exam (Is it an exam that you're wanting to give me)?

FULVIA — ⁵Qualcosa del gènere. ⁶Da chi fu fondata Roma?

FULVIA — ⁵Something of the kind. ⁶By whom was Rome founded?

PIETRO — ⁷Ohibò, questa è un'offesa! ⁸Da Ròmolo e Remo, naturalmente.

PETER — ⁷Shame on you! That's an insult! ⁸By Romulus and Remus, naturally.

FULVIA — ⁹Bene, quanti fùrono i re di Roma?

FULVIA — ⁹Very good; how many kings did Rome have (were the kings of Rome)?

PIETRO — ¹⁰Sette, se non mi sbaglio.

PETER — ¹⁰Seven, if I'm not mistaken.

FULVIA — ¹¹Ah! Ah! È qui che ti volevo! ¹²Non ti ricordi che Napoleone nominò suo figlio re di Roma?

FULVIA — ¹¹Ha, ha! I've got you where I wanted you! ¹²Don't you remember that Napoleon named his son king of Rome?

PIETRO — ¹³Ma questa è una domanda a trucco. ¹⁴Il figlio di Napoleone non salì mai al trono.

PETER — ¹³But this is a tricky question. ¹⁴Napoleon's son never ascended the throne.

FULVIA — ¹⁵Va bene, va bene, passiamo ad altro. ¹⁶Chi fu allora il primo imperatore e contro chi combattè?

FULVIA — ¹⁵All right, all right, let's go on to something else. ¹⁶Who was, then, the first emperor and against whom did he fight?

Colonna Traiana
Foto ISTO

PIETRO — ¹⁷Ottaviano Augusto, il quale sconfisse prima Bruto e poi Antonio. ¹⁸Dopo èssere stato nominato imperatore chiuse il tempio di Giano per simboleggiare l'inizio di un lungo perìodo di pace.

FULVIA — ¹⁹Bravìssimo, e chi fu l'imperatore che suonava la lira? ²⁰Cosa fece?

PIETRO — ²¹Nerone, il quale, dopo aver incendiato Roma, assistette all'incendio cantando e suonando la lira.

FULVIA — ²²Congratulazioni, e dieci con lode.

PETER — ¹⁷Octavian Augustus, who defeated first Brutus and then Antony, ¹⁸After being named emperor, he closed the temple of Janus to symbolize the beginning of a long period of peace.

FULVIA — ¹⁹Very good, and who was the emperor who played the lyre? ²⁰What did he do?

PETER — ²¹Nero, who, after having set fire to Rome, was present at the fire singing and playing the lyre.

FULVIA — ²²Congratulations, and ten with praise.

NOTES

1. **Fare un esame a qualcuno** = *to give an examination to somebody. To take an examination* is **dare un esame**.
2. **È qui che ti volevo,** literally *It's here that I wanted you.*
3. **Dieci con lode:** in high school examinations, the highest mark is usually ten, to which is added **la lode** (*praise*) for an especially fine performance.

Terme di Caracalla

VERB FORMS

chiùdere *to close;* past participle **chiuso** *closed.*
ritornare *to return;* takes **èssere** as normal auxiliary.
sconfìggere *to defeat;* past participe **sconfitto** *defeated.*
For past absolutes, see Grammar Unit XIII.

Esercizi

A. *Risponda in italiano alle seguenti domande basate sul testo:*

1. Da quanto tempo Pietro è in Italia?   2. Che cosa ha visitato?   3. Fulvia gli vuol fare un esame?   4. Chi fondò Roma?
5. Chi fùrono Ròmolo e Remo?   6. Quanti fùrono i re di Roma?   7. Chi nominò suo figlio re di Roma?   8. Questo ragazzo è salito al trono di Roma, o no?   9. Chi fu il primo imperatore di Roma?
10. Chi sconfisse?   11. Che cosa fece per simboleggiare l'inizio di un lungo perìodo di pace?   12. Chi incendiò Roma e poi assistette all' incendio cantando e suonando la lira?

B. *Domandi a un altro studente (a un'altra studentessa) :*

1. se è stato in Italia, e per quanto tempo.   2. se ha visitato i monumenti del-
l'antichità.   3. quanto gli è ritornato alla memoria della storia di Roma.
4. se vuol farLe un esame.
5. se sa da chi fu fondata Roma.   6. se ci fùrono sette od otto re di Roma.   7.
chi fu Napoleone.   8. chi fu suo figlio.   9. chi combattè contro Augusto.
10. perché Augusto chiuse il tempio di Giano.

C. *Dica a un altro studente (a un'altra studentessa) :*

1. che Lei è in Italia da sei mesi.   2. che ha visitato molti monumenti.   3. che
ci fùrono sette re di Roma, se Lei non si sbaglia.   4. che Lei non è mai
salito al trono, e che non spera mai di salirvi.
5. che Lei non è mai stato nominato imperatore (imperatrice [*empress*]).   6. che
Lei e i suoi amici non hanno mai incendiato una città.   7. che Le piace
cantare e suonare.

D. Revisione del Condizionale. *Dica o scriva in italiano:*

1. We'd be in Italy now.   2. It would come back to my memory.   3. He
would name his son emperor.   4. It would symbolize a period of peace.
5. That would be a trick question.   6. You (**voi**) would be present.   7. They
would visit all the museums.   8. Would you (**tu**) sing and play?   9. I
would have ten with praises.   10. He would combat against his friends.

E. *Dica o scriva in italiano:*

1. We have been in Italy one year.   2. I don't remember anything.   3. We're
never mistaken.   4. Those examinations aren't difficult.
5. No, but they're never really easy.   6. Has your aunt returned from Florence?   7. This isn't an examination, but it's something of the kind.   8.
They have named him emperor.   9. Rome was founded by Romulus and
Remus.
10. Romulus and Remus were twins.

F. Conversations:

1. A mock examination, in which one person asks questions and another
answers.
2. Two persons tell each other what they know about Roman history.

Foto Henle — Monkmeyer

Ostia Antica

Un Po' di Storia Romana

(Ostia Antica)

(Conversations 21-25)

¹**organizzare** to organize.
²**gli scavi** the excavations.
³**Ostia Antica** literally ancient Ostia, the port town of ancient Rome near the mouth of the Tiber.
⁴**non vede l'ora** he is impatient (literally, he does not see the time).
⁵**tanto più che** all the more so because.
⁶**archeologìa** *(f.)* archeology.
⁷**guida** *(f.)* guide (**farà da guida** he will act as a guide).
⁸**conferenza** *(f.)* lecture (**tenere una conferenza** to give a lecture).
⁹**vicenda** *(f)* event, happening
¹⁰**stòrico** historic(al).
¹¹**introduzione** *(f.)* introduction.
¹²**notizie** *(f. pl.)* information.
¹³**sviluppo** *(m.)* development.
¹⁴**dati** *(m. pl.)* data, information.
¹⁵**ricavare** to extract.
¹⁶**iscrizione** *(f.)* inscription.
¹⁷**edificio** *(m.)* building.
¹⁸**secondo** according to.
¹⁹**sbarcare** to disembark.
²⁰**Enea** *(m.)* Aeneas, the legendary ancestor of the Romans.
²¹**laborioso** painful, troublesome.
²²**viaggio** *(m.)* trip.
²³**Troia** *(f.)* Troy, ancient city of Asia Minor destroyed in the Trojan War.
²⁴**ricerca** *(f.)* research.
²⁵**archeològico** archaeological.
²⁶**viceversa** [*here*] on the other hand.
²⁷**stabilire** (II/isc) to establish.
²⁸**risalire** to go back (in time).
²⁹**quarto** fourth.
³⁰**nessun'altra** no other.
³¹**esistere** to exist (takes auxiliary **èssere** in compound tenses).
³²**precedentemente** before (in time).
³³**repubblicano** republican.
³⁴**notévole** notable.
³⁵**importanza** *(f.)* importance.
³⁶**sebbene** = **benché**, although.
³⁷**usare** to use.

All'Università è stata organizzata¹ una gita agli scavi² di Ostia Antica.³ Pietro non vede l'ora⁴ di andare, tanto più che⁵ uno dei più bravi professori di archeologìa⁶ fará da guida.⁷ Il giorno prima, lo stesso professore tiene una breve conferenza⁸ sulle vicende⁹ stòriche¹⁰ della città come introduzione¹¹ alla visita.

"Purtroppo non ci sono notizie¹² stòriche molto sicure sullo sviluppo¹³ della città" — spiega il professore — "e molti dati¹⁴ si ricàvano¹⁵ dalle iscrizioni¹⁶ trovate sul luogo e dalla architettura degli edifici¹⁷ rimasti".

Secondo¹⁸ la leggenda Ostia fu fondata nel luogo dove sbarcò¹⁹ Enea²⁰ dopo il suo lungo e laborioso²¹ viaggio²² da Troia.²³ Le ricerche²⁴ archeològiche,²⁵ viceversa,²⁶ hanno stabilito²⁷ che la città risale²⁸ alla fine del quarto²⁹ sècolo e che nessun'altra³⁰ città è mai esistita³¹ precedentemente³² in quel luogo. Durante il perìodo repubblicano³³ Ostia ebbe una notévole³⁴ importanza³⁵ sebbene³⁶ non fosse usata³⁷ come porto[38] di Roma. Si può dire, però, che essa segna[39] la prima affermazione[40] di Roma sul mare.

Fu soltanto[41] con Augusto e gli imperatori successivi[42] che Ostia fiorì[43] grandemente[44] fino a diventare non solo porto di Roma ma empòrio[45] dell'impero.[46] Lo sviluppo della città è dimostrato[47] dall'intensa attività[48] edilizia[49] di quel perìodo. Le sémplici case di tufo[50] vèngono demolite,[51] si sostituìscono[52] con costruzioni[53] in mattoni[54] e vèngono arricchite[55] di marmi[56] pregiati.[57]

Poiché[58] il fiume[59] non bastava[60] più al tráffico[61] delle navi[62] che cresceva[63] ogni anno, l'imperatore Clàudio[64] pensò di far costruire un vero e pròprio[65] porto.

Potete immaginare quanto fosse difficile l'impresa:[66] la foce[67] del Tévere si trovava[68] a diversi[69] chilòmetri da Ostia e il porto doveva èssere scavato[70] tutto artificialmente.[71] Ma i romani non si perdèttero d'animo[72] e iniziàrono i lavori. Ci vòllero ben dódici anni per terminarli[73] ma infine il porto fu completato e funzionava alla perfezione.[74]

Pietro ascolta[75] la conferenza affascinato.[76] Non sa réndersi conto[77] di come già all'època dei romani si potèssero risòlvere[78] dei problemi di ingegnerìa[79] così complessi.[80] I romani èrano davvero degli ingegneri[81] provetti[82] e a provarlo[83] basta vedere il sistema[84] stradale[85] da loro costruito, gli acquedotti,[86] il perfetto funzionamento[87] dell'acqua e delle fognature[88] della città e così via. Per di più[89] èrano degli artisti, perché oltre a[90] curare[91] la funzionalità[92] dei loro edifici si preoccupàvano anche della parte estètica.[93]

"Era davvero un pòpolo[94] civile[95] da cui abbiamo molto da imparare[96]", pensa Pietro, e forse la vìsita agli scavi di Ostia Antica non sarà che una conferma[97] di questo suo pensiero.[98]

[38]**porto** (m.) port.
[39]**segnare** to mark.
[40]**affermazione** (f.) affirmation, assertion of strength.
[41]**soltanto** only.
[42]**successivo** following.
[43]**fiorire** (II/isc) to flourish.
[44]**grandemente** greatly.
[45]**empòrio** (m.) warehouse.
[46]**impèro** (m.) empire.
[47]**dimostrare** to demonstrate, show.
[48]**attività** (f.) activity.
[49]**edilìzio** pertaining to building.
[50]**tufo** (m.) tufa (a kind of soft volcanic rock).
[51]**demolire** (II/isc) to demolish.
[52]**sostituire** (II/isc) to substitute, replace.
[53]**costruzione** (f.) construction, building.
[54]**mattone** (m.) tile.
[55]**arricchire** (II/isc) to enrich.
[56]**marmo** (m.) marble.
[57]**pregiato** valuable.
[58]**poiché** since.
[59]**fiume** (m.) river.
[60]**bastare** to be enough, to be sufficient.
[61]**tráffico** (m.) traffic.
[62]**nave** (f.) ship.
[63]**créscere** to grow.
[64]**Clàudio** (m.) Claudius, Roman emperor.
[65]**vero e pròprio** real.
[66]**impresa** (f.) undertaking.
[67]**foce** (f.) mouth (of a river).
[68]**trovarsi** to be located.
[69]**diversi** (adj., pl.) several.
[70]**scavare** to excavate.
[71]**artificialmente** artificially.
[72]**ànimo** (m.) spirit (**pèrdersi d'ànimo** to lose heart, become discouraged).
[73]**terminare** to terminate, finish, end.
[74]**perfezione** (f.) perfection (**funzionare alla perfezione** to work perfectly).
[75]**ascoltare** to listen to.
[76]**affascinare** to fascinate.
[77]**réndersi conto di** to realize.
[78]**risòlvere** to resolve.
[79]**ingegnerìa** (f.) engineering.
[80]**complesso** complex, complicated.
[81]**ingegnère** (m.) engineer.
[82]**provetto** skilled.
[83]**provare** to prove.
[84]**sistema** (m.) system.
[85]**stradale** pertaining to roads, of roads.
[86]**acquedotto** (m.) aqueduct.
[87]**funzionamento** (m.) functioning.
[88]**fognatura** (f.) sewer.
[89]**per di più** moreover.
[90]**oltre a** in addition to.
[91]**curare** to take care of.
[92]**funzionalità** (f.) functional nature
[93]**estètico** aesthetic.
[94]**pòpolo** (m.) people (in sense of *nation, race*).
[95]**civile** civilized.
[96]**imparare** to learn (**molto da imparare** a great deal to learn).
[97]**conferma** (f.) confirmation.
[98]**pensiero** (m.) thought, idea.

IN ALTO: Ulisse e Penelope, Pompei
IN BASSO: Nel Museo, Ostia Antica

On the Telephone

Peter finds that telephone numbers in Italy are very long and difficult to remember.

FULVIA — [1]Pietro, sto per telefonare ad Anna per darle gli auguri di Natale. [2]Vuoi parlarle anche tu?

PIETRO — [3]Sì, per favore; pàssamela appena hai finito.

FULVIA — [4]Non mi ricordo più il suo nùmero di telèfono. [5]Tu lo sai a memoria per caso?

PIETRO — [6]No, temo che dobbiamo guardarlo sull'elenco.

FULVIA — [7]Eccolo qui: trentacinque — settantanove — quattro — cinquantacinque.

PIETRO — [8]Accipìcchia, quant'è lungo! [9]Non finisce mai! [10]Non capisco perché in Italia non ùsino le léttere invece dei primi due nùmeri. [11]Sarebbe molto più facile ricordarsi i nùmeri degli amici.

FULVIA — [12]Sì, lo so, ma credo che costerebbe troppo cambiare tutti i teléfoni. [13]Accidèmpoli, la linea è occupata! [14]Quando si attàccano al telèfono in quella casa, non la sméttono più.

FULVIA — [1]Peter, I'm about to telephone (to) Anna to wish her a merry Christmas (give her Christmas greetings). [2]Do you want to talk to her too?

PETER — [3]Yes, please; let me speak to her as soon as you've finished.

FULVIA — [4]I don't remember her telephone number any more. [5]Do you know it by heart, by any chance?

PETER — [6]No, I'm afraid that we have to look it up in the phone book.

FULVIA —[7]Here it is, here: 35-79-4-55.

PETER — [8]Gosh, how long it is! [9]It never ends! [10]I don't understand why in Italy they don't use letters instead of the first two numerals. [11]It would be much easier to remember one's friends' numbers.

FULVIA — [12]Yes, I know, but I think that it would cost too much to change all the telephones. [13]Gosh, the line is busy! [14]When they get on the phone in that house, they never stop.

Foto Bright — Rapho-Guillumette

PIETRO — ¹⁵Senti chi parla! ¹⁶Tu sei la prima a stare al telèfono per delle mezze ore.

FULVIA — ¹⁷Taci, taci, ché è lìbero. ¹⁸Pronto? ¹⁹C'è Anna, per favore?

DALL'ALTRO CAPO DELLA LINEA — ²⁰Qui casa Biondi, chi parla?

FULVIA — ²¹Sono la sua amica Fulvia. ²²Vorrei parlare con Anna.

RISPOSTA — ²³Un momento, signo-.rina, Gliela chiamo sùbito.

PETER — ¹⁵Listen who's talking! ¹⁶You are the first to be on the telephone for half an hour at a time.

FULVIA — ¹⁷Hush, hush; the line's free. ¹⁸Hello? ¹⁹Is Anna there, please?

FROM THE OTHER END OF THE LINE — ²⁰This is Biondis'; who's speaking?

FULVIA — ²¹I am her friend Fulvia. ²²I'd like to talk with Anna.

ANSWER — ²³One minute, miss; I'll call her for you right away.

NOTES

1. **Pàssamela,** literally *Pass her to me.*
2. **Lo sai a memoria,** literally *Do you know it by memory.*
3. **si attàccano al telèfono,** literally *they attach themselves to the telephone.*
4. **per delle mezze ore,** literally *for some half-hours.*
5. **casa Biondi,** literally *(the) Biondi house.*

VERB FORMS

finire *to finish;* II/**isc**

tacere *to be silent;* present **taccio, taci, tace, tacciamo, tacete, tàcciono**; subjunctive command forms 3rd. sg. **taccia,** 3rd. pl. **tàcciano**

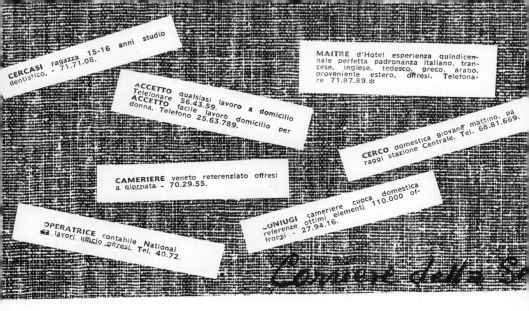

CERCASI ragazza 15-16 anni studio dentìstico. - 71.71.08.

ACCETTO qualsiasi lavoro a domicilio Telefonare 56.43.59. ACCETTO facile lavoro domicilio per donna. Telefono 25.63.789.

MAITRE d'Hotel esperienza quindicennale perfetta padronanza italiano, francese, inglese, tedesco, greco, arabo, proveniente estero, offresi. Telefonare 71.87.89.✳

CERCO domestica giovane mattino, pa raggi stazione Centrale. Tel. 68.81.669.

CAMERIERE veneto referenziato offresi a giornata. - 70.29.55.

CONIUGI cameriere cuoca domestica referenze ottimi elementi 110.000 offrorsi - 27.94.16.

OPERATRICE contabile National ea lavori ufficio offresi. Tel. 40.72.

Esercizi

A. *Risponda in italiano alle seguenti domande basate sul testo:*

1. A chi sta per telefonare Fulvia? 2. Che cosa vuol darle? 3. Anche Pietro vuol parlarle? 4. Si ricorda Fulvia il nùmero di telèfono di Anna?
5. Lo sa a memoria Pietro? 6. Che cosa dévono guardare per trovarlo? 7. È molto lungo il nùmero di telèfono di Anna? 8. Perché non ùsano le léttere invece dei primi due nùmeri in Italia? 9. Quando Fulvia telèfona, è lìbera la lìnea?
10. Di che cosa Pietro accusa (*accuses*) Fulvia? 11. Che cosa gli risponde Fulvia? 12. Che cosa si dice quando si telèfona a qualcuno in Italia?

B. *Domandi a un altro studente (a un'altra studentessa):*

1. se Natale è vicino. 2. se vuol dar gli auguri di Natale a un suo amico (a una sua amica). 3. se sta per telefonare a un suo amico (a una sua amica). 4. di passarGlielo (di passarGliela) appena ha finito.
5. se si ricorda del nùmero di telèfono. 6. se sa a memoria i nùmeri di telèfono dei suoi amici. 7. se deve guardare sull'elenco quando vuol sapere un nùmero di telèfono. 8. perché in Italia non ùsano le léttere nei nùmeri di telèfono. 9. se sta al telèfono a chiacchierare per delle ore.
10. se smette di parlare quando altre persone vògliono telefonare.

CONVERSATION UNIT TWENTY-SIX

C. *Dica a un altro studente (a un'altra studentessa), sempre nella prima persona plurale:*

1. che Loro stanno per telefonare a un amico (a un'amica).   2. che vorrèbbero parlargli (parlarle) anche Loro.   3. che non si ricórdano il nùmero di telèfono.   4. che dévono guardarlo sull'elenco.
5. che non vògliono tacere.   6. che vorrèbbero parlare con la signorina Bianchi.

D. REVISIONE DELLE FORME NEGATIVE (Review of negative forms). *Dica o scriva in italiano:*

1. They are never silent.   2. I'm not saying anything to her.   3. The lines aren't busy at all.   4. Nobody gets on (attaches himself to) the telephone.
5. You (**tu**) won't ever finish .   6. She doesn't understand anything.   7. Don't (**Loro**) say anything to her about it.   8. We weren't talking with anyone.
9. Don't (**voi**) telephone them..   10. That certainly wouldn't cost too much.

E. *Dica o scriva in italiano:*

1. They have wished us a merry Christmas (given us Christmas greetings).
2. Golly, how funny you (**tu**) are!   3. Why wasn't the line free?   4. Hello; may I speak to Mr. Bruni?
5. Let me speak to Mr. Bruni, please.   6. We'll call him for you (**tu**) immediately.   7. I can't find their names in (= on) the telephone book.   8. Let's telephone instead of writing them.   9. Are they finishing, by chance?
10. All the lines were busy.

F. CONVERSATIONS:

1. You call a friend and chat with him (her) about the weather, shopping, or any other subject. A third person butts in and wants the telephone and the conversation finally stops.
2. You compare American and Italian telephone numbers, and discuss whether or not it is easier, if the first two numbers are letters. Make up sample numbers to illustrate your points.

⬤ **50. THE PAST ABSOLUTE.**

For regular verbs of the three conjugations, the past absolute is formed on the root + the characteristic vowel of each conjugation and the endings shown here for the three typical verbs **nominare** *to name*, **finire** *to finish*, and **véndere** *to sell*.

THE PAST ABSOLUTE-REGULAR VERBS			
FIRST CONJUGATION			
nominare *to name* **nomin-**			
nominai	I named	nomin**ammo**	we named
nomin**asti**	you (*fam. sg.*) named	nomin**aste**	you (*fam. pl.*) named
nomin**ò**	he, she, it named; you (*formal sg.*) named	nomin**àrono**	they named; you (*formal pl.*) named
SECOND CONJUGATION			
finire *to finish* **fin-**			
fin**ii**	I finished	fin**immo**	we finished
fin**isti**	you (*fam. sg.*) finished	fin**iste**	you (*fam. pl.*) finished
fin**ii**	he, she, it finished; you (*formal sg.*) finished	fin**ìrono**	they finished; you (*formal pl.*) finished
THIRD CONJUGATION			
véndere *to sell* **vend-**			
vend**ei**	I sold	vend**emmo**	we sold
vend**esti**	you (*fam. sg.*) sold	vend**este**	you (*fam. pl.*) sold
vend**è**	he, she, it sold; you (*formal sg.*) sold	vend**èrono**	they sold; you (*formal pl.*) sold

This tense refers to action taking place at a clearly identifiable and definable time in the past as opposed to the imperfect (Grammar Unit **X**, *Sec.* **38**) which refers to action at a time in the past whose beginning and end are left unclear.

PAST ABSOLUTE	IMPERFECT
Augusto **chiuse** il tempio. Augustus *closed* the temple (*on one specific occasion*).	Augusto **chiudeva** il tempio ogni anno. Augustus *used to close* the temple every year.
Non **salì** mai al trono. He never *ascended* the throne.	**Saliva** al trono quando cadde e si ruppe la gamba. He *was ascending* the throne when he fell and broke his leg.
Nerone **assistette** all'incendio. Nero *was present* at the fire (*at a particular point of time*).	Nero **assisteva** spesso ad incendi del gènere. Nero often *was present* at fires of this kind.

The parallelism in the endings of the three conjugations will be noted. In addition to the endings for **véndere**, verbs of the -ere conjugation, which are regular in their past absolute, have alternative forms, for the 1st sg., 3rd sg., and 3rd pl., ending in **-etti**, **-ette** and **-èttero** respectively (**vendetti** *I sold* **vendette** *he, she it sold*; **vendèttero** *they sold*).

Many verbs (mostly those in **-ere** and -ere) have irregular past absolutes. Three verbs (**èssere** *to be*, **dare** *to give*, and **stare** *to stand*) show irregularity in all six forms of the past absolute.

PAST ABSOLUTE-IRREGULAR VERBS

essere *to be*		dare *to give*		stare *to stand*	
fui	fummo	diedi (detti)	demmo	stetti	stemmo
fosti	foste	desti	deste	stesti	steste
fu	fùrono	diede (dette)	diédero	stette	stéttero
			(dèttero)		

In other verbs with irregular past absolutes, the irregularity is limited to the 1st sg. and 3rd pl., in which there is always a special irregular verb to which are added the endings **-i**, **-e**, and **-ero** respectively. The forms for the other persons (2nd sg., 1st pl., and 2nd pl.) are based on the normal stem of the verb for whichever conjugation it belongs to and have the normal past absolute endings for the person involved.

PAST ABSOLUTE

fare *to do*		chiùdere *to close*	
feci	facemmo	chiusi	chiudemmo
facesti	faceste	chiudesti	chiudeste
fece	fécero	chiuse	chiùsero

In addition to **èssere**, **dare**, **stare**, **fare**, and **chiudere**, the following verbs have irregular past absolutes:

INFINITIVE		PAST ABSOLUTE
amméttere	to admit	ammisi, ammettesti, *etc.*
aprire	to open	apersi, apristi, *etc.*
avere	to have	ebbi, avesti, *etc.*
chièdere	to ask for	chiesi, chiedesti, *etc.*
conóscere	to know	conobbi, conoscesti, *etc.*
coprire	to cover	copersi, copristi, *etc.*
costruire	to construct	costrussi, costruisti, *etc.*
decìdere	to decide	decisi, decidesti, *etc.*
descrìvere	to describe	descrissi, descrivesti, *etc.*
dipéndere	to depend	dipesi, dipendesti, *etc.*
dire	to say	dissi, dicesti, *etc.*
dispiacere	to give displeasure	dispiacqui, dispiacesti, *etc.*
distrùggere	to destroy	distrussi, distruggesti, *etc.*
divenire	to become	divenni, divenisti, *etc.*
lèggere	to read	lessi, leggesti, *etc.*
méttere	to put	misi, mettesti, *etc.*
offéndere	to offend	offesi, offendesti, *etc.*
piacere	to please	piacqui, piacesti, *etc.*
piàngere	to cry, weep	piansi, piangesti, *etc.*
préndere	to take	presi, prendesti *etc.*
protèggere	to protect	protessi, proteggesti, *etc.*
sapere	to know	seppi, sapesti, *etc.*
scomméttere	to bet	scommisi, scommettesti, *etc.*
sconfìggere	to defeat	sconfissi, sconfiggesti, *etc.*
scrìvere	to write	scrissi, scrivesti, *etc.*
sméttere	to cease, stop	smisi, smettesti, *etc.*
tacere	to be silent	tacqui, tacesti, *etc.*
tenere	to hold	tenni, tenesti, *etc.*
tògliere	to take away	tolsi, togliesti, *etc.*
vedere	to see	vidi, vedesti, *etc.*
venire	to come	venni, venisti, *etc.*
vìvere	to live	vissi, vivesti, *etc.*
volere	to wish, want	volli, volesti, *etc.*

In addition, the verb **accadere** *to happen* has the 3rd sg. and 3rd pl. forms **accade**, **accàddero** (the verb is not normally used in the other persons); and the impersonal verb **piòvere** *to rain* has **piovve** *it rained.*

51. Dative of Person Affected.

In Italian, a dative phrase (a *to, for* + object) or a dative personal pronoun is often used with a verb to indicate the person affected by the action. In such instances, the accompanying noun normally has a definite article instead of (as in English) a possesive adjective.

Non sapete **godervi la vita.**	You don't know how *to enjoy life (for yourselves).*
Il cameriere **Le porterà** su la valigia.	(The bellboy *will carry* up *for you the suitcase* =) The bellboy *will carry up your suitcase.*
Me lo faccia personale.	*Make it* personal *for me.*
Può **cambiarmi** diecimila lire?	Can you *change* ten thousand lire *for me?*
Ti fa male **la testa?**	(Does *the head* do evil *to you* =) Does *your head ache?*

52. Ecco + Pro-Complements.

Although it is invariable, the form **ecco** *here is, here are; there is, there are; behold* behaves like an imperative verb in that any pro-complement or combination of pro-complements can occur suffixed to it.

Ecco tuo figlio.	*Here is* your son.	**Èccolo.**	*Here he is.*
Ecco tua madre.	*Here is* your mother.	**Èccola.**	*Here she is.*
Ecco i miei amici.	*Here are* my friends.	**Èccoli.**	*Here they are.*
Ecco le cravatte.	*Here are* the ties.	**Èccole.**	*Here they are.*
Ecco delle cravatte.	*Here are* some ties.	**Èccone.**	*Here are some.*
Ecco delle cravatte per te.)	*Here are* some ties for you.	**Èccotene.**	*Here are some for you.*
Èccomi.	*Here I am.*		

Grammatical Exercises

A. Substitutions.

1. *For each infinitive in the list of verbs on* p. 202, *give the 3rd sg. past absolute: e.g.,* **amméttere** to admit: **ammise** he admitted. 2. *As in Exercise A, 1, but giving the 3rd pl. past absolute.* 3. *As in Exercise A, 1, but giving the 1st pl. past absolute.* 4. *As in Exercise A, 1, but giving the 2nd pl. past absolute.* 5. *In each of the following sentences, replace the dative phrase (introduced by* **a** *or* **per** *by the appropriate dative personal pronoun :*

¹A lei fa male il braccio.	*Her arm hurts.*
²Il cassiere cambia cinquemila lire per me.	*The cashier changes five thousand lire for me.*
³A te fa male lo stòmaco?	*Does your stomach ache?*

6. *In each of the following sentences, replace the direct or indirect object, or partitive expression, by the appropriate pro-complement suffixed to* **ecco**:

¹Ecco dei fiammiferi.	*Here are some matches.*
²Ecco dei fiammiferi per voi.	*Here are some matches for you.*
³Ecco le case.	*Here are the houses.*
⁴Ecco la cattedrale.	*There is the cathedral.*
⁵Ecco gli studenti.	*There are the students.*
⁶Ecco lo zio.	*There is the uncle.*
⁷Ecco lui.	*There he is.*
⁸Ecco noi.	*Here we are.*
⁹Ecco te.	*Here you are.*
¹⁰Ecco me.	*Here I am.*

B. PROGRESSIVE VARIATIONS.

(1) ¹To live.
²They lived.
³They took.
⁴We took.
⁵We wept.
⁶She wept.
⁷She did.

⁸You *(fam. sg.)* did.
⁹You *(fam. sg.)* saw.
¹⁰You *(fam. pl.)* saw.
¹¹You *(fam. pl.)* decided.
¹²I decided.
¹³I lived.
¹⁴To live.

(2) ¹To study.
²We studied.
³We met.
⁴I met.
⁵I returned.
⁶You *(formal pl.)* returned.
⁷You *(formal pl.)* brought.

⁸She brought.
⁹She ate.
¹⁰You *(fam. sg.)* ate.
¹¹You *(fam. sg.)* continued.
¹²You *(fam. pl.)* continued.
¹³You *(fam. pl.)* studied.
¹⁴We studied.

(3) ¹To be.
²You *(formal sg.)* were.
³You *(formal sg.)* did.
⁴We did.
⁵We gave.
⁶You *(formal pl.)* gave.
⁷You *(formal pl.)* stood.
⁸I stood.
⁹I did.

¹⁰You *(fam. sg.)* did.
¹¹You *(fam. sg.)* were.
¹²You *(fam. pl.)* were.
¹³You *(fam. pl.)* gave.
¹⁴They gave.
¹⁵They did.
¹⁶You *(formal sg.)* did.
¹⁷You *(formal sg.)* were.

(4) ¹My head hurts.
  ²My stomach hurts.
  ³His stomach hurts.
  ⁴His arm hurts.
  ⁵Your *(fam. sg.)* arm hurts.
  ⁶Your *(fam. sg.)* arms hurt.
  ⁷Our arms hurt.
  ⁸Our feet hurt.
  ⁹Your *(fam. pl.)* feet hurt.
  ¹⁰Your *(fam. pl.)* arms hurt.
  ¹¹My arms hurt.
  ¹²My arm hurts.
  ¹³Her arm hurts.
  ¹⁴Her foot hurts.
  ¹⁵His foot hurts.
  ¹⁶His stomach hurts.
  ¹⁷My stomach hurts.

(5) ¹There he is.
  ²There they are.
  ³There are the boys.
  ⁴There are the girls.
  ⁵There they are.
  ⁶There she is.
  ⁷There you *(fam. sg.)* are.
  ⁸There you *(fam. pl.)* are.
  ⁹There he is.

(6) ¹Here is some bread.
  ²Here is some.
  ³Here is some for you *(fam. pl.)*.
  ⁴Here is some white wine for you.
  ⁵Here are some cigarettes for you.
  ⁶Here are some for you.
  ⁷Here are some for us.
  ⁸Here we are.
  ⁹Here is some.
  ¹⁰Here is some bread.

C. *Say or write in Italian (using the past absolute wherever possible):*

1. We continued to eat. 2. Dante spoke of it in the *Divine Comedy*. 3. Where did your brother get married? 4. They greeted him cordially. 5. Did you *(fam. pl.)* meet each other in the Roman Forum? 6. He used to make eyes at all the girls. 7. They gave us a free concert. 8. I liked the church very much. 9. Romulus and Remus founded Rome. 10. We used to eat a lot of potatoes.

After Christmas Vacation

The Carso and its rugged landscape fascinate Peter who plans a return trip during warmer weather.

PÀOLO — [1]Ben tornato! [2]Come hai passato le vacanze?

PIETRO — [3]Magnificamente. [4]Mi dispiace solo che sìano finite.

PÀOLO — [5]Dove sei stato?

PAUL — [1]Welcome back! [2]How did you spend the vacation?

PETER — [3]Wonderfully. [4]I'm sorry only that they're over.

PAUL — [5]Where did you go (were you)?

Nelle Dolomiti

Foto ISTO

PIETRO — ⁶Siamo andati in montagna a sciare. ⁷Prima sulle Dolomiti e poi sul Carso.

PÀOLO — ⁸E cosa ti è piaciuto di più?

PIETRO — ⁹Ma non so; mi sono piaciuti molto tutti e due i posti. ¹⁰In maniera diversa, naturalmente. ¹¹Il Carso ha un paesaggio molto aspro, ma è veramente interessantìssimo. ¹²Voglio tornarci nella bella stagione per vedere le grotte sotterrannee.

PÀOLO — ¹³Mi piacerebbe venire con te.

PIETRO — ¹⁴Benìssimo. ¹⁵Mio zio ha una casa lì e potremo èssere ospitati da lùi.

PÀOLO — ¹⁶Chi? ¹⁷Di chi è la casa?

PIETRO — ¹⁸Mio zio, il padre di Fulvia, ha costruito una casetta in un paesino in cima ad una montagna. ¹⁹Quei posti gli sono molto cari, perché ci combattè durante la prima guerra mondiale.

PÀOLO — ²⁰Dev'èssere stato un viaggio bellìssimo. ²¹Io invece ho passasato Natale con i miei qui a Roma. ²²Però la notte di Capodanno siamo andati ad un veglione stupendo.

PETER — ⁶We went to the mountains to ski. ⁷First to the Dolomites and afterwards to the Carso.

PAUL — ⁸And you what did you like more?

PETER — ⁹But I don't know, I liked both the places very much. ¹⁰In a different way, naturally. ¹¹The Carso has a very rugged landscape, but it is really most interesting. ¹²I want to go back there during the good season to see the underground grottoes.

PAUL — ¹³I'd like to come with you.

PETER — ¹⁴Excellent. ¹⁵My uncle has a house there and we can be put up by him.

PAUL — ¹⁶Who? Whose house is it ¹⁷(Whose is the house)?

PETER — ¹⁸My uncle, Fulvia's father, has built a little house in a little village on top of a mountain. ¹⁹Those places are very dear to him, because he fought there during the First World War.

PAUL — ²⁰It must have been a very beautiful trip. ²¹I, on the other hand, passed Christmas with my folks here at Rome. ²²However, on New Year's Eve we went to a wonderful all-night ball.

NOTES

1. **Ben tornato**, literally *Well returned*! parallel to **ben venuto** *Welcome*! (*well come*): These expressions vary in gender and number with the person(s) addressed.
2. The *Dolomites*, mountains north of Venice and east of Trent.
3. The *Carso*, a high rocky limestone plateau north and east of Trieste, characterized by very uneven terrain and many water-worn caves. They were the scene of heavy fighting in the First World War. Both the Dolomites and the Carso are favorite winter resorts for skiing, etc.

Foto ISTO

Di una grotta nelle Dolomiti

Esercizi

A. *Risponda in italiano alle seguenti domande basate sul testo:*

1. Come ha passato Pietro le vacanze?   2. Dove è stato?   3. Che cosa gli è piaciuto di più?   4. Dove sono le Dolomiti?
5. Dove è il Carso?   6. Che cosa c'è d'interessante nel Carso?   7. Che cosa ha lo zio di Pietro?   8. Che cosa potrebbe fare lo zio di Pietro per i due ragazzi?   9. Perché quei posti sono cari allo zio di Pietro?
10. Dove ha passato il Natale Pàolo?   11. Che cosa ha fatto la notte di Capodanno?

B. *Domandi a un altro studente (a un'altra studentessa):*

1. come ha passato le vacanze.   2. dove ha passato le vacanze.   3. se gli dispiace che sìano finite.   4. se gli piace andare in montagna a sciare.
5. se conosce le Dolomiti.   6. se conosce il Carso.   7. dove ci sono delle grotte sotterranee.   8. se suo padre o suo zio combattè nella guerra mondiale (prima o seconda).   9. se ha passato Natale con i suoi.
10. come ha passato la notte di Capodanno.   11. come è il paesaggio del Carso.

C. *Dica a un altro studente (a un'altra studentessa) :*

1. che Le piàcciono le Dolomiti e il Carso.   2. che vorrebbe vedere le grotte sotterranee del Carso.   3. che Suo zio ha una casetta lì.   4. dove Suo zio l'ha costruita.

5. perché quei posti gli sono cari.   6. che Lei ha fatto un viaggio bellìssimo. 7. Che ha passato Natale con i Suoi genitori.   8. che la notte di Capodanno Lei è andato (andata) a un veglione stupendo.

D. REVISIONE DEL PASSATO REMOTO (Review of past absolute). *Dica o scriva in italiano:*

1. I wrote to him last year.   2. We saw them (*m.*) last summer.   3. They dined at eight.   4. It displeased me greatly.

5. Did you (**Lei**) fight in the Dolomites?   6. Where did she spend Christmas? 7. They put it on the table.   8. The children slept well.   9. My mother sold her house.

10. Did they admit that you (**tu**) were right?

E. *Dica o scriva in italiano:*

1. We'll go to ski on the Carso.   2. Did you (**voi**) like the underground grottoes?   3. I haven't seen them [the grottoes] yet.   4. I'll spend the summer on top of a mountain.

5. Why would you (**tu**) go back there?   6. Because the landscape is very rugged, and there is no one there.   7. Do you (**tu**) like the Dolomites too? 8. Yes, but in a different way.   9. There are many people, and I'll ski all winter.

10. I am glad that vacation is over, because now I can work.

F. CONVERSATION:

1. Two or more persons discuss winter sports, and the places where one can ski in Italy (Dolomites, Carso).
2. Two or more persons discuss spending vacation in the city, and possible amusements (*e.g.,* all-night balls).

CONVERSATION UNIT
—— 28 ——

At a Pensione in Perugia

Mrs. Longhi, Peter, and Henry Schneider, a German student, are seated at a table in a **pensione** *(boarding-house) in Perugia, a picturesque city in Umbria (central Italy).*

LA SIG.RA LONGHI — ¹È la prima volta che viene a Perugia Lei?

PIETRO — ²Sì, era tanto che volevo venire. ³Ma non mi è stato mai possìbile venire. ⁴Ho molti amici che sono in Italia con una borsa di studio Fulbright. ⁵Come Lei sa, loro vèngono sempre qui per il corso d'orientamento.

LA SIG.RA LONGHI — ⁶Sì, certo, ne abbiamo ospitati parecchi anche quest'anno. ⁷A Perugia ci sono molti studenti stranieri che vèngono a studiare l'italiano. ⁸C'è un ambiente veramente internazionale. ⁹Ma insomma Le piace Perugia?

PIETRO — ¹⁰Ah sì, moltìssimo. ¹¹Le sue case medioevali, le sue salite e discese, le sue mura di cinta sono veramente pittoresche. ¹²Ma ciò che mi diverte di più è il passeggio della sera.

MRS. LONGHI — ¹Is this the first time that you have come to Perugia?

PETER — ²Yes, I had wanted to come for a long time. ³But it was never possible for me to come. ⁴I have many friends who are in Italy on [*lit.*, with] a Fulbright scholarship. ⁵As you know, they always come here for the orientation course.

MRS. LONGHI — ⁶Yes, certainly, we have put up several of them this year, too. ⁷In Perugia there are many foreign students who come to study Italian. ⁸There is a truly international atmosphere. ⁹But, in short, do you like Perugia?

PETER — ¹⁰Oh, yes, very much, ¹¹Its mediaeval houses, its steep streets, its encircling walls, are truly picturesque. ¹²But what amuses me most is the evening promenade.

ENRICO — ¹³Che cos'è il passeggio? ¹⁴Sono arrivato a Perugia soltanto stamattina e ancora non conosco le abitùdini della città.

LA SIG.RA LONGHI — ¹⁵Veramente questa non è una caratterìstica particolare di Perugia. ¹⁶Direi che sia piuttosto di tutte le città pìccole in Italia.

PIETRO — ¹⁷La signora ha ragione. ¹⁸A tutti gli italiani piace incontrarsi con gli amici la sera, fare due passi e due chiàcchiere insieme nella strada principale della città, nel *Corso*.

ENRICO — ¹⁹Ho capito, ùsano la strada come se fosse una grande sala di ricevimenti.

PIETRO — ²⁰Proprio così, e noi americani che ci vantiamo di aver inventato le grandi attività sociali!

HENRY — ¹³What's the promenade? ¹⁴I arrived in Perugia only this morning, and I still am not familiar with the customs of the city.

MRS. LONGHI — ¹⁵Really this is not a peculiar characteristic of Perugia. ¹⁶Rather I'd say that it is of all the small cities in Italy.

PETER — ¹⁷You are right (The lady is right). ¹⁸All Italians like to meet their friends in the evening, to take a short walk and have a little chat together on the main street of the town, on the *Corso*.

HENRY — ¹⁹I see, they use the street as if it were a big reception hall.

PETER — ²⁰Just so, and we Americans who boast of having invented big social activities!

NOTES

1. **Era tanto che volevo venire**, literally *It was so much [time] that I was wanting to come.*
2. **ambiente**, literally *environment, surroundings*; *atmosphere* only in figurative sense.
3. **le sue salite e discese**, literally *its rises and descents*: a **salita** is any street which goes up steeply, and a **discesa** is one which goes down steeply.
4. **le sue mura di cinta**, literally *its walls of encirclement*.
5. **fare due passi**, literally *to make two steps.*
6. **fare due chiàcchiere**, literally *to make two chats.*

Palazzo Comunale e Fontana Maggiore

Foto ISTO

Esercizi

A. *Risponda in italiano alle seguenti domande basate sul testo:*

1. Lei è mai stato a Perugia? 2. Vorrebbe andare a Perugia? 3. Perché?
4. Ha degli amici che sono stati a Perugia?
5. Perché ci vanno quelli che hanno una borsa Fulbright? 6. Perché ci vanno anche altri studenti stranieri? 7. Come è l'ambiente? 8. Come sono le case di Perugia? 9. Come sono le sue strade?
10. Come sono le sue mura di cinta? 11. Che cos'è il passeggio? 12. Perché il passeggio è una caratterìstica di tutte le città pìccole in Italia? 13. Come ùsano la strada durante il passeggio?

B. *Domandi a un altro studente (a un'altra studentessa):*

1. se gli (le) è stato mai possìbile andare a Perugia. 2. se vorrebbe andare a Perugia. 3. se conosce delle persone che sono state a Perugia. 4. dove vanno gli studenti che hanno delle borse di studio Fulbright.
5. se e perché gli (le) piacerebbe Perugia. 6. se conosce le abitùdini delle pìccole città italiane. 7. come si chiama l'abitùdine di fare due passi e due chiàcchiere insieme, la sera. 8. come si chiama la strada principale di molte città italiane.

C. *Dica a un altro studente (a un'altra studentessa):*

1. che questa è la prima volta che Lei viene a Perugia. 2. che voleva venire prima. 3. che non Le è stato possìbile venire prima. 4. che Lei ha ospitato molti studenti stranieri.
5. che Le piace Perugia. 6. che Le piàcciono le città pìccole. 7. che Lei non conosce le abitùdini della città. 8. che Lei s'incontrerà con i suoi amici. 9. che Lei farà due passi e due chiàcchiere con loro.
10. che Lei non si vanta di aver inventato le grandi attività sociali.

D. REVISIONE DI **ecco.** *Dica o scriva in italiano:*

1. Here is the descent. 2. Here it is. 3. Here is a rise. 4. Here is one of them.
5. There are my friends. 6. There they are. 7. There are the cities. 8. There they are. 9. There are some students.
10. There are some of them. 11. Here is some coffee for *you* (*fam. sg.*). 12 Here is some coffee for you (*use conjunctive dative pronoun*). 13. Here is some for you. 14. Here we are!
15. There you (*fam. pl.*) are!

Foto ISTO

Porta Sant'Angelo, Perugia

E. *Dica o scriva in italiano:*

1. Does he have a scholarship? 2. Where do they hold the orientation course? 3. How many foreign students are there in Perugia? 4. We don't like mediaeval houses.
5. But the evening promenade amuses us. 6. Many Americans, also, like to take a short walk and have a little chat together with their friends. 7. Every little city has its *Corso*. 8. The promenade is a very amusing social activity. 9. He likes to take tea at four o'clock in the afternoon.
10. Why would they use the street as if it were a reception hall?

F. CONVERSATIONS:

1. You talk about Perugia, its appearance, and the kind of students who go there (including Americans, English [*inglese, sg.*] and German [*tedesco, sg.*]).
2. You discuss the small-town custom of the promenade and what one does during the promenade.

53. VERBS: THE SUBJUNCTIVE.

There exist in Italian two tenses, the present subjunctive and the past subjunctive, which have special functions in both dependent and independent clauses. In the regular conjugations, the present subjunctive has the characteristic vowel **-i-** for verbs ending in **-are**, and **-a-** for verbs ending in **-ire** and **-ere**:

PRESENT SUBJUNCTIVE	
FIRST CONJUGATION	

nominare   *to name*
nomin-

nòmini	(that) I name	nominiamo	(that) we name
nòmini	(that) you (*fam.*) name	nominiate	(that) you (*fam. pl.*) name
nòmini	(that) he, she, it name; (that) you (*formal sg.*) name	nòminino	(that) they name; (that) you (*formal pl.*) name

SECOND CONJUGATION		THIRD CONJUGATION
dormire *to sleep* **dorm-**	**capire** *to understand* **cap-**	**véndere** *to sell* **vend-**
dorma (that) I sleep, *etc.*	capisca (that) I understand, *etc.*	venda (that) I sell *etc.*
dorma	capisca	venda
dorma	capisca	venda
dormiamo	capiamo	vendiamo
dormiate	capiate	vendiate
dòrmano	capiscano	vèndano

Note that, for all subjunctives, both regular and irregular, the three persons of the singular are the same. The 1st pl. ends in **-iamo** and is always identical with the 1st pl. of the present; and the 2nd pl. always in **-iate**. For **-ire** verbs in **-isc-** (like **capire**, **finire**, *etc.*), the element **-isc-** is always added to the root in the present subjunctive singular and third person plural.

A number of verbs have irregular stems in part or all of the present subjunctive. The following verbs which you have had to date show irregularities in this tense:

INFINITIVE		PRESENT SUBJUNCTIVE
andare	to go	vada; andiamo, andiate, vàdano
avere	to have	abbia; abbiamo, abbiate, àbbiano
dare	to give	dia; diamo, diate, dìano
dire	to say	dica; diciamo, diciate, dìcano
divenire	to become	divenga; diveniamo, diveniate, divèngano
dovere	to owe, have to	debba or deva; dobbiamo, dobbiate, dèbbano or dévano
èssere	to be	sia; siamo, siate, siano
fare	to do, make	faccia; facciamo, facciate, fàcciano
morire	to die	muoia; moriamo, moriate, muòiano
piacere	to be pleasing to	piaccia; piacciamo, piacciate, piàcciano
riempire	to fill	riempia; riempiano, riempiate, riémpiano
rimanere	to remain	rimanga; rimaniamo, rimaniate, rimàngano
salire	to go up	salga; saliamo, saliate, sàlgano
sapere	to know	sappia; sappiamo, sappiate, sàppiano
sedersi	to seat oneself, sit down	mi (ti, si) sieda; ci sediamo, vi sediate, si sièdano
soddisfare	to satisfy	soddisfaccia; soddisfacciamo, soddisfacciate, soddisfàcciano or regular, like verbs in -are (soddisfi, etc.)
stare	to stand, be located	stia; stiamo, stiate, stìano
tacere	to be silent	taccia; tacciamo, tacciate, tàcciano
tenere	to hold	tenga; teniamo, teniate, tèngano
uscire	to go out	esca; usciamo, usciate, èscano
venire	to come	venga; veniamo, veniate, vèngano
volere	to want, wish	voglia; vogliamo, vogliate, vògliano

Verbs in -care, -gare and in -ciare -giare, -sciare keep the same pronunciation of the final consonant of the root throughout the present subjunctive, and hence have the same automatic alternations in spelling as in the present tense (cf. Grammar Unit III, Sec. 9): e.g., for elencare to list: elenchi; elenchiamo, elenchiate, elènchino; for pagare to pay: paghi; paghiamo, pàghiate, pàghino; for mangiare to eat: mangi; mangiamo, mangiate, màngino; for lasciare to leave: lasci; lasciamo, lasciate, làscino.

When used in independent sentences, the present subjunctive has the meaning of a wish, desire or command expressed by the speaker: *e.g.*, **Venga**! *Let him come*!; **Tàcciano**! *Let them be silent*! The subjunctive giving a command in this way is used primarilly in the third person. The command given in formal direct address (*3rd person*, **Lei** *sg.*, **Loro** *pl.*; Grammar Unit **VII**, *Sec.* **25**) is a special case of this use of the subjunctive: *e.g.*, **Venga (Lei)**! *Come*! **Tàcciano (Loro)**! *Be silent*!

The use of the subjunctive in dependent clauses will be discussed in Grammar Units XV and XVI, *Secs.* **56** and **60**.

54. Verbs: Perfect Phrases.

The so-called "compound past" (Grammar Unit **VIII**, *Sec.* **29**), corresponds in its structure to the English present perfect, in that it consists of the present tense of an auxiliary verb + the past participle of a main verb. Both in English and in Italian, other tenses of the auxiliary besides the present can be used to form further perfect phrases, such as the past perfect (*I had gone*), the future perfect (*I shall have gone*), the conditional perfect (*I should have gone*), *etc.* Examples of these formations in Italian:

Pluperfect (Past Perfect) = Imperfect of Auxiliary + Past Participle: **avevo lavorato** *I had worked*; **era andata** *she had gone.*

Future Perfect = Future of Auxiliary + Past Participle: **avrai mangiato** *you (fam. sg.) will have eaten*; **saranno partite** *they (f.) will have departed.*

Conditional Perfect = Conditional of Auxiliary + Past Participle: **avremmo pagato** *we would have paid*; **sareste arrivati** *you (m. fam. pl.) would have arrived.*

Present Subjunctive Perfect = Present Subjunctive of Auxiliary + Past Participle: (**che**) **abbia saputo** (*that*) *he have known*; (**che**) **siate usciti** (*that*) *you (fam. pl.) have gone out.*

In these perfect phrases, the agreement of the past participle with subject or object is, of course, determined by the auxiliary verb (**èssere** or **avere**, as the case may be), as explained in Grammar Units **VIII** and **X** (*Secs.* **29, 39**).

55. Relative Pronoun Phrases: il quale, etc.

In addition to the relative pronoun forms **che** *who, whom, which* and **cui** *whom, which*; *of whom, of which*; *to whom, to which* (*cf.* Grammar Unit **XI**, *Sec.* **44**), there also exists in Italian a phrase, consisting of the definite article + the adjective **quale**, which serves as a relative pronoun.

Nerone, **il quale**, dopo aver incendiato Roma, assistette all'incendio.	Nero, *who* after having burned Rome, was present at the fire.
La zia di mio marito, **la quale** arriverà domani.	My husband's aunt, *who* [the aunt, not the husband] will arrive tomorrow.
Le zie di mio marito, **le quali** arriveranno domani.	My husband's aunts, *who* will arrive tomorrow.

In relative pronoun phrases of this type, the definite article agrees in gender and number, and the form **quale** agrees in number, with the antecedent of the relative expression. The phrase **il quale** is somewhat heavy and literary and is used chiefly to make clear the gender and number of an antecedent which would otherwise be unclear.

Grammatical Exercises

A. SUBSTITUTIONS.

1. *On the model of* **èssere** *to be* > **sia** *let him be, transform the following infinitives into third person singular commands*:

[1]camminare	*to walk*		[5]lavorare	*to work*
[2]dare	*to give*		[6]méttere	*to put*
[3]dormire	*to sleep*		[7]tacere	*to be silent*
[4]finire	*to end*		[8]uscire	*to go out*

2. *On the model of* **avere** *to have* > **àbbiano** *let them have, transform the following into third person plural commands*:

[1]capire	*to understand*		[5]pagare	*to pay*
[2]chiamare	*to call*		[6]sentire	*to listen*
[3]morire	*to die*		[7]telefonare	*to telephone*
[4]offéndere	*to offend*		[8]venire	*to come*

3. *On the model of* **fare** *to do* > **Faccia**! Do! (**Lei**), *transform the following into commands in formal singular direct address*:

[1]cominciare	*to begin*		[5]rimanere	*to remain*
[2]dire	*to say*		[6]sapere	*to know*
[3]fumare	*to smoke*		[7]sedersi	*to seat oneself*
[4]riempire	*to fill*		[8]véndere	*to sell*

4. *On the model of* **uscire** to go out > **Èscano**! Go out! (**Loro**), *transform the following into commands in formal plural direct address:*

¹andare	*to go*	⁵sedersi	*to seat oneself*
²decidere	*to decide*	⁶stare	*to stand*
³mangiare	*to eat*	⁷restare	*to remain*
⁴salire	*to go up*	⁸vedere	*to see*

5. *Make negative all the positive commands formed in Exercises A, 1-4.*

6. *On the model* of **cominciare** to begin > **aver cominciato** to have gone, *form perfect infinitive phrases on:*

¹attribuire	*to attribute*	⁵invitare	*to invite*
²camminare	*to walk*	⁶istruire	*to instruct*
³decidere	*to decide*	⁷préndere	*to take*
⁴dormire	*to sleep*	⁸volere	*to wish, want*

and on the model of **restare** to remain > **èssere restato** to have remained, *form similar phrases on:*

¹andare	*to go*	⁵rimanere	*to remain*
²èssere	*to be*	⁶salire	*to go up*
³morire	*to die*	⁷uscire	*to go out*
⁴partire	*to depart*	⁸venire	*to come*

7. *On the model of* **aver cominciato** to have begun > **avevo cominciato** I had begun, *form past perfect phrases on the perfect infinitive phrases developed in Exercise A, 6.*

8. *On the model of* **aver cominciato** to have begun > **avrà**, *cominciato* he will have begun, *form future perfect phrases on the perfect infinitive phrases developed in Exercise A, 6.*

9. *On the model of* **aver cominciato** to have begun > **avremmo cominciato** we would have begun, *form conditional perfect phrases on the perfect infinitive phrases developed in Exercise A, 6.*
   The other persons and numbers of the auxiliary verbs may be used in extending the past perfect, future perfect and conditional perfect phrases formed in Exercises A, 7-9.

10. *On the model of* **le léttere che ho lette** > **le léttere, le quali ho lette** the letters which I have read *replace* **che** *or* **cui** *by forms of* **il quale** *in the following expressions:*

¹Ho molti amici **che** sono in Italia.   *I have many friends who are in Italy.*

²Molte studentesse **che** vèngono a studiare l'italiano.   *Many students who come to study Italian.*

³l'automobile **che** ho comprata.   *the automobile which I have bought.*

⁴Ottaviano Augusto, **che** sconfisse Marco Antònio.   *Octavian Augustus, who defeated Mark Antony.*

⁵Quella ragazza a **cui** hai fatto l'occhiolino.   *That girl at whom you made eyes.*

B. PROGRESSIVE VARIATION. *Say or write in Italian:*

(1) ¹To go.
²Let him go!
³Let them go!
⁴Let them work!
⁵Let her work!
⁶To work.
⁷To have worked.
⁸I have worked.
⁹I had worked.
¹⁰They had worked.
¹¹They had slept.
¹²He had slept.
¹³He had gone.
¹⁴To have gone.
¹⁵To go.

(2) ¹We have departed.
²We will have departed.
³We will have begun.
⁴She will have begun.
⁵She would have begun.
⁶She would have gone out.
⁷She had gone out.
⁸She goes out.
⁹Let her go out!
¹⁰Let them go out!
¹¹Let them write!
¹²They write.
¹³They have written.
¹⁴They had written.
¹⁵They had departed.
¹⁶We had departed.
¹⁷We have departed.

C. *Say or write in Italian:*

1. When had you (*fam. pl.*) arrived?   2. We had arrived before ten o'clock. 3. Why do they boast of having gone up on the mountain?   4. Will I never have seen Florence or Rome?

5. You (*fam. pl.*) would have been right.   6. I would have liked (it would have been pleasing to me) to meet with my friends.   7. Where would they have gone?   8. Let my friends write to me!*   9. Let him invent a new machine! 10. Let her buy a new skirt!

---

*Note that these and similar English sentences with *let* + a verb are not requests to allow someone to do something, but are commands for someone to do something, and therefore should not be translated with Italian **lasciare** *to allow, let* + infinitive.

Going to a Concert

Henry buys tickets for the concert at the box-office (**il botteghino**).

ENRICO — [1]Domani c'è un bel concerto. [2]Ti piacerebbe venire con me? [3]Hai altri impegni?

HENRY — [1]Tomorrow there's a nice concert. [2]Would you like to come with me? [3]Have you anything else to do?

PIETRO — [4]Veramente no. [5]Ma di che si tratta?

PETER — [4]As a matter of fact, no. [5]But what's it about?

ENRICO — [6]Il programma è òttimo, e mi hanno detto che anche l'orchestra è molto buona. [7]Io veramente non la conosco, ma conviene tentare.

HENRY — [6]The program is excellent, and they've told me that the orchestra is very good, too. [7]I really don't know it, but we'll have to try and see.

PIETRO — [8]Va bene. [9]Potresti préndere tu i biglietti?

PETER — [8]All right. [9]Could you get the tickets.

ENRICO — [10]Va bene. [11]Ci penso io.

HENRY — [10]Very well. [11]I'll see to it.

Al botteghino

ENRICO — [12]Che tipo di posti ci sono?

At the box-office

HENRY — [12]What kind of places are there?

L'IMPIEGATO — [13]Di tutti i tipi, signore: dalle poltrone di platea che cóstano tremila cinquecento lire, al loggione che costa solo quattrocento lire.

THE CLERK — [13](Of) all kinds, sir: from the orchestra seats, which cost 3500 lire, to the top galery, which costs only 400 lire.

ENRICO — [14]E le poltroncine di prima galleria quanto cóstano?

HENRY — [14]And how much do the seats in the first balcony cost?

L'IMPIEGATO — [15]La prima e la seconda fila duemila lire, e le altre mille cinquecento. [16]Ma Le posso assicurare che anche da lì si sente molto bene.

THE CLERK — [15]The first and the second row, two thousand lire, and the others, 1500. [16]But I can assure you that you can hear very well from there too.

ENRICO — [17]Bene, mi dia alloradue biglietti di terza fila. [18]Me ne dia due al centro se sono ancora liberi.

HENRY — [17]Very well, then give me two tickets in the third row. [18]Give me two of them in the center if they are still available.

Teatro alla Scala

L'Impiegato — ¹⁹Guardi, queste poltrone qui sono un po' laterali, ma non molto.

Enrico — ²⁰Benìssimo. ²¹Il concerto comincia alle otto, vero?

L'Impiegato — ²²Sì signore alle otto in punto il direttore alzerà la bacchetta e l'orchestra comincerà a suonare.

The Clerk — ¹⁹Look, these seats here are a little to one side, but not much.

Henry — ²⁰Excellent. ²¹The concert starts at eight, doesn't it?

The Clerk — ²²Yes, sir, at eight o'clock sharp the director will raise his baton and the orchestra will start to play.

NOTES

1. **Hai altri impegni?**, literally *Have you other engagements?*
2. **Di che si tratta?**, literally *Of what does it treat itself = what's it about?*
3. **Conviene tentare,** literally *it's necessary to try.*
4. **La platea** is the floor of the orchestra in a theater.
5. **Suonare** = English *play* in connection with instruments. For games, *play* = **giocare.**

VERB FORMS

convenire   *to be fitting* — like **venire.** Normally used only in the third person.

Esercizi

A. *Risponda in italiano alle seguenti domande basate sul testo:*

1. Quando c'è un concerto? 2. Ha altri impegni Pietro? 3. Che cosa vuol sapere Pietro da Enrico? 4. Che cosa pensa Enrico del programma e dell' orchestra? 5. Conosce l'orchestra Enrico? 6. Chi prenderà i biglietti? 7. Che cosa domanda Enrico all'impiegato del botteghino? 8. Quanto cóstano le poltrone di platea? 9. Quanto cóstano i posti di loggione? 10. Quelli di prima galleria? 11. Che tipo di biglietti prende Enrico? 12. Quanto cóstano i due biglietti? 13. A che ora comincia il concerto? 14. Che cosa fa il direttore quando l'orchestra comincia a suonare?

B. *Domandi a un altro studente (a un'altra studentessa):*

1. Se gli piacerebbe venire con Lei al concerto. 2. se ha altri impegni. 3. di che cosa si tratta. 4. se il programma è buono. 5. se sa se l'orchestra è buona. 6. se conosce l'orchestra. 7. quanto cóstano i posti. 8. se si sente bene dalla galleria. 9. se si sente bene dal loggione. 10. di darLe quattro biglietti di platea. 11. a che ora comincia il concerto. 12. che cosa fa l'orchestra quando il direttore alza la bacchetta.

C. *Dica a un altro studente (a un'altra studentessa):*

1. che Le piacerebbe accompagnarlo al concerto. 2. che Lei non ha altri impegni. 3. che Lei crede che il programma è ottimo. 4. che Lei potrebbe préndere i biglietti. 5. che Lei preferisce le poltrone di platea. 6. che Lei vorrebbe cinque biglietti di prima fila. 7. che se non ce ne sono, Lei prenderà cinque posti di seconda fila.

D. REVISIONE DEI TEMPI DEL PERFETTO (Review of Perfect Tenses). *Dica o scriva in italiano:*

1. They had had other engagements. 2. He would have given me some places in the third row. 3. The conductor will have raised his baton. 4. The orchestra will have begun to play. 5. She had come with me. 6. What would you (**tu**) have said? 7. I hadn't said anything. 8. They had played a beautiful symphony (**sinfonia,** *f.*). 9. When had she arrived? 10. Won't he have departed yet?

E. *Dica o scriva in italiano:*

trattarsi di *to be a question of*

(a) 1. It's a question of working (*use infinitive after* **di**).   2. Is it a question of a symphony?   3. Isn't it a question of writing?   4. Of what was it a question?
  5. Will it be a question of a concert?   6. It would be a question of money.

suonare, giocare *to play*

(b) 1. The orchestra is playing.   2. The children are playing.   3. What was the orchestra playing?   4. When will the boy play?
  5. They have played a symphony of Beethoven.

convenire *to be fitting, necessary*

(c) 1. It's necessary to eat.   2. Is it necessary to work so much?   3. Will it be necessary to write to him?   4. Why was it necessary to depart?
  5. It would be necessary to invent a new machine.

F. *Dica o scriva in italiano:*

  1. It would please us to hear the symphony.   2. There are places of all kinds.
  3. I've already gotten the tickets.   4. There is an excellent program.
  5. The concert began late.   6. The conductor was not good.   7. The orchestra did not play well.   8. Our seats were too much to one side.   9. We had places in the last row.
 10. From there, one heard very badly.

G. CONVERSATIONS:

  1. You talk over the situation with regard to concerts (Is there a concert? How is the program? Are the orchestra and conductor good?) and decide whether to go or not.
  2. At the box-office: a customer inquires of the clerk whether seats are available, in what price range and in what parts of the house, and finally buys tickets.

In the Tuscan Hills

Henry and Pietro are driving through the hills of Upper Tuscany looking for a perfect example of Romanesque art.

PIETRO — [1]Mi pare che la tua idea di andare a caccia di chiese romàniche sconosciute non sia stata troppo brillante. [2]È già un'ora che abbiamo lasciato Arezzo, mentre ci hanno detto che Grópina era soltanto a trenta chilòmetri di distanza.

ENRICO — [3]Càlmati, amico mio. [4]Forse abbiamo sbagliato strada. [5]Intanto gòditi la campagna toscana. [6]Guarda che meraviglia!

PIETRO (*ad un contadino*) — [7]Scusi, è questa la strada per Grópina?

CONTADINO — [8]Grópina? [9]Mai sentita nominare!

PIETRO — [10]Ma sì, è un paese vicino a Loro Ciuffenna.

CONTADINO — [11]Ah sì, allora questa non è la strada giusta, signori. [12]Loro è al di là di questa collina.

PIETRO — [13]Uffa, che rabbia! [14]È molto lontano di qui?

CONTADINO — [15]Non moltìssimo, signore, una diecina di chilòmetri, ma la strada è tutta in salita e piuttosto brutta.

PIETRO — [16]Che bellezza! [17]Con il caldo che fa c'è da stare allegri!

PETER — [1]It seems to me that your idea of going hunting for unknown Romanesque churches wasn't too brilliant. [2]It's already an hour since we left Arezzo, whereas they told us that Grópina was only thirty kilometers away.

HENRY — [3]Calm down (yourself), my friend. [4]Perhaps we've taken the wrong road. [5]Meanwhile, enjoy the Tuscan countryside. [6]Look how beautiful (what a marvel)!

PETER (*to a farmer*) — [7]Excuse me, is this the road for Grópina?

FARMER — [8]Grópina? [9]Never heard tell of it!

PETER — [10]But yes, it's a town near Loro Ciuffenna.

FARMER — [11]Ah yes, then this isn't the right road, gentlemen. [12]Loro is beyond this hill.

PETER — [13]Phew, how irritating! [14]Is it very far from here?

FARMER — [15]Not terribly far, sir, about ten kilometers, but the road is all uphill and rather nasty.

PETER — [16]How wonderful! [17]With this hot weather, there's reason to be cheerful!

ENRICO ¹⁸C'è un paese prima di Loro dove potremmo fermarci a riposare?

CONTADINO — ¹⁹Certo signore: a tre chilòmetri su questa strada c'è un paesino. ²⁰Lì potranno trovare anche una trattoria. ²¹È proprio di fronte alla chiesa. ²²Vi si mangia a meraviglia. ²³Per di più, c'è un'acqua di sorgente speciale fresca e leggera.

HENRY — ¹⁸Is there a town before Loro where we could stop to rest?

FARMER — ¹⁹Certainly, sir; three kilometers from here on this road there's a little town. ²⁰There you'll be able to find a restaurant, too. ²¹It's just opposite the church. ²²The food is marvelous there. ²³Furthermore, there's a special spring water, cool and light.

NOTES

1. **Sbagliare strada** *to take the wrong road*, literally *to mistake [the] road.*
2. **Mai sentita nominare,** short for **Non l'ho mai sentita nominare** *I have never heard it mentioned.*
3. **Uffa, che rabbia!** literally *Phew, what anger!*
4. Sentences 16 and 17, literally *What a beauty! With the heat that it makes, there is [reason] for being cheerful!*
5. **Vi si mangia a meraviglia,** literally *One eats marvellously there.*
6. Loro Ciuffenna and Grópina are two small towns in the upper Arno valley, northeast of Montevarchi. The twelfth century Romanesque church of St. Peter is in Grópina.

VERB FORMS

gòditi   imperative 2nd sg. of **godersi** *to enjoy (for oneself).* reflexive of **godere** *to enjoy.*

calmarsi   *to calm oneself* and **fermarsi** *to stop oneself* are reflexives of the transitive verbs **calmare** *to calm* and **fermare** *to stop,* respectively.

Villaggio nel Centro

Esercizi

A. *Risponda alle seguenti domande basate sul testo:*

1. Che idea aveva avuto Enrico?   2. Che cosa ne pensa Pietro?   3. Perché?
4. Che cosa avevano detto a Pietro ed Enrico?
5. Che cosa risponde Enrico a Pietro?   6. Che cosa gli dice di guardare?

7. Con chi pàrlano Pietro ed Enrico? 8. Il contadino ha mai sentito nominare Grópina? 9. Grópina è vicina a quale altro paese? 10. Dove si trova quest'altro paese? 11. A che distanza si trova? 12. Com'è la strada? 13. Dove è possìbile (*possible*) fermarsi a riposare? 14. Che cosa vi si trova? 15. Dove si trova? 16. Come vi si mangia? 17. Che tipo d'acqua c'è?

B. *Domandi a un altro studente (a un'altra studentessa):*

1. se gli (le) pare che la Sua idea sia stata brillante. 2. se vuol andare a caccia di chiese romàniche. 3. da quando ha lasciato la città. 4. se Loro hanno sbagliato strada. 5. se questa è la strada per Grópina. 6. dove si trova Loro Ciuffenna. 7. se Grópina è molto lontana da qui. 8. com'è la strada per Grópina. 9. se c'è un paese dove Lei si può fermare a riposarsi. 10. se c'è una trattoria dove Lei potrà mangiare.

C. *Dica a un altro studente (a un'altra studentessa):*

1. che non Le pare che la sua idea sia stata brillante. 2. che è già un'ora che Lei ha lasciato la città. 3. che Lei ha sbagliato strada. 4. che Lei si gode la campagna toscana. 5. di guardare la campagna toscana. 6. che c'è un paese dove lùi (lei) può fermarsi a riposare. 7. che lì troverà una buona trattoria.

D. Revisione del congiuntivo (Review of the subjunctive). *Dica o scriva in italiano:*

1. Let him be silent. 2. Let them find a restaurant. 3. Let her work tomorrow. 4. Let him go. 5. Let them go up. 6. Let her not mistake the road. 7. Let them enjoy the countryside. 8. Let her take (an) ice cream. 9. Let him walk to the Forum. 10. Let them leave Arezzo. 11. Let him go hunting for Roman ruins.

E. *Dica o scriva in Italiano:*

> **fare due passi** *to take a walk*
> **fare due chiàcchiere** *to have a chat*

1. Let's take a walk. 2. They'd like to have a chat. 3. We had a chat. 4. Do you (**tu**) want to take a walk? 5. Why haven't they taken a walk? 6. Will she have a chat with her friend? 7. I took a walk on the encircling walls.

sapere a memoria *to know by heart*

1. Does she know the book by heart?   2. I don't know it by heart.   3. We used to know it by heart.   4. They will know the books by heart.
5. She would know them by heart.   6. Do you (**Lei**) know them by heart?
7. No one knew them by heart.

farsi vivo *to show signs of life, come around*

1. He never comes around here.   2. Show some signs of life (**tu**)!
3. I always used to come around here.   4. They won't come around here.
5. We would come around.   6. When will you (**voi**) show some signs of life?   7. She came around (*use Past Absolute* = she made herself alive).

F. *Dica o scriva in Italiano:*

1. Where is that town of which you (**tu**) spoke?   2. Do you like Romanesque churches?   3. Florence is only forty kilometers away.   4. The road was all uphill.
5. Have you ever heard of Grópina? (= Have you ever heard Grópina named?).   6. Here's a farmer. Let's talk to him.   7. Is there a town beyond this hill?   8. We can't be cheerful today.   9. What kind of water is there in this spring?
10. It is very cool and light.

G. CONVERSATIONS:

1. You talk about the kind of churches you like (Gothic? Romanesque? Baroque?) and where the best churches are.
2. A city person meeting a farmer along the road and asks whether he is on the road to Arezzo (Florence, Rome, *etc.*). The farmer tells him how far it is, what kind of roads there are, *etc.*

LETTURA SESTA

Una Vacanza a Porto S. Stèfano[1]

(Conversations 26-30)

Pietro ha invitato Pàolo a passare qualche giorno con lui nella casa di suo zio a Porto S. Stèfano. Così una bella mattina i due amici decìdono di partire.

C'è molta pace là: i villeggianti[2] non sono ancora arrivati e il porto è pieno di pescherecci[3] dalle vele[4] colorate[5].

Alle sette del mattino Pàolo e Pietro sàlgono su un tassì e si fanno portare alla stazione. Pàolo ha fatto tardi,[6] come al sòlito, per cui non c'è tempo da pèrdere, non si può préndere l'àutobus. Il treno parte alle *7.52* e arriva a Orbetello alle *11*. A quell'ora ci dovrebbe èssere la coincidenza[7] per Porto S. Stèfano, ma se si perde quella, bisogna aspettare[8] la corriera[9] delle *12.20* che arriva alle *13*. Per quel che riguarda gli orari Pietro lascia fare[10] al suo amico, poveretto! è ancora molto confuso[11] con tutte queste ore: *13, 15, 20* ecc. Deve sempre fare un certo sforzo[12] per capire di che ora si stia parlando.

Il treno è molto pieno, ma per fortuna i nostri amici tròvano due posti vicino al finestrino di un scompartimento[13] di seconda classe.[14] Dopo una mezz'oretta[15] di viaggio si vede già il mare: è di un azzurro intenso e molto calmo,[16] fa venir voglia di tuffarsi[17] e

[1]**Porto Santo Stèfano** a small port on the Tyrrhenian coast about 75 miles northwest of Rome.
[2]**villeggiante** *(m.)* vacationer.
[3]**peschereccio** *(m.)* fishing-boat.
[4]**vela** *(f.)* sail.
[5]**colorato** colored.
[6]**far tardi** to be late.
[7]**coincidenza** *(f.)* connection.
[8]**aspettare** to wait for.
[9]**corriera** *(f.)* (suburban or interurban) bus.
[10]**lasciar fare** to leave it up to
[11]**confuso** confused.
[12]**sforzo** *(m.)* effort.
[13]**scompartimento** *(m.)* compartment.
[14]**classe** *(f.)* class.
[15]**una mezz'oretta** about half an hour.
[16]**calmo** calm.
[17]**tuffarsi** to dive.

farsi un bel bagno. Anche la campagna circostante[18] è molto bella: i prati sono tutti in fiore e le pècore,[19] i cavalli,[20] le mucche[21] che pàscolano[22] plàcidi[23] nella radura[24] complétano questo quadro campestre.[25]

Il treno fa parécchie[26] fermate[27] prima di arrivare ad Orbetello perché è un accelerato,[28] ma in fondo[29] non importa, tanto[30] il viaggio è breve.[31]

Orbetello è una brutta[32] città, ma ci sono delle cose interesanti da vedere. Nei dintorni[33] difatti,[34] ci sono delle fortezze[35] saracene.[36] Proseguendo[37] con la corriera, Pàolo e Pietro si meravigliano[38] della bellezza[39] straordinària[40] del panorama.[41] Porto S. Stèfano si trova ai piedi del monte[42] Argentàrio[43] che è a picco[44] sul mare.

Pietro spiega a Pàolo che durante l'ùltima guerra mondiale Porto S. Stèfano è stata una delle città più bombardate[45] d'Italia. „Mi ha detto lo zio" — prosegue Pietro — „che era diventato un porto militare[46] tedesco ed è per questo che è stata tanto colpita.[47] Infatti anche gli zii hanno dovuto ospitare in casa loro molti sfollati[48]". „Ora capisco perché ci sono tante case nuove" — dice Pàolo.

I due gióvani pàssano davvero una bella vacanza: gìrano[49] tutto il promontòrio,[50] fanno lunghe passeggiate a piedi e in un giorno particolarmente[51] caldo fanno anche il bagno. Alla fine di aprile l'acqua è ancora freddissima, ma dopo un po' che uno sta dentro è piacévole e rinvigorante[52] e il freddo non si sente più.

[18]**circostante** surrounding.
[19]**pècora** *(f.)* sheep.
[20]**cavallo** *(m.)* horse.
[21]**mucca** *(f.)* milch-cow.
[22]**pascolare** to graze.
[23]**plàcido** placid, calm.
[24]**radura** *(f.)* meadow.
[25]**campestre** rustic.
[26]**parecchi** *(m.),* **parécchie** *(f.)* several.
[27]**fermata** *(f.)* stop.
[28]**accelerato** *(m.)* local (train).
[29]**in fondo** after all.
[30]**tanto** *[here]* in any case.
[31]**breve** short, brief.
[32]**brutto** ugly.
[33]**dintorni** *(m. pl.)* surroundings, environs.
[34]**difatti** in fact.
[35]**fortezza** *(f.)* fort.
[36]**saraceno** Saracen.
[37]**proseguire** to continue.
[38]**meravigliarsi** to be amazed.
[39]**bellezza** *(f.)* beauty.
[40]**straordinàrio** extraordinary.
[41]**panorama** *(m.)* panorama.
[42]**monte** *(m.)* mountain, Mount.
[43]**Argentàrio** name of the mountain near Porto S. Stèfano.
[44]**a picco su** jutting out over.
[45]**bombardare** to bomb.
[46]**militare** military.
[47]**colpire** (II/isc) to hit, strike.
[48]**sfollati** *(m. pl.)* war refugees.
[49]**girare** to go around.
[50]**promontòrio** *(m.)* promontory, cape.
[51]**particolarmente** particularly.
[52]**rinvigorante** invigorating.

XV

GRAMMAR UNIT

56. VERBS: THE SUBJUNCTIVE—AUTOMATIC USES.

In some grammatical constructions the use of the subjunctive is obligatory and hence automatic. Among these constructions are:

1. Clauses, normally introduced by **che** *that*, after such verbs as **convenire, occórrere, bisognare** and such phrases as **èssere necessàrio** (all meaning *to be necessary*), and similar verbs or phrases referring to *necessity, obligation, desirability, advisability, etc.*:

Conviene che lo fàcciano.	*It's necessary that* they do it.
Occorre che ci vada.	*It's necessary that* he go there.
Bisogna che vi fermiate.	*It's necessary that* you stop.
Sarà necessàrio che parta.	*It will be necessary that* you (**tu**) depart.

2. Clauses, normally introduced by **che**, after verbs such as **crédere** *to believe*, **pensare** *to think*, **parere** *to seem*, and other expressions referring to *thought, opinion, etc.* The indicative is often found in this construction in modern usage.

Mi pare che la tua idea non sia stata brillante.	*It seems to me* that your idea was not brilliant.
Crede che occorra partire.	*He thinks that* it's necessary to depart.
Non penso che sia l'ora giusta.	*I don't think that* it's the right time.

3. Clauses dependent on the negative of such verbs as **capire** *to understand*, **èssere chiaro** *to be clear*, **risultare** *to be evident*, **sapere** *to know*, or **vedere** *to see*, referring to the speaker's perception of the facts referred to in the dependent clause:

Non capisco perché l'abbia detto.	*I don't understand* why he said it.
Non so se questo sia giusto.	*I don't know* whether this is right.
Non risulta che àbbiano ragione.	*It's not clear* that they are right.

4. Clauses dependent on such verbs and expressions as **piacere** *to please*, **dispiacere** *to displease*, **desiderare** *to desire*, **volere** *to wish*, and **peccato** (*it's a*) *pity*; and on predicates containing such adjectives as **contento** *glad*, **scontento** *discontented*, **possìbile** *possible*, **impossìbile** *impossible*, **probàbile** *probable*, **improbàbile** *improbable*, and other expressions referring to the speaker's emotional attitude towards the situation or his evaluation of it. For example:

Mi dispiace che Lei sia arrivato in ritardo.	*I'm sorry* that you arrived late.
Desìderano che lo faccia.	*They desire* that he do it *or They desire him* to do it.
Vuole che Le porti dell'insalata?	*Do you want* that I bring you some salad (= *Do you want* me to bring you some salad)?
Peccato che abbia sbagliato strada.	*It's a pity* that he took the wrong road.

In all constructions of the types discussed above, note that the conjunction **che**, *that*, may not be omitted in Italian. In English, a sentence like *I'm sorry that you arrived late* has an optional transformation *I'm sorry you arrived late*, but such a transformation is not possible in Italian, and one must always say **Mi dispiace che Lei sia arrivato in ritardo.**

● 57. ORDINAL ADJECTIVES.

The ordinal numerals in Italian are adjectives in **-o -a -i -e.** For the first ten numbers, they are:

primo	first	**quinto**	fifth	**ottavo**	eighth
secondo	second	**sesto**	sixth	**nono**	ninth
terzo	third	**sèttimo**	seventh	**dècimo**	tenth
quarto	fourth				

For numbers from *eleven* upwards, ordinals are formed by adding **-ésimo** to the stem of the corresponding cardinal number. Before this suffix, the unstressed vowel is lost, but it is added directly to numerals ending in **-tre** *-three, e.g.,* **ventitreésimo** *twenty-third.*

undicésimo	eleventh	**ventunésimo**	twenty-first
dodicésimo	twelfth	**ventiduésimo**	twenty-second
	etc., to	**ventitreésimo**	twenty-third
sedicésimo	sixteenth	**ventiquattrésimo**	twenty-fourth, *etc.*
diciassettésimo	seventeenth	**trentésimo**	thirtieth
diciottésimo	eighteenth	**trentunésimo**	thirty-first, *etc.*
diciannovésimo	nineteenth	**centésimo**	hundredth
ventésimo	twentieth	**millésimo**	thousandth

● 58. COLLECTIVES ON NUMERALS.

Nouns with the suffix **-ina**, *a group of about* ..., are formed on the numerals **dieci** *ten*, **quindici** *fifteen*, and the tens from **venti** *twenty* through **novanta** *ninety*. There exist also special nouns for *dozen, about a hundred* and *about a thousand*, as shown in the following table.

GRAMMAR UNIT FIFTEEN

una diecina	a group of about ten
una dozzina	a group of about twelve, a dozen
una quindicina	a group of about fifteen
una ventina	a group of about twenty
una trentina	a group of about thirty
una quarantina	a group of about forty *etc.*
un centinaio	a group of about a hundred; *pl.* (**delle**) **centinaia** hundreds
un migliaio	a group of about a thousand; *pl.* (**delle**) **migliaia** thousands

Note that the plurals of **centinaio** and **migliaio** are feminines in -a, like **le mura, le uova, le braccia,** *etc.* (*cf.* Grammar Unit **IX,** *Sec.* **33**).

● 59. Pre-Vocalic Forms of Prepositions and Conjunctions.

Certain prepositions and conjunctions have special forms for use before a following vowel: **ad** (**a** *to*), **ed** (**e** *and*) **od** (**o** *or*). In earlier usage, these special forms were used before any word beginning with a vowel:: *e.g.,* **ed io** *and I,* **od Alberto** *or Albert,* **ad entrare** *to enter.* In modern Italian. the special forms are used only before a word beginning with the same vowel as that contained in the preposition or conjunction: *e.g.,* **ed entrare** *and to enter;* **ad Alberto** *to Albert,* **od otto** *or eight.* Before other vowels, the ordinary form of the preposition or conjunction is now used: **e io, o Alberto, a entrare.**

Grammatical Exercises

A. Substitutions.

1. *Make sentences consisting of* **occorre che** it's necessary that, *followed by each of the following expressions in a dependent clause, with the necessary change of the verb to a subjunctive form:*

¹Il direttore alza la bacchetta.	*The conductor raises his baton.*
²I concerti comìnciano alle otto.	*The concerts start at eight.*
³Tu prendi i biglietti.	*You get the tickets.*
⁴Andiamo a caccia di chiese romàniche.	*We go hunting Romanesque churches.*

2. *As in Exercise A, 1, transform the following sentences into clauses dependent on* **bisognerà** it will be necessary:

¹Mangio a mezzogiorno.	*I eat at noon.*
²Loro véndono la casa.	*You sell the house.*
³Capìscono meglio	*They understand better.*
⁴Trovate una trattoria.	*You find a restaurant.*

3. *Transform the following into clauses dependent on* **crédono** they think:

¹Questa sinfonìa è bella.
²So tutto.
³Le sue idee son brillanti.
⁴Potete rimanere a casa.

This symphony is beautiful.
I know everything.
His ideas are brilliant.
You can remain at home.

4. *Make the following dependent on* **sono contento (-a)** I am glad:

¹La linea non è occupata.
²Sai il nùmero a memoria.
³Avete visitato tutti i monumenti.
⁴Deve tornare a casa.

The line isn't busy.
You know the number by heart.
You've visited all the monuments.
She has to go back home.

5. *Make the following dependent on* **non capìscono** they don't understand:

¹Perché non usano le léttere invece dei primi due nùmeri?
²Perché non la smette più?
³Perché vuol parlare con Anna?
⁴Perché le scarpe cóstano tanto?

Why don't they use letters instead of the first two numbers?
Why doesn't she ever stop?
Why does she want to talk with Anna?
Why do the shoes cost so much?

6. *On the analogy of* **primo** first: **uno** one, *give the ordinal numerals for the numbers from* **uno** *through* **dieci**; *from* **ùndici** *through* **venti**; *from* **ventuno** *through* **trenta**; *and so on up through the tens to* **cento**, *and for* **mille**.

7. *On the analogy of* **una diecina** a group of about ten, *form collective nouns (with their plurals) for the numerals* **dódici** twelve, **quìndici** fifteen, **venti** twenty, **trenta** thirty, *and the further tens through* **cento** a hundred, *and for* **mille** a thousand.

B. PROGRESSIVE VARIATION. *Say or write in Italian:*

(1) ¹He's coming.
²It's necessary that he come.
³They believe that he's coming.
⁴They believe that he's working.
⁵We believe that he's working.
⁶We believe that they're working.

⁷We're glad that they're working.
⁸We're glad that they're coming.
⁹It's probable that they're coming.
¹⁰It's probable that he's coming.
¹¹He's coming.

(2) ¹She doesn't remember the number.
²It's probable that she doesn't remember the number.
³It's probable that they remember the number.

⁴It's necessary that they remember the number.
⁵It's necessary that I continue to work.
⁶They're glad that I continue to work.

GRAMMAR UNIT FIFTEEN

⁷They're glad that she continues to work.

⁸We're sorry that she continues to work.

⁹We're sorry that there are no restaurants here.

¹⁰Too bad that there are no restaurants here.

¹¹Too bad that she doesn't remember the number.

¹²She doesn't remember the number.

(3) ¹They're studying singing.

²I don't know why they're studying singing.

³I don't know why she gives herself airs.

⁴She gives herself airs.

⁵She doesn't give herself airs.

⁶It's possible that she doesn't give herself airs.

⁷It's possible that she is likeable.

⁸She is likeable.

⁹You (**voi**) are not likeable.

¹⁰Too bad that you aren't likeable.

¹¹Too bad that she's not studying singing.

¹²I don't understand why she's not studying singing.

¹³I don't understand why they're studying singing.

¹⁴They're studying singing.

(4) *On the model of* **una dozzina di case** a dozen (of) houses, *form the following expressions:*

¹a dozen houses

²about ten houses (= a group-of-about-ten of houses)

³about ten men

⁴about fifty men

⁵about fifty lawyers

⁶about a hundred lawyers

⁷about a hundred companies

⁸hundreds of companies

⁹hundreds of cigarettes

¹⁰thousands of cigarettes

¹¹about a thousand cigarettes

¹²about eighty cigarettes

¹³about eighty matches

¹⁴a score of matches

¹⁵a score of houses

¹⁶a dozen houses.

C. *Say or write in Italian:*

1. I don't know where the station is. 2. It's in the third square on the left.
3. Do you understand why he says that? 4. This is the eighth cigarette that she's smoked today.
5. Too bad you (**voi**) haven't understood. 6. She's sorry that you (**tu**) have taken the wrong road. 7. It will be necessary that she talk with her friends.
8. They smoke thousands of cigarettes every day. 9. Why do they desire that I give them those gloves?
10. It's not clear whether (= if) he is working today.

CONVERSATION UNIT——31

Trains vs. Automobiles

Fulvia and Pietro are traveling together on an Italian train.

PIETRO — ¹A te piace di più viaggiare in treno o in màcchina?

FULVIA — ²Io sono come mio padre. ³Per me il treno è il mezzo migliore: il più ràpido, il più còmodo, il più divertente.

PIETRO — ⁴T'invidio. ⁵Io non lo posso soffrire. ⁶In quanto a divertimento, poi, viaggiare in màcchina è senz'altro più piacévole che viaggiare in treno.

FULVIA — ⁷Ah no, mi dispiace, ma non sono d'accordo. ⁸Quando mai trovi l'occasione di farti lunghe chiacchierate con la gente come le trovi facendo un lungo viaggio in ferrovia?

PETER — ¹Do you prefer to travel by train or by auto?

FULVIA — ²I'm like my father. ³For me, the train is the best means [of transportation]: the fastest, the most comfortable, the most entertaining.

PETER — ⁴I envy you. ⁵*I* can't stand it. ⁶With regard to entertainment, for that matter, travelling by auto is undoubtedly more pleasant than travelling by train.

FULVIA — ⁷Ah, no, I'm sorry, but I don't agree. ⁸When do you ever find the opportunity to hold long conversation with people as you do [when] making a long trip by railroad?

PIETRO — [9]Sì, lo so. [10]Generalmente, però, sono discorsi superficiali e senza troppo senso.

FULVIA — [11]Dipende. [12]A volte proprio perché si sa che la persona che ti sta accanto o di fronte non ti conosce, uno è portato a parlare di cose molto personali.

PIETRO — [13]Ma che valore hanno questi discorsi? [14]Generalmente sono più noiosi che altro.

FULVIA — [15]Mio caro, questo dipende dalla tua sensibilità.

PIETRO — [16]Che c'entra ora la mia sensibilità? [17]Io sto dicendo semplicemente che non ha nessun significato ricévere questa specie di confessioni.

FULVIA — [18]Chiàmale così, se vuoi. [19]Se non altro, ìndicano molto chiaramente il bisogno umano di trovare una persona comprensiva che ti stia ad ascoltare. [20]In parole pòvere: il bisogno di sfogarsi.

PIETRO — [9]Yes, I know. [10]Generally, however, they are superficial conversations and without too much sense.

FULVIA — [11]It depends. [12]At times, just because you know that the person who is beside you or opposite you doesn't know you, you're impelled to talk about very personal matters.

PETER — [13]But what value do these conversations have? [14]Generally, they are more annoying than anything else.

FULVIA — [15]My dear fellow, this depends on your sensitivity.

PETER — [16]Now what's my sensitivity got to do with it? [17]I'm saying simply that there's no sense in receiving this kind of confession.

FULVIA — [18]Call them that, if you want. [19]If nothing else, they show very clearly the human need to find an understanding person who will listen to you. [20]In words of one syllable: the need to express oneself.

NOTES

1. **A te piace di più**, literally *to you does it please more?*
2. **soffrire**, literally *to suffer*
3. **Non sono d'accordo**, literally *I'm not in agreement*
4. **Che c'entra la mia sensibilità** literally *[In] what [way] does my sensitivity enter into it?*
5. **Non ha nessun significato ricévere...**, literally *to receive... has no meaning.*
6. **Chiàmale così**, literally *call them thus.*
7. **In parole pòvere**, literally *in poor words.*

Foto Bright — Rapho-Guillumette

VERB FORMS

dipéndere   *to depend*: past absolute **dipesi, dipendesti,** *etc.*; past participle
dipeso

soffrire   *to suffer*: past absolute **soffersi, soffristi,** *etc.*; past participle **sofferto**

Esercizi

A. *Risponda in italiano alle seguenti domande basate sul testo:*

1. Pietro che mezzo preferisce?   2. Fulvia che mezzo preferisce?   3. Che cosa pensa Fulvia del treno?   4. Pietro che cosa ne pensa?
5. Che cosa si può fare, facendo un lungo viaggio in ferrovia?   6. Che cosa pensa Pietro dei discorsi che si fanno in treno?   7. Perché uno è portato a parlare di cose molto personali in treno?   8. Da che cosa dipende l'opinione che si ha di questi discorsi?   9. Che significato ha ricévere questa specie di confessioni?
10. Che cosa ìndicano?

B. *Domandi a un altro studente (a un'altra studentessa):*

1. se gli (le) piace di più viaggiare in treno o in màcchina.   2. se crede che il treno sia più ràpido della màcchina.   3. se crede che il treno sia più còmodo della màcchina.   4. se crede che il treno sia più divertente della màcchina.
5. se gli (le) piace fare lunghe chiacchierate con la gente.   6. se crede che queste chiacchierate sìano discorsi superficiali.   7. se è portato (portata) a parlare di cose molto personali con persone che non conosce.   8. se ha significato ricévere questa specie di confessioni.   9. se sente il bisogno di trovare una persona che lo (la) stia ad ascoltare.
10. se ha mai sentito il bisogno di sfogarsi.

C. *Dica a un altro studente (a un'altra studentessa):*

1. che Le piace di più viaggiare in màcchina.   2. che per Lei la màcchina è il mezzo migliore.   3. che Lei l'invidia.   4. che non Le piace fare lunghe chiacchierate con persone che Lei non conosce.
5. che trova più noiosi che altro questi discorsi.   6. che non sente nessun bisogno di ricévere questa specie di confessioni.   7. che non desìdera di trovare una persona comprensiva che La stia ad ascoltare.

D. REVISIONE DEL CONGIUNTIVO. *Dica o scriva in italiano:*

1. I'm sorry that you don't like trains.   2. Does he wish that they listen to him?   3. Is it necessary that he make a long trip?   4. We don't believe that they envy us.

5. Pietro doesn't understand why Fulvia likes the train more. 6. Is it necessary that you (**voi**) talk about these personal matters? 7. We don't know why these confessions have no meaning. 8. Why is it necessary that they express themselves? 9. Are you (**tu**) glad that I'm beside you?
10. It seems to Fulvia that Pietro is not right.

E. *Dica o scriva in italiano:*

piacere di più *to be more pleasing*

(a) 1. Do you prefer white wine or red wine? 2. My aunt prefers travelling by automobile. 3. I don't understand why she prefers to listen. 4. They prefer singing.
5. He likes the Forum more.

èssere d'accordo *to agree*

(b) 1. Why don't you (**Lei**) agree with me? 2. She has never agreed with her father. 3. Will they agree with him? 4. We don't agree with you (**voi**).
5. Would he agree?

entrarci *to enter into it?*

(c) 1. How do *I* enter into it? 2. The need to express oneself doesn't enter into it. 3. The persons who are opposite you don't enter into it.
4. How would *we* enter into it?
5. The conductor of the orchestra didn't enter into it.

F. *Dica o scriva in italiano:*

1. What means [of transportation] do you (**Loro**) find most comfortable and amusing? 2. Why do we have to endure his long conversation? 3. I've never had the opportunity to travel by railroad. 4. This trip has been very tiresome.
5. I like to receive confessions from people that I don't know. 6. We don't understand; say it to us in words of one syllable. 7. Who sat (was) opposite you in the train? 8. Dining in a restaurant is more pleasant than eating at home. 9. With regard to sensitivity, *you* (**tu**) don't have any.
10. She never felt the human need of expressing herself.

G. CONVERSATIONS:

1. Two or more students argue their preferences for automobiles *vs.* trains.
2. Two or more students discuss whether one should or should not talk of personal matters with people one doesn't know.

Foto Bright — Rapho-Guillumette

CONVERSATION UNIT————32

In the Dining Car

A comfortable dining car, a good meal and a fine view enchant Peter.

FULVIA — [1]Vedi i vantaggi dei treni? [2]Quando mai ti sogneresti di mangiare un pasto così buono ed avere per di più una vista incantévole?

PIETRO — [3]Ammesso e non concesso che il cibo sia òttimo — "così buono" come dici tu — [4]devi riconóscere che siamo venuti di qua per sfuggire quella calca infernale del corridoio.

FULVIA — [5]Ecco lo snob: "la calca infernale" della seconda classe.

FULVIA — [1]Do you see the advantages of trains? [2]When would you ever dream of eating such a good meal and of having, furthermore, an enchanting view?

PETER — [3]Admitting and not granting that the food is excellent — "so good", as you say — [4]you have to admit that we came in here to get away from that infernal crush in the corridor.

FULVIA — [5]There's a snob for you: "the infernal crush" of the second class.

PIETRO — [6]Ma no, tu mi interpreti sempre male. [7]Hai più idee fisse e pregiudizi che capelli in testa.

FULVIA — [8]Povera me! Sono ridotta proprio male allora!

PIETRO — [9]No, scherzavo. [10]Avanti, però! [11]Riconosci che, malgrado i tuoi princìpi democratici, eri stanca anche tu di stare in mezzo a tutta quella gente, così stretta come una sardina.

FULVIA — [12]Sì, ti confesso che non ce la facevo più. [13]Era peggio degli àutobus nelle ore di punta.

PIETRO — [14]Il vagone ristorante è molto carino, però, vero?

FULVIA — [15]Lo dici a me? [16]Io lo trovo simpaticìssimo, e mi diverte molto mangiarci. [17]Mi sento veramente in vacanza.

PIETRO — [18]A che ora arriveremo a destinazione? [19]Mi pare che ci sia più ritardo del sòlito oggi.

FULVIA — [20]Molto spesso recùperano in viaggio, e si arriva ugualmente in oràrio

PETER — [6]Oh no, you're always misinterpreting me. [7]You have more fixed ideas and prejudices than [you have] hair on your head.

FULVIA — [8]Poor me! I'm really in a bad way then!

PETER — [9]No, I was joking. [10]But go on! [11]Admit that, despite your democratic principles, you too were tired of standing in the midst of all those people, squashed as tight as a sardine.

FULVIA — [12]Yes, I'll confess that I couldn't stand it any longer. [13]It was worse than the buses in the rush hour.

PETER — [14]The dining car is very nice, though, isn't it?

FULVIA — [15]Are you telling me? [16]I find it very pleasant, and enjoy eating here very much. [17]I really feel on vacation.

PETER — [18]At what time will we arrive at our destination? [19]It seems to me that today there's more delay than usual.

FULVIA — [20]Very often they make up time along the way, and they arrive on time all the same.

NOTES

1. **Ammesso e non concesso**, literally *admitted and not conceded*.
2. **La seconda classe**: Italian trains have two classes, first and second. On long-distance express trains, the second class is usually crowded.
3. **mi interpreti male**, literally *you interpret me badly*.
4. Sentence 8 is literally *Poor me! I'm reduced really badly, then!* In the exclamation **povero -a me**, the adjective **povero** agrees in gender and number with the person speaking.
5. **così stretta come una sardina**, literally *so squeezed as a sardine*. **Stretto** is past participle of **stringere** *to squeeze*.
6. **non fàrcela più**, *not to be able to stand it any longer*.
7. **in oràrio**, literally *in [accordance with the] time table*.

VERB FORMS

amméttere   *to admit*: past absolute **ammisi ammettesti**, *etc.*; past participle **ammesso**

concédere   *to concede*: past absolute **concessi, concedesti**, *etc.*; past participle **concesso**

riconóscere   *to recognize*, like **conóscere**

ridurre   *to reduce*: root **riduc-**, and hence present **riduco, riduci**, *etc.*; imperfect **riducevo**; future **ridurrò**, conditional **ridurrei**; past absolute **ridussi, riducesti**, *etc.*; present subjunctive **riduca**, *etc.*; past participle **ridotto**

stríngere   *to squeeze*: past absolute **strinsi, stringesti**, *etc.*; past participle **stretto**

Esercizi

A. *Risponda in italiano alle seguenti domande basate sul testo:*

1. Quali, secondo [*according to*] Fulvia, sono i vantaggi dei treni?   2. Crede Pietro che il cibo sia òttimo nel vagone ristorante?   3. Perché sono entrati Fulvia e Pietro nel vagone ristorante?   4. Che cosa pensa Fulvia delle idee di Pietro sulla seconda classe?

5. Come crede Pietro che Fulvia lo interpreti?   6. Secondo Pietro, quante idee fisse ha Fulvia?   7. Come è ridotta Fulvia?   8. Come si sentiva Fulvia, stando in mezzo a tutta la gente nel corridoio?   9. Come trova Pietro il vagone ristorante?

10. Fulvia è d'accordo con Pietro?   11. Come si sente Fulvia nel vagone ristorante?   12. Che cosa dice Pietro del ritardo del treno?   13. Che cosa fanno spesso in viaggio quando il treno è in ritardo?

B. *Domandi a un altro studente (a un'altra studentessa):*

1. se concede che i treni sono migliori delle màcchine. 2. quando si sognerebbe di mangiare e di avere nello stesso tempo una vista incantévole. 3. che
cosa pensa della calca del corridoio in seconda classe. 4. se La interpreta
male.

5. se ha dei princìpi democratici. 6. se gli (le) piace stare in mezzo alla gente.
7. se gli (le) piace stare stretto (stretta) come una sardina negli àutobus alle
ore di punta. 8. se trova simpàtico il vagone ristorante. 9. se si diverte a
mangiare nel vagone ristorante.

10. se c'è più ritardo del sòlito oggi. 11. se arriveranno in oràrio. 12. se
recupereranno in viaggio.

C. *Dica a un altro studente (a un'altra studentessa):*

1. che Lei non sognerebbe di mangiare in un vagone ristorante. 2. che Lei
riconosce di èssere uno snob. 3. che Lei non ha né idee fisse né pregiudizi. 4. che Lei è ridotto male.

5. che Lei non scherzava. 6. che i Suoi princìpi sono veramente democratici.
7. che Lei non è stanco di stare in mezzo alla gente. 8. che Lei si sente
veramente in vacanza.

D. REVISIONE DEI NUMERI ORDINALI. *Dica o scriva in italiano:*

1. This is the first time that I'm travelling in Italy. 2. She has written her
thirty-seventh book. 3. Let's seat ourselves in the third car. 4. I'm
eating my third meal. 5. That's the fifteenth sardine you (**tu**) have eaten.

E. *Dica o scriva in italiano:*

1. I admit, but I don't grant, that this automobile is very nice. 2. Do you
(**voi**) recognize your friends when you see them? 3. His hair is too long.
4. Will they arrive late?

5. We always eat sardines with the antipasto. 6. He was really in a bad way.
7. Will they catch up along the way. 8. We can't stand it any longer. 9.
His sister is a very likeable person.

10. It seems to us that they are misinterpreting us.

F. CONVERSATIONS:

1. Two or more people are standing in the crowded corridor of an Italian
train talking about how uncomfortable it is, *etc.*
2. A young man and a girl are seated in a dining car talking about the food,
the view, *etc.* They give their order to the waiter.

60. VERBS: THE SUBJUNCTIVE—MEANINGFUL USES.

When used in independent sentences, the subjunctive has the meaning of a wish or command (*cf.* Grammar Unit **XIV**, *Sec.* **53**). In certain types of dependent clauses, it is possible to have either a subjunctive or a non-subjunctive verb. If the verb is in the subjunctive in such clauses, its use is meaningful, *i.e.*, conveys a special meaning. In clauses modifying nouns, use of the subjunctive indicates that a particular characteristic is desired:

una persona che ti **stia** ad ascoltare	a person who [such that he] *listens* to you
una casa che **sia** vicina al mare	a house which [such that it] *is* near the sea
dei ragazzi che non **fàcciano** troppo rumore	children that [such that they] *do* not make too much noise

Clauses of this type are normally found modifying the objects of such verbs as **cercare** *to look for*, **desiderare** *to desire*, **volere** *to want*, and the subjects of such verbs as **occórrere**, **bisognare** or **èssere necessàrio** *to be necessary*.

il bisogno umano di trovare una persona che ti **stia** ad ascoltare	the human *need* to find a person who, *will* listen to you
Vogliamo una casa che **sia** vicina al mare.	We *need* a house which *is* near the sea.
Occórrono dei ragazzi che non **fàcciano** troppo rumore.	Children that don't *make* too much noise *are necessary*.

After such verbs as **sperare** *to hope*, **dire** *to say*, **affermare** *to affirm*, **dichiarare** *to declare*, use of the subjunctive implies that the speaker doubts the accuracy or likelihood of the declaration or hope:

Speriamo che **venga**.	We *hope* that he'll *come* (*but rather doubt, it*).
Dice che il treno **sia** in ritardo.	He *says* that the train *is* late (*that's what he says, but I'm not sure of it*).

Use of a non-subjunctive implies that the speaker accepts what is said:

Speriamo che **verrà**	We *hope* that he *will come* (*and think he will*).
Dice che il treno é in ritardo.	He *says* that the train *is* late (*and I see no reason to doubt it.*)

Foto ISTO

"Viaggiare in aèreo è più piacevole che viaggiare in 'autobus."
Acroporto Leonardo da Vinci, Roma

🌑 61. TERM OF COMPARISON OTHER THAN NOUN OR PRONOUN.

After a comparative, the term of comparison is normally introduced by **di** *than*, if it is a noun or a pronoun (*cf.* Grammar Unit **VIII**, *Sec.* **27**). If the term of comparison is not a noun or a pronoun, it is normally introduced by **che** in the meaning of *than*.

Viaggiare in màcchina è più piacévole **che** viaggiare in treno.	To travel by auto is more pleasant *than* to travel by train.
Generalmente sono più noiosi **che** altro.	Generally they are more annoying *than* [they are] anything else.
Questo viaggio è più lungo **che** interessante.	This trip is more long *than* [it is] interesting.

⬤ 62. Prepositions and Prepositional Phrases.

Most Italian prepositions are fairly close in meaning to certain other preposi-
tions in English: *e.g.*, **a** *to*, **di** *of*, **con** *with*, **su** *on*, *etc*. However, other Italian
prepositions have meanings which cannot be translated by single words in
English: *e.g.*, **da** *at my house* and also *suitable for, fit for*:

scarpe **da** uomo	shoes *for* men (*suitable for men*)
Mangeremo **da** mio zio.	We'll eat *at* my uncle's (*house*).
Compreremo **da** mangiare.	We'll buy (*something*) to eat.

Particularly with verbs, many Italian prepositions have uses which do not
correspond to their literal English equivalents:

pensare **a** qualche cosa	to think *of* [= direct one's thoughts to-wards] something.
Roma fu fondata **da** Romolo e Remo.	Rome was founded *by* Romulus and Remus.
Dobbiamo guardare il nùmero **sul -** l'elenco	We'll have to look up the number *in* (*literally*, on) the telephone book.

In Italian as in English, there are many sequences of two, three or four words
(usually ending in **di** *of*) which have the same function as single prepositions:

Loro è **al di là di** questa collina.	Loro *is beyond* this hill.
C'è un paese **prima di** Loro?	Is there a town *before* Loro?
L'ufficio postale è **di fronte** alla stazione.	The post office is *opposite* the station.

⬤ 63. Elision.

Elision, or the loss of an unstressed vowel before a following vowel (normally
symbolized in writing by an apostrophe), is obligatory in modern Italian only
with certain forms of the definite and indefinite article (*cf.* Grammar Unit **I**,
Sec. **1** and **2**). With other forms, it is normally optional in present-day usage.
In speech, two like vowels are usually run together into a single vowel sound;
but in writing, they may be written separately even when two like vowels are
in adjacent words.

Mi ha visto (*or* **M'ha visto**).	He has seen me.
Glielo invìdio (*or* **Gliel'invìdio**).	I envy you it.
Ci é entrato (*or* **C'é entrato**).	He went in there.
le ferrovìe d'Italia	the railways of Italy

Grammatical Exercises

A. SUBSTITUTIONS.

1. *Combine as many of the expressions on the left with as many of those on the right as possible, to form dependent clauses using the subjunctive to indicate a desired characteristic:*

[1]Cércano *they're seeking*

[2]desìdera *she desires*

[3]occorre (occórrono) *is (are) necessary*

[4]vorremmo trovare *we'd like to find*

[5]vuoi? *do you want?*

[1]una donna che non chiàcchiera *a woman who doesn't jabber*

[2]un marito che non fuma *a husband who doesn't smoke*

[3]un'orchestra che suona bène *an orchestra that plays well*

[4]delle persone che ci stanno ad ascoltare *some persons who listen to us*

[5]degli studenti che tàcciono *some students who are silent*

[6]dei treni che arrìvano in oràrio *trains that arrive on time.*

2. *Combine the verb forms on the left with the clauses on the right, to form sentences containing subjunctives indicating doubt:*

[1]afferma *he affirms*
[2]dichiari? *do you declare?*

[3]dìcono *they say*

[4]spero *I hope*

[1]è vero *it's true*
[2]il professore non fa nulla *the professor isn't doing anything*
[3]questi discorsi non hanno nessun significato *this talk hasn't any meaning*
[4]non costa troppo *it doesn't cost too much.*

3. *On the model of* **È più buono che cattivo** He (it) is more good than bad, *form sentences with the following pairs of adjectives:*

[1]biondo *blond* — bruno *dark-haired*
[2]brutto *ugly* — bello *beautiful*
[3]diffìcile *difficult* — facile *easy*
[4]divertente *amusing* — noioso *tiresome*
[5]freddo *cold* — caldo *hot*
[6]gòtico *Gothic* — barocco *baroque*

4. *On the model of* **È meno interessante dormire che mangiare** (It is less interesting to sleep than to eat), *form sentences with the following pairs of infinitives*:

¹capire *to understand* — interpretare *to interpret*
²chiùdere una porta *to close a door* — aprirla *to open it*
³far colazione *to breakfast* — cenare *to have supper*
⁴restare a casa *to stay at home* — viaggiare *to travel*
⁵tacere *to he silent* — chiacchierare *to chatter*
⁶tornare *to return* — partire *to depart*

B. PROGRESSIVE VARIATION. *Say or write in Italian:*

(1) ¹Here is a boy who wants to work.
²We need a boy who wants to work.
³We need a boy who can work.
⁴I've found a boy who can work.
⁵I've found a conductor who understands the orchestra.
⁶I'm looking for a conductor who understands the orchestra.
⁷I'm looking for some cigarettes that aren't too strong.
⁸I've bought some cigarettes that aren't too strong.
⁹I've bought a book that is interesting.
¹⁰She needs (= to her is necessary) a book that is interesting.
¹¹She needs a husband who wants to work.
¹²She has a husband who wants to work.
¹³Here is a husband who wants to work.
¹⁴Here is a boy who wants to work.

(2) ¹Florence is more interesting than Rome.
²Florence is more interesting than beautiful.
³To travel is more interesting than beautiful.
⁴To travel is more interesting than to work.
⁵To travel is less interesting than to work.
⁶To travel is less agreeable than to work.
⁷To travel is less agreeable than expensive.
⁸Florence is less agreeable than expensive.
⁹Florence is less agreeable than Rome.
¹⁰Florence is less interesting than Rome.
¹¹Florence is more interesting than Rome.

(3) ¹The restaurant is opposite the hotel.
²The restaurant is next to the hotel.
³The tobacconist's is next to the hotel.
⁴The tobacconist's is in the hotel.
⁵The tobacconist's is in the station.
⁶The tracks are in the station.
⁷The tracks are beyond the station.
⁸The street is beyond the station.
⁹The street is beyond the garden.
¹⁰There's a house beyond the garden.
¹¹There's a house opposite the garden.
¹²There's a restaurant opposite the garden.
¹³There's a restaurant opposite the hotel.
¹⁴The restaurant is opposite the hotel.

C. *Say or write in Italian:*

1. I'll go to Aversa or to Ostia.   2. Is it better to complain than to suffer?
   3. Give me seven or eight of them.   4. I've never had the opportunity to
   talk to him.
5. Please give me some cigarettes that (such that they) are not too strong.
   6. All depends on the meaning of this letter. 7. This city is more beautiful
   than cordial.   8. Do you like standing in the midst of that crush?   9.
   Tell (**voi**) it to me in words of one syllable.
10. She feels (that she is) more on a vacation than on a trip.

Foto Stefani — Monkmeyer

CONVERSATION UNIT————33

At the Beach

Fulvia, Anna, Silvana and Pietro are at the beach at Ostia, with Mrs. Tucci and her little son Paoletto.

FULVIA — ¹Avanti, venite a fare il bagno, ché l'acqua è un brodo.

ANNA — ²Tu dici sempre così perché non hai mai freddo. ³Ma sai che io sono una freddolosa!

PIETRO — ⁴Va bene, andiamo. ⁵Venga anche Lei, signora, si faccia corragio.

FULVIA — ¹Come on, come and go bathing, for the water is quite warm.

ANNA — ²You always say that because you're never cold. ³But you know that I'm a chilly one!

PETER — ⁴O.K., let's go. ⁵You come too, ma'am, be brave,

SIG.RA TUCCI — [6]No, ragazzi, io resto qui a préndere il sole. [7]Voglio abbronzarmi un po' prima di tornare in città.

SILVANA — [8]Anche la signora ha la mania della tintarella, eh? [9]Non si scotti, però, altrimenti ci son dolori! [10]Possiamo portare Paoletto con noi a nuotare?

SIG.RA TUCCI — [11]Certamente, grazie mille. [12]Ma tu, Paoletto, non starci troppo dentro, ché hai ancora un po' di tosse. [13]Poi quando esci dall'acqua, càmbiati sùbito il costume. [14]Hai capito?

PAOLETTO — [15]Va bene, mammina. [16]Ora làsciami andare sùbito, però. [17]Andiamo?

PIETRO — [18]Noleggiamo una barca? [19]Così andiamo a nuotare al largo e ci tuffiamo dove l'acqua è più pulita.

ANNA — [20]Ecco là il bagnino che dà a nolo i pattini. [21]Accipìcchia, quanto brucia la sàbbia!

FULVIA — [22]Ti sei messa abbastanza crema sulla pelle? [23]Se no, domani sarai tutta scottata. [24]Méttiti anche qualcosa in testa per protèggerti dal sole.

MRS. TUCCI — [6]No, kids, I'll stay here and take a sun bath. [7]I want to get tanned a little before going back to town.

SILVANA — [8]You've got the sun-tan craze too, have you, ma'am? [9]Don't get burned though, otherwise it hurts! [10]May we take Paoletto with us to swim?

MRS. TUCCI — [11]Certainly, thanks a lot. [12]But you, Paoletto, don't stay in too much, for you still have a bit of cough. [13]Then when you come out of the water, change your bathing suit immediately. [14]Have you understood?

PAOLETTO — [15]O.K., mommy. [16]But let me go now right away, though. [17]Shall we go?

PETER — [18]Shall we hire a boat? [19]In that way we'll go and swim farther out, and we'll dive where the water's cleaner.

ANNA — [20]There's the beach attendant who rents out the rowboats. [21]Golly, how the sand burns!

FULVIA — [22]Did you put enough cream on your skin? [23]If not, tomorrow you'll be all burned. [24]Put something on your head, too, to protect you from the sun.

NOTES

1. **l'acqua è un brodo**, literally *the water is a broth*.
2. **freddoloso** (*adj.*), literally *chilly*.
3. Sentence 8 = literally *The lady, too, has the craze for sun tan, eh?* In very courteous speech, persons spoken to are often referred to by their titles, in the third person.
4. **altrimenti ci son dolori**, literally *otherwise there are pains*.

VERB FORMS

protèggere   *to protect*: past absolute **protessi, proteggesti**, *etc.*; past participle **protetto**.

Esercizi

A. *Risponda in italiano alle seguenti domande basate sul testo:*

1. Perché vuole Fulvia che i suoi amici vèngano a fare il bagno? 2. Com'è l'acqua? 3. Sente il freddo Fulvia? 4. Anna lo sente? 5. Che cosa vuol Fulvia che la Sig.ra Tucci venga a fare? 6. Che cosa decide la Sig.ra Tucci? 7. Che cosa vuol fare la signora? 8. Che mania ha la signora Tucci? 9. Che cosa le dice Silvana di evitare? 10. Che cosa domanda Silvana alla sig.ra Tucci? 11. Che cosa dice la signora a Paoletto? 12. Che cosa risponde Paoletto? 13. Che cosa vuol fare Pietro? 14. Perché vuole che vàdano a nuotare al largo? 15. Chi dà a nolo i pattini? 16. Com'è la sabbia? 17. Che cosa accade, se non ci mettiamo abbastanza crema sulla pelle? 18. Perché si mette qualche cosa anche sulla testa?

B. *Domandi a un altro studente (a un'altra studentessa):*

1. di venire a fare il bagno. 2. se non ha mai freddo. 3. se è un freddoloso (una freddolosa). 4. se vuol préndere il sole. 5. se ha la mania della tintarella. 6. se si è scottato (scottata). 7. se ha un po' di tosse. 8. se vuol noleggiare una barca. 9. dove vuol andare a nuotare. 10. dove vuol tuffarsi. 11. chi dà a nolo i pattini. 12. se si è messo (messa) della crema sulla pelle. 13. se si é messo (messa) qualcosa in testa.

C. *Dica a un altro studente (a un'altra studentessa):*

1. che Lei non ha mai freddo. 2. di farsi coraggio. 3. che Lei vuol abbronzarsi. 4. che Lei non ha la mania della tintarella. 5. di non scottarsi. 6. di non stare troppo dentro all'acqua. 7. di cambiarsi il costume quando sarà uscito dall'acqua. 8. di lasciarLa andare sùbito. 9. che Lei non si è messo (messa) abbastanza crema sulla pelle. 10. che domani Lei sarà tutto scottato.

D. Revisione del Congiuntivo (Review of the Subjunctive). *Dica o scriva in italiano:*

1. Let him go bathing. 2. Do not let them get tanned. 3. I need a cream which will protect me (such that it protect me) from the sun. 4. We're looking for a place where the water is clean. 5. Although I have gotten tanned, I have not burned myself. 6. Where is a beach attendant who (such that he) rents rowboats?

E. *Dica o scriva in italiano:*

1. The water was quite warm. 2. They're often cold. 3. We don't want to be courageous! 4. Put on your bathing suit before going to swim.
5. They took Anna and Silvana with them to swim. 6. He has hired a boat.
7. They went to swim farther out. 8. The pain was very strong. 9. The sand has burned my feet (= has burned to me the feet).
10. I used to have the craze for sun tan.

F. CONVERSATIONS:

1. Two or more persons talk about the sun tan craze and the harm that can result if one doesn't use enough cream, doesn't put something on one's head, *etc.*
2. Scene at a beach: One or more persons rent a boat from a beach attendant and talk about what they intend to do (swim farther out, dive, *etc.*) .

A Recent Movie

Peter has been too busy studying to go to the movies, but decides he must see the one recommended by Anna.

ANNA — ¹Sei andato a vedere *Marco e le sue Sorelle?*

PIETRO — ²No, cos'è? ³Di chi è?

ANNA — ⁴Ma dove vivi — sulla luna? ⁵Non hai letto i giornali ultimamente?

PIETRO — ⁶Dovessi dirti la verità, no. ⁷Sono stato molto occupato con lo studio.

ANNA — ⁸È un film molto discusso, ma *Il Messaggero* ne ha fatto una recensione bellissima. ⁹Devi assolutamente andarci, sai? ¹⁰A mio parere, è uno dei film più belli che abbia mai visto.

PIETRO — ¹¹È per caso quello di Giorgio Casagrande? ¹²Ah sì, ora mi ricordo di averne sentito parlare. ¹³Ma temevo di non capire niente perché pàrlano in dialetto.

ANNA — ¹⁴Non dar retta a nessuno. ¹⁵Lo capirai benìssimo.

PIETRO — ¹⁶Ma cos'è che ti ha colpito e commosso tanto in questo film?

ANNA — ¹Did you go to see *Mark and His Sisters?*

PETER — ²No, what is it? ³Whose is it?

ANNA — ⁴But where are you living — on the moon? ⁵Haven't you read the newspapers recently?

PETER — ⁶[Should I have] to tell you the truth, no. ⁷I've been very busy [with] studying.

ANNA — ⁸It's a very much talked about film, but *The Messagero* gave it a very fine review. ⁹You absolutely must go and see it, do you know? ¹⁰In my opinion, it's one of the most beautiful films I've ever seen.

PETER — ¹¹Is it, by chance, the one by Giorgio Casagrande? ¹²Ah, yes now I remember that I've heard [people] tell of it. ¹³But I was afraid I wouldn't understand anything because they speak in dialect.

ANNA — ¹⁴Don't pay attention to anybody. ¹⁵You'll understand it very well.

PETER — ¹⁶But what is it that has struck you and moved you so much in this film?

La Stampa,
10.21.62

al Cine **CORSO**
GIOVEDI' 25 OTTOBRE
L'ATTESISSIMA «PRIMA»

DINO DE LAURENTIIS PRESENTA

ALBERTO
SORDI
mafioso

con
NORMA BENGELL   REGIA DI **ALBERTO LATTUADA**
PRODOTTO DA **ANTONIO CERVI**

ANNA — [17]Non vorrei sciupàrtelo raccontàndotelo. [18]Ma ti assicuro che per me Casagrande ha colto dei punti fondamentali della nostra società. [19]Non solo, ma li ha sviluppati con tanta sensibilità e profondità che ne ha fatto un'òpera d'arte, un vero capolavoro.

PIETRO — [20]Devo proprio vederlo allora. [21]E gli attori come sono? [22]Rècitano bene?

ANNA — [23]Altroché, la recitazione è superba e anche la fotografìa è eccellente.

ANNA — [17]I wouldn't want to spoil it for you by telling it to you. [18]But I assure you that, for me, Casagrande has grasped some fundamental points of our society. [19]Not only [that], but he has developed them with so much sensitivity and profundity that he has made of it a work of art, a real masterpiece.

PETER — [20]I really must see it, then. [21]And how are the actors? [22]Do they act well?

ANNA — [23]Of course, the acting is superb and the photography is excellent too.

NOTES

1. **Devi assolutamente andarci,** literally *you must absolutely go there.*
2. **Un film molto discusso,** literally *a much discussed film.*

**cò
gliere**	*to grasp, seize, take hold of*: present **colgo, cogli, coglie, cogliamo, cogliete, còlgono**; present subjunctive **colga, cogliamo, cogliate, còlgano**; past absolute **colsi, cogliesti**, *etc.*; past participle **colto**.
colpire	*to strike*. II-*isc*.
commuovere	*to move* (emotionally): like **muòvere**.
discùtere	*to discuss*: past absolute **discussi, discutesti**, *etc.*; past participle **discusso**.

Esercizi

A. *Risponda in italiano alle seguenti domande basate sul testo:*

1. Quale film ha visto Anna? 2. Di chi è questo film? 3. Che cosa ne pensa Anna? 4. Ne ha sentito parlare Pietro?
5. Perché non è andato a vederlo? 6. Perché non glielo racconta Anna? 7. Che cosa crede che Casagrande abbia fatto in questo film? 8. Che cosa ne ha fatto? 9. Che cosa fanno gli attori?
10. Com'è la recitazione e la fotografia di questo film?

B. *Domandi a un altro studente (a un'altra studentessa):*

1. Che cos'è *Marco e le sue Sorelle*. 2. di chi è. 3. se ne ha sentito parlare.
4. se ha letto i giornali ultimamente.
5. se vive sulla luna. 6. se teme di non capire i film parlati in dialetto. 7. che cosa l'ha colpito in questo film. 8. come sono gli attori. 9. se la fotografia è buona.

C. *Dica a un altro studente (a un'altra studentessa):*

1. che Lei ha visto un òttimo film. 2. che ne ha letto una recensione bellìssima. 3. che non dà retta a nessuno. 4. che Le piàcciono i film fatti con sensibilità e profondità.
5. che Lei è stato (stata) commosso (commossa) dal film. 6. che Lei teme di non capire un film in cùi pàrlano in dialetto. 7. che Lei rècita bene. 8. che Lei è molto occupato con lo studio.

D. REVISIONE DEL COMPARATIVO E DEL SUPERLATIVO. *Dica o scriva in italiano:*

1. This film is better than that one.   2. It is better to speak in Italian than in dialect.   3. The film has been made more with sensitivity than with profundity.   4. This is the most beautiful film that I've ever seen.
5. This is a very beautiful film (*do not use* **molto bello**).   6. The sun is less beautiful than the moon   7. She is less occupied than I.   8. This is the most fundamental point of their society.   9. Casagrande acts better than Martucci.
10. They have travelled more in Italy than in the United States.

E. *Dica o scriva in italiano:*

1. They always tell the truth.   2. The newspapers have made very fine reviews of these films.   3. In your society, do the newspapers dare to (**di**) tell the truth?   4. These films move me very much.
5. Why don't they pay attention to us?   6. They're afraid that they won't understand anything.   7. The best works of art are called masterpieces.
8. She spoiled the film for me by telling me about it (to to me).   9. Have you heard tell about those films?
10. We're very busy (with) studying.

F. CONVERSATIONS:

1. You ask your friend whether he (she) has been to this concert, seen that film, *etc.* It turns out that he (she) has been too busy studying and you tease him (her) about not knowing what's happening, living on the moon, *etc.*
2. You talk about recent films, which ones you have or haven't seen, and whether they have moved you or not, and why.

64. THE PAST SUBJUNCTIVE.

The past subjunctive of almost all Italian verbs is regular and formed according to the following pattern:

THE PAST SUBJUNCTIVE		
FIRST CONJUGATION	SECOND CONJUGATION	THIRD CONJUGATION
recitare *to act*	**dormire** *to sleep*	**vendere** *to sell*
recit-	**dorm-**	**vend-**
recit**assi** *(that)* I recited, etc.	dorm**issi** *(that)* I slept, etc.	vend**essi** *(that)* I sold, etc.
recit**assi**	dorm**issi**	vend**essi**
recit**asse**	dorm**isse**	vend**esse**
recit**àssimo**	dorm**ìssimo**	vend**éssimo**
recit**aste**	dorm**iste**	vend**este**
recit**àssero**	dorm**ìssero**	vend**éssero**

All Italian past subjunctives are formed with the endings shown in the above paradigms: **-ssi, -ssi, -sse; -ssimo, -ste, -ssero.** A few verbs have special stem forms to which these endings are added:

dare	to give	**dessi,** *etc.*
éssere	to be	**fossi,** *etc.*
stare	to stand, be located	**stessi,** *etc.*

In the case of verbs with shortened infinitives, it is of course the main root of the verb to which the past subjunctive endings are added.

dire	to say	**dicessi,** *etc.*
fare	to do, make	**facessi,** *etc.*

In independent clauses, the past subjunctive is normally used to express a wish contrary to fact (*Oh, that ... would ...* or *Would that ... were ...* ,) often with the emphasizing adverb **pure** *indeed* or with the introductory word **magari,** which gives a slightly optimistic tone to the wish.

Venìssero pure!	*Oh, that* they *would come!*
Magari **venìssero!**	If they *would* only *come!* (Implication: it would be nice if they'd come, and perhaps they might even do so.)
Fosse pur vero!	I only wish it *were* true (*were* it but true)!
Lavorasse almeno un poco!	If he *would work* at least a little!

The past subjunctive can, on occasion, also indicate a condition contrary to fact without the introductory conjunction **se** *if*.

Dovessi dirti la verità.	*If I had* to tell you the truth.

In dependent clauses, the past subjunctive has two chief uses. It takes the place of a present subjunctive, automatically, if the main verb of the sentence is in a past tense (or also, in conservative usage, in the conditional):

MAIN VERB IN PRESENT OR FUTURE	MAIN VERB IN A PAST TENSE
Voglio che **venga** (*I want* that he come) *I want* him *to come.*	**Volevo** che **venisse.** (*I wanted* that he come) *I wanted* him *to come.*
Non **dico** che **sia** vero. *I don't* say that it *is* true.	No **ho detto** che **fosse** vero. I *have* not said that it *was* true.
Mi **pare** che questo **sia** giusto. It *seems* to me that this *is* right.	Non mi **era** parso che questo **fosse** giusto. It *had* not seemed to me that this *was* right.
Non **so** se **sia** *arrivato. I don't* know whether he *has* arrived.	Non **sapevo** se **fosse** arrivato. I *did* not *know* whether he *had* arrived.

The other main use of the past subjunctive in dependent clauses is after **se** *if,* referring to conditions which are contrary to fact, when the main verb of the sentence is in the conditional:

Se non mi fossi messa abbastanza crema sulla pelle, mi sarei scottata.	*If I hadn't put* enough cream on my skin, I'd have gotten burned.
Se avéssimo centomila dollari, saremmo contenti.	*If we had* a hundred thousand dollars, we'd be happy.
Noleggerèbbero una barca, **se potéssero.**	They'd hire a boat, *if they could.*

● 65. Transformations of Dependent Clauses.

If an Italian clause with a given subject is dependent on such a verb as **dire** *to say* (**dichiarare** *to declare*, **affermare** *to affirm, etc.*) or **crédere** *to believe* with the same subject, then the verb of the dependent clause is replaced by an infinitive introduced by **di**.

Luisa dice Louise says + **Luisa è stanca** Louise is tired > **Luisa dice di èssere stanca.** Louise says she's tired. (*lit.* Louise says of being tired).

Questi signori afférmano These gentlemen affirm + **Questi signori sono italiani** These gentlemen are Italian > **Questi signori afférmano di èssere italiani.** These gentlemen affirm that they are Italian (*lit.* ... of being Italian).

Non credo I don't believe + **ho delle idee fisse** I have fixed ideas > **Non credo di aver idee fisse.** I don't believe I have fixed ideas.

Because of this Italian pattern of transformation, Italians speaking English often produce such sentences as *She says of being tired.* = *She says she's tired.*

On the other hand, there is a certain English dependent-clause transformation which has no counterpart in Italian: *e.g.,* *I want* + *he does it* > *I want him to do it.* Here an English subject and verb are replaced by an object + infinitive phrase when they depend on such verbs as *want, desire, etc.* In Italian, such a transformation cannot take place. Clauses dependent on **volere, desiderare,** *etc.,* must be introduced by **che** *that*, and the dependent verb transformed into the appropriate tense of the subjunctive.

Voglio I want + **lo fa** he does it > **Voglio che lo faccia.** I want that he do it = I want him to do it.

Volevo I wanted + **lo fa** he does it > **Volevo che lo facesse.** I wanted that he do it = I wanted him to do it.

Desìderano *They desire* + **state ad ascoltare** you listen > **Desìderano che stiate ad ascoltare.** They want that you listen = They want you to listen.

● 66. Pro-Complements in Modal Phrases.

The verbs **dovere** *to have to*, **potere** *to be able to* and **volere** *to want to* are called *modal auxiliaries* (Grammar Unit **III**, *Sec.* **11**), and phrases formed of one of these modal auxiliaries + a dependent infinitive are known as *modal phrases.* If the dependent verb in a modal phrase has one or two pro-complements, the pro-complement(s) may either precede the modal auxiliary and be written as a separate word, or follow the infinitive and be suffixed to it. Thus:

Non lo **posso soffrire** _or_ Non **posso soffrirlo.**   I can't stand it.

Ne **vorremmo comprare** cinque _or_ **Vorremmo comprarne** cinque.   We'd like to buy five of them.

Ci deve tornare _or_ **Deve tornarci.**   He was to go back there.

Grammatical Exercises

A. TRANSFORMATIONS.

1. _Transform each of the following sentences into the past, making the main verb imperfect and making the necessary adjustments in the dependent subjunctive verbs_:

[1]Bisogna che ci vada.	_It's necessary that he go there._
[2]Mi pare che ci sia più ritardo del sòlito.	_It seems to me that there's more delay than usual._
[3]Crede che il treno sia il mezzo migliore.	_He thinks the train is the best means of transportation._
[4]Vògliono che tu lavori.	_They want you to work._
[5]Benché arriviamo in ritardo, non siamo stanchi.	_Although we're arriving late, we're not tired._
[6]Non credete che il treno arrivi in orario?	_Don't you think the train's arriving on time?_
[7]Spero che venga.	_I hope he'll come._
[8]Cércano una casa che sia vicina al mare.	_They're looking for a house that's near the sea._
[9]Credete che occorra partire?	_Do you think it's necessary to depart?_
[10]Vi dispiace che partiamo?	_Are you sorry that we're leaving?_

2. _Transform the following statements into wishes contrary to fact, using the past subjunctive_:

[1]Non ho sbagliato strada.	_I've not taken the wrong road._
[2]L'abbiamo vista a Roma.	_We have seen her in Rome._
[3]Mi sta ad ascoltare.	_She's listening to me._
[4]Non mi interpreti male.	_You don't misinterpret me._
[5]Schérzano.	_They're joking._
[6]Si arriva in oràrio.	_One arrives on time._
[7]Siamo in vacanza.	_We're on vacation._
[8]Non fanno tanto rumore.	_They're not making so much noise._
[9]Ti piace anche il barocco.	_You like the Baroque too._
[10]Sai nuotare.	_You know how to swim._

3. *Transform the sentences in the right-hand column into clauses depending on those in the left-hand and introduced by the conjuction* **se** *if*:

¹Lo faremmo. *We'd do it.*
²Viaggerebbe. *He'd travel.*
³Mi sarei scottato. *I'd be burned.*

⁴Potresti andare a nuotare. *You could go to swim.*
⁵Camminerebbe sulla sabbia? *Would you walk on the sand?*
⁶Il film mi piacerebbe. *I'd like the picture.*
⁷Sareste molto occupati. *You'd be very busy.*

¹Abbiamo il tempo. *We have the time.*
²È ricco. *He's rich.*
³Non mi metto abbastanza crema sulla pelle. *I don't put enough cream on my skin.*
⁴Non hai un po' di tosse. *You don't have a little bit of cough.*
⁵Non brucia. *It doesn't burn.*

⁶Gli attori rècitano bene. *The actors act well.*
⁷Studiate un poco. *You study a little.*

4. *Make the sentences in the right-hand column dependent on those in the left-hand column, assuming the subjects in each pair of clauses to be the same:*

¹Credo. *I believe.*
²Giovanni dice. *John says.*
³Temiamo. *We're afraid.*

⁴Mi pare. *It seems to me.*
⁵Affermava. *He used to affirm.*

¹Ho capito. *I've understood.*
²Vuol partire. *He wants to depart.*
³Non capiamo niente. *We don't understand anything.*
⁴So nuotare. *I know how to swim.*
⁵Aveva studiato a Roma. *He had studied at Rome.*

5. *In the following modal phrases, replace the direct or indirect object, or the phrase introduced by a preposition, by a pro-complement, framing each replacement sentence in two ways, on the model of* **Deve tornare a Firenze** > **Ci deve tornare** *or* **Deve tornarci.**

¹Può leggere il giornale.
²Dobbiamo comprare delle scarpe.
³Non potevamo vedere i nostri amici.
⁴Vuole andare a Firenze?
⁵Dovette véndere la casa.
⁶Vorreste mangiare in questa trattoria?

He can read the newspaper.
We have to buy some shoes.
We couldn't see our friends.
Do you want to go to Florence?
He had to sell the house.
Would you like to eat in this restaurant?

B. PROGRESSIVE VARIATIONS. *Say or write in Italian:*

(1) ¹He wants us to work.
²He wanted us to work.
³He wanted us to depart.
⁴They wanted us to depart.
⁵They wanted me to depart.
⁶You (**voi**) wanted me to depart.
⁷You believed that I was departing.
⁸You believed that you were departing.
⁹He believed that he *(himself)* was departing.
¹⁰He believed that he *(someone else)* was departing.
¹¹He believed that we were working.
¹²He wanted us to work.

(2) ¹If I take a sunbath, I get tanned.
²If I took a sunbath, I'd get tanned.
³If we took a sunbath, we'd get tanned.
⁴If we take a sunbath, we get tanned.
⁵If he takes a sunbath, he gets tanned.
⁶If he takes a sunbath, he gets sunburned.
⁷If he took a sunbath, he'd get sunburned.
⁸If he went to swim, he'd get sunburned.
⁹If they went to swim, they'd get sunburned.
¹⁰If they go to swim, they get sunburned.
¹¹If they take a sunbath, they get burned.
¹²If they took a sunbath, they'd get burned.
¹³If they took a sunbath, they'd get tanned.
¹⁴If I took a sunbath, I'd get tanned.

(3) ¹I want to see this film.
²I want to see it.
³We want to see it.
⁴We want him to see it.
⁵We wanted him to see it.
⁶He wanted to see it.
⁷He was able to see it.
⁸He thought he was able to see it.
⁹He thought he was able to see them.
¹⁰He thought he was able to see the films.
¹¹I thought I was able to see the films.
¹²I was able to see the films.
¹³I was able to see them.
¹⁴I wanted to see them.
¹⁵I wanted to see it.
¹⁶I wanted to see this film.
¹⁷I want to see this film.

C. *Say or write in Italian:*

1. If only the sand didn't burn!   2. If we hired a boat, we could swim where the water's clean.   3. I want him to change his bathing suit immediately. 4. Do you think you've made a real masterpiece?
5. I wouldn't want you to spoil it for me.   6. If the acting were really excellent, Casagrande would have made a work of art.   7. In my opinion, if he hasn't read the newspapers, he ought to read them.   8. They're afraid they won't see him.   9. Although he was tired, he continued to work.
10. Do you remember that you've seen that film?

Foto ISTO

Learning a Foreign Language

Peter finds irregular Italian nouns difficult to remember.

FULVIA — ¹A che cosa stai pensando? ²Sembra che hai qualche grosso problema da risòlvere.

PIETRO — ³Infatti non ti sbagli. ⁴Ti giuro che con questi sostantivi italiani non ci capisco proprio un bel niente.

FULVIA — ⁵Meno male che te ne accorgi adesso! ⁶Ma di che ti lamenti, tu che parli l'italiano così bene? ⁷Magari parlassi io l'inglese come tu parli l'italiano.

PIETRO — ⁸Sì, va bene, va bene, ma intanto perché prima hai detto: "ha le braccia lunghe come una scimmia", invece di dire "bracci"?

ANNA — ⁹Mio caro, perché **braccio** al plurale è irregolare, come **ginòcchio**, **ciglio**, **orècchio**, **uovo**, **lenzuolo**, eccètera.

FULVIA — ¹What are you thinking of? ²It seems that you have some big problem to solve.

PETER — ³In fact, you're not mistaken. ⁴I swear to you that I can't make head or tail out of these Italian nouns.

FULVIA — ⁵It's a good thing that you're noticing it now! ⁶But what are you complaining about, you who speak Italian so well? ⁷If I could only speak English as well as you speak Italian!

PETER — ⁸Yes, O.K., O.K., but meanwhile why did you say earlier "He has arms (**braccia**) as long as a monkey," instead of saying **bracci**?

ANNA — ⁹My dear fellow, because **braccio** is irregular in the plural, like **ginòcchio** (knee), **ciglio** (eyelash), **orècchio** (ear), **uovo** (egg), **lenzuolo** (sheet), etc.

PIETRO — ¹⁰E come si fa a ricordarli tutti?

ANNA — ¹¹Avanti, non fare storie. ¹²Basta imparàrseli a memòria.

PIETRO — ¹³E ti sembra fàcile, no?

ANNA — ¹⁴Certo, facilìssimo. ¹⁵Intanto ricòrdati che l'irregolarità in queste parole è costante: genere maschile per il singolare e femminile per il plurale. ¹⁶A volte, però, queste parole hanno anche il plurale regolare — con un significato diverso, naturalmente. ¹⁷Così, per esempio, si dice: "i bracci del lume" o "i cigli della strada" e così via. ¹⁸Consòlati, però, perché ci sono anche irregolarità di altro tipo.

PIETRO — ¹⁹Basta, per carità! ²⁰Ne ho abbastanza per questa volta.

PETER — ¹⁰And what does one do to remember them all?

ANNA — ¹¹Come on, don't make a fuss. ¹²It's enough to learn them by heart.

PETER — ¹³And that seems easy to you, doesn't it?

ANNA — ¹⁴Certainly, very easy. ¹⁵Meanwhile remember that the irregularity in these words is constant: masculine gender for the singular and feminine for the plural. ¹⁶Sometimes, however, these words have the regular plural too—with a different meaning, naturally. ¹⁷Thus, for example, one says "The arms (**bracci**) of the lamp" or "the edges (**cigli**) of the road", and so on. ¹⁸Console yourself, however, because there are irregularities of other kinds too.

PETER — ¹⁹Enough, for heaven's sake! ²⁰I have enough of it for this time.

NOTES

1. Sentence 4, literally *I swear to you that with these Italian nouns I don't understand in it absolutely ·a fine nothing.*
2. **Meno male**, literally *not so bad*; used when one feels that a situation is turning out better than might be expected.
3. **Braccio** and the other nouns mentioned in sentence 9 all have plurals ending in -a: **braccia, ginòcchia**, *etc.* (*cf.* Grammar Unit **IX**, *Sec.* **33**). As pointed out in sentence 16, many of these nouns also have regular masculine plurals in -i, normally with special or transferred meaning.
4. **Non fare storie**, literally *Don't make histories* (an imitation of French **faire des histoires** *to make a fuss*).

VERB FORMS

accorgersi	*to notice*: past absolute **mi accorsi, ti accorgesti**, *etc.*; past participle **accorto** (**mi sono accorto -a** *I have noticed, etc.*)
risòlvere	*to resolve*: past absolute **risolsi, risolvesti**, *etc.*; past participle **risolto**

Esercizi

A. *Risponda alle seguenti domande basate sul testo:*

1. Che cosa vuol sapere Fulvia da Pietro? 2. Si sbaglia Fulvia? 3. Capisce i sostantivi italiani Pietro? 4. Quando se n'è accorto?
5. Che cosa vorrebbe poter fare Fulvia? 6. Che cosa ha detto Fulvia poco prima? 7. Che cosa spiega Anna a Pietro sul plurale dei sostantivi come "braccio"? 8. Pietro trova fàcile ricordare tutti i plurali irregolari? 9. I plurali femminili in -a sono le sole forme (*forms*) irregolari in italiano?
10. È soddisfatto Pietro?

B. *Domandi a un altro studente (a un'altra studentessa):*

1. a che cosa sta pensando. 2. se ha qualche problema da risòlvere. 3. se ha risolto il suo problema. 4. se si è accorto del suo problema.
5. se capisce i sostantivi italiani. 6. di che cosa si lamenta. 7. perché si dice "braccia" invece di "bracci", o "uova" invece di "uovi". 8. se la parola "sostantivo" è irregolare al plurale. 9. come si fa a ricordare tutti i plurali irregolari.
10. qual'è il plurale di "il braccio del lume". 11. qual'è il plurale di "il ciglio della strada". 12. se ci sono anche irregolarità di altro tipo.

C. *Dica a un altro studente (a un'altra studentessa):*

1. che Lei ha un grosso problema da risòlvere. 2. che lo risolverà domani.
3. che Lei non si sbaglia mai. 4. che Lei se n'è già accorto.
5. che Lei non fa storie. 6. che Le sembra fàcile imparare a memória le forme irregolari. 7. che il gènere di "braccio" è maschile per il singolare e femminile per il plurale. 8. che Lei non si consola. 9. che delle irregolarità, Lei ne ha avuto abbastanza per questa volta.

D. Revisione del Passato del Congiuntivo (Review of the past subjunctive). *Dica o scriva in italiano:*

1. If Italian didn't have these irregular plurals, I'd understand it more easily.
2. If only I had learned them by heart! 3. It seemed to me that it wasn't easy. 4. If they would only console themselves!
5. I wasn't saying that the irregularity in these plurals was constant. 6. If the regular plurals didn't have a different meaning, we wouldn't make such a fuss (= so many stories). 7. If we could only speak Italian as they speak English!

E. *Dica o scriva in italiano:*

1. We won't make a fuss.   2. Are there eggs in this salad?   3. Has she made a mistake?   4. She was always complaining and making a fuss.
5. The monkey's arms were long.   6. We haven't learned these words by heart.   7. We never learn anything by heart.   8. I'm looking for some monkeys which (such that they) have long ears.   9. I don't think that there are any.
10. Why are you on your (= the) knees?

F. CONVERSATIONS:

1. Two or more people discuss the trouble they have learning the irregularities of Italian.
2. Two or more people argue as to whether Italian is better than English.

LETTURA SETTIMA

Foto ISTO

Un Concerto a Castel Sant'Angelo[1]

(Conversations 31-35)

¹Castel Sant'Àngelo the modern name for the mausoleum of Hadrian, located on the right bank of the Tiber in Rome, near the Vatican. During the Middle Ages it was a fortress.

²accettare, to accept.

³invito *(m.)* invitation.

⁴entusiasmo *(m.)* enthusiasm.

⁵informare to inform.

⁶brano *(m.)* piece, part.

⁷La Tosca an opera (1900) by Giàcomo Puccini (see below, n. 35); part of the scene of **Tosca** is set in Castel Sant'-Àngelo.

⁸adatto suited.

⁹illuminare to illuminate, light up.

¹⁰sfondo *(m.)* background.

¹¹cùpola *(f.)* cupola, dome.

¹²imponente imposing.

¹³scórrere to flow.

¹⁴lento slow; [*here*] slowly.

¹⁵silenzioso silent; [*here*] silently.

¹⁶ponte *(m.)* bridge.

¹⁷scala *(f.)* stair.

¹⁸piano soft(ly); **piano piano** very softly.

¹⁹quasi [*here*] as if *(conjunction)*.

²⁰rómpere to break.

²¹incanto *(m.)* enchantment.

²²salone *(m.)* salon.

²³arma *(f. pl.* **armi***)* arm, weapon.

²⁴addobare to deck out.

²⁵pianta *(f.)* plant.

²⁶tappeto *(m.)* carpet.

²⁷sèdia *(f.)* chair.

²⁸fondo *(m.)* back; **in fondo** at the back.

Una sera il dottor Dossi e sua moglie invìtano Fulvia e Pietro ad un concerto a Castel Sant'Àngelo. I ragazzi accèttano² l'invito³ con molto entusiasmo.⁴ "Sono davvero contento di questa occasione" — dice Pietro — "sono passato mille volte vicino a Castel Sant'Àngelo e non sono mai entrato. Finalmente lo vedrò anche dentro". Fulvia informa⁵ suo cugino che il concerto sarà vocale e che anche la figlia del Dossi vi prenderà parte. "Pensa che canterà brani⁶ della 'Tosca'⁷". Non c'è luogo più adatto⁸ per cantare la 'Tosca'.

Quella sera Castel Sant'Àngelo è tutto illuminato.⁹ Da dietro, sullo sfondo,¹⁰ si vede San Pietro con la sua cùpola¹¹ imponente,¹² mentre il fiume scorre¹³ lento¹⁴ e silenzioso¹⁵ sotto il ponte.¹⁶ Tutto è così tranquillo e sereno in quella notte di primavera che sembra quasi che il tempo si sia fermato per qualche sècolo.

Tutti sàlgono le scale¹⁷ di Castel Sant'-Àngelo piano piano¹⁸ quasi¹⁹ non volèssero rómpere²⁰ l'incanto.²¹

Il salone²² delle armi²³ è stato addobbato²⁴ per il concerto: vi hanno messo piante,²⁵ fiori, tappeti,²⁶ sèdie²⁷ e in fondo²⁸ un bellìssimo

Opera nel Teatro alla Scala

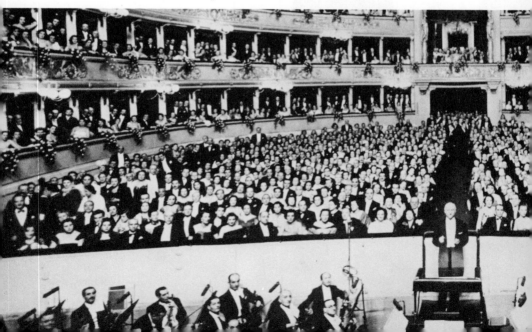

piano a coda.[29] All'entrata[30] si véndono i programmi: còstano duecento lire l'uno. Pietro e Fulvia ne cómprano uno che si divideranno.[31] C'è un bel programme: se eseguiranno[32] delle mùsiche[33] di Verdi,[34] Puccini,[35] Donizetti[36] e Mozart.[37]

L'orchestra attacca[38] le prime note[39] e tutti ascóltano con il fiato[40] sospeso.[41] Il fatto è che questi gióvani cantanti sono dei debuttanti[42] è l'udienza[43] è formata[44] per lo più[45] di parenti[46] e amici. "Saranno molto emozionati[47]" — bisbiglia[48] Fulvia all'orecchio di Pietro — "è la prima volta che càntano di fronte[49] a un pùbblico".

Nel complesso[50] la serata[51] va molto bene: i cantanti hanno tutti una bella voce anche se alcuni[52] dévono ancora studiare molto per sfruttarla[53] al màssimo.[54]

Tutti applàudono[55] con calore[56] e due dei cantanti, un tenore[57] e un soprano,[58] concédono[59] anche un bis.[60]

Dopo il concerto c'è un pìccolo rinfresco[61] in onore[62] delle gióvani promesse[63] del canto italiano. Anche Fulvia e Pietro vi partécipano[64] per congratularsi[65] con la sig.na Dossi, la quale, per la verità,[66] ha eseguito il suo pezzo[67] con moltà sensibilità[68] e freschezza.[69]

[29]**coda** *(f.)* tail; **piano a coda** grand piano.
[30]**entrata** *(f.)* entrance.
[31]**divìdere** to divide (**dividersi** to divide among themselves).
[32]**eseguire** (II/isc) to perform.
[33]**mùsica** *(f.)* music, piece of music.
[34]**Giuseppe Verdi** (1813-1901) the composer of **Rigoletto** (1851), **Il Trovatore** ("The Troubadour", 1853), **La Traviata** ("The Girl Who Went Wrong", 1853), **Aïda** (1871), and many other popular operas.
[35]**Giàcomo Puccini** (1856-1924) the composer of **La Bohème** ("Bohemian Life", 1896), **La Tosca** (1900), **Madame Butterfly** (1904), etc.
[36]**Gaetano Donizetti** (1797-1848), whose best-known opera is **Lucia di Lammermoor** (1835).
[37]**Wolfgang Amadeus Mozart** (1756-1791) the composer of **Don Giovanni** (1787), and many other operas.
[38]**attacare** to attack, strike up.
[39]**nota** *(f.)* note.
[40]**fiato** *(m.)* breath.
[41]**sospeso** suspended (**sospéndere** to suspend); **con il fiato sospeso** with bated breath.
[42]**debuttante** *(m. or f.)* person making a début (performing for the first time).
[43]**udienza** *(f.)* audience.
[44]**formare** to form.
[45]**per lo più** for the most part.
[46]**parente** *(m. or f.)* relative (NOT parent;).
[47]**emozionare** to thrill.
[48]**bisbigliare** to whisper.
[49]**di fronte a** facing.
[50]**nel complesso** taken as a whole.
[51]**serata** *(f.)* evening.
[52]**alcuni** *(m.; f.* **alcune**) some.
[53]**sfruttare** to exploit.
[54]**al màssimo** to the greatest extent.
[55]**applaudire** to applaud.
[56]**calore** *(m.)* warmth (**con calore** warmly).
[57]**tenore** *(m.)* tenor.
[58]**soprano** *(m.)* soprano.
[59]**concédere** to grant.
[60]**bis** *(m.)* encore; *a² adverb*, twice. To get an encore, Italian audiences shout "Bis! Bis!"
[61]**rinfresco** *(m.)* refreshment.
[62]**onore** *(m.)* honor.
[63]**promessa** *(f.)* promise; [*here*] future star.
[64]**partecipare a** to participate in.
[65]**congratularsi con** to congratulate.
[66]**verità** *(f.)* truth; **per la verità** to tell the truth.
[67]**pezzo** *(m.)* piece.
[68]**sensibilità** *(f.)* sensitivity.
[69]**freschezza** *(f.)* freshness.

Foto ISTO

The Italian Elections

Paul and Peter cannot see eye to eye on the Italian Elections.

PIETRO — ¹Pàolo, ti vedo piuttosto abbattuto. ²Non starai mica pensando ancora alle elezioni?

PÀOLO — ³E invece sì. ⁴Gli italiani mi hanno proprio deluso. ⁵Capisci che la campagna elettorale non ha smosso nessuno? ⁶Si cùllano sul borghesismo mediocre.

PIETRO — ⁷Via, non esagerare ora. ⁸In fondo hanno fatto tutti il loro dovere di cittadini.

PETER — ¹Paul, I see you rather dejected. ²You aren't still thinking of the elections?

PAUL — ³On the contrary, yes. ⁴The Italians have really disillusioned me. ⁵Do you understand that the electoral campaign didn't excite anybody? ⁶They're pinning their hopes on mediocre middle-class attitudes.

PETER — ⁷Come on, don't exaggerate now. ⁸In the last analysis, they've all done their duty as citizens.

Foto Morin — Monkmeyer

PÀOLO — [9]Fino ad un certo punto. [10]Infatti la percentuale dei votanti si è abbassata moltìssimo.

PIETRO — [11]Méttila come ti pare, tu vuoi l'impossìbile. [12]Io ti dico che il novanta per cento è una mèdia buonìssima. [13]A propòsito, dimmi, come si chiàmano le adunanze in cùi i candidati fanno dei discorsi in pùbblico?

PÀOLO — [14]Si chiàmano comizi. [15]Io non vedo l'ora che ci sìano le elezioni polìtiche.

PIETRO — [16]Che differenza c'è?

PÀOLO — [17]Quelle scorse èrano le amministrative. [18]Cioè, riguardàvano semplicemente l'amministrazione delle varie città e provincie. [19]Nelle pròssime, invece, si eleggeranno i deputati e i senatori. [20]E si formerà il nuovo governo.

PIETRO — [21]A me sembra che gli italiani non discùtano altro che di polìtica o di sport.

PAUL — [9]Up to a certain point. [10]In fact, the percentage of those voting has gone down very greatly.

PETER — [11]Put it as you wish, you want the impossible. [12]I tell you that ninety per cent is a very good average. [13]By the way, tell me, what's the name of the meetings in which the candidates make speeches in public?

PAUL — [14]They are called political meetings. [15]I can't wait for [there to be] the political elections.

PETER — [16]What difference is there?

PAUL — [17]Those just past were the administrative ones. [18]That is, they concerned simply the administration of the various cities and provinces. [19]In the forthcoming [elections], on the other hand, the deputies and senators will be elected [20]And the new government will be formed.

PETER — [21]It seems to me that the Italians don't talk about anything else but politics or sport.

NOTES

1. **si cùllano,** literally *they are cradling themselves.*
2. A **comìzio** (from the Latin **comitium**) is a special meeting held for making political speeches. To hold such a meeting and make an oration at it is **tenere un comìzio.**
3. **non vedo l'ora,** literally *I don't see the hour.*

VERB FORMS

delùdere   *to disappoint (not to delude!)*: past absolute **delusi, deludesti,** *etc.*; past participle **deluso**

elèggere   *to elect*: past absolute **elessi, eleggesti,** *etc.*; past participle **eletto**

smuòvere   *to move* (something or someone from a position): past absolute **smossi, smuovesti,** *etc.*; past participle **smosso**

Esercizi

A. *Risponda alle seguenti domande basate sul testo:*

1. Perché è abbattuto Paolo? 2. A che cosa pensa? 3. Che cosa pensa degli italiani? 4. Chi è stato smosso dalla campagna elettorale? 5. Su che cosa si cùllano? 6. Che cosa risponde Pietro a Pàolo? 7. Che cosa crede Pietro che tutti àbbiano fatto? 8. Che cosa è accaduto con la percentuale dei votanti? 9. Secondo Pietro, quale sarebbe una buona media?
10. Come si chiàmano le adunanze in cui si fanno dei discorsi elettorali? 11. Che differenza c'è tra le elezioni amministrative e quelle polìtiche? 12. In quali elezioni si elèggono i deputati e i senatori? 13. Di che cosa discùtono gli italiani?

B. *Domandi a un altro studente (a un'altra studentessa) :*

1. se è abbattuto (abbattuta) e perché. 2. se sta pensando alle elezioni. 3. se è mai stato deluso (stato delusa). 4. che cosa pensa della campagna elettorale. 5. di non esagerare. 6. se non vede l'ora che ci sìano le elezioni.

C. *Dica a un altro studente (a un'altra studentessa) :*

1. che Lei sta pensando alle elezioni. 2. che Lei non esàgera. 3. che Lei fa il suo dovere di cittadino. 4. che Lei non vuole l'impossìbile. 5. che Lei discute di molte cose, non solamente di polìtica o di sport.

D. REVISIONE DELLE CLÀUSOLE SUBORDINATE (Review of dependent clauses). *Dica o scriva in italiano:*

1. It seems to me that he wants the impossible. 2. It doesn't seem to me that I want the impossible. 3. I can't wait for them to leave for Italy. 4. I can't wait to leave for Italy. 5. Do you want to elect the deputies? 6. Do you want them to elect the deputies? 7. The Italians don't discuss anything but sports. 8. It seems me that the Italians don't discuss anything but sports.

E. *Dica o scriva in italiano:*

1. Do the electoral campaigns move people? 2. Up to a certain point, yes. 3. Fifty per cent is not a very good average. 4. The candidate held a political meeting.

Annunci politici, Bologna

5. The political elections don't concern the administration of the cities.   6.
When do the deputies and the senators form the new government?   7.
Are we doing our duty as citizens?   8. Why has the percentage of voters
gone down?   9. It goes down when people pin their hopes on middle-
class attitudes.

F. CONVERSATIONS:

1. Discussion of Italian parties and politics (look up in encyclopaedia or newspaper).
2. Comparison of Italian and American politics.

◐ 67. VERBS: ADJECTIVES IN -ante, -ente.

Adjectives ending in **-ante** (for **-are** verbs) or in **-ente** (for **-ire or -ere** verbs) can be formed from almost all verbs. They are inflected like other adjectives ending in **-e** (*cf.* Grammar Unit **IV**, *Sec.* **12**) and correspond, in general, to the *-ing* form of English verbs used as an adjective.

votare	to vote	**votante**	*voting*	**dormire**	to sleep	**dormente**	*sleeping*
cantare	to sing	**cantante**	*singing*	**vìvere**	to live	**vivente**	*living*
parlare	to talk	**parlante**	*talking*	**fare**	to do	**facente**	*making*

These forms can also be used as nouns, meaning *person or thing doing the action named by the verb*: e.g., **il votante** *the person voting, the voter*; **un cantante** *the singer*; and likewise in the feminine, *e.g.*, **una cantante** *a (woman) singer*.

◐ 68. VERB + PREPOSITION + INFINITIVE.

After a number of Italian verbs, a dependent infinitive must be introduced by a preposition, as in:

L'orchestra comincia **a suonare.**   The orchestra begins *to play*.
Ci vantiamo di **aver inventato** le grandi   We boast *of having invented* the great
  attività sociali.   social activities.

The choice of preposition to be used depends on the main verb of the sentence, on which the infinitive depends. The preposition **a** is used before a dependent infinitive, after such verbs as:

andare	to go	**imparare**	to learn	**mandare**	to send
cominciare	to begin	**insegnare**	to teach	**méttersi**	to start
continuare	to continue	**(a qualcuno)**	*(somebody)*	**riuscire**	to succeed
costrìngere	to force	**invitare**	to invite	**venire**	to come

The preposition **di** must be used before an infinitive depending on such verbs as:

chièdere (a qualcuno) to ask *(somebody)*   **pregare** to pray, beg
consolare to console   **perméttere (a qualcuno)** to permit
desiderare to desire   *(somebody)*
ordinare (a qualcuno) to order *(some-*   **ricordarsi** to remember
  body)   **vantarsi** to boast

69. VERBS: PRO-COMPLEMENTS WITH IMPERSONAL si.

When an impersonal verb is formed with the reflexive **si**, *e.g.*, **si fa** *one does*, **si mangia** *one eats, etc.*, any pro-complements used with such a verb normally precede the element **si**, except for **ne**, which follows:

Lo si fa.	*One* does it.
Vi si mangia.	*One* eats there.
Non se ne parla più.	*One* doesn't talk about it any more.

If such an impersonal construction is formed on a verb which is already reflexive (*e.g.* **accorgersi** *to notice*; **abbronzarsi** *to get tanned*), then the impersonal of the reflexive is formed with **ci si** and not with two **si**'s as might be expected.

Ci si accorge.	*One* notices.
Ci si abbronza.	*One* gets tanned.

70. VERBS: FUTURE OF PROBABILITY.

The future is often used in Italian (as in French and Spanish) to indicate a state of affairs which is not actually in the future, but simply probable in the present:

Non **starai** mica pensando alle elezioni.	You *can* not *be* (probably aren't) thinking of the elections.
Sarà già partita.	She *must have* departed already.
Vi **sarete** scottati.	You *must have gotten* burned.
Avranno esagerato.	They *must have been* exaggerating.

71. VERBS: SUBJUNCTIVES WITH ADJECTIVES INDICATING EXTREMES.

In clauses depending on nouns modified by adjectives indicating extremes (positive or negative superlatives; **primo** *first*; **ùltimo** *last, etc.*), a subjunctive is often found, though it is not obligatory in modern usage.

È uno dei film **più belli** che **abbia** mai visto.	It's one of the *most beautiful* films that I *have* ever *seen*.
Questo è **l'ùltimo** nùmero che **sia** uscito.	This is the *last* number that *has come out*.
È **il migliore** professore che **conosca**.	He's the *best* teacher I *know*.

Grammatical Exercises

A. SUBSTITUTIONS AND TRANSFORMATIONS.

1. *Form adjectives or nouns in* **-ante** *or* **-ente** *on the following verbs, making words or expressions as suggested*:

¹andare *(to go)* going
²assìstere *(to be present)* those present [use definite article + present participle in the plural]
³combàttere *(to combat)* the combatants
⁴crédere *(to believe)* a believer
⁵commòvere *(to move—emotionally)* a moving story
⁶depositare *(to deposit)* our depositors
⁷firmare *(to sign)* the signers
⁸importare *(to be important)* an important person

⁹insìstere *(to insist)* some insistent children
¹⁰mancare *(to be missing)* the missing books
¹¹morire *(to die)* a dying voice
¹²passare *(to pass)* a passerby
¹³potere *(to be able)* a powerful (potent) idea
¹⁴soffrire *(to suffer)* a suffering boy
¹⁵vìvere *(to live)* some living persons

2. *Combine each of the verbs in the left-hand column with the infinitives in the right-hand column, to form as many sentences as possible in which the verb and dependent infinitive are linked by* **a**:

¹cominceremo	*we'll start*		¹ascoltare	*to listen*	
²continuate!	*keep on!*		²capire	*to understand*	
³fui costretto	*I was forced*		³esagerare	*to exaggerate*	
⁴non ha imparato	*he hasn't learned*		⁴guardare	*to look*	
⁵gli insegnàrono	*they taught him*	+ a +	⁵mangiare	*to eat*	
⁶invitiàmolo	*let's invite him*		⁶parlare	*to speak*	
⁷non riuscì	*he didn't succeed*		⁷pensare	*to think*	
⁸si metterebbe	*he'd start*		⁸scherzare	*to joke*	
⁹andava	*he used to go*		⁹suonare	*to play*	
¹⁰verranno	*they'll come*		¹⁰viaggiare	*to travel*	

GRAMMAR UNIT EIGHTEEN

3. *As in Exercise A, 2, combine the verbs in the left-hand column with the infinitives in the right-hand column preceded by* **di**:

¹le chiediamo	*we ask her*		¹andarci	*to go there*
²desideravo	*I desired*		²lavorare	*to work*
³gli ordinàrono	*they ordered him*	+ di +	³nuotare	*to swim*
⁴mi pregheranno	*they will beg me*		⁴partire	*to depart*
⁵non permisi loro	*I didn't permit them*		⁵tacere	*to be silent*
⁶si ricordi	*remember!*		⁶venire	*to come*

4. *On the model of* **si prende il pasto** one eats the meal > **lo si prende** one eats it, *transform the following sentences with noun objects into sentences with pronoun objects replacing the noun objects*:

¹Si mangia la cotoletta.	One eats the cutlet.
²Si vede la cattedrale.	One sees the cathedral.
³Si guarda il Foro.	One looks at the Forum.
⁴Non si sente più il rumore.	One doesn't hear the noise any more.
⁵Non si ascolta il discorso.	One doesn't listen to the speech.

5. *As in Exercise A, 4, transform the following sentences containing phrases introduced by* **a**, *etc., into sentences with the pro-phrases* **ci** *or* **vi** *replacing the phrases introduced by prepositions*:

¹Si va a San Pietro.	One goes to St. Peter's.
²Si arriva a Roma.	One arrives at Rome.
³Si resta nell'albergo.	One stays in the hotel.
⁴Perché si cena sul Palatino?	Why does one dine on the Palatine?
⁵Non si riesce a capire?	Doesn't one succeed in understanding?

6. *As in Exercise A, 5 but replacing the phrases introduced by the prepositions* **di** *or* **da** *with the pro-phrase* **ne**:

¹Si parla di tutto.	One talks about everything.
²Si torna dalla stazione alle cinque.	One comes back from the station at five.
³Si fuma del tabacco.	One smokes tobacco.
⁴Non si discute di polìtica in questa casa.	One doesn't talk about politics in this house.
⁵Si risparmia del denaro.	One saves money.

7. *Form indefinite reflexives on the following verbs, on the model of* **accòrgersi** *to notice* > **ci si accorge** *one notices:*

¹abbronzarsi	*to get tanned*	⁶ricordarsi	*to remember*
²avvicinarsi	*to draw near*	⁷sbagliarsi	*to make a mistake*
³consolarsi	*to console oneself*	⁸sfogarsi	*to express oneself*
⁴fermarsi	*to stop (oneself)*	⁹tuffarsi	*to dive*
⁵lamentarsi	*to complain*	¹⁰vantarsi	*to boast*

8. *Form expressions using the future to indicate probability, by transforming the following sentences which contain present tense forms:*

¹Lavora moltìssimo.	He's working a great deal.
²Il treno è in ritardo.	The train's late.
³Hanno sbagliato strada.	They've taken the wrong road.
⁴È in vacanza	She's on vacation.
⁵Hai studiato a Firenze.	You've studied in Florence.

9. *Combine as many as possible of the expressions on the left with the clauses on the right, using subjunctive verb forms in the latter:*

¹La ragazza più intelligente *The most intelligent girl*
²Il palazzo più grande *The biggest palace*
³I paesi meno ricchi *The least rich countries*

+ che +

¹c'è *there is*
²conosce *he knows*
³avete visto *you have seen*
⁴hanno visitato *they've visited*

B. PROGRESSIVE VARIATION. *Say or write in Italian:*

(1) ¹The orchestra begins to play.
²The orchestra desires to play.
³We desire to play.
⁴We desire to work.
⁵We learn to work.
⁶We learn to swim.
⁷They learn to swim.
⁸They ask me to swim.
⁹They ask me to be silent.
¹⁰They are forced to be silent.
¹¹They are forced to travel.
¹²We permit him to travel.
¹³We permit him to play.
¹⁴We begin to play.

(2) ¹One looks at the cathedral.
²One looks at it.
³One looks at some.
⁴One eats some.
⁵One eats some bread.
⁶One eats in the restaurant.
⁷One eats there.
⁸One saves there.
⁹One saves some.
¹⁰One saves some money.
¹¹One looks at the money.
¹²One looks at the cathedral.

C. *Say or write in Italian:*

1. Fifty percent of the voters didn't vote. 2. I've ordered her to bring me some white wine. 3. If one didn't discuss (about) it, one wouldn't remember to go to the meeting. 4. He's probably rather dejected.
5. They begged me to return. 6. That was the longest electoral campaign that there has been up to now. 7. She must have noticed it. 8. We've asked them to continue working. 9. Why doesn't one talk about it?
10. They must have invited a lot of people.

At a Café in
Via Vèneto

Foto Silberstein —
Rapho-Guillumette

CONVERSATION UNIT————37

Peter, Fulvia and Anna are seated at an outdoor table of a café in Via Vèneto,
the main fashionable thoroughfare of Rome.

PIETRO — ¹Questa strada sarà bella quanto ti pare, però a me è antipàtica.

ANNA — ²Io la trovo divertente. ³C'è un ambiente veramente internazionale.

PIETRO — ⁴Sì, però è piena di gente che si dà un mùcchio di àrie. ⁵E tu sai che questo è un atteggiamento che non sopporto.

FULVIA — ⁶A Via Vèneto, però, si védono sempre le ùltime novità della moda. ⁷Gente strana e originale che si comporta nel modo più impensato.

PETER — ¹This street may be as beautiful as you like, but it is disagreeable to me.

ANNA — ²*I* find it amusing. ³There's a truly international atmosphere.

PETER — ⁴Yes, but it's full of people who put on (a heap of) airs. ⁵And you know that this is an attitude that I can't stand.

FULVIA — ⁶In Via Vèneto, though, you always see the latest novelties of fashion. ⁷Strange and peculiar people who behave in the most unexpected manner.

ANNA — [8]Fulvia ha ragione. [9]L'altro giorno, per esempio, ho visto una bellìssima donna che era ad un tàvolo in compagnia di un signore a bere un aperitivo. [10]Ad un certo punto si avvicina un altro signore distintìssimo che, senza dire né tanto né quanto, dà due schiaffoni sonori alla signora.

PIETRO — [11]E poi cos'è successo?

ANNA — [12]Non ti dico che parapiglia! [13]Come al sòlito si è formato un cròcchio di gente intorno ai due signori al bar, i quali, poveretti, non sapévano più che pesci préndere.

FULVIA — [14]Questa è davvero una scena da film!

PIETRO — [15]Ammetto che possa èssere stata divertente, ma io non la giustìfico. [16]Sarò un orso, ma a me la gente che si mette tanto in mostra non va a gènio.

FULVIA — [17]Avanti, sii un po' più sportivo!

ANNA — [18]Sméttila di fare tanto il puritano!

ANNA — [8]Fulvia's right. [9]The other day, for example, I saw a very beautiful woman who was at a table in the company of a gentleman drinking an apéritif. [10]At a certain point there approaches another very distinguished gentleman, who, without saying yea or nay, gives the lady two resounding slaps.

PETER — [11]And then what happened?

ANNA — [12]I can't tell you what a mêlée [there was]! [13]As usual, a knot of people formed around the lady and gentleman at the bar, who poor things, didn't know which way to turn.

FULVIA — [14]This is really a scene fit for a film!

PETER — [15]I admit that it may have been amusing, but I don't excuse it. [16]I may be grouchy (a bear), but people who put themselves so much on display aren't to my liking.

FULVIA — [17]Come on, be a little more sporting!

ANNA — [18]Stop being such a Puritan!

NOTES

1. **bella quanto ti pare**, literally *beautiful as much as it pleases you.*
2. **un atteggiamento che non sopporto**, literally *an attitude that I don't stand (support)*
3. **senza dire né tanto né quanto**, literally *without saying neither so much nor how much.*
4. **due schiaffoni**, literally *two big slaps* (**schiaffo** *slap*)
5. Sentence 12 means literally *I don't tell you what a mêlée!*
6. **non sapere più che pesci préndere**, literally *not to know any longer what fish to take*
7. **andare a gènio a qualcuno**, *to be to someone's liking*
8. **fare il puritano**, *to act like a Puritan*

bere *to drink* (root **bev-**) present **bevo, bevi, beve, beviamo, bevete, bévono**; imperfect **bevevo,** *etc.*; present subjunctive **beva,** *etc.*; future **berrò** *etc.*; past subjunctive **bevessi,** *etc.*; past absolute **bevvi, bevesti,** *etc.*; past participle **bevuto**

succédere *to happen* past absolute **successe** (3rd *sg.*), **succéssero** (3rd pl.); past participle **successo** (auxiliary **éssere**)

Esercizi

A. *Risponda alle seguenti domande basate sul testo:*

1. Dove sono Fulvia, Anna e Pietro? 2. Di che cosa pàrlano? 3. A Pietro piace Via Vèneto? 4. Piace ad Anna?
5. Perché piace (o non piace) a ciascuno dei due? 6. Che cosa pensa Pietro dell'atteggiamento della gente che si dà un mùcchio di àrie? 7. Che cosa si vede a Via Vèneto? 8. Che cosa ha visto Anna? 9. Che cosa ha dato il secondo signore alla signora?
10. Poi che cos'è successo? 11. Come si sono comportati i due signori? 12. Che cosa pensa Pietro della scena che Anna ha visto? 13. Va a gènio a Pietro la gente che si mette in mostra? 14. Come vuole Fulvia che Pietro si comporti? 15. Che cosa vuole Anna che Pietro smetta di fare?

B. *Domandi a un altro studente (a un'altra studentessa):*

1. se Via Vèneto gli (le) pare bella. 2. se gli (le) è antipàtica. 3. che tipo di gente si vede a Via Vèneto. 4. se sopporta la gente che si mette in mostra.
5. se gli (le) piàcciono le ùltime novità della moda. 6. se ha mai bevuto un aperitivo. 7. se ha mai ricevuto uno schiaffone. 8. se crede giustificata la scena descritta da Anna. 9. se è una persona sportiva,
10. se è un puritano (una puritana).

C. *Dica a un altro studente (a un'altra studentessa):*

1. che Via Vèneto non Le è antipàtica. 2. che Lei trova divertente l'ambiente di Via Vèneto. 3. che Le piace darsi delle àrie. 4. che Lei trova interessanti le ùltime novità della moda.
5. che Lei non sa più che pesci préndere. 6. che Lei non è un orso (un'orsa). 7. che Lei si diverte a méttersi in mostra. 8. che Lei è molto sportivo (sportiva). 9. che Lei non fa il puritano (la puritana).

D. Revisione delle Preposizioni (Review of prepositions). *Dica o scriva in italiano:*

1. They began to behave in the most unexpected manner. 2. I don't permit anybody to give me a slap. 3. Let's teach him to behave himself better. 4. Do you (**Lei**) desire to drink an apéritif?
5. I begged him to give himself airs. 6. How can you (**tu**) justify yourself? 7. Why did they ask you (**voi**) to be more sporting? 8. They forced the poor fellows to depart.

E. *Dica o scriva in italiano:*

1. I find those people quite disagreeable. 2. How can you stand the attitude of such people? 3. The slaps that he gave her were very resounding. 4. The Puritans were not at all strange nor peculiar.
5. The poor fellow doesn't know which way to turn. 6. If you (**tu**) want to see bears, you have to go on an expedition to the North Pole. 7. How many scenes are there in that film? 8. The international atmosphere of Florence is very distinguished. 9. He was in the midst of a knot of people.
10. These latest novelties aren't to her liking.

F. Conversations:

1. Two or more girls talk about the latest fashions (gloves, shoes, *etc.*).
2. One person takes the Puritan point of view and another opposes him, with regard to the way in which some people behave.

At Santa Maria Sopra Minerva

Pietro, Fulvia and Anna visit the Gothic church of Santa Maria Sopra Minerva, in the center of Rome near the Pantheon.

PIETRO — ¹Quant'è bella questa chiesa! ²Come si chiama?

FULVIA — ³Questa è Santa Maria Sopra Minerva. ⁴È l'ùnica chiesa che la Roma papale abbia avuta in stile gòtico.

ANNA — ⁵Si chiama "sopra Minerva" perché fu costruita su un tempio dedicato alla dea Minerva?

FULVIA — ⁶Esatto. ⁷Con l'andar del tempo la chiesa si arricchì di tombe e ornamenti per lo più barocchi. ⁸Fu solo nell'Ottocento che si cercò di riportarla alla forma primitiva.

PIETRO — ⁹Guarda queste làpidi qui sulla facciata. ¹⁰Cosa stanno ad indicare?

FULVIA — ¹¹Credo che ci stìano a ricordo delle inondazioni del Tévere. ¹²Pensate che ce ne fu una che coprì la chiesa per quattro metri.

PETER — ¹How beautiful this church is! ²What's its name?

FULVIA — ³This is Santa Maria Sopra Minerva. ⁴It's the only church that papal Rome had in Gothic style.

ANNA — ⁵Is it called "on Minerva" because it was built on a temple dedicated to the goddess Minerva?

FULVIA — ⁶Exactly. ⁷With the passage of time, the church was enriched with tombs and ornaments, for the most part baroque. ⁸It was only in the nineteenth century that an attempt was made to bring it back to its original state (primitive form).

PETER — ⁹Look at these stones here on the façade. ¹⁰What do they stand for (are they to show)?

FULVIA — ¹¹I think that they're there as a record of the inundations of the Tiber. ¹²Think that there was one which covered the church to a depth of four meters!

ANNA — [13]Dio mio! [14]E poi come finìrono?

FULVIA — [15]Fu il Governo italiano che fece costruire dei muraglioni sul Tévere, per farle cessare.

PIETRO — [16]L'interno è interessante?

FULVIA — [17]Ah sì, moltìssimo. [18]Fra l'altro, ci sono il famoso Cristo che porta la Croce di Michelàngelo, e i cèlebri affreschi di Filippino Lippi. [19]C'è anche la tomba del Beato Angélico che fu chiamato "il più dolce poeta dell'arte pittòrica".

PIETRO — [20]Bisogna che entriamo sùbito, non possiamo pèrdere una miniera di tesori come questa.

ANNA — [21]Anch'io non vedo l'ora. [22]Sembra che in un posto solo ci sìano radunati gioielli di tutte le èpoche.

ANNA — [13]Good Heavens! [14]And then how did they end?

FULVIA — [15]It was the Italian government that had high walls built along the Tiber, to make them cease.

PETER — [16]Is the interior interesting?

FULVIA — [17]Oh, yes, very much so. [19]Among other things, there are the famous *Christ carrying the Cross* by Michelangelo, and the celebrated frescoes of Filippino Lippi. [19]There's also the tomb of the Blessed Angèlico, who was called "the sweetest poet of the art of painting".

PETER — [20]We must go in right away, we can't miss a mine of treasures like this one.

ANNA — [21]I'm very impatient too. [22]It seems that in one single place there are collected jewels from all epochs.

NOTES

1. "Papal Rome", *i.e.* Rome, while it was under the direct rule of the popes, roughly from the time of Gregory I (590-604) to 1870.
2. Michelàngelo Buonarroti, one of the most famous Renaissance painters and sculptors (1475-1564).
3. Filippino Lippi, an early Renaissance painter (1457-1504), son of the more famous Fra Lippi Lippi (1406-1469).
4. **Il Beato Angèlico**, more commonly known as Fra Angèlico, a fifteenth-century painter (1387-1455).
5. Sentence 21, literally *I, too, do not see the hour* [*of entering the church*]

VERBS

arricchire to enrich, II/**isc**

Esercizi

A. *Risponda alle seguenti domande basate sul testo:*

1. Dove sono Fulvia, Anna e Pietro?   2. Come si chiama l'ùnica chiesa che la Roma papale abbia avuto in stile gòtico?   3. Perché si chiama così?   4. Di che tipo di tombe e ornamenti si arricchì con il passar del tempo?
5. Quando si cercò di riportarla alla forma primitiva?   6. Che cosa stanno ad indicare le lapidi sulla facciata?   7. Come finìrono le inondazioni?   8. Cosa c'è nell'interno della chiesa?   9. Di chi è il "Cristo che porta la Croce"?
10. Come fu chiamato il Beato Angèlico?   11. Che cosa pensa Anna dei tesori di questa chiesa?

B. *Domandi a un altro studente (a un'altra studentessa):*

1. se crede che Santa Maria Sopra Minerva sia una chiesa bella.   2. che cosa pensa dello stile gòtico e dello stile barocco.   3. perché questa chiesa ebbe il nome di Santa Maria Sopra Minerva.   4. fino a quanti metri la chiesa fu coperta da un'inondazione.
5. se l'interno di Santa Maria Sopra Minerva è interessante.   6. di chi sono gli affreschi di Santa Maria Sopra Minerva.   7. chi fu il Beato Angèlico.   8. che cosa vuol dire una "miniera di tesori".

C. REVISIONE DI **si** IMPERSONALE. *Dica o scriva in italiano:*

1. One is trying to bring it back to its original state.   2. They are building a big wall.   3. One can go in at nine o'clock.   4. We can't miss a jewel like this.
5. In Santa Maria Sopra Minerva, one sees Michelàngelo's "Christ Carrying the Cross".   6. The church gets rich.   7. One gets rich. 8. They are building a new church.   9. They are building it in Gothic style.

D. *Dica o scriva in italiano:*

1. What's the name of this church?   2. It's probably called St. Anne.   3. Is this the only fresco you've seen?   4. Here is a temple dedicated to the goddess Minerva.

5. I don't think that this baroque facade is very interesting.   6. The inundation covered the city to a depth of ten meters.   7. Why don't they build big walls to make them cease?   8. We're very impatient to (**di**) look at the treasures of the church.   9. They have collected many treasures in this place alone.
10. Where is the tomb of Michelàngelo?   11. It's in the church of Santa Croce, in Florence.

E. CONVERSATIONS:

1. Two or more people talk about the river Tiber and its inundations (how deep, when it stopped).
2. Look up as many pictures by as many Italian painters as you can and base Italian conversations on them.

● 72. Verbs: Passive Phrases.

As in English, passive phrases are constructed in Italian by using the auxiliary verb **èssere** (in any possible tense, including perfect phrases) + the past participle of a main verb, agreeing in gender and number with the subject.

Traiano **fu risuscitato** da Gregorio Magno.	Trajan *was resuscitated* by Gregory the Great.
Fu così battezzato.	He *was baptized* in this way.
Da chi **fu fondata** Roma? Da Romolo e Remo.	By whom *was* Rome *founded*? By Romulus and Remus.
Fu costruita su un tempio.	It *was constructed* on a temple.
È stata riportata alla forma primitiva,	It *has been brought back* to its original state (the primitive form).
Questi gioielli **èrano stati radunati** dall'imperatore.	These jewels *had been gathered* by the emperor.

The person or thing performing the action (the *agent*), which in English is indicated with the preposition *by*, is indicated by **da** in Italian.

This type of passive construction can be formed in Italian only when the true subject of an active verb is transformed into an expression of agent introduced by **da**, with the direct object of the active verb becoming the subject of a passive verb: *e.g.*, **Gregorio Magno resuscitò Traiano.** > **Traiano fu resuscitato da Gregorio Magno.** *Gregory the Great resuscitated Trajan.* > *Trajan was resuscitated by Gregory the Great.*

In English, another type of transformation is possible, in which an indirect object of an active verb can become the subject of a passive verb: *e.g.*, *The gentleman gave the lady a slap.* > *The lady was given a slap by the gentleman* (where *the lady* is indirect object in the active sentence). This latter transformation is not possible in Italian. The only passive that could be made from, say, **il signore diede uno schiaffone alla signora** is **alla signora fu dato uno schiaffone dal signore** (literally, *To the lady was given a slap by the gentleman*).

● 73. Verbs—Causative Phrases.

The combination of **fare** + infinitive forms a phrase in Italian meaning *to cause to ..., to make ..., to have ... -ed.*

... per **far cessare** le inondazioni	*to make* the inundations *stop*
... per **farle cessare**	*to make them stop*
Il governo **fece costruire** dei muraglioni.	The government *had* big walls *built* (*lit.*, caused to be built some big walls).
Ci **faceva parlare** in latino.	He *made* us *talk* in Latin.
Gregorio Magno **fece salire** in cielo l'ànima di Traiano.	Gregory the Great *caused* Trajan's soul *to rise* to Heaven.
Si **fa portare** un gelato.	She *has* an ice cream *brought* to herself.

In sentences of this type, pro-complements are attached to the verb **fare** (suffixed if it is imperative or non-finite, otherwise preceding), as shown in the fourth and sixth sentences given as examples.

● 74. VERBS: **fare** AND IMPERSONAL METEOROLOGICAL EXPRESSIONS.

In expression referring to the state of the weather, forms of the verb **fare** are used in the 3rd. sg. of the various tenses, followed by an adjective or by the noun **tempo** *weather* modified by an adjective.

Fa bello.	It's fine (*lit.* it makes beautiful).
Fa freddo.	It's cold.
Faceva caldo.	It was hot.
Farà bel tempo.	It will be fine weather.
Farebbe fresco.	It would be hot.

Other verbs occur normally only in the third person singular, referring to phenomena of weather.

Piove.	It's raining.
Nevicava.	It was snowing.
Grandinerà.	It will hail.

● 75. EXCLAMATIONS.

English exclamations constructed with *what, how, etc.*, normally have the structure: exclamatory word + *a(n)* + adjective + noun : *e.g., What a beautiful church! What a stupid remark!* The corresponding exclamations in Italian have no definite article.

Che piacere!	*What a* pleasure!
Che bella chiesa!	*What a* beautiful church!
Che libro interessante!	*What an* interesting book!

Full exclamatory sentences in English are often introduced by *How* ..., with the rest of the sentence in inverted order, the predicate adjective immediately following *How* ...! In Italian, the corresponding exclamatory sentence-type contains **Quanto** *How much* ...! followed by the predicate and then the subject:

Quant' è bella questa chiesa!   *How* beautiful this church is (*lit.*, how much is beautiful this church)!

Quanto sono intelligenti questi ragazzi!   *How* intelligent these boys are!

Quanto mi piace questo ristorante!   *How* I like this restautaurant (*lit.*, how much to-me pleases this restaurant)!

76. Noun-Suffixes: Augmentative and Pejorative.

Among the suffixes which can be added to nouns are **-one**, **-accio** and **-uccio**. The suffix **-one** indicates largeness of size (increase or augmentation), as in·

uno schiaffo	a slap	uno schiaff**one**	a *big* slap
un ragazzo	a boy	un ragazz**one**	a *big* boy
quel libro	that book	quel libr**one**	that *big* book
un pesce	a fish	un pesc**ione**	a *big* fish

When added to feminines, this suffix often assumes the form **-ona** (*f.*).

una ragazza	a girl	una ragazz**ona**	a *big* girl
mia sorella	my sister	la mia sorell**ona**	my *great big* sister
una chiesa	a church	una chies**ona**	a *huge* church

On occasion, however, the suffix **-one** is added to a feminine noun, and the noun thus formed is masculine.

donna	woman	un donn**one** a *big* (and rather mannish) woman

The suffix **-accio -a** means *bad* ..., *nasty* ..., *unpleasant* ... and is used to give a pejorative (worsening) meaning to nouns.

un libro	a book	un libr**accio**	a *bad* book
un giornale	a newspaper	un giornal**accio**	a *nasty* newspaper
uno scherzo	a joke	uno scherz**accio**	a *mean* joke
una commèdia	a comedy	una commedi**accia**	a *nasty* comedy

The suffix **-uccio -a** means *contemptible little* ...; but added to proper names, it adds an overtone of endearment.

un libro	a book	un lib**ruccio**	a *measly little* book
un professore	a teacher	un professor**uccio**	a *contemptible little* teacher
una commèdia	a comedy	una commedi**uccia**	a *worthless little* comedy
Roberto	Robert	Robert**uccio**	*dear little* Robert
Maso	Tom (< **Tom-maso** Thomas)	Mas**uccio**	*dear* Tommy

Grammatical Exercises

A. TRANSFORMATIONS.

1. *Change the following sentences from active to passive*:

1. L'imperatore Vespasiano costruì questo tempio.   2. Pàolo ha salutato le ragazze.
3. Il tabaccaio gli consiglia le sigarette *Granfiltro*.   4. Il governo ci mette queste tasse.
5. Il dottor Dossi invita Fulvia e Pietro per il tè.   6. Nerone aveva incendiato Roma.
7. Il professore ha bocciato lo studente.   8. Mio zio ci ha ospitati.   9. Gli americani non hanno inventato le grandi attività sociali.
10. La sàbbia mi ha bruciato.

2. *Combine the expressions in the left-hand column with those in the right-hand column to form causative phrases, e.g.* **faccio** I make, cause + **costruire una chiesa** to build a church > **faccio costruire una chiesa** I cause to be built a church, I have a church built.

¹Faccio		¹véndere la casa
²Ha fatto		²recitare una commèdia
³Farete		³risòlvere il problema
⁴Avessi fatto ...!	+	⁴formare un nuovo governo
⁵Fece		⁵dargli uno schiaffone
⁶Facèssero ...!		⁶arricchire di affreschi la chiesa
⁷Avevamo fatto		⁷riempire questa distinta di versamento
⁸Avrebbe fatto		⁸portarle un gelato

3. *Form exclamations consisting of* **che** what a ...! + *the following expressions*:

1. vita   2. rabbia   3. tabaccaccio   4. bel tempo   5. gente originale   6. leggenda curiosa   7. persona seria   8. calca infernale.

4. *Form exclamatory sentences by prefixing* **Quanto** ...! *to the following sentences and making the necessary changes in the order of subject and predicate:*

¹Questa famiglia è simpàtica.	*This family is likeable.*
²Quella ragazza era snella.	*That girl was slender.*
³Questi paesi mi sono cari.	*Those towns are dear to me.*
⁴La stagione è bella.	*The season is beautiful.*
⁵Le grotte sono magnifiche.	*The grottoes are magnificent.*
⁶Le mura di Perugia sono pittoresche.	*The walls of Perugia are picturesque.*

5. *Form derivatives in* **-one** big ... *on the following:*

¹**amico**	friend	⁴**pedante**	pedant
²**assegno**	check	⁵**sacco**	sack
³**màcchina**	machine	⁶**tàvolo**	table

6. *Form derivatives in* **-accio -a** nasty ... *on the following:*

¹**ària**	air	⁴**sapore**	flavor
²**avvocato**	lawyer	⁵**scimmia**	monkey
³**léttera**	letter	⁶**vita**	life

7. *Form derivatives in* **-uccio -a** contemptible little ... *on:*

¹**albergo**	hotel	⁴**negòzio**	business
²**attore**	actor	⁵**rumore**	noise
³**idea**	idea	⁶**stanza**	room

B. PROGRESSIVE VARIATION. *Say or write in Italian:*

(1) ¹He has built this house.
²This house has been built by him.
³This house has been built by them.
⁴This house had been built by them.
⁵Those houses had been built by them.
⁶Those houses had been sold by them.
⁷They had sold those houses.
⁸We had sold those houses.
⁹We had sold those restaurants.
¹⁰We will sell those restaurants.
¹¹Those restaurants will be sold by us.
¹²Those restaurants will be sold by him.
¹³These houses will be sold by him.
¹⁴This house will be sold by him.
¹⁵This house will be built by him.
¹⁶He will build this house.

(2) ¹He has built a house.
²He has had a house built.
³He has had a political meeting held.
⁴He would have a political meeting held.
⁵He would have a speech made.
⁶He would have made a speech.
⁷He would have formed a government.
⁸He has formed a government.
⁹He has built a house.

(3) ¹A comedy.
²A contemptible little comedy.
³A contemptible little newspaper.
⁴A nasty newspaper.
⁵A nasty girl.
⁶A big girl.

⁷A big problem.
⁸A bad problem.
⁹Nasty people.
¹⁰Nasty weather.
¹¹A nasty comedy.
¹²A comedy.

C. *Say or write in Italian:*

1. All the preparations were made by Fulvia and Theodora. 2. Her father's letter was given to Fulvia by Dr. Dossi. 3. What a worthless little comedy! 4. How intelligent Anna and Maria are!

5. I don't like that nasty teacher. 6. She was given a ticket to the concert. 7. Fulvia's suitcase was brought up to her by the bellboy. 8. What really marvelous pictures! 9. I don't like that nasty newspaper; please don't (**Lei**) give it to me.

A Street Accident

A driver who ignores a "Stop" sign and an improperly parked truck cause an accident.

PÀOLO — ¹Hai visto che scontro?

PIETRO — ²No, chi ha scontrato?

PÀOLA — ³Non vedi? ⁴Quella Seicento e quella Appia.

PIETRO — ⁵Mamma mia! ⁶Il còfano della Seicento è tutto schiacciato. ⁷Ma come è avvenuto?

PÀOLO — ⁸Veramente, non l'ho visto quando è accaduto. ⁹Ma l'autista della Appia non deve aver visto il cartello di stop. ¹⁰Ha proseguito dritto e ha preso la Seicento in pieno.

PIETRO — ¹¹Però, se non ci fosse stato quel càmion posteggiato lì all'àngolo, forse l'incidente non sarebbe avvenuto.

PAUL — ¹Did you see what a collision?

PETER — ²No, who collided?

PAUL — ³Don't you see? ⁴That 600 and that Appia.

PETER — ⁵My gosh! ⁶The hood of the 600 is (all) smashed in. ⁷But how did it happen?

PAUL — ⁸In truth, I didn't see it when it happened. ⁹But the driver of the Appia must not have seen the stop sign. ¹⁰He went straight ahead and hit the 600 full on.

PETER — ¹¹However, if that truck hadn't been parked there at the corner, perhaps the accident wouldn't have happened.

Foto Bright — Rapho-Guillumette

PÀOLO — ¹²Mah! ¹³Non ne sono si-curo. ¹⁴Credo che non avrebbe fatto ugualmente in tempo a fer-marsi, anche se l'avesse visto.

PIETRO — ¹⁵Però, con tutti questi sensi vietati e divieti di sosta, non si riesce a girare più per le strade di Roma.

PÀOLO — ¹⁶Questo è vero. ¹⁷Però, credo che ora ci sìano molti meno ingorghi di prima.

PIETRO — ¹⁸ Sì, ed é anche vero che con tutte queste circolazioni rotato-rie che hanno messo ultimamente, non c'è più bisogno di tanti semà-fori, che rallentavano il tràffico tremendamente.

PÀCLO — ¹⁹Che ci sìano dei vantaggi è indiscutìbile. ²⁰Ci vorrebbe ora che la gente avesse un po' più di coscienza nel guidare.

PAUL — ¹²Oh well! ¹³I'm not sure of that. ¹⁴I think he wouldn't have been in time to stop, anyhow, even if he had seen him.

PETER — ¹⁵However, with all these one-way streets and "no parking" signs, you can't circulate through the streets of Rome any more.

PAUL — ¹⁶That's true. ¹⁷However, I think that now there are many less bottlenecks than before.

PETER — ¹⁸Yes, and it's also true that with all these traffic circles which they've put in recently, there's no longer any need for so many traf-fic lights, which used to slow down the traffic tremendously.

PAUL — ¹⁹That there are advantages (in it) is undeniable. ²⁰It would be desirable now that people have a bit more conscience in driving.

NOTES

1. The **Seicento** and the **Appia** are two well-known makes of Italian automobiles.
2. Sentence 14, literally *I think that he would not have made equally in time to stop...* **Fare in tempo a...** *to be in time to...*
3. **Senso vietato** literally *forbidden direction*; **divieto di sosta**, literally *prohibition of parking.*
4. **non si riesce a girare più**, literally *one doesn't succeed in turning any more.*
5. **circolazione rotatoria**, literally *rotatory circulation.*

VERB FORMS

accadere	*to happen:* normally used only in 3rd person singular and plural; past absolute **accadde, accàddero**; past participle **accaduto**; future **accadrà, accadranno**	
avvenire	*to happen:* normally used only in 3rd person singular and plural; like **venire**	
riuscire	*to succeed* like **uscire** (inherent auxiliary **èssere** in compound past tenses.)	

Esercizi

A. *Risponda alle seguenti domande basate sul testo:*

1. Che cosa ha visto Pàolo?   2. Chi ha scontrato?   3. Com'è il còfano della Seicento?   4. Che cosa avrà fatto l'autista dell'altra màcchina?
5. Come c'entra il càmion?   6. L'autista avrebbe fatto in tempo a fermarsi se non ci fosse stato il càmion?   7. È facile girare ora per le strade di Roma? 8. Ci sono ora meno inghorghi di prima, o no?   9. Perché c'è meno bisogno di semàfori ora?
10. I semàfori che effetto (*effect*) hanno sul tràffico?   11. Le circolazioni rotatorie pòrtano dei vantaggi?   12. Che cosa ci vorrebbe che la gente avesse nel guidare?

B. *Domandi a un altro studente (a un'altra studentessa):*

1. se c'è stato uno scontro.   2. se lui (lei) l'ha visto.   3. che cosa è avvenuto. 4. chi ha scontrato.
5. che cosa ha fatto l'autista della Appia.   6. se è sicuro (sicura) che l'incidente sarebbe avvenuto, anche se non ci fosse stato un càmion posteggiato all'àngolo.   7. se ci sono meno ingorghi di prima.   8. se ce ne sono meno, perché.   9. perché non c'è più bisogno di tanti semàfori.
10. se è indiscutìbile che ci sìano dei vantaggi.   11. se la gente ha un po' di coscienza nel guidare.   12. se ci vorrebbe che ne avesse un po' più.

C. *Dica a un altro studente (a un'altra studentessa):*

1. che Lei ha visto uno scontro.   2. quali màcchine hanno scontrato.   3. come è avvenuto lo scontro.   4. che cosa vuol dire "senso vietato".
5. che cosa vuol dire "divieto di sosta".   6. quale è l'effetto delle circolazioni rotatorie sul tràffico.

D. REVISIONE DEL PASSIVO. *Dica o scriva in italiano:*

1. The hood of the "600" was smashed in.   2. The "600" was hit full on by the driver of the Appia.   3. A stop sign was put [up] by the government. 4. The church was covered to a depth of four meters by the water of the Tiber.
5. The stones were put on the facade by the Popes.   6. This church was built in Gothic style.   7. Paul has been disillusioned by the Italians.

E. *Dica o scriva in italiano:*

1. A "600" and a "Appia" collided.   2. The driver of the "Appia" smashed in the hood of the "600".   3. Why didn't they see the stops signs?   4. Tell (**Lei**) me why you went straight ahead.
5. Why did the accident happen?   6. Can't you see that sign which says "No Parking"?   7. We like circulating through the streets of the city. 8. There's need for a traffic light at this corner.   9. It's undeniable that traffic circles have advantages.
10. Don't you [**Lei**] know how to drive?

F. CONVERSATIONS:

1. A motorist has collided with another auto, and a policeman interrogates him as to what happened.
2. An argument as to the respective merits of traffic circles *vs.* traffic lights, and the desirability that people show some conscience in driving.

Un agente morto e tre feriti in uno scontro fra 5 mezzi

(Dal nostro corrispondente)
Bologna, 20 ottobre.

(c. c.) Un tenente della polizia ha perduto la vita e tre agenti sono rimasti feriti in un pauroso incidente avvenuto nel pomeriggio sulla Bologna-Ferrara, nei pressi di Altedo.

Una Dauphine proveniente da Bologna si era fermata al centro della carreggiata stradale azionando il segnale di svolta a sinistra per immettersi nella strada per Bentivoglio. L'auto però sostava a lungo al centro della strada perché in senso contrario stava transitando una colonna della polizia composta di diciotto camion, reduci dalla festa della P.S. a Trieste. Sopraggiungeva nel frattempo da Bologna un camion dei carabinieri che, per cause imprecisate, tamponava la Dauphine ferma e la scaraventava nella carreggiata di sinistra.

In quel momento, dall'altra parte, giungeva l'ultimo camion dell'autocolonna, seguito a breve distanza da una 600 e da un milite motociclista della polizia stradale. Il camion della polizia, che portava a bordo dodici guardie e un maresciallo, cozzava contro il muso della Dauphine, usciva di strada e si ribaltava nel fosso latera-

le. L'agente Angelo Sassi, di 28 anni, da Isermia, che era al volante, riportava leggere ferite.

Il camion dei carabinieri intanto, proseguendo la corsa dopo il tamponamento, sbandava a sinistra e piombava sulla 600, a bordo della quale viaggiava il tenente di polizia Iantorni in compagnia d'una guardia di P.S. L'urto era fortissimo e la 600 veniva letteralmente schiacciata: il tenente Iantorni, che era alla guida, rimaneva ucciso sul colpo; l'agente al suo fianco Onofrio Impellittieri, di 27 anni, da Alcamo, restava leggermente ferito.

Il motociclista della polizia stradale che chiudeva la colonna urtava a sua volta contro la 600 procurandosi alcune ferite.

Parroco muore precipi† dà un'impalcatura i̇

Padova, 2⸱

Un sacerdote è tre sorvegliava in chiesa, prec' altezza di d' vittima è dor di 59 anni, a rocchia di spari era catura della con' la r

La Stampa
10.21.62

Veii and the Etruscans

*Fulvia, Anna, Peter, Paul and Stephen are on an excursion to Veii (It., **Veio**), an Etruscan town whose ruins are about 10 miles northwest of Rome.*

STÈFANO — ¹Le signore pòrtano "calzettoni all'alpina", come consigliato dalla guida turìstica?

ANNA — ²Èccolo lùi, sempre il sòlito. ³Se non fa lo spiritoso, muore.

PÀOLO — ⁴Scherzi a parte, ci sono cardi e erbe spinose dappertutto.

(A Veio)

FULVIA — ⁵Che pòpolo misterioso questi Etruschi. ⁶Spariti così senza lasciar traccia.

PIETRO — ⁷Eppure sì che dai resti che ci rimàngono delle loro sculture e dei loro utensili, si pensa che dovesse èssere un pòpolo civilìssimo.

STÈFANO — ⁸Qualcosa si sa sulla loro civiltà. ⁹Che i romani conquistàrono Veio, si può arguire dai resti di civiltà romana trovati in questi luoghi.

STEPHEN — ¹Are the ladies wearing "heavy stockings, Alpine style", as advised by the tourist guide?

ANNA — ²There *he* is, always the same as usual. ³If he can't be a "wise guy", he'll die.

PAUL — ⁴Joking aside, there are thistles and spiky grasses everywhere.

(At Veii:)

FULVIA — ⁵What a mysterious people, these Etruscans. ⁶[They have] disappeared in this way without leaving any trace.

PETER — ⁷And yet from the remains that are left to us of their sculptures and their utensils, we do think that they must have been a very civilized people.

STEPHEN — ⁸Something is known about their civilization. ⁹That the Romans conquered Veii, can be deduced from remains of Roman civilization found in these places.

Foto ISTO

Foto Bright — Rapho-Guillumette

PIETRO — ¹⁰Mi pare di aver letto che in una famosìssima battaglia Camillo sembra fosse penetrato nella città e l'avesse conquistata.

FULVIA — ¹¹Che bella questa idea di costruire tombe come se fòssero delle case. ¹²Gli Etruschi le arredàvano e le riempìvano di tutto il necessàrio, perché pensàvano che forse i loro cari morti ne potèssero aver bisogno nell'altra vita.

ANNA — ¹³È un atteggiamento molto ottimista della vita. ¹⁴O meglio della morte.

PETER — ¹⁰It seems to me that I've read that in a very famous battle, Camillus seems to have penetrated into the city and to have conquered it.

FULVIA — ¹¹How beautiful [was] this idea of building tombs as if they were houses. ¹²The Etruscans furnished them and filled them with everything necessary, because they thought that perhaps their dear departed might have need of these things in the next life.

ANNA — ¹³That's a very optimistic attitude towards life. ¹⁴Or better towards death.

STÈFANO — [15]Ti piacerebbe avere una tomba come questa? [16]Pensa che disgrazia avere la tomba di tua moglie attaccata alla tua. [17]Come se non bastasse èssersela sopportata tutta una vita!

FULVIA — [18]Andiamo, tanto sappiamo che posi a fare il disfattista, senza ragione. [19]Ti serva da esempio invece, guardare la coppia di sposi al Museo di Valle Giulia per rénderti conto di quanto fòssero sereni e felici di stare insieme.

STEPHEN — [15]Would you like to have a tomb like this? [16]Just think, what a misfortune to have your wife's tomb attached to your own. [17] As if it weren't enough to have put up with her all through one life!

FULVIA — [18]Come on, we know anyhow that you like to pose as a defeatist, without reason. [19]On the other hand, let it serve as an example to you, to look at the bride and groom in the Valle Giulia Museum to realize how serene and happy they were to be together.

NOTES

1. **all'alpina**, *after the Alpine fashion*; similarly, **all'italiana** *after the Italian fashion;* **alla fiorentina** *after the Florentine fashion*; **alla romana** *after the Roman fashion, etc.*
2. Sentence 3, literally *if he doesn't act like a witty person, he dies*
3. **Camillo** (*Marcus Furius Camillus*), *the Roman general said by the historian Livy to have captured Veii after a ten-year siege (406-396 B.C.).*
4. **èssersela sopportata**, literally *to have supported her for oneself*
5. **la coppia di sposi**, literally *the couple of newlyweds*
6. **réndersi conto (di)** *to realize*, literally *to render to oneself an account (of)*
7. The Museum of Valle Giulia, in Rome, contains collections of pre-Roman (including Etruscan) antiquities from Rome and the surrounding territory.

VERB FORMS

arguire	*to deduce, conclude*: II-**isc**
lèggere	*to read*: past absolute **lessi, leggesti,** *etc.*; past participle **letto**
réndere	*to render, give back*: past absolute **resi, rendesti,** *etc.*; past participle **reso**
riempire	*to fill up*: II-**isc**
sparire	*to disappear*: II-**isc**; inherent auxiliary **essère** in compound past

Esercizi

A. *Risponda alle seguenti domande basate sul testo:*

1. Che cosa consiglia la guida turistica di portare alle signore? 2. Crede Anna che Stéfano sia serio? 3. Perché le signore dovrèbbero portare "calzettoni all'alpina"? 4. Gli Etruschi sono veramente spariti senza lasciar traccia?

5. Che cosa ci rimane della civiltà degli Etruschi?   6. Che cosa si può arguire dai resti di civiltà romana trovati a Veio?   7. Chi fu Camillo e che cosa fece?   8. Come costruìvano gli Etruschi le loro tombe?   9. Di che cosa credévano che i loro morti potèssero aver bisogno nell'altra vita?
10. Che tipo di atteggiamento è questo?   11. Stèfano che cosa pensa dell'idea di avere la tomba della moglie attaccata a quella del marito?   12. Che cosa ne pensa Fulvia?

B. *Domandi a un altro studente (a un'altra studentessa):*

1. se gli (le) piace fare lo spiritoso (la spiritosa).   2. che cosa sa sulla civiltà degli Etruschi.   3. se vorrebbe che le tombe fossero costruite come se fóssero delle case.   4. se ha un atteggiamento ottimista della vita e della morte.
5. se posa a fare il (la) disfattista.   6. se gli (le) piacerebbe avere una tomba come quelle degli Etruschi.

C. Revisione del Verbo **fare.** *Dica o scriva in italiano:*

1. The Etruscans had tombs built for their dear departed.   2. It was beautiful weather when we went to Veii.   3. Why do you act like a "wise guy"?
4. We aren't acting like defeatists.
5. Will it be hot in the next life?   6. I'll have my wife's tomb attached to mine.   7. We've had our house furnished with everything necessary.

D. *Dica o scriva in italiano:*

1. At Veii, there were thistles and spiky grass everywhere.   2. I hope not to disappear without leaving a trace.   3. Who was the Roman who penetrated into Veii and conquered the city?   4. He used to like to act like an optimist.
5. The tourist guide advises us to wear "big stockings, Alpine style".   6. The sculptures and utensils of the Etruscans were very interesting.   7. The Etruscans had a fine civilization.   8. The newlyweds were very happy to be together.   9. My attitude towards life is not at all defeatist.
10. This will serve us as an example.

E. Conversations:

1. Look up (preferably in the **Enciclopedia italiana,** if possible) and report on what you can find about Veii, amplifying what is contained in Conversation 40.
2. Hold an argument over whether it is or is not a misfortune to have a wife (husband), and whether one would like to have her (him) with one in the next life.

Cervèteri[1]

(Conversations 36-40)

[1]A town northwest of Rome, near which is located an ancient Etruscan necropolis.
[2]almeno   at least.
[3]necròpoli (f.)   necropolis (city of tombs).
[4]presso   near.
[5]estèndere   extend.
[6]gente (f.)   people.
[7]interesse (m.)   interest.
[8]culturale   cultural.
[9]unire (II/isc)   to unite (unirsi   to be joined).
[10]apparenza (f.)   appearance.
[11]esterno   exterior, outward.
[12]collina (f.)   hill (collinetta   little hill)
[13]sparso   scattered.
[14]qua   here, hither (qua e là   hither and yon).
[15]apparentemente   apparently.
[16]òrdine (m.)   order.
[17]preciso   precise.
[18]ondulatura (f.)   undulation.
[19]terreno (m.)   terrain.
[20]sospettare   to suspect.
[21]realtà (f.)   reality.
[22]esse (f.; m. essi)   these.
[23]rappresentare   to represent.
[24]architettònico   architectural.
[25]fornire (II/isc)   to furnish.
[26]separare   to separate.
[27]modello (m.)   model.
[28]notare   to notice.
[29]imitazione (f.)   imitation.
[30]sepolcro (m.)   sepulchre, tomb.
[31]tùmulo (m.)   mound (sepolcro a tùmulo   mound-shaped sepulchre).
[32]sopraelevazione (f.)   super-elevation.
[33]terra (f.)   earth.
[34]varietà (f.)   variety.
[35]roccia (f.)   rock.
[36]pietra (f.)   stone.
[37]tufàceo   tufa-like, of tufa.
[38]rievocare   to recall, call to mind.
[39]edilizio   pertaining to building.
[40]temporaneamente   temporarily.

Dopo aver visitato il museo etrusco di Valle Giulia, bisogna vedere almeno[2] una necròpoli[3] per avere una idea più esatta della civiltà etrusca.

La più vicina è presso[4] Cervèteri che si estende[5] a nord di Roma non lontana dal mare.

Molta gente[6] va a visitarla anche perché c'è tanto verde intorno e all'interesse[7] culturale[8] si unisce[9] il piacere di stàrsene qualche ora all'ària aperta. L'apparenza[10] esterna[11] della necròpoli è molto strana: appena si entre si védono soltanto delle collinette[12] sparse[13] qua[14] e là apparentemente[15] senza un òrdine[16] preciso,[17] che sémbrano più che altro un'ondulatura[18] del terreno.[19] Non si sospetterebbe[20] mai che in realtà[21] esse[22] rappreséntano[23] delle vere e pròprie costruzioni architettòniche[24] e che ci hanno fornito[25] tante informazioni sulla civiltà etrusca. La strada che separa[26] le tombe da una parte e dall'altra, per esempio, sembra èssere fatta sul modello[27] della via principale di una città etrusca, così come nelle tombe stesse, persino le più antiche, si nota[28] un'imitazione[29] delle loro case. I sepolcri[30] a tùmulo[31] (cioè a sopraelevazione[32] di terra[33] a forma di cùpola) sono solo una varietà[34] architettònica di tombe, altri infatti sono scavati nella roccia[35] e altri sono costruiti con pietra[36] tufàcea.[37] Tutte le tombe etrusche, però, rièvocano[38] l'architettura edilizia[39] di questo pòpolo. Entrando in alcune di queste tombe, sembra quasi di entrare in casa di qualcuno che sia uscito temporaneamente[40] e stia per tornare.

La disposizione[41] degli ambienti[42] varia, ma la forma più comune[43] consiste[44] di un vestìbolo[45] (o ingresso[46]) su cui si àprono due stanze laterali e una in fondo. A volte, poi, ci sono scolpiti[47] in pietra letti[48] con cuscini[49] e sèdie e ci sono persino dei dipinti[50] alle pareti.[51] Quando le tombe fùrono aperte c'èrano anche utensili[52] da cucina,[53] vasi[54] di varia grandezza,[55] gioielli[56] ecc. che fùrono poi portati nei musei.

Gli stòrici[57] ci dìcono che la religione[58] era un aspetto[59] molto importante della civiltà etrusca e la loro visione dell'oltretomba[60] assai diversa sia[61] da quella greca[62] che da quella romana. Questo spiega[63] il grande culto[64] degli Etruschi per i morti. Gli Etruschi infatti credévano che le persone dopo morte[65] continuàssero a vìvere nell'aldilà.[66] Bisognava provvedere dunque le tombe di tutto il necessario[67] per dare ai loro cari la possibilità[68] di avere una vita gioiosa[69] e serena.

[41]**disposizione** *(f.)* arrangement.
[42]**ambiente** *(m.)* surroundings.
[43]**comune** common.
[44]**consistere** to consist.
[45]**vestibolo** *(m.)* vestibule.
[46]**ingresso** *(m.)* entry.
[47]**scolpire** (II/isc) to carve.
[48]**letto** *(m.)* bed.
[49]**cuscino** *(m.)* cushion, pillow.
[50]**dipinto** *(m.)* painting.
[51]**parete** *(f.)* wall.
[52]**utensile** *(m.)* utensil
[53]**cucina** *(f.)* kitchen.
[54]**vaso** *(m.)* vessel.
[55]**grandezza** *(f.)* size.
[56]**gioiello** *(m.)* jewel.
[57]**stòrico** *(m.)* historian.
[58]**religione** *(f.)* religion.
[59]**aspetto** *(m.)* aspect.
[60]**oltretomba** *(m.)* life beyond the tomb.
[61]**sia ... che ...** , both ... and ... .
[62]**greco** Greek.
[63]**spiegare** to explain.
[64]**culto** *(m.)* cult, worship.
[65]**morte** *(f.)* death.
[66]**aldilà** *(m.)* the beyond (life after death).
[67]**necessario** necessary; **tutto il necessario** everything necessary.
[68]**possibilità** *(f.)* possibility.
[69]**gioioso** happy.

⬤ 77. VERBS: SUBJUNCTIVE WITH **sembrare, parere,** ETC.

In clauses dependent on verbs meaning *seem, appear, etc.,* such as **sembrare** and **parere,** the dependent verb is often (not always) in the subjunctive.

Sembra che in un posto solo ci **siano** radunati gioielli di tutte le èpoche.	It *seems* that in a single place there *are* collected jewels of all epochs.
A me **sembra** che gli italiani non **discùtano** altro che di politica o di sport.	It *seems* to me that the Italians *discuss* nothing else but politics and sports.
Mi **pare** che la tua idea non **sia** stata troppo brillante.	It *seems* to me that your idea *was* not too brilliant.
Gli **pareva** che ci **fosse** più ritardo del solito.	It *seemed* to me that there *was* more delay than usual.

If the subject of the dependent clause is the same as that of **parere** or **sembrare,** the subject may also precede the verb meaning *seem, appear,* and the conjunction **che** may then be cancelled out. This construction corresponds to the English construction *to seem to* + verb.

Camillo **sembra fosse** penetrato nella città e l'**avesse** conquistata.	Camillus *seems to have penetrated* into the city and *to have* conquered it.
Giovanni **pare sia** stanco.	John *seems to be* tired.

⬤ 78. VERBS: PAST SUBJUNCTIVE WITH **come se** OR **quasi.**

After these two conjunctions, both meaning *as if,* the past subjunctive is normally used:

... **come se fosse** una grande sala da ricevimenti	... *as if it were* a big reception hall
... **come se non bastasse**	... *as if it were* not enough
Parla **quasi** gli Etruschi **fóssero** spariti senza lasciar **traccia.**	She talks *as if* the Etruscans *had* disappeared without leaving any trace.

⬤ 79. FURTHER CONSTRUCTIONS WITH **fare.**

The construction **fare** + definite article + noun or adjective is equivalent to the English expression *to act like ..., to play the ...*:

Non fate i pedanti	*Don't act* like pedants.
Sméttila di **fare** tanto il puritano!	*Stop acting* so much *like* a Puritan!
Se non **fa** lo spiritoso, muore.	If he *does* not play the 'wise guy', he dies.

With the pro-complement cluster **ce la**, the expression **fàrcela** means *to be able to stand it*, especially with **non** ... **più** *not any longer*.

Non ce la facevo più.	*I couldn't stand it any longer.*
Ce la fai?	*Can you hold out?*

80. Uses of the Preposition **da**.

This preposition has several functions in Italian, as shown by the different types of pro-complements which replace it in its different uses. When **da** indicates the location from which movement takes place, the source, or the agent (in a passsive construction), it is replaced by the pro-phrase **ne**:

Vengo **da Firenze**. I come *from Florence*. > **Ne** vengo. I come *from there*.
Ho imparato molte cose **da questo libro**. I've learned many things *from this book*. >
 Ne ho imparato molte cose. I've learned many things *from it*.
Giovanni fu ucciso **dall'urto**. John was killed by *the impact*. > Giovanni **ne** fu ucciso.
 John was killed *by it*.

As a preposition telling where an action took place or to which motion was made, **da** means *at ... 's place*, *where ... hangs out*, and in this function it is replaced by the pro-phrases **ci** or **vi**:

Vado **da mio zio**. I'm going *to my uncle's house*. > **Ci** vado. I'm going *there*.
L'ho vista **dal professor Riccio**. I saw her at *Professor Riccio's*. > **Ce** l'ho vista. I
 saw her *there*.

Da can also be used in phrases modifying nouns, or also after the adjective **tale** *such*. In this function, it indicates suitability, purpose, or characteristic of what is referred to and is not replaceable by a pro-phrase:

un tipo **da** fare l'occhiolino alle ragazze	a character *who makes* [*such as to make*] eyes at girls.
un grosso problema **da** risolvere	a big problem *to* be resolved
qualcosa **da** mangiare	something *to* eat
un costume **da** bagno	a bathing suit, *lit.*, a costume *for* [*the*] bath
la sala **da** pranzo	the dining room, *lit.*, the hall *for* dinner
roba **da** matti	nonsense, *lit.*, stuff *for* crazy people

81. Prepositions after Adjectives.

Italian adjectives often have infinitives depending on them, as in **felici di vì-vere insieme** *happy to live together*. Normally, such infinitives dependent on adjectives are introduced by prepositions; the choice of preposition is determined by the particular adjective involved. **Di** is used after such adjectives as **certo** *certain*, **contento** *happy*, **felice** *happy*, **sicuro** *sure*, **stanco** *tired* and many others. After **buono** *good*, **fàcile** *easy*, **pronto** *ready*, **sìmile**, *similar, like, etc.*, **a** *to, for* is used; and **da** is used after **differente** and **diverso** *different*, **indipendente** *independent*, **lontano** *far away*, *etc.*

Siamo **certi di** farlo.	We're *certain to* do it.
Sono **felici di** stare insieme.	They're *happy to* be together.
Sei **sicuro di** arrivarci?	Are you *sure* you'll get there?
Eri **stanca di** stare in mezzo a quella gente.	You *were tired of* standing in the middle of those people.
Non è **buono a** nulla.	He isn't *good for* anything.
Siete **pronti a** partire?	Are you *ready to* depart?
Vorrei dei guanti **sìmili a** questi.	I'd like some gloves *similar* to (*like*) these.
Questo guanto è **diverso dall**'altro.	This glove is *different from* the other one.
Siamo ancora **lontani da** Firenze.	We're still *far from* Florence.

Grammatical Exercises

A. Transformations.

1. *Make the following sentences dependent on* **sembra che** it seems that ...:

[1]Non osa parlare.	*He doesn't dare to speak.*
[2]Fa l'occhiolino alle ragazze.	*He makes eyes at the girls.*
[3]Non vògliono smétterla di pettegolare.	*They don't want to stop gossiping.*
[4]Giovanni e Pàolo hanno ragione.	*John and Paul are right.*
[5]Non ce la fa.	*He can't stand it.*
[6]Si sono istruiti sulle rovine romane.	*They've improved their minds on the Roman ruins.*
[7]Chiacchieràvano tutto il pomeriggio.	*They were chatting all afternoon.*
[8]Non avévano sigarette americane.	*They didn't have American cigarettes.*
[9]Le sigarette èrano monopòlio di stato.	*The cigarettes were a state monopoly.*
[10]Non sentìrono niente.	*They didn't hear anything.*

2. *Make the sentences of Exercise A, 1 dependent on* **sembrava che** *it seemed that ...*

3. *On the model of* **Giovanni è stanco** John is tired + **sembra** he seems >
Giovanni sembra sia stanco John seems to be tired, *introduce the verb*
sembra seems *or* **pare** appears *after the subject, with the requisite change of the
main verb to the subjunctive, in the following:*

¹Giorgio lavora molto.	*George works a lot.*
²I nostri amici sono andati in montagna a sciare.	*Our friends have gone to the mountains to ski.*
³Perugia è una bella città.	*Perugia is a beautiful city.*
⁴L'ambiente è veramente internazionale.	*The atmosphere is truly international.*
⁵Anna non ce la fa più.	*Anna can't stand it any longer.*
⁶I contadini non capìscono niente.	*The farmers don't understand anything.*
⁷La campagna elettorale non smuove nessuno.	*The electoral campaign doesn't move anyone.*
⁸Queste elezioni riguàrdano soltanto l'amministrazione.	*These elections concern only the administration.*
⁹Quella gente si dà un mùcchio d'arie.	*Those people put on a heap of airs.*
¹⁰L'autista del càmion non ha fatto in tempo a fermarsi.	*The driver of the truck wasn't in time to stop.*

4. *Instead of using the present, use the imperfect* **sembrava** it seemed *or* **pareva** it
appeared *and make all the sentences of* Exercise A, 3 *dependent, with the necessary
change of the verbs to the past subjunctive.*

5. *Make the sentences of* Exercise A, 3 *dependent on* **Parla come se ...** He talks as
if ..., *with the necessary change of the verbs to the past subjunctive.*

6. *In each of the following sentences, replace the phrase introduced by* **da** *with the
appropriate pro-phrase, either* **ne** *or* **ci** (**vi**):

¹Èrano arrivati **da** Roma.	*They had arrived from Rome.*
²Èrano arrivati **dai** loro zii.	*They had arrived at their aunt and uncle's.*
³Èrano abbronzati **dal** sole.	*They were tanned by the sun.*
⁴Entrai **dal** tabaccaio.	*I went into the tobacconist's.*
⁵Partiremmo **dalla** città.	*We would depart from the city.*
⁶Sarete mangiati **dai** pesci.	*You'll be eaten by the fish.*
⁷Andiamo **da** mia sorella!	*Let's go to my sister's!*
⁸Èscono **dall'** albergo.	*They go out of the hotel.*
⁹Il suo male viene **dallo** stòmaco.	*His sickness comes from his stomach.*
¹⁰Fùrono veduti **da** un cane.	*They were seen by a dog.*

7. *Combine the adjectives in the left-hand column with as many as possible of the expressions in the right-hand column, e.g.,* **era contento** he was glad + **rimanere** to remain > **era contento di rimanere** he was glad to remain.

¹Mio cugino è certo	*My cousin is certain*		¹andare a caccia	*to go hunting*
²Eravamo contenti	*We were glad*		²guidare	*to drive*
³Sei felice ...?	*Are you happy ...?*	+	³parlare	*to speak*
⁴Sareste pronti	*You would be ready*		⁴partire	*to depart*
⁵Sono sicuri	*They are sure*		⁵riuscire	*to succeed*
⁶Fulvia è stanca	*Fulvia is tired*		⁶ritornare a casa	*to return home*

8. *As in Exercise 7, combining the expressions in the left-hand column with those in the right-hand column.*

¹La Sicilia è indipendente *Sicily is independent*		¹gli Stati Uniti	*the United States*
²In certe cose, l'Itàlia è simile *In certain things, Italy is similar*	+	²la Francia	*France*
³La Germània è diversa *Germany is different*		³l'Inghilterra	*England*

B. Progressive Variations.

(1) ¹They have departed.
²It seems that they have departed.
³It seems that she has departed.
⁴Anna seems to have departed.
⁵Anna seems to have spoken.
⁶Anna seemed to have spoken.
⁷It seemed that they had spoken.
⁸It seemed that they had been tired.
⁹It seemed that they were tired.
¹⁰It seemed that my uncle was tired.
¹¹My uncle seemed to be tired.
¹²My uncle seems to be tired.
¹³My uncle seems to have departed.
¹⁴It seems that my uncle has departed.
¹⁵My uncle has departed.
¹⁶He has departed.
¹⁷They have departed.

(2) ¹He goes to Henry's.
²He goes there.
³He arrives there.
⁴He arrives from there.
⁵He arrives from France.
⁶He talks about France.
⁷He talks about it.
⁸He has talked about it.
⁹He has gone out from it (from there).
¹⁰He is burned by it.
¹¹He is burned by the sand.
¹²He is burned by the sun.
¹³He is tanned by the sun.
¹⁴He is tanned by it.
¹⁵He is tanned there.
¹⁶He has arrived there.
¹⁷He arrives there.
¹⁸He arrives at Henry's.
¹⁹He goes to Henry's.

(3) ¹I'm ready to work.
²I was ready to work.
³I was ready to go out.
⁴I was certain to go out.
⁵I was tired of going out.
⁶I was tired of driving.
⁷This automobile is easy to drive.
⁸This automobile is similar to mine.
⁹That house is similar to mine.
¹⁰That house is far from the center.

¹¹The university is far from the center.
¹²The university is independent of the government.
¹³The teachers are independent of the government.
¹⁴The teachers are glad to talk.
¹⁵I'm glad to talk.
¹⁶I'm ready to talk.
¹⁷I'm ready to work.

C. *Say or write in Italian:*

1. It seemed that there had been a tremendous collision.   2. The "600" hit the truck full on.   3. I don't know why the driver of the truck didn't see the stop sign.   4. He continued as if nothing had happened.

5. People don't seem to have any conscience in driving.   6. Have the thistles hurt you?   7. Stephen always used to act like a "wise guy".   8. I don't like her attitude.   9. What can you deduce from these remains of Etruscan civilization?

10. Do you realize how happy I am?

Appendices

I. ITALIAN PHONETICS AND ORTHOGRAPHY

II. ITALIAN SUBSTANTIVE AND VERB
INFLECTION

III. VOCABULARIES

I. Italian Phonetics and Orthography

Both the phonetics and the orthography of Italian are relatively simple as compared with those of English, and Italian spelling is almost wholly phonemically based.

● 1. Vowels.

There is a maximum of seven vowel phonemes in stressed syllables in standard Italian, as exemplified in the following words:

VOWEL	EXAMPLE		APPROXIMATE DESCRIPTION
i	**vino**	*wine*	Like the *i* of Eng. *machine*
é	**fede**	*faith*	Like the *ay* of Eng. *day*
è	**terra**	*earth*	Like the *e* of Eng. *bed*
a	**mano**	*hand*	Like the *a* of "General American" Eng. *father*
ò	**porta**	*door*	Like the vowel sound of Eng. *bought*
o	**coda**	*tail*	Like the *o* of Eng. *code*
u	**muro**	*wall*	Like the *oo* of Eng. *boot*

All of these vowels are pronounced with the tongue muscles tense and without any final off-glide such as is customary in English pronunciation with the vowel sounds of *machine, day, code, boot, etc.*

The distinction between **é** (close vowel) and **è** (open vowel), and that between **ó** (close) and **ò** (open) is normally made by Central Italian speakers (from Florence and Rome, and from Tuscany, Umbria and Latium), but is frequently not made by speakers in other parts of Italy. In this book, the distinction between close and open **e** and **o** has not been marked except in a few special instances. Where it is indicated, the close vowels are marked with an acute accent ('), and the open vowels with a grave accent (`).

In unstressed syllables, there is no contrast between close and open **e** and **o**, and only five vowel contrasts exist, those indicated by the five vowel letters **i, e, a, o** and **u**. Standard Italian has no central or "obscure" vowel comparable to the final *a* of English *sofa*, and speakers of English must be careful to give every Italian unstressed vowel its full sound.

● 2. Consonants.

Most Italian consonant phonemes are represented in conventional spelling by only one letter or digraph; a few have double representation; and one has triple representation.

2.1. SINGLE REPRESENTATION is afforded for the following:

CONSONANT	EXAMPLE		APPROXIMATE DESCRIPTION
b	**babbo**	*dad*	Like the *b* of Eng. *baby*
d	**dato**	*given*	Like the *d* of Eng. *date* (but see below)
f	**fato**	*fate*	Like the *f* of Eng. *fate*
gn	**ogni**	*every*	A sound whose beginning is like *n* and whose ending is like *y*; often compared to the *ni* of Eng. *onion*, but a single palatal sound.
l	**lato**	*side*	Like the *l* of Eng. *late*, but never pronounced in the back of the mouth as done at the end of a syllable in English (e.g. *bell*).
m	**mano**	*hand*	Like the *m* of Eng. *main*
n	**nano**	*dwarf*	Like the *n* of Eng. *nice*
p	**papa**	*pope*	Like the *p* of Eng. *pope*
r	**raro**	*rare*	A flap of the tongue against the inner side of the upper front teeth, such as most Americans make for *d* in *muddy*; when double, *rr* is a trill or series of flaps made in the same way.
s	**sete**	*thirst*	Like the *s* of Eng. *sate*, when at the beginning or end of a word, and before a voiceless consonant; like the *z* of Eng. *zeal* when before a voiced consonant; and like either *s* or *z* when between vowels.
t	**tutto**	*all*	Like the *t* of Eng. *total* (but see below)
v	**verità**	*truth*	Like the *v* of Eng. *verity*
z	**pazzo**	*crazy*	A single sound whose beginning is like *t* and whose ending is like *s*
ẓ	**mezzo**	*half*	A single sound whose beginning is like *d* and whose ending is like *z*

The two last-mentioned sounds are both normally spelled with the letter **z** in Italian orthography; in dictionaries and grammars the voiced sound (similar to *dz*) is often marked with a dot above or below the letter, or by some similar device.

The dental sounds **d, n, r, s, t, z** and **z** are all pronounced with the tip of the tongue against the inside of the upper front teeth, instead of against the gum-ridge as in English.

The sounds **p, t** and "hard" **c** (*see* below, *Sec.* **2.3**), known as "stop" consonants because their pronunciation involves complete stoppage of the breath-stream, are pronounced without any puff of breath following them such as is found in English.

2.2. DOUBLE REPRESENTATION is found for:

PHONEMIC TRANSCRIPTION	ITALIAN LETTER(S)	EXAMPLES	DESCRIPTION
č	c before e, i	cena *supper*; cinque *five*	Like *ch* in Eng. *church*
	ci before a, o, u	ciarla *chat*; ciuffo *forelock*	
ǧ	g before e, i	gelo *cold*; gita *excursion*	Like *g* in Eng. *gem*
	gi before a, o, u	giacca *jacket*; giorno *day*	
š	sc before e, i	scemo *foolish*; scimmia *monkey*	Like *sh* in Eng. *show*
	sci before a, o, u	sciame *swarm*; sciocco *foolish*; sciupare *to ruin*	
g ("hard" *g*)	gh before *e, i*	Gherardo *Gerard*; ghiro *dormouse*	Like *g* in Eng. *go*
	g elsewhere	gamba *leg*; gomma *rubber*; gufo *owl*	
ʎ	gl before i; gli before e, a, o, u	gli *the* (m. *pl.*); moglie *wife*; figlia *daughter*; aglio *garlic*	A sound with the beginning of *l* and the ending of *y*; often compared to the *lli* in Eng. *million*, but a single sound.

2.3. TRIPLE REPRESENTATION is found for the phoneme /k/ ("hard" *c*), as follows:

q before u when immediately followed by another vowel	qui *here*; quando *when*; questo *this*; quota *dues*
ch before e, i	cheto *quiet*; chi *who?*
c elsewhere	caro *dear*; come *how*; cute *skin*

The letters **j, k, w** and **y** are not used in the normal spelling of Italian words; **x** occurs in a few words, with the value of *ks*, as in **uxoricida** *wife-killer*.

The letter **h** is used only in four forms of the verb **avere** *to have*: **ho** *I have*, **hai** *you* (*2nd sg.*) *have*, *he, she it has*, and **hanno** *they have*; and in the interjections **ah, eh, ih** *ow!*, **oh** and **uh** *ooh!* It never stands for any sound, and words beginning with **h** are treated as if they began (as, in speech, they do begin) with a vowel: *e.g.,* **lo** *it* + **ho visto** *I've seen* > **l'ho visto** *I've seen it*.

2.4. DOUBLE CONSONANTS. All Italian consonant phonemes except those written **sc(i)**, **gl(i)** and **gn** occur both single (short) and double (long). Those written **sc(i)**, **gl(i)** and **gn** occur only long in pronunciation. Examples; **fato** *fate vs.* **fatto** *done*; **stese** *extended (f. pl.) vs.* **stesse** *the same (f. pl.); etc.* Long consonant last between one-and-a-half and two times as long in their time of pronunciation as do short consonants. The spelling of long **q** is usually **cq**, as in **acqua** *water*; other long consonants are written by doubling the letter or the first letter of the digraph involved, as in **panna** *whipped cream*, **mucche** *milch-cows, etc.*

2.5. AUTOMATIC ALTERNATIONS OF CONSONANTS. In many words whose roots end in the phonemes listed in Sections **2.2** and **2.3**, when there is a change in the vowel following the root, the spelling of the root automatically changes: *e.g.*, in forming the plural, as in **moglie** *wife vs.* **mogli** *wives*; or in certain tenses and persons of the verb, as in **mangiare** *to eat vs* **mangi** *you eat (2nd sg.)*, or as in **mancare** *to be lacking vs.* **mancherà** *it will be lacking*. These changes do not constitute grammatical irregularities, since they are wholly automatic in the framework of double and triple representation of phonemes given in Sections **2.2** and **2.3**.

3. SYLLABIFICATION.

In pronunciation and spelling, the division between syllables in Italian words is clearly marked. A single consonant sound between two vowels belongs with the following vowel, as does any combination of consonant + **r**, consonant + **l**, or (in spelling but not in pronunciation) **s** + consonant: *e.g.* **be-ne** *well*, **da-to** *given*, **pa-dre** *father*, **ci-clo** *cycle*, **pa-sta** *paste*. Other combinations of two consonants (including double consonants) are divided with the first consonant in the syllable of the preceding vowel and the second in that of the following vowel: *e.g.*, **cam-po** *field*, **smal-to** *enamel*, **ac-qua** *water*, **pet-to** *chest, etc.* These principles must be strictly observed in breaking the spelling of Italian words at the end of a line.

4. STRESS AND ACCENT MARKS.

In an Italian word, the main stress may fall on any syllable from the last to the fourth-from-the-last: *e.g.*, **città** *city*; **modo** *manner*; **pòpolo** *people*; **andiàmo-cene** *let's go away*. Words ending in a consonant are normally not accented on the last syllable, but on the next-to-the-last or third-from-the-last: *e.g.* **nàilon** *nylon*; **vèronal** *veronal* (a sleep-inducing drug). In conventional Italian spelling, the stress is required to be marked (normally with the grave accent) only on words stressed on the last syllables: *e.g.*, **tribù** *tribe*; **perdè** *he lost*;

capì *he understood.* In this book, we have followed the practice of dictionaries and grammars in marking also all other words in which the stress does not fall on the next-to-the-last syllable: *e.g.*, **pèrdono** *they lose*; **diàmogliene** *let's give him some.*

The accent mark normally used in Italian spelling is the grave (`); some use also the acute (´) to indicate the close vowel sounds of **é** and **ó** (*cf. Sec.* 1), as is done in this book. The circumflex is occasionally used over final unstressed **i** when it stands for **ii**: *e.g.* **studî** *studies* = **studii**.

II. Italian Substantive and Verb Inflection

⬤ **1.** NOUN INFLECTION.

The great majority of Italian nouns are inflected according to one of the five following patterns:

		SINGULAR	PLURAL	EXAMPLES
FINAL VOWEL	1a.	-a	-e	**casa** *house,* **case** *houses*
	1b.	-a	-i	**artista** *artist,* **artisti** *artists*
	2a.	-o	-i	**pezzo** *piece,* **pezzi** *pieces*
	2b.	-o	-a	**uovo** *egg,* **uova** *eggs*
	3.	-e	-i	**luce** *light,* **luci** *lights*

Almost all nouns not belonging to these five types are invariable in the plural, including nouns ending in a stressed vowel (**città** *city*), in **-i** (**anàlisi** *analysis*), or in a consonant (**làpis** *pencil*), as well as abbreviations (**àuto** *auto*) and family names (**i Marotta** *the Marotta's*).

The gender of Italian nouns is not predictable on the basis of their grammatical form or of their meaning, except that all nouns of type 1b above are masculine (**l'artista** *the artist*, **gli artisti** *the artists*), and that all nouns of type 2b are masculine in the singular and feminine in the plural (*e.g.*, **il ginòcchio** *the knee*, **le ginòcchia** *the knees*). Most nouns of type 1a are feminine, and most nouns of type 2a are masculine (except for **la mano** the hand, **le mani** *the hands*). Those of type 3 are about equally distributed between masculine and feminine.

⬤ **2.** ADJECTIVE INFLECTION.

Italian adjectives are of two main types. One type has four distinctive forms, one each for masculine singular and plural, and for feminine singular and plural, combining the patterns of noun types 1a and 2a (*Sec.* **1**, above):

	SINGULAR	PLURAL	
MASCULINE	**caro**	**cari**	} *dear*
FEMININE	**cara**	**care**	

Another type has no contrast between masculine and feminine, and has distinctive forms only for singular and plural:

SINGULAR	PLURAL	
forte	forti	*strong*

A few adjectives have special shortened forms for use only before a following noun, for the most part in the masculine singular:

ADJECTIVE	SHORTENED FORM	CONDITIONS OF USE
bello *fine*	**bel** *m. sg.* **bei** *m. pl.*	Before "pure" consonant*
	begli *m. pl.*	Before "impure" consonant* or vowel
buono *good*	**buon** *m. sg.*	Before "pure" consonant
grande *big*	**gran** *sg.*	Before "pure" consonant
quello *that*	**quel** *m. sg.* **quei** *m. pl.*	Before "pure" consonant
	quell' *f. sg.*	Before vowel
	quegli *m. pl.*	Before "impure" consonant or vowel
santo *Saint*	**san** *m. sg.*	Before "pure" consonant
	sant' *m., f. sg.*	Before vowel
uno *a, an*	**un** *m. sg.*	Before "pure" consonant
	un' *f. sg.*	Before vowel

The adjective **pari** *equal* does not change for gender or number.

🌑 3. DEFINITE ARTICLE INFLECTION.

The definite article has seven forms, used under the following conditions:

MASCULINE	SINGULAR	PLURAL
Before "pure" consonant	il	i
Before "impure" consonant	lo	gli
Before vowel	l'	
FEMININE		
Before consonant	la	le
Before vowel	l'	

---

*An "impure" consonant is one of the following: **s** when followed by another consonant; **z** ([*ts*] or [*dz*]); **ps**; **gn**. A "pure" consonant is any other consonant or group of consonants.

4. VERB INFLECTION.

In the following sections will be given sample paradigms of the simple tenses of regular verbs; the conjugation of the two auxiliary verbs **avere** *to have* and **èssere** *to be*; sample compound tenses; and a list of the irregular verbs used in this book, with an indication of the pecularities of each.

4.1. REGULAR VERBS are inflected according to the following patterns:

CONJUGATION	I	II	II/**isc**	III
SAMPLE VERB (INFINITIVE)	**parlare** *to speak*	**dormire** *to sleep*	**finire** *to finish*	**véndere** *to sell*
PRESENT	parlo	dormo	finisco	vendo
	parli	dormi	finisci	vendi
	parla	dorme	finisce	vende
	parliamo	dormíamo	finiamo	vendiamo
	parlate	dormite	finite	vendete
	pàrlano	dòrmono	finìscono	véndono
IMPERFECT	parlavo	dormivo	finivo	vendevo
	parlavi	dormivi	finivi	vendevi
	parlava	dormiva	finiva	vendeva
	parlavamo	dormivamo	finivamo	vendevamo
	parlavate	dormivate	finivate	vendevate
	parlàvano	dormìvano	finìvano	vendévano
PRESENT SUBJUNCTIVE	parli	dorma	finisca	venda
	parli	dorma	finisca	venda
	parli	dorma	finisca	venda
	parliamo	dormiamo	finiamo	vendiamo
	parliate	dormiate	finiate	vendiate
	pàrlino	dòrmano	finìscano	véndano
IMPERATIVE	parla	dormi	finisci	vendi
	parliamo	dormiamo	finiamo	vendiamo
	parlate	dormite	finite	vendete
FUTURE	parlerò	dormirò	finirò	venderò
	parlerai	dormirai	finirai	venderai
	parlerà	dormirà	finirà	venderà
	parleremo	dormiremo	finiremo	venderemo
	parlerete	dormirete	finirete	venderete
	parleranno	dormiranno	finiranno	venderanno
CONDITIONAL	parlerei	dormirei	finirei	venderei
	parleresti	dormiresti	finiresti	venderesti
	parlerebbe	dormirebbe	finirebbe	venderebbe

SUBSTANTIVE AND VERB INFLECTION

	parleremmo	dormiremmo	finiremmo	venderemmo
	perlereste	dormireste	finireste	vendereste
	parlerèbbero	dormirèbbero	finirèbbero	venderèbbero
PAST ABSOLUTE	parlai	dormii	finii	vendei
	parlasti	dormisti	finisti	vendesti
	parlò	dormì	finì	vendè
	parlammo	dormimmo	finimmo	vendemmo
	parlaste	dormiste	finiste	vendeste
	parlàrono	dormìrono	finìrono	vendérono
PAST SUBJUNCTIVE	parlassi	dormissi	finissi	vendessi
	parlassi	dormissi	finissi	vendessi
	parlasse	dormisse	finisse	vendesse
	parlàssimo	dormìssimo	finìssimo	vendéssimo
	parlaste	dormiste	finiste	vendeste
	parlàssero	dormìssero	finìssero	vendéssero
PRESENT PARTICIPLE	parlando	dormendo	finendo	vendendo
PAST PARTICIPLE	parlato	dormito	finito	venduto

4.2. CONJUGATION OF **avere** *to have* AND **èssere** *to be*.

PRESENT	ho	abbiamo	sono	siamo
	hai	avete	sei	siete
	ha	hanno	è	sono
IMPERFECT	avevo	avevamo	ero	eravamo
	avevi	avevate	eri	eravate
	aveva	avévano	era	èrano
PRESENT	abbia	abbiamo	sia	siamo
SUBJUNCTIVE	abbia	abbiate	sia	siate
	abbia	àbbiano	sia	sìano
IMPERATIVE		abbiamo		siamo
	abbi	abbiate	sii	siate
FUTURE	avrò	avremo	sarò	saremo
	avrai	avrete	sarai	sarete
	avrà	avranno	sarà	saranno
CONDITIONAL	avrei	avremmo	sarei	saremmo
	avresti	avreste	saresti	sareste
	avrebbe	avrèbbero	sarebbe	sarèbbero
PAST ABSOLUTE	ebbi	avemmo	fui	fummo
	avesti	aveste	fosti	foste
	ebbe	èbbero	fu	fùrono

PAST SUBJUNCTIVE	avessi	avéssimo	fossi	fòssimo
	avessi	aveste	fossi	foste
	avesse	avéssero	fosse	fòssero
PRESENT PARTICIPLE	avendo		essendo	
PAST PARTICIPLE	avuto		stato	

The compound tenses of **èssere** are formed with **èssere** as auxiliary: *e.g.,* **sono stato -a** *I have been, etc.*

4.3. SAMPLE COMPOUND TENSES.   These are all formed using an auxiliary verb (either **avere** or **èssere** with non-reflexive verbs, always **èssere** with reflexive verbs) + the past participle of the main verb. As sample verbs are given **parlare** *to speak,* **partire** *to depart,* and **vedersi** *to see oneself.* Only the first person singular and first person plural are given for each tense.

PRESENT PERFECT	ho parlato abbiamo parlato	sono partito -a siamo partiti -e	mi sono visto -a ci siamo visti -e
PAST PERFECT	avevo parlato avevamo parlato	ero partito eravamo partiti -e	mi ero visto -a ci eravamo visti -e
SUBJUNCTIVE PERFECT	abbia parlato abbiamo parlato	sia partito -a siamo partiti -e	mi sia visto -a ci siamo visti -e
FUTURE PERFECT	avrò parlato avremo parlato	sarò partito -a saremo partiti -e	mi sarò visto -a ci saremo visti -e
CONDITIONAL PERFECT	avrei parlato avremmo parlato	sarei partito -a saremmo partiti -e	mi sarei visto -a ci saremmo visti -e
PRETERITE PERFECT*	ebbi parlato avemmo parlato	fui partito -a fummo partiti -e	mi fui visto -a ci fummo visti -e
PAST SUBJUNCTIVE PERFECT	avessi parlato avéssimo parlato	fossi partito -a fòssimo partiti -e	mi fossi visto -a ci fòssimo visti -e
PERFECT INFINITIVE	aver parlato	èsser partito -a	èssermi visto -a
PRESENT PERFECT PARTICIPLE	avendo parlato	essendo partito -a	essèndomi visto -a

4.4. IRREGULAR VERBS.   In this section are listed only the irregular features of such irregular verbs as occur in this book, in the order in which the forms are given in Sections **4.2.** and **4.3** above. In a few instances, verbs have roots which differ in shape from the form in which they appear in the infinitive; in these instances, the root is given in parentheses after the infinitive: *e.g.,* **dire** *to say* (root **dic-**).

---

*A literary tense, used primarily after conjunctions of time such as **quando** *when*: *e.g.,* **quando ebbe parlato** *when he had spoken.*

accadere *to happen:* PAST ABSOLUTE **accadde** (*3rd sg.*) **accàddero** (*3rd pl.*); AUXILIARY VERB **èssere** in compound tenses: **è accaduto,** *etc.*

accòrgersi *to notice:* PAST ABSOLUTE **mi accorsi, ti accorgesti,** *etc.*; PAST PARTICIPLE **accorto.**

amméttere *to admit:* PAST ABSOLUTE **ammisi, ammettesti,** *etc.*; PAST PARTICIPLE **ammesso.**

andare *to go:* PRESENT **vado, vai, va, andiamo, andate, vanno;** PRESENT SUBJUNCTIVE **vada, vada, vada, andiamo, andiate, vàdano;** IMPERATIVE *2nd sg.* **va';** Future **andrò,** etc.; CONDITIONAL **andrei,** *etc.* Auxiliary verb **èssere** in compound tenses **sono andato –a,** *etc.*

aprire *to open:* PAST PARTICIPLE **aperto,**

arrivare *to arrive:* Auxiliary Verb **èssere** in compound tenses: **sono arrivato -a,** *etc.*

assìstere *to be present:* PAST PARTICIPLE **assistito.**

avere *to have* — *See* PARADIGMS *Sec.* **4.2.**

bastare *to be enough:* Auxiliary verb **èssere** in compound tenses: **è bastato -a,** *etc.*

bere *to drink* (root **bev-**) Regular as if from *****bévere,** except for FUTURE **berrò,** etc.; CONDITIONAL **berrei** *etc.*; PAST ABSOLUTE **bevvi, bevesti,** *etc.*

bisognare *to be necessary:* Auxiliary verb **èssere** in compound tenses: **è bisognato,** *etc.*

chièdere *to request:* PAST ABSOLUTE **chiesi, chiedesti,** *etc.*; PAST PARTICIPLE **chiesto.**

chiùdere *to close:* PAST ABSOLUTE **chiusi, chiudesti,** *etc.*; PAST PARTICIPLE **chiuso.**

concédere *to concede:* PAST ABSOLUTE **concessi, concedesti,** *etc.*; PAST PARTICIPLE **concesso.**

conóscere *to know:* PAST ABSOLUTE **conobbi, conoscesti,** *etc.*

consìstere *to consist:* PAST PARTICIPLE **consistito;** Auxiliary verb **èssere** in compound tenses: **è consistito,** *etc.*

convenire *to be fitting, necessary:* PRESENT *3rd sg.* **conviene;** PRESENT SUBJUNCTIVE *3rd sg.* **convenga;** FUTURE *3rd sg.* **converrà;** CONDITIONAL *3rd sg.* **converrebbe;** PAST ABSOLUTE *3rd sg.* **convenne;** PAST PARTICIPLE **convenuto;** Auxiliary verb **èssere** in compound tenses: **è convenuto,** *etc.*

coprire *to cover:* PAST PARTICIPLE **coperto.**

costrìngere *to force:* PAST ABSOLUTE **costrinsi, costringesti,** *etc.*; PAST PARTICIPLE **costretto.**

crèscere *to grow:* PAST ABSOLUTE **crebbi, crescesti,** *etc.*; PAST PARTICIPLE **cresciuto;** Auxiliary verb **èssere** in compound tenses: **sono cresciuto -a,** *etc.*

dare *to give:* PRESENT **do, dai, dà, diamo, date, dànno;** IMPERFECT **davo;** PRESENT SUBJUNCTIVE **dia, dia, dia, diamo, diate, dìano;** IMPERATIVE **da', diamo, date;** FUTURE **darò,** *etc.*; CONDITIONAL **darei,** *etc.*; PAST ABSOLUTE **diedi, desti, diede, demmo, deste, dièdero;** PAST SUBJUNCTIVE **dessi, dessi, desse, dèssimo, deste, dèssero.**

decìdere *to decide:* PAST ABSOLUTE **decisi, decidesti,** *etc.*; PAST PARTICIPLE **deciso.**

delùdere *to disappoint:* PAST ABSOLUTE **delusi, deludesti,** *etc.*; PAST PARTICIPLE **deluso.**

descrìvere *to descrire:* PAST ABSOLUTE **descrissi, descrivesti,** *etc.*; PAST PARTICIPLE **descritto.**

dipèndere *to depend:* PAST ABSOLUTE **dipesi, dipendesti,** *etc.*; PAST PARTICIPLE **dipeso.**

dire *to say* (root **dic-**) regular as if from **dìcere*, except for: PRESENT and IMPERATIVE *2nd pl.* **dite**; IMPERATIVE *2. sg.* **di'**; FUTURE **dirò,** *etc.*; CONDITIONAL **direi,** *etc.*; PAST ABSOLUTE **dissi, dicesti,** *etc.*; PAST PARTICIPLE **detto.**

discùtere *to discuss:* PAST ABSOLUTE **discussi, discutesti,** *etc.*; PAST PARTICIPLE **discusso.**

dispiacere *to displease:* PRESENT *1st sg.* **dispiaccio,** *1st pl.* **dispiacciamo,** *3rd pl.* **dispiàcciono**; PRESENT SUBJUNCTIVE **dispiaccia, dispiaccia, dispiaccia dispiacciamo, dispiacciate, dispiàcciano**; PAST ABSOLUTE **dispiacqui, dispiacesti,** *etc.*; PAST PARTICIPLE **dispiaciuto.** Auxiliary verb **èssere** in compound tenses: **sono dispiaciuto -a,** *etc.*

distrùggere *to destroy:* PAST ABSOLUTE **distrussi, distruggesti,** *etc.*; PAST PARTICIPLE **distrutto.**

divenire *to become:* PRESENT **divengo, divieni, diviene, diveniamo, divenite, divèngono**; PRESENT SUBJUNCTIVE *1st, 2nd, 3rd sg.* **divenga,** *3rd pl.* **divèngono**; FUTURE **diverrò,** *etc.*; CONDITIONAL **diverrei,** *etc.*; PAST ABSOLUTE **divenni, divenisti,** *etc.*; PAST PARTICIPLE **divenuto.** Auxilliary verb **èssere** in compound tenses: **sono divenuto -a,** *etc.*

divìdere *to divide* PAST ABSOLUTE **divisi, dividesti,**,*etc.*; PAST PARTICIPLE **diviso.**

diventare *to become*; Auxiliary verb **èssere** in compound tenses: **sono diventato -a,** *etc.*

dovere *to owe, have to:* PRESENT **devo** (*or* **debbo**)**, devi, deve, dobbiamo, dovete, dévono** (*or* **débbono**)**;** PRESENT SUBJUNCTIVE *1st, 2nd, 3rd sg.* **deva** (*or* **debba**)**, dobbiamo, dobbiate, dévano** (*or* **débbano**)**;** FUTURE **dovrò,** *etc.*; CONDITIONAL **dovrei,** *etc.*

elèggere *to elect:* PAST ABSOLUTE **elessi, eleggesti,** *etc.*; PAST PARTICIPLE **eletto.**

entrare *to enter:* Auxiliary verb **èssere** in compound tenses: **sono entrato -a,** *etc.*

esìstere *to exist:* PAST PARTICIPLE **esistito**; Auxillary verb **èssere** in compound tenses: **sono esistito -a,** *etc.*

èssere *to be* — See Paradigms, *Sec.* **4.2.**

estèndere *to extend:* PAST ABSOLUTE **estesi, estendesti,** *etc.*; PAST PARTICIPLE **esteso.**

fare *to do* (root **fac-**) Regular as if from **fàcere*, except for Present **faccio, fai, fa, facciamo, fate, fanno**; PRESENT SUBJUNCTIVE **faccia, faccia, faccia, facciamo, facciate, fàcciano**; IMPERATIVE **fa', facciamo, fate**; FUTURE **faro,** *etc.*; CONDITIONAL **farei,** *etc*; PAST ABSOLUTE **faci, facesti,** *etc.*; PAST PARTICIPLE **fatto.**

godere *to enjoy:* FUTURE **godrò**, *etc.*; CONDITIONAL **godrei**, *etc.*

incùtere *to strike into:* PAST ABSOLUTE **incussi, incutesti**, *etc.*, *or* regular; PAST PARTI-
CIPLE **incusso**.

insìstere *to insist:* PAST PARTICIPLE **insistito**.

lèggere *to read:* PAST ABSOLUTE **lessi, leggesti**, *etc.*; PAST PARTICIPLE **letto**.

méttere *to put:* PAST ABSOLUTE **misi, mettesti**, *etc.*; PAST PARTICIPLE **messo**.

morire *to die:* PRESENT **muoio, muori, muore, moriamo, morite, muoiono**;
PRESENT SUBJUNCTIVE *1st, 2nd, 3sg.* **muoia**, *3rd pl.* **muòiano**; FUTURE **morrò**;
CONDITIONAL **morrei**; PAST PARTICIPLE **morto**. Auxiliary verb **èssere** in com-
pound tenses: **sono morto -a**, *etc.*

occórrere *to be necessary:* PAST ABSOLUTE *3rd sg.* **occorse**, *3rd pl.* **occórsero**; Auxiliary
verb **èssere** in compound tenses: **è occorso -a**, *etc.*

offéndere *to offend:* PAST ABSOLUTE **offesi, offendesti**, *etc.*; PAST PARTICIPLE **offeso**.

partire *to depart* (II/**isc**): Auxiliary verb **èssere** in compound tenses: **sono partito**
-a, *etc.*

passare *to pass:* Auxiliary verb **èssere** in compound tenses: **sono passato -a**. *etc.*

pèrdere *to lose:* PAST ABSOLUTE **persi, perdesti**, *etc.*, *or* regular; PAST PARTICIPLE
perso *or* **perduto**.

perméttere *to permit:* PAST ABSOLUTE **permisi, permettesti**, *etc.*; PAST PARTICIPLE
permesso.

piacere *to give pleasure:* PRESENT *1 st sg.* **piaccio**, *1st pl.* **piacciamo**, *3rd pl.* **piàcciono**;
PRESENT SUBJUNCTIVE **piaccia, piaccia, piaccia, piacciamo, piacciate, piàc-
ciano**; PAST ABSOLUTE **piacqui, piacesti**, *etc.*; PAST PARTICIPLE **piaciuto**; Auxiliary verb **èssere** in compound tenses: **sono piaciuto -a**, *etc.*

piàngere *to weep:* PAST ABSOLUTE **piansi, piangesti**, *etc.*; PAST PARTICIPLE **pianto**.

pióvere *to rain:* PAST ABSOLUTE *3rd sg.* **piovve**. Auxiliary verb **èssere** in compound
tenses optional: **è piovuto** *or* **ha piovuto**, *etc.*

potere *to be able:* PRESENT **posso, puoi, puo, possiamo, potete, possono**; PRESENT
SUBJUNCTIVE **possa, possa, possa, possiamo, possiate, possano**; FUTURE
potrò, *etc.*; CONDITIONAL **potrei**, *etc.*

préndere *to take:* PAST ABSOLUTE **presi, prendesti**, *etc.*; PAST PARTICIPLE **preso**.

protèggere *to protect:* PAST ABSOLUTE **protessi, proteggesti**, *etc.*; PAST PARTICIPLE
protetto.

provvedere *to provide:* FUTURE **provvedrò**, *etc.*; CONDITIONAL **provvedrai**, *etc.*;
PAST ABSOLUTE **provvidi, provvedesti**, *etc.*

réndere *to give back, render:* PAST ABSOLUTE **resi, rendesti**, *etc.*; PAST PARTICIPLE **reso**.

restare *to stay:* Auxiliary verb **èssere** in compound tenses: **sono restato -a**, *etc.*

riconóscere *to recognize:* PAST PARTICIPLE **riconosciuto**.

rimanere *to remain:* PRESENT *1st sg.* **rimango,** *3rd pl.* **rimàngono;** PRESENT SUBJUNCTIVE *1st, 2nd, 3rd sg.* **rimanga,** *3rd pl.* **rimàngano;** FUTURE **rimarro,** *etc.;* CONDITIONAL **rimarrà** *,etc.;* PAST ABSOLUTE **rimasi, rimanesti,** *etc.;* PAST PARTICIPLE **rimasto;** Auxiliary verb **èssere** in compound tenses: **sono rimasto -a,** *etc.*

risalire *to go back:* PRESENT *1st sg.* **risalgo,** *3rd pl.* **risàlgono;** PRESENT SUBJUNCTIVE *1st, 2nd, 3rd sg.* **risalga,** *3rd pl.* **risàlgano;** Auxiliary verb **èssere** in compound tenses: **sono risalito,** *etc.*

risòlvere *to resolve:* PAST ABSOLUTE **risolsi, risolvesti,** *etc.;* PAST PARTICIPLE **risolto.**

ritornare *to return:* Auxiliary verb **èssere** in compound tenses: **sono ritornato -a,** *etc.*

riuscire *to succeed:* PRESENT **riesco, riesci, riesce, riusciamo, riuscite, rièscano;** PRESENT SUBJUNCTIVE *1st, 2nd, 3rd sg.* **riesca,** *3rd pl.* **rièscano;** IMPERATIVE *2nd sg.* **riesci;** Auxiliary verb **èssere** in compound tenses: **sono riuscito -a,** *etc.*

rómpere *to break:* PAST ABSOLUTE **ruppi, rompesti,** *etc.;* PAST PARTICIPLE **rotto.**

salire *to go up:* PRESENT *1st sg.* **salgo** *3rd pl.* **sàlgono;** PRESENT SUBJUNCTIVE *1st, 2nd, 3rd. pl.* **sàlgano;** Auxiliary verb **èssere** in compound tenses: **sono salito -a,** *etc.*

sapere *to know:* PRESENT **so, sai, sa, sappiamo, sapete, sanno;** PRESENT SUBJUNCTIVE **sappia, sappia, sappia, sappiamo, sappiate, sàppiano;** IMPERATIVE **sappi, sappiamo, sappiate;** FUTURE **saprò,** *etc.;* CONDITIONAL **saprei,** *etc.;* PAST ABSOLUTE **seppi, sapesti,** *etc.*

scomméttere *to be:* PAST ABSOLUTE **scommisi, scommettesti,** *etc.;* PAST PARTICIPLE **scommesso.**

sconfìggere *to defeat:* PAIt ABSOLUTE **sconfissi, sconfiggesti,** *etc.;* PAST PARTICIPLE **sconfitto.**

scórrere *to run along, flow:* PAST ABSOLUTE **scorsi, scorresti,** *etc.;* PAST PARTICIPLE **scorso.**

scrìvere *to write:* PAST ABSOLUTE **scrissi, scrivesti,** *etc.;* PAST PARTICIPLE **scritto.**

sfuggire *to escape* (II-isc)*:* Auxiliary verb **èssere** in compound tenses: **sono sfuggito -a,** *etc.*

sméttere *to stop:* PAST ABSOLUTE **smisi, smettesti,** *etc.;* PAST PARTICIPLE **smesso.**

smuòvere *to move* PAST ABSOLUTE **smossi, smuovesti,** *etc.;* PAST PARTICIPLE **smosso.**

soffrire *to suffer:* PAST PARTICIPLE **sofferto.**

sorpréndere *to surprise:* PAST ABSOLUTE **sorpresi, sorprendesti,** *etc.;* PAST PARTICIPLE **sorpreso.**

stare *to stand:* PRESENT **sto, stai, sta, stiamo, state, stanno;** IMPERFECT **stavo,** *etc.;* PRESENT SUBJUNCTIVE **stia, stia, stia, stiamo, stiate, stiano;** IMPERATIVE *2nd sg.* **sta';** FUTURE **starò,** *etc.;* CONDITIONAL **starei,** *etc.;* PAST ABSOLUTE **stetti, stesti, stette, stemmo, steste, stèttero;** PAST SUBJUNCTIVE **stessi,** *etc.;* PAST PARTICIPLE **stato.** Auxiliary verb **èssere** in compound tenses: **sono stato -a,** *etc.*

strìngere *to squeeze:* PAST ABSOLUTE **strinsi, stringesti,** *etc.*; PAST PARTICIPLE **stretto.**

succédere *to happen* PAST ABSOLUTE *3rd sg.* **successe,** *3rd pl.* **succèssero;** PAST PARTI-
CIPLE **successo;** Auxiliary verb **èssere** in compound tenses: **è successo -a,**
etc.

tacere *to be silent:* PRESENT *1st sg.* **taccio,** *1st pl.* **tacciamo,** *3rd pl.* **tacciono;** PRESENT
SUBJUNCTIVE **taccia, taccia, taccia, tacciamo, tacciate, tàcciano;** PAST ABSOLUTE
tacqui, tacesti, *etc.*; PAST PARTICIPLE **taciuto.**

tenere *to hold:* PRESENT **tengo, tieni, tiene, teniamo, tenete, tèngono;** PRESENT
SUBJUNCTIVE **tenga, tenga, tenga, teniamo, teniate, tèngano;** IMPERATIVE
2rd sg. **tieni;** FUTURE **terrò,** *etc.*; CONDITIONAL **terrei,** *etc.*; PAST ABSOLUTE **tenni,
tenesti,** *etc.*; PAST PARTICIPLE **tenuto.**

tògliere *to take away:* PRESENT *1st sg.* **tolgo,** *3rd pl.* **tòlgono;** PRESENT SUBJUNCTIVE
1st, 2rd, 3rd sg. **tolga,** *3rd pl.* **tòlgano;** FUTURE **torrò,** *etc.*; CONDITIONAL **torrei,**
etc.; PAST ABSOLUTE **tolsi, togliesti,** *etc.*; PAST PARTICIPLE **tolto.**

tornare *to return:* Auxiliary verb **èssere** in compound tenses: **sono tornato -a,** *etc.*

uscire *to go out:* PRESENT **esco, esci, esce, usciamo, uscite, èscono;** PRESENT SUB-
JUNCTIVE *1st, 2nd, 3rd sg.* **esca,** *3rd pl.* **èscano;** IMPERATIVE *2nd sg.* **esci;** Auxiliary verb **èssere** in compound tenses: **sono uscito -a,** *etc.*

vedere *to see:* FUTURE **vedro,** *etc.*; CONDITIONAL **vedrei,** *etc.*; PAST ABSOLUTE **vidi,
vedesti,** *etc.*; PAST PARTICIPLE **visto** *or* **veduto.**

venire *to come:* PRESENT **vengo, vieni, viene, veniamo, venite, véngono;** PRESENT
SUBJUNCTIVE *1st, 2rd, 3sg.* **venga,** *3rd pl.* **vèngano;** IMPERATIVE *2rd sg.* **vieni;**
Future **verrò,** *etc.*; CONDITIONAL **verrei,** *etc.*; PAST ABSOLUTE **venni, venisti,** *etc.*;
PAST PARTICIPLE **venuto.** Auxiliary verb **èssere** in compound tenses: **sono
venuto -a,** *etc.*

vìvere *to live:* FUTURE **vivrò,** *etc.*; CONDITIONAL **vivrei,** *etc.*; PAST ABSOLUTE **vissi,
vivesti,** *etc.*; PAST PARTICIPLE **vissuto;** Auxiliary verb **èssere** in compound
tenses optional: **ho vissuto** *or* **sono vissuto -a,** *etc.*

volere *to wish:* PRESENT **voglio, vuoi, vuole, vogliamo, volete, vògliono;** PRESENT
SUBJUNCTIVE **voglia, voglia, voglia, vogliamo, vogliate, vògliano;** IMPERA-
TIVE **voglia, vogliamo, vogliate;** FUTURE **vorrò,** *etc.*; CONDITIONAL **vorrei,** *etc.*;
PAST ABSOLUTE **volli, volesti,** *etc.*; PAST PARTICIPLE **voluto.**

III. VOCABULARIES

NOTE

This vocabulary is intended to be complete. Gender of nouns is indicated by *m* (for masculine) and *f* (for feminine). Adjectives are given in the masculine form. Idiomatic expressions containing a noun are listed under the noun; all others will be found under the main word of each phrase.

A list of abbreviations used in the vocabulary follows.

ABBREVIATIONS

abbrev	abbreviated	*num*	numeral
adj	adjective	*obj*	object
adv	adverb	*part*	participle
art	article	*pers*	person, personal
conj	conjunction	*phr*	phrase
conjv	conjunctive	*pl*	plural
dat	dative	*poss*	possessive
def	definite	*prep*	preposition, prepositional
dem	demonstrative	*pron*	pronoun, pronominal
dir	direct	*pro-phr*	pro-phrase
disjv	disjunctive	*refl*	reflexive
exclam	exclamation	*rel*	relative
f	feminine	*sg*	singular
II/*isc*	verb of second conjugation with	*subj*	subject
	infix -*isc*- in certain forms	*subjv*	subjunctive
imperf	imperfect	*vb*	verb, verbal
indef	indefinite		
interj	interjection		
interr	interrogative		
invar	invariable		
m	masculine		
n	noun		
neg	negative		

A

a, ad   at, to
abbassarsi   to go down, become lower
abbastanza   enough
abbàttere   to beat down, deject
abbigliamento *m*   clothing
abbronzarsi   to get tanned
abitùdine *f*   habit, custom
accadere   to happen
accanto   next, beside; **accanto a** next to
accelerato *m*   local (*train*)
accettare   to accept
accidèmpoli   gosh!
accipìcchia   golly!
accogliere   to receive
accomodarsi   to sit down; to go
accompagnare to accompany; to go (come) along with
accordo *m*   agreement; **èssere d'accordo** to agree
accòrgersi (di ...) to notice
acqua *f*   water
aquedotto *m*   aqueduct
ad   at, to
adatto   suited
addìo   good-bye
adesso   now
addobbare   to deck out
adunanza *f*   meeting
aèreo   aerial, pertaining to the air
affannato   breathless; troubled
affascinare   to fascinate
affatto   (not) at all
affermazione *f*   affirmation, assertion of strength
affresco *m*   fresco
agente *m* (*police*)   officer, policeman
agiato   wealthy, well-to-do
agosto *m*   August
aiutare   to help
albergatore *m*   hotel-keeper
albergo *m*   hotel
àlbero *m*   tree
alcuni *m* (*f* **alcune**)   some
aldilà *m*   the beyond (*life after death*)

al di là di *prep*   beyond
alimento *m*   food
alla *f sg*   to the
all'aperto   in the open air
alle *f pl*   at the, to the
allegro   cheerful, merry
allora   then
almeno   at least
alt. = **altitùdine**   altitude
altare *m*   altar
altrimenti   otherwise
altro *adj* other; *pron* something else; **fra l'altro** among other things; **senz'altro** right away; undoubtedly
altroché! *interj*   certainly!
alzare to raise; **alzarsi** to get up
ambiente *m* environment, surroundings; atmosphere
americano   American
amica *f*   friend
amico *m*   friend
amméttere   to admit
amministrativo   administrative
amministrazione *f*   administration
ammirare   to admire
anche   also
ancora   still, yet
andare   to go
ànima *f*   soul
ànimo *m* spirit; **pèrdersi d'ànimo** to lose heart, become discouraged
Anna *f*   Anna, Ann(e)
anno *m*   year
antichità *f*   antiquity
antìcipo: in antìcipo   in advance
antico *m*   ancient, old
antipasto *m sg*   hors d'œuvres
antipàtico   disagreeable
Antònio *m*   Anthony
aperitivo *m*   apéritif
aperto *past part*   open
apòstolo *m*   apostle
apparentemente   apparently
apparenza *f*   appearance
appena *adv* scarcely; *conj* as soon as

applaudire to applaud
approfittare to profit
appuntamento *m* appointment, date
aprile *m* April
aprire to open
aranciata *f* orangeade
arancio *m* orange
archeologìa *f* archaeology
archeològico archaeological
architettònico architectural
architettura *f* architecture
Arezzo *f* Arezzo (*a city in S.E. Tuscany*)
Argentàrio (**Monte**) *m* Mount Argentàrio (*near Porto S. Stèfano*)
ària *f* air; manner; **darsi delle àrie** to put on airs
Ariete *m* Aries; ram
arma *f* (*pl* armi) arm, weapon
aromàtico aromatic, sweet-smelling
arricchire (II/*isc*) to enrich
arrivare to arrive
arrivederLa good-bye
arrosto *invar* roasted
arte *f* art
artìcolo *m* article
artificialmente artificially
artista *m* artist
ascoltare to listen to; **stare ad ascoltare** to listen to
aspettare to wait (for)
aspetto *m* aspect
aspro harsh, rugged
assegno *m* cheque; **assegno viaggiatori** travelers' cheque
assicurare to assure
assicurazione *f* insurance; **società d'assicurazioni** *f* insurance company
assìstere to be present
assolutamente absolutely
attaccare to attack, strike up
attaccarsi to attach oneself
atteggiamento *m* attitude
attesissimo long-awaited
attività *f* activity
attore *m* actor
attribuire (II/*isc*) to attribute
augùrio *m* greeting
Augusto *m* Augustus

àutobus *m* (auto) bus
automòbile *f* automobile
autunno *m* autumn
avanti forward; go ahead; come on
avere to have
avevo *imperf* I had
avvicinarsi to come near, approach
avvocato *m* lawyer
azzurro blue

B

bacchetta *f* baton
bagnino *m* beach attendant
bagno *m* bath; **fare il bagno** to take a bath
bambino *m* child
banana *f* banana
banco *m* counter
bar *m* espresso bar
barca *f* boat
barocco baroque
basato *past part* based
basìlica *f* basilica
basso low; **in basso** below
bastare to be enough; **basta!** (it's) enough!
battezzare to baptize
beato blessed
bellezza *f* beauty
bellìssimo very beautiful
bello beautiful
bene well; **ben tornato** welcome back; **va bene** all right
benestante well-to-do
benìssimo very well
benone very well indeed
bere to drink
bevanda *f* drink, beverage
bianco white
bìbita *f* drink
biglietto *m* ticket; (*bank*) note; **fare il biglietto** to get one's ticket
bilancia *f sg* scales
bimbo *m* child
binàrio *m* track
biondo blond
birra *f* beer
bis *m* encore

bisbigliare to whisper
bisognare to be necessary
bisogno *m* need
bistecca *f* steak; **bistecca ai ferri** grilled steak
bocciare to reject, flunk
bombardare to bomb
borghesismo *m* middle-class (*bourgeois*) attitudes
borsa *f* purse; **borsa di stùdio** *f* scholarship
botteghino *m* box-office
braccio *m* (*pl* **le braccia** *f*) arm
brano *m* piece, part
bravo excellent, fine
breve short, brief
brillante brilliant
brodo *m* broth
bruno dark, brunet(te)
Bruto *m* Brutus
brutto ugly; nasty
budino *m* pudding
bue *m* (*pl* **buoi**) ox
buffo funny
buonìssimo very good
buono good
burro *m* butter

C

caccia *f* hunt; **andare a caccia (di ..).** to go hunting
cacciare to hunt; **cacciarsi** to hide (*oneself*)
caffè *m* coffee
calca *f* crush
caldo *adj* warm, hot; *n* heat; **far caldo** to be hot
calligrafia *f* handwriting, calligraphy
calmarsi to calm oneself, calm down
calmo calm
calore *m* warmth; **con calore** warmly
calzino *m* sock
cambiare to change
cameriere *m* waiter; bell-boy
camicetta *f* blouse
camminare to walk

campagna *f* country (*as opposed to city*); countryside; campaign
campestre rustic
candidato *m* candidate
cane *m* dog
cantante *m or f* singer
cantare to sing
canto *m* singing; song
cantoria *f* choir
capello *m* (*single*) hair
capire (II/*isc*) to understand; **non capire un bel niente** not to understand anything
capitale *f* capital
capo *m* end
Capodanno *m* New Year's
capolavoro *m* masterpiece
capra *f* goat
caratterìstica *f* characteristic
carino nice, attractive, pretty
carìssimo very expensive
carità *f* charity; **per carità** for heaven's sake! good heavens!
caro dear, expensive; **costare caro** to be expensive, cost a lot
carrozza *f* carriage
Carso *m* Carso (*limestone plateau in N.E. Italy*)
cartolina *f* post card
casa *f* house, home
casalingo homely, domestic
casetta *f* little house
caso *m* chance; **per caso** by (any) chance
cassa *f* cashier's desk or window
castello *m* castle; **Castelli (Romani)** *m pl* the Alban Hills
cattedrale *f* cathdral
cavaliere *m* knight; gentleman
cavallo *m* horse
càvolo *m* cabbage
c'è there is
cèlebre celebrated
cena *f* dinner (*evening meal*)
cenare to dine
centinaio *m* (*pl* **le centinaia** *f*) group of about a hundred
cento a hundred; **per cento** percent
centro *m* center; **in centro** downtown
cercare to seek, try

cerino *m* wax match

certamente certainly

certo certain; certainly

cessare to cease

cestinarsi to be refused, thrown into the wastebasket

che *rel pron* which, who, whom; *interrog pron, adj* what; *exclam adj* what a ...!

ché *conj* for

chi *interrog pron* who?; **di chi** whose?

chiàcchiera *f* chat; **fare due chiàcchiere** to have a little chat

chiacchierare to chat, jabber

chiacchierata *f* chat, conversation

chiamare to call; **chiamarsi** to be called, be named

Chianti *m* Chianti (*a kind of Italian wine*)

chiaramente clearly

chiaro clear

chiave *f* key

chièdere to ask for, request

chiesa *f* church

chilòmetro *m* kilometer

chìmica *f* chemistry

chiosco *m* kiosk, stand

chiùdere to close

ci *I pl pers pron* us, to us; *pro-phr* there, on it, in it, etc. (*replacing phrases introduced by prepositions of place where or to which*)

ciao hi (*used only to people whom one would address with* **tu**)

ciascuno each

cibo *m* food

cicerone *m* guide

cielo *m* sky, heaven

ciglio *m* (*pl* **le ciglia** *f*) eyelash

cima *f* summit, top; **in cima a** on top of

cìnema *m* (*invar*) movie-house

cinematògrafo *m* cinematograph, movie-house

cinquanta fifty

cinque five

cinquecento five hundred

cinquemila five thousand

cinta: **mura di cinta** *f pl* encircling walls

cioè that is

circostante surrounding

ci sono there are

città *f* city; **in città** to, in town

cittadino *m* citizen

civile civilized

civiltà *f* civilization

classe *f* class

Clàudio *m* Claudius

coda *f* tail; **piano a coda** *m* grand piano

cògliere to grasp, seize, pick

cognata *f* sister-in-law

cognato *m* brother-in-law

coincidenza *f* connection (*train, bus, etc.*)

colazione *f* breakfast

collina *f* hill

collinetta *f* little hill

colonna *f* column

colonnato *m* colonnade

colorato colored

colore *m* color

colpire (II/*isc*) to strike

coltello *m* knife

colto cultured

combàttere to fight, combat

come *interr adv* how; *prep* as

cominciare to begin

comitiva *f* party

comìzio *m* (*political*) meeting

commèdia *f* comedy

commemorare to commemorate

commessa *f* saleswoman

commuòvere to move (*emotionally*)

comodamente comfortably

còmodo convenient, comfortable

compagnìa *f* company

companàtico *m* what is eaten along with bread; "fixin's"

compiere to accomplish

complesso complex, complicated; **nel complesso** taken as a whole

completamente completely

completare to complete

completo *m* suit (*women's clothing*)

complimento *m* compliment

comportarsi to behave

comprare to buy

comunale: **palazzo comunale** town-hall

comune common

comunque however

con with

concédere to concede. yield, grant
concerto *m* concert
conferenza *f* lecture; **tenere una conferenza** to give a lecture
conferma *f* confirmation
confessare to confess
confessione *f* confession
confuso confused
congratularsi (**con** ...) to congratulate
congratulazione *f* congratulation
conòscere to know, be acquainted with, get acquainted with
conoscenza *f* acquaintance
consigliare to advise
consìstere to consist
consolarsi to console oneself.
contadino *m* farmer, peasant
contento glad
continuare to continue
conto *m* bill, account; **conto corrente** *m* current account, checking account; **réndersi conto di** to realize
contorno *m* vegetables (*accompanying a meat dish*)
contrastare to contrast
contro against
convenire to be fitting, be necessary, be better
conversazione *f* conversation
coppa *f* sundae
coperto *past part* covered
coprire to cover
coraggio *m* courage; **farsi coraggio** to be courageous
cordiale cordial
cordialmente cordially
corredare to equip, furnish. (with)
corrente current
corridoio corridor
corriera *f* (*suburban or interurban*) bus
corriere *m* messenger, courier; post (*mail*)
corso *m* course
Corso *m* "Corso", avenue
cosa *f* thing, matter; *interrog pron* what ?
così thus, so, in this (that) way; **così così** so-so; **così via** so forth
costante constant
Costantino *m* Constantine

costare to cost; **costare caro** to be expensive, cost a lot
costrìngere to force
costruire (II/*isc*) to construct
costruzione *f* construction
costume *m* costume, (*bathing*) suit
cotoletta *f* cutlet; **cotoletta alla milanese** *f* breaded veal cutlet
cotone *m* cotton
cravatta *f* necktie
crédere to believe
crema *f* cream
créscere to grow
cristallo *m* crystal
Cristo *m* Christ
cròcchio *m* group, knot (*of people*)
croce *f* cross
cucchiaio *m* spoon
cucina *f* kitchen
cucinare to cook
cugina *f* cousin
cugino *m* cousin
cùi *rel pron* whose; to which, to whom; which, whom
cullarsi (**su** ...) to cradle oneself; to pin one's hopes (on ...)
culto *m* cult, worship
culturale cultural
cuoca *f* cook
cùpola *f* cupola, dome
cura: **a cura di** by
curare to take care of
cuscino *m* cushion, pillow

D

da from; fit for; for the purpose of; of (*amount of bank note, postage stamp etc.*); such as, likely to; as; **fare da** to act as
da at ... 's place, where ... is to be found
dà he, she, it gives; **dà su** it looks out over
d'accordo in agreement; all right; **èssere d'accordo** to agree
dannoso harmful
dapprima at first
dare to give; **dare su** to look out over
dati *m pl* data, information

davvero really

dea *f* goddess

debuttante *m or f* person making a début

decapitazione *f* beheading

decìdere to decide

dècimo tenth

dedicare to dedicate

dei *m pl* of the; some

del *m sg* of the

delitto *m* crime

delle *f pl* of the

delùdere to disappoint

democràtico democratic

demolire (II/*isc*) to demolish

denaro *m* money

dente *m* tooth

dentista *m* dentist

dentro *adv, prep* inside; **dentro a** *prep* inside

depositare to deposit

depòsito *m* deposit

deputato *m* deputy

descrìvere to describe

descrizione *f* description

desiderare to desire

destinazione *f* destination

destra : **a destra** to (on) the right

destro right

devo I have to

di of

dia give

dialetto *m* dialect

dica say, speak

dicembre *m* December

diciannove nineteen

diciassette seventeen

diciotto eighteen

dieci ten

diecimila ten thousand

diecina *f* (*a group of*) about ten

dietro behind

difatti in fact

differenza *f* difference

diffìcile difficult, hard

dimenticare to forget

dimostrare to demonstrate, show

dintorni *m pl* surroundings, environs

dio *m* (*pl* **dei**) god; **Dio mio**! good heavens!

dipéndere to depend

dipinto *m* painting

dire to say; **senza dire né tanto né quanto** without saying yea or nay

direttore *m* director; conductor (*of orchestra*)

discesa *f* descent; sharply descending street

discorso *m* discourse, conversation; speech

discùtere to discuss

dispiacere to be displeasing; **mi dispiace** I'm sorry

disposizione *f* arrangement

distanza *f* distance

distinta *f* slip (*sales*)

distinto distinguished

distrùggere to destroy

divenire to become

diventare to become

diverso diverse, different; *pl* several

divertente amusing

divertimento *m* amusement, entertainment

divertire to amuse; **divertirsi** to amuse oneself, to have a good time

divìdere to divide

divino divine

dobbiamo we have to

doccia *f* shower

dòdici twelve

dolce sweet

dòllaro *m* dollar

Dolomiti *f pl* Dolomites (*mountains in N. Italy*)

dolore *m* pain

domanda *f* question; **domanda a trucco** *f* trick question; **fare una domanda** to ask a question

domani tomorrow

doménica *f* Sunday

donna *f* woman; **prima donna** *f* opera star

dopo after

dòppio double

dorato *past part* gilded, golden

dormire to sleep

dote *f* dowry; **doti** gifts, qualities, accomplishments

dove where
dov'è where is ... ?
dovere to owe, to have to; *m* duty
dovessi (if) I had to
dovunque wherever
dozzina *f* dozen
dritto straight
dùbbio *m* doubt
due two
duecento two hundred
duemila two thousand
durante during
durare to last

E

e, ed and
è is; (you) are
eccellente excellent
eccètera etcetera
eccezione *f* exception
ecco *defective vb* here is, here are, there is,
   there are; ecco fatto here it is done
econòmico economical, cheap
e così via and so forth
edificio *m* building
edilìzio (*pertaining to*) building
educazione *f* education
elèggere to elect
elencare to list
elenco *m* list, (*telephone*) book
elettorale electoral
elezione *f* election
emozionare to thrill
empòrio *m* warehouse
Enea *m* Aeneas
Enrico *m* Henry
entrare to enter, go in
entrata *f* entrance
entusiasmo *m* enthusiasm
entusiasta *m* enthusiast
època *f* epoch, time of year
equivalente *n m adj* equivalent
era *imperf* he, she, it was
esagerare to exaggerate
esame *m* examination; fare un esame a
   to give an examination to
esattamente exactly
esatto exact

eseguire (II/*isc*) to perform
esèmpio *m* example
esìstere to exist
esplorare to explore
espresso *m* espresso coffee
èssere to be
esso *dem pron* this
estate *f* summer
estèndere to extend
esterno exterior, outward
èstero foreign
estètico aesthetic
età *f* age

F

faccia make
facciata *f* façade
fàcile easy
fagiolini *m pl* string beans
fallimento *m* bankruptcy
fame *f* hunger; aver fame to be hungry
familiarizzarsi to get familiar, to get
   acquainted
fantino *m* jockey
fare to do, make, cause, (*of weather*) be;
   fare da to act as; farsi to become; il
   da farsi what is to be done; non fàrcela
   più not to be able to stand it any longer
fatto *m* fact, deed, activity; vanno per i
   fatti loro they go on about their business
favore *m* favor; per favore please
fazzoletto *m* handkerchief
febbraio *m* February
febbre *f* fever
febbrile feverish
femminile feminine
ferito wounded, injured
fermarsi to stop (*oneself*)
fermata *f* stop
ferro *m* iron
ferrovìa *f* railroad
ferroviàrio (*of the*) railroad
fiammìfero *m* match
fianco *m* side
fiato *m* breath; con il fiato sospeso with
   bated breath
figlia *f* daughter

figlio *m* son
figùrati 2 *sg pres* just imagine; don't mention it
figurativo representational
figurarsi to imagine (*to oneself*)
fila *f* row (*of seats, etc.*)
film *m* film (*moving picture*)
filobus *m* trolley-bus
filtro *m* filter
finalmente finally
fine *f* end
finestrino *m* window
finire (II/*isc*) to finish; **farla finita** to stop it
fino a(d) as far as, to the point of
fiore *m* flower
fiorentino Florentine
fiorire (II/*isc*) to flourish
Firenze *f* Florence (*city in Tuscany*)
firmare to sign
fìsica *f* physics
fìsico *m* physique
fisso fixed
fiume *m* river
foce *f* mouth (*of a river*)
foglia *f* leaf
fognatura *f* sewer
fondamentale fundamental
fondare to found
fondo *m* bottom, back; **in fondo** at the back, in the background, after all, in the last analysis
fontana *f* fountain
forchetta *f* fork
forma *f* form
formaggio *m* cheese
formare to form
fornire (II/*isc*) to furnish
Foro *m* Forum
forse perhaps
forte strong
fortezza *f* fort
fortuna *f* fortune; **per fortuna** fortunately
fotografare to photograph
fotografìa *f* photograph, photography
fotogràfico photographic
fra among, between
fràgola *f* strawberry

Francesca *f* Frances
Francia *f* France
francobollo *m* postage stamp
fratello *m* brother
freddo cold; **aver freddo** to be (feel) cold
freddoloso chilly, cold-blooded
freschezza *f* freshness
fresco cool, fresh
fretta *f* haste, hurry; **in fretta** in a hurry rapidly
fritto fried
fronte : di fronte opposite; **di fronte a** facing
frutta *f* fruit
Fùlvia *f* Fulvia
fumare to smoke
funzionalità *f* functional nature
funzionamento *m* functioning
funzionare to function, to work
fuori outside

G

gabinetto *m* toilet
gallerìa *f* gallery
gamba *f* leg; **in gamba** smart
gatto *m* cat
gelaterìa ice-cream shop
gelato *m* ice-cream
gemelli *m pl* twins
generale general
generalmente generally
gènere *m* kind; (*grammatical*) gender
gènero *m* son-in-law
gènio *m* genius; **andare a genio a qualcuno** to be to someone's liking
genitore *m* parent
gennaio *m* January
gente *f* people
gentile nice, kind
ghiàccio *m* ice
già already; yes indeed; of course
giacca *f* jacket
giallo yellow
Giano *m* Janus
giardino *m* garden
ginócchio *m* (*pl* **le ginócchia** *f*) knee
giocare to play

gioco *m* play, game
gioiello *m* jewel
gioioso happy
giornalaio *m* newsdealer
giornale *m* newspaper
giornata *f* day (*cf* Conversation 9, *note 2*)
giorno *m* day; **buon giorno** good morning
gióvane young
giovedì *m* Thursday
gioviale jovial
girare to go around
giro *m* turn; trip (*around a place*); **préndere in giro** to make fun of
gita *f* excursion
giugno *m* June
giurare to swear
giustificare to justify, excuse
giusto right
gli *pers pron* to him
Glielo *pers pron* it to you
goccia *f* drop
godere to enjoy; **godersi** to enjoy (*for oneself*)
gola *f* throat
gonna *f* skirt
gòtico Gothic
governo *m* government
grande big, large, great
grandemente greatly
grandezza *f* size
grandinare to hail
"Granfiltro" (*invar*) a brand of cigarette
granita *f* ice (*crushed ice with syrup or flavoring poured over it*)
gratis free for nothing, gratis
grave serious
grazie *f pl* thanks; thank you
grazioso pretty, graceful
greco Greek
Gregòrio *m* Gregory
Gròpina *f* Gròpina (*village in the upper Arno valley*)
grosso big
grotta *f* grotto
gruppo *m* group
guanto *m* glove
guardare to look at
guarire to recover (*one's health*)

guerra *f* war
guida *f* guide; steering wheel
gusto *m* taste

H

ho I have

I

idèa *f* idea
ideale ideal
identificazione *f* identification
ieri yesterday
illùdersi to delude oneself
illuminare to illuminate, light up
imitazione *f* imitation
immaginare to imagine
imparare to learn
impegno *m* engagement
impensato unexpected
imperatore *m* emperor
imperatrice *f* empress
impermeàbile *m* raincoat
impèro *m* empire
impiegato *m* employee, clerk
impiego *m* employment, job
imponente imposing
importante important
importanza *f* importance
importare to matter, be important
impossìbile impossible
impresa *f* undertaking
improbàbile improbable
in in
incantato *past part* enchanted
incantévole enchanting
incanto *m* enchantment
incaricare to charge, entrust
incendiare to set fire to
incèndio *m* fire
incontrare to meet
incùtere to strike in; to command (*respect*)
indicare to indicate, show
indigestione *f* indigestion
infatti in fact
infernale infernal
inferno *m* hell
infine finally

influenza *f* influence
informare to inform
informazione *f* piece of information
ingegnere *m* engineer
ingegnerìa *f* engineering
Inghilterra *f* England
ingiallire (II/*isc*) to grow yellow
inglese English
ingresso *m* entrance
iniziare to begin
inìzio *m* beginning
innocente innocent
inoltre besides, moreover
inondazione *f* inundation
insalata *f* salad
insegnare to teach
insieme together; **insieme a(d)** together with
insistente insistent
insistentemente insistently
insìstere to insist
insomma in short
intanto meanwhile
intelligente intelligent
intenso intense
interessante interesting
interessarsi (**di** ...) to be interested (in ...)
interesse *m* interest
internazionale international
interno *n and adj* interior; domestic (*mail*)
interpretare to interpret; **interpretar male** to misinterpret
interrogazione *f* interrogation
intorno *adv* around; **intorno a** around
introduzione *f* introduction
invece instead, on the other hand; **invece di** instead of
inventare to invent
inverno *m* winter
invidiare to envy
invitare to invite
invito *m* invitation
ìo *pers pron* I
irregolare irregular
irregolarità *f* irregularity
iscrizione *f* inscription
istante *m* instant

istruire (II/*isc*) to instruct; **istruirsi** to instruct oneself, improve one's mind
Italia *f* Italy
italiano Italian

K

kilometro (**chilometro**), *abbreviation* **km.** *m* kilometer

L

la *pers pron* her, it
la *art* the
La *pers pron* you
là there, over there; **al di là di** beyond
labbro *m* (*pl* **le labbra** *f*) lip
laborioso painful, troublesome
laggiù down there, over there
Lambretta *f* a kind of motor-scooter
lamentarsi to complain
lana *f* wool
làpide *f* stone
largo broad
lasciare to leave, let, allow; **lasciar fare a** to leave it up to
laterale lateral, to one side
latino Latin
lato *m* side
latte *m* milk
lavare to wash
lavorare to work
lavoro *m* work
le *pers pron* to her; them (*f pl*)
Le *pers pron* you; to you; for you
leale faithful, loyal
legge *f* law
leggenda *f* legend
lèggere to read
leggèro light
Lei *pers pron* you
lento slow
lenzuolo *m* (*pl* **le lenzuola** *f* [*by pairs*], **i lenzuoli** *m* [*not by pairs*]) sheet
léttera *f* letter
letto *m* bed
lettore *m* reader
lezione *f* lesson, lecture, class
li *pers pron m pl* them

Li *pers pron 3 pl m* you
lì there
lìbero free, available
libretto *m* booklet
libro *m* book
limone *m* lemon
lìmpido limpid, clear
lìnea *f* line
lingua *f* language
liquidazione *f* liquidation; **in liquidazione** on sale
lìquido liquid; in cash
lira *f* lira (*Italian monetary unit*)
lira *f* lyre
lista *f* list
lo *pers pron* him, it
lode *f* praise
loggione *m* top-gallery
logicamente logically, naturally
lontano distant, far away
loro *pers pron* they; their; them; to them
Loro *pers pron* you; your; to you
Loro Ciuffenna *a small town in the upper Arno valley*
luce *f* light
luglio *m* July
lùi *pers pron* he, him
lume *m* light, lamp
luna *f* moon
lunedì *m* Monday
lungo long
luogo *m* place
lusso *m* luxury; **di lusso** de luxe

M

màcchina *f* machine, automobile; **màcchina fotografica** *f* camera
madre *f* mother
magari perhaps even (*normally used with past subjunctive*)
maggio *m* May
maggiore main, greater, larger
magnificamente magnificently
magnìfico magnificent
magno: Gregòrio Magno *m* Gregory the Great
mai never

malanno *m* sickness, trouble
malato sick
male *n* evil, pain, hurt; **far male (a)** to hurt
male *adv* badly; **meno male** it's a good thing
malgrado in spite of
malincònico melancholy
mamma *f* mother; **mamma mia!** *interj* golly!
mammina *f* little mother, mommy
mancare to be lacking
mancia *f* tip
mandare to send
mangiare to eat
mania *f* mania, craze
maniera *f* manner, way
mano *f* hand
mare *m* sea; **per via mare** by ocean (regular) mail
Marìa *f* Mary
marito *m* husband
marmo *m* marble
marrone brown
martedì *m* Tuesday
Martino *m* Martin
marzo *m* March
maschile masculine, men's
Maso *m* Tom
màssimo greatest; **al màssimo** to the greatest extent
Masuccio *m* dear Tommy
matrìcola (*always f*) freshman
mattina *f* morning
mattone *m* tile
me *pers pron* me
mèdia *f* average
medicina *f* medicine
mèdico *m* doctor
mediocre mediocre
medioevale mediaeval
meglio *adv* better
memòria *f* memory; **a memòria** by heart
meno less; **per lo meno** at least
mensile monthly
mente *f* mind
mentire (*optionally II/isc*) to lie (*tell a falsehood*)

mentre while

menù *m* menu

meraviglia *f* marvel; **a meraviglia** marvellously

meravigliarsi to be amazed

meraviglioso marvellous

mercato *m* market; **a buon mercato** cheap

mercoledì *m* Wednesday

mese *m* month

messaggero *m* messenger; **Il Messaggeró** name of a Roman newspaper

metà *f* half; middle

metro *m* meter

méttere to put; **méttersi a** to start

mezzo *m* means (*especially of transport*)

mezzo *adj* half; **in mezzo a** in the midst of

mezzogiorno *m* noon

mi *pers pron* me, to me, for me

mica not at all, certainly not

mi dispiace I'm sorry

migliaio *m* (*pl* **le migliaia** *f*) group of about a thousand

migliore *adj* better; **il migliore** the best

milanese Milanese

militare military

mille a thousand

minerale mineral

Minerva *f* Minerva (*Roman goddess*)

miniera *f* mine

minuto *m* minute

mio *poss adj* my, mine

miràcolo *m* miracle

misto *m* mixture

moda *f* fashion

modello *m* model

moderno modern

modificazione *f* modification

modo *m* manner

moglie *f* wife

molte *f pl*, **molti** *m pl* many

moltìssimo very much

molto *adj* much, *pl* many; *adv* very, greatly, a lot

momento *m* moment, minute

mònaco monk; **mònaca** nun

mondiale world-wide; **guerra mondiale** *f* World War

monopòlio *m* monopoly

montagna *f* mountain; **in montagna** to (in) the mountains

monte *m* mountain, Mount

monumento *m* monument

morigerato moderate, temperate, of simple habits

morire to die

morte *f* death

morto *past part* dead; **stanco morto** dead tired

mosso rough (*of the sea*)

mostra *f* show, display; **méttersi in mostra** to put oneself on display

mucca *f* milch-cow

mùcchio *m* heap

multicolore multicolored, many-colored

muore he, she, it dies

muòversi to move (*oneself*)

muraglione *m* big wall

muro *m* (*pl* **le mura** *f* [city walls]; **i muri** *m* [house walls]) wall; **mura di cinta** *f pl* encircling walls

musèo *m* museum

mùsica *f* music, piece of music

N

Napoleone *m* Napoleon

napolitano Neapolitan

Natale *m* Christmas

natura *f* nature

naturalmente naturally

nave *f* ship

nazionale national

ne *pro-phr* some, any; from there (*replacing phrases introduced by* **da** "from" *or* **di**)

necessàrio necessary

necròpoli *f* necropolis

negòzio *m* store, business

nel *m sg* in the

nella *f sg* in the

neppure not even

nero black

Nerone *m* Nero

nessuno *pron* nobody; *adj* no

nevicare to snow

nevvero? isn't that so? isn't it?

niente *neg pron* nothing; **niente affatto** not at all; **non capire un bel niente** not to understand anything

noioso tiresome, annoying

nipote *m* nephew, grandson; *f* niece, granddaughter

no no

noleggiare to hire

nolo *m* hire; **dare a nolo** to rent out

nome *m* name

nominare to name

non not; **non ... affatto** not at all; **non c'è male** (*as answer to inquiry after health*) not badly

nonna *f* grandmother

nonno *m* grandfather

nono ninth

Nord *m* north

nostalgìa *f* nostalgia, homesickness, yearning

nostro *1 pl poss adj* our, ours

nota *f* note

notare to notice

notévole notable

notìzie *f pl* information, news

notte *f* night

novanta ninety

nove nine

novecento nine hundred

novembre *m* November

novemila nine thousand

novità *f* novelty

nulla *neg pron* nothing

nullatenente *m* wage-earner, propertyless

nuora *f* daughter-in-law

nuotare to swim

nuovo new; **di nuovo** again, anew

nuvolosità *f* cloudiness

nuvoloso cloudy

O

o, od *conj* or

obbligare to oblige

obiezione *f* objection

occasione *f* opportunity

òcchio *m* eye

occhiolino : fare l'occhiolino a qualcuno to make eyes at someone

occórrere to be necessary

occupato busy

od or

offéndere to offend

offesa *f* offense, insult

oggetto *m* object

oggi today

ogni every; **ogni tanto** every so often

ognuno everyone

oh oh

ohibò! for shame! shame on you!

oliva *f* olive

oltre a in addition to

oltretomba *m* life beyond the tomb

ombra *f* shadow

ombrello *m* umbrella

ondulatura *f* undulation

ònore *m* honor

opera *f* work; opera

operàio *m* workman; **operàia** *f* operator, employee

ora *f* hour, time; **di buon ora** early; **non veder l'ora (di)** to be impatient (for), not be able to wait (until)

ora *adv* now

oràrio *m* timetable; **in oràrio** on time

Orbetello *a city on the Tyrrhenian coast*

orchestra *f* orchestra

ordinare to order

òrdine *m* order

orécchio *m* (*pl* **le orécchia** *f*) ear

oretta *f* little hour; **tra un'oretta** in an hour or so; **una mezz'oretta** about half an hour

organizzare to organize

organizzatore *m* organizer

organizzatrice *f* organizer

orientamento *m* orientation

originale queer

originàrio original

ornamento *m* ornament

orsa *f* she-bear

orso *m* bear

osare to dare

ospitare to put up (*as a guest*)

Òstia *f* Ostia (*ancient seaport of Rome*)

ottanta eighty

Ottaviano *m* Octavian
ottavo eight
òttimo excellent
otto eight
ottobre *m* October
ottocento eight hundred; **l'Ottocento** the nineteenth century
ottomila eight thousand
otturare to stop up, fill (*tooth*)

P

pacchetto *m* little package
pace *f* peace, quiet
padre *m* father
padronanza *f* command, mastery
paese *m* country; town
paesino *m* little village
pagamento *m* payment
pagare to pay
Palatino *m* Palatine (*a hill of ancient Rome*)
palazzo *m* palace
palestra *f* gymnasium; practice
panchina *f* bench
pane *m* bread
panino *m* roll, sandwich; **panino imbottito** *m* sandwich
panna *f* whipped cream
panorama *m* panorama
Pàolo *m* Paul
papa *m* pope
papale papal
paraggi *m pl* neighborhood
parapiglia *m* (*invar*) mêlée
parecchi *m pl* (*f pl* **parécchie**) several
parente *m or f* relative (*NOT* parent!)
parere to seem, appear; to please; **che ve ne pare?** what do you think of it?; **quando ci pare** when we like
parere *m* opinion
parete *f* wall
pari equal, like
parlare to speak, talk
parola *f* word; **in parole pòvere** in words of one syllable, in a few words
parte *f* part, side; **da una parte** on one side, from one point of view
parte you leave; he, she, it leaves

partecipare (*a*) to participate (in)
partenza *f* departure
particolare peculiar
particolarmente particularly
partire to depart, leave
pascolare to graze
passaporto *m* passport
passare to pass
passeggiata *f* walk
passeggio *m* promenade
passo *m* step; **fare due passi** to take a little, (short) walk
pasta *f* dough; bread-paste; macaroni, etc.
pasticcerìa *f* pastry-shop
pasto *m* meal; **fine pasto** *f* dessert
patata *f* potato
pattino *m* (*light*) rowboat
pauroso fearful, frightful
pazienza *f* patience
peccato *m* sin; *exclam* what a pity! too bad!
pècora *f* sheep
pedante *m* pedant
peggio *adv* worse
peggiore *adj* worse
pelle *f* skin, leather
pellìcola *f* film (*e.g. in a camera*)
pensare to think; **pensarci** to see to it
pensianato *m* pensioner, one receiving a pension
pensiero *m* thought, idea
pensione *f* boarding-house
per for; **per cùi** for which reason; **per di più** moreover; **per lo meno** at least; **per lo più** for the most part
pera *f* pear
percentuale *f* percentage
perché because; why?
pèrdere to lose, miss
perfetto perfect
perfezione *f* perfection; **funzionare alla perfezione** to work perfectly
perfino even
perìodo *m* period
perméttere to permit
però however
persino even
persona *f* person

personale personal
Perugia *f a city in Umbria*
pesare to weigh
pesca *f* peach
pesce *m* fish; **non sapere più che pesci
  préndere** not to know which way to
  turn
peschereccio *m* fishing-boat
pettegolare to gossip
pezzo *m* piece
piacere to be pleasing, give pleasure;
  m pleasure
piacévole pleasant
piàngere to weep, cry
piano *adv* soft
pianta *f* plant
pianura *f* plain
piatto *m* dish
piazza *f* square
picco *m* peak; **a picco su** jutting out over
pìccolo little, small
piede *m* foot; **a piede** on foot
piemontese Piedmontese, *from Piemonte*
pieno full
pietra *f* stone
Pietro *m* Peter
Pincio *m a hill in Rome*
pioġgia *f* rain
pióvere to rain
pipa *f* pipe
pittoresco picturesque
pittòrico *(of or pertaining to)* painting
più more; **di più** most; **non ... più** not ...
  any more; **per di più** moreover; **tanto
  più che** all the more so because
piuttosto rather
pizzetta *f* little pizza
plàcido placid, calm
platèa *f* orchestra *(floor of theater)*
plurale *m* plural
po': **un po'** a little
poeta *m* poet
poi afterwards
poiché since
polìtica *f* politics
polìtico political
polo *m* pole
pòpolo *m* people, nation, race

poltrona *f* arm-chair; seat
poltroncina *f* little arm-chair; seat (*smaller
  than* **poltrona**)
pomeriggio *m* afternoon
pomodoro *m* (*pl* **i pomodori** *or* **i pomidoro**)
  tomato
ponte *m* bridge
portare to carry, bring; to impel; to
  take
portatore *m* bearer
pòrtico *m* portico; porch
portiera *f* door-keeper's wife
portiere *m* door-keeper, concierge
porto *m* port
Porto Santo Stèfano *a city on the Tyrrhenian
  coast*
possiamo we can
possìbile possible
possibilità *f* possibility
postale postal
posto *m* place; **èssere a posto** to be
  all set
potere to be able, can
poveretto *m* poor fellow
pòvero poor
prato *m* field
precedentemente previously, before (*in
  time*)
preciso precise
preferire (II/*isc*) to prefer
pregare to pray, beg
pregiato prized, valuable
pregiudìzio *m* prejudice
prego you're welcome
préndere to take, get; **préndersela** to get
  angry, be offended
prenotazione *f* reservation
preoccuparsi to worry, be concerned
preparativi *m pl* preparations
presenza *f* presence; **presenza 1.85**
  1.85 meters tall
presso near
presto quickly
prezzo *m* price
prima *adv* first, earlier; **prima di** *prep phr*
  before
primavera *f* spring
primitivo primitive

primo first; **prima donna** *f* opera star; **prima mattina** early morning

principale principal, main

princìpio *m* principle

probàbile probable

problema *m* problem

procurare to procure, get

professione *f* profession; **far la professione lìbera** to be on one's own (*professionally*)

professore *m* professor, teacher

profondità *f* profundity

programma *m* program

proibitivo prohibitive

promessa *f* promise

promontòrio *m* promontory, cape

pronto ready; (*on telephone*) hello

pronuncia *f* pronunciation

propòsito : a propòsito by the way

proprietario *m* owner; man of property

pròprio *adj* one's own; **vero e pròprio** real

pròprio *adv* just, right, really

prosciutto *m* ham

proseguire to continue

pròssimo next; forthcoming

protèggere to protect

provare to prove; to try; to feel, experience

proveniente coming (from), originating (in)

provetto skilled

provincia *f* province

provvedere (a) to provide (for), to look out (for), to take care (of)

pùbblico *adj and n m* public

pulito clean

punta : ora di punta *f* rush hour

punto *m* point; **in punto** on the dot, (*of time*) sharp

può you can; he, she, it can

pure *adv* just

puré *m* purée; **puré di patate** *m* mashed potatoes

puritano Puritan

puro pure

purtroppo unfortunately

Q

qua here, over here

quadro *m* picture

qualche *indef adj* some (*always with singular*)

qualcosa *indef pron m* something

qualcuno *indef pron m* somebody, someone

quale *interrog adj* which; **il quale** *rel pron phr* which, who

qualsiasi any

quanto *interrog adj, adv* how much, how many; *rel adj, adv* as much as, as many as; **senza dire né tanto né quanto** without saying yea or nay

quaranta forty

quarantacinque forty-five

quarto *adj* fourth; *n m* quarter

quasi *adv* almost; *conj* as if

quattòrdici fourteen

quattro four

quattrocento four hundred

quattromila four thousand

quello *dem adj, pron* that, that one, the one

questo *dem adj, pron* this

qui here

quìndici fifteen

quinto fifth

R

rabbia *f* anger; **che rabbia!** *exclam* how irritating!

raccomandata *f* registered letter

raccontare to tell, recount, narrate

radunare to collect, gather

radura *f* open space

raffreddore *m* cold

ragazza *f* girl

ragazzo *m* boy

ragione *f* reason; **aver ragione** to be right

ràpido rapid, fast

rappresentare to represent

re *m* (*invar*) king

realtà *f* reality

recensione *f* review; **fare una recensione di un film** to give a film a review

recitare to act

recitazione *f* acting
recuperare to make up time
regina *f* queen
regolare regular
regolarmente regularly
religione *f* religion
Remo *m* Remus (*legendary founder of Rome*)
réndere to give back, render
reparto *m* department
repubblicano republican
restare to remain
restaurazione *f* restoration
restauro *m* restoration; remodeling
resto *m* change
retta *f* attention; **dar retta** to pay attention
ribàttere to reply, retort
ricavare to extract
ricerca *f* research
ricévere to receive
ricevimento *m* reception
ricevuta *f* receipt
ricordare to remember; **ricordarsi** to remember
ricordo *m* record
riconòscere to recognise; to acknowledge, admit
ridurre to reduce; **ridotto male** "in a bad way"
riempire to fill out
riesce he, she, it succeeds
rievocare to recall, call to mind
riguardare to regard, concern; **riguardarsi** to take care of oneself
rimanere to remain, be
rincontrarsi to meet again
rinfrescare to cool off
rinfresco *m* refreshment
rinvigorante invigorating
ripétere to repeat
riportare to bring back
riposare to rest
riposo *m* rest
risalire to go back (*in time*)
rìschio *m* risk
risòlvere to resolve
risparmiare to save
rispàrmio *m* savings
risposta *f* answer

ristorante *m* restaurant
risuscitare to resuscitate
ritardo *m* delay; **in ritardo** late
ritirare to withdraw
ritornare to return
ritorno *m* return
riuscire to succeed
Roberto *m* Robert
robusto robust
roccia *f* rock
Roma *f* Rome
romànico Romanesque
romano Roman
Ròmolo *m* Romulus (*legendary founder of Rome*)
rómpere to break
rosso red
rovina *f* ruin
rubare to steal
rumore *m* noise

S

sa you know
sàbato *m* Saturday
sàbbia *f* sand
sacco *m* sack; **sacco a pelo** *m* sleeping-bag
sagra *f* festival
sala *f* hall
salame *m* salame
salire to go up, rise, get onto; **salire a** to ascend
salita *f* rise, steeply rising street; **in salita** uphill
salone *m* salon
saltimbocca alla romana *m a rolled-up slice of veal with various kinds of piquant sauces*
salumerìa *f* pork-butcher shop
salutare to greet, to say good-bye to
salute *f* health
saluto *m* greeting
salvare to save; **salvare capre e càvoli** to eat one's cake and have it too
salve hello
sano healthy; wholesome
santo holy; Saint

sapere to know
sapore *m* flavor
saraceno Saracen
sardina *f* sardine
sbagliare to mistake; **sbagliarsi** to make a mistake, be mistaken
sbaglio *m* mistake
sbarcare to disembark
scala *f* stair
scalino *m* step
scarpa *f* shoe
scarso scarce
scartare to eliminate
scavare to excavate
scena *f* scene
scherzare to joke
scherzo *m* joke
schiacciare to crush
schiaffone *m* (*big*) slap
sciare to ski
scìmmia *f* monkey, ape
sciupare to spoil
scolpire (II/*isc*) to carve
scomméttere to bet
scòmodo uncomfortable
scompartimento *m* compartment (*on a train*)
sconfìggere to defeat
sconosciuto unknown
scontento discontented
scontro *m* collision; **scontro fra cinque mezzi** collision of five different types of vehicles
scopo *m* purpose, aim, object
scòrrere to flow
scorso last (*most recent*)
scottare to burn; **scottarsi** to get burned, get sunburned
scrìvere to write
scudo *m* shield, escutcheon
scuro dark
scuola *f* school
scusare to excuse
se if; whether
sé *3 sg, pl refl pron* him-, her-, itself; themselves
sebbene although
sècolo *m* century

scondo *adj* second; *prep* according to
sèdia chair
sediàmoci let's sit down
sédici sixteen
seduto *past part* seated
segnare to mark
seguente following
seguitare to continue, keep on
sei six
sei you are
seicento six hundred; *n f* "600" (*kind of automobile*)
seimila six thousand
sellare to saddle
sembrare to seem
semifreddo *m* frozen custard
sémplice simple
semplicemente simply
sempre always, ever; **sempre dritto** straight ahead
senatore *m* senator
sensibilità *f* sensitivity
senso *m* sense
sentimentale *adj* sentimental; *n m* sentimentalist
sentire to feel, to hear; **sentirsi** to feel (*in health*)
senza without
senz'altro right away; undoubtedly
separare to separate
sepolcro *m* sepulchre, tomb
sera *f* evening; **buona sera** good evening
serata *f* evening
sereno clear
sèrio serious
servire to serve, help, assist
sessanta sixty
sessione *f* session; examination period
sesto sixth
sete *f* thirst
settanta seventy
sette seven
settecento seven hundred
settembre *m* September
settemila seven thousand
settentrionale north, northern; northerner
settimana *f* week
sèttimo seventh

sfogarsi to express oneself
sfollato *m* war refugee
sfondo *m* background
sforzo *m* effort
sfruttare to exploit
sfuggire to get away from, escape from (a)
si *3 sg, pl refl pron* (to) himself, (to) herself, (to) itself, (to) yourself; (to) themselves, (to) yourselves
sì yes
sia (that) it be; sia ... che ... both ... and ...
si accòmodi sit down; please go
sicuro sure, certain; di sicuro certainly
si fa one does, we do
si figuri don't mention it
sigaretta *f* cigarette
significato *m* meaning
signora *f* lady; Mrs.
signore *m* gentleman, lord; sir; Mr.
Signorìa: Piazza della Signorìa *f* a square in Florence
signorina *f* young lady; Miss
silenzioso silent
simboleggiare to symbolise
simpàtico likeable
sinfonìa *f* symphony
singolare singular
sìngolo single
sinistra: a sinistra to (on) the left
si prova one experiences
si riesce one succeeds
si ritorna one returns
si sièdono they sit down
sistema *m* system
si va one goes
s.m. = sopra (il livello del) mare above sea level
sméttere to cease; smétterla to cease, stop it
smuòvere to move (*from a previous position*)
snello slender; agile, nimble
snob *m* snob
so I know
sociale social
società *f* society, company
soddisfare to satisfy
sòffice soft

soffrire to suffer, stand, endure
soggiorno *m* sojourn
sognare to dream
sogno *m* dream
solamente only
sole *m* sun; préndere il sole to take a sun-bath
sòlito usual, customary; al sòlito as usual; del sòlito than usual
solo *adj* only, single; *adv* only
soltanto *adv* only
somigliare (a) to resemble
sono I am
sonoro sonorous, refreshing
sopportare to support, stand
sopra above, on; sopra a on (to)
sopraelevazione *f* super-elevation
soprano *m* soprano
sorella *f* sister
sorellina *f* little sister
sorgente *f* spring (*of water*)
sorpresa *f* surprise
sospéndere to suspend; con il fiato sospeso with bated breath
sospettare to suspect
sostantivo *m* noun
sostanzioso substantial
sostituire to substitute, replace
sotterraneo underground, subterranean
sottovoce in a low voice
sparso scattered
spécchio *m* mirror
speciale special
specialità *f* specialty
specialmente especially
specie *f* kind, species
spedire (II/*isc*) to send
spedizione *f* expedition
sperare to hope
spesa *f* expense, expenditure; fare delle spese to do some shopping
spesso often
spiegare to explain
spiritoso witty, humorous; "wise guy"
splendore *m* splendor
sport *m* sport
sportello *m* ticket-window
sportivo sporting

sposare to marry; **sposarsi** to get married

sposi *m pl* married couple

sposo *m* bridegroom

sta he, she, it is; you are (*with regard to health*)

stabilire (II/*isc*) to establish

stagione *f* season

stai you are (*with regard to health*)

stamattina this morning

stampa *f* press (*newspaper*)

stanco tired; **stanco morto** dead tired

stanno they are, you are (*with regard to health*)

stanza *f* room

stare to stand, be located; to be (*with regard to health*); **stare per** to be about to; **stare ad ascoltare** to listen ; **stàrsene** to remain

Stati Uniti *m pl* United States

stato *m* state

stato *past part* been

statua *f* statue

stazione *f* station

Stèfano *m* Stephen

stella *f* star

stile *m* style

stòmaco *m* stomach

stòria *f* history; **fare delle stòrie** to make a fuss

stòrico *adj* historic(al); *n m* historian

strada *f* street, road; **per la strada** along the way; **sbagliare strada** to take the wrong road

stradale pertaining to roads, of the road

straniero *adj* foreign; *n m* foreigner

strano strange

straordinàrio extraordinary

strapazzare to overwork

stretto tight

strìngere to squeeze, squash

struttura *f* structure

studente *m* student

studiare to study

stùdio *m* study, studying

stupendo wonderful, stupendous

stupire (II/*isc*) to amaze

su on

subire (II/*isc*) to undergo, fall under (*influence*)

sùbito immediately

succédere to happen

successivo following

suddetto above-mentioned, aforesaid

suo his, her, its; your

suòcera *f* mother-in-law

suòcero *m* father-in-law

suonare to play (*a musical instrument*)

superbo superb

superficiale superficial

surgelati *m pl* frozen foods

sviluppare to develop

sviluppo *m* development

T

tabaccaio *m* tobacconist

tabacco *m* tobacco

tacere to be silent, shut up

tale such

tanto *dem adj* so much, so many; **tanto più che** all the more so because

tanto *adv* in any case

tappeto *m* carpet

tardi *adv* late; **far tardi** to be late

tassa *f* tax

tassì *m* taxi

tàvola *f* table

tàvolo *m* table

te *2 sg pers pron* you

tè *m* tea

tedesco German

telefonare to telephone

telèfono *m* telephone

temere to fear, be afraid

tèmpio *m* temple

tempo *m* time; **un tempo** once upon a time; **con l'andar del tempo** with the passage of time

temporale *m* storm

temporaneamente temporarily

tenda *f* tent

tenente *m* lieutenant

tenere to hold

tenore *m* tenor

tentare to try

Teodora *f* Theodora
terme *f pl* hot springs; baths
terminare to terminate, finish, end
terra *f* earth
terrazza *f* terrace
terreno *m* terrain
terzo third
tesoro *m* treasure
testa *f* head
testo *m* text
Tévere *m* Tiber
ti *2 sg pers pron* (to) you
tièpido tepid, lukewarm
tintarella *f* sun-tan
tipo *m* type, sort
tirare to pull
tògliere to take away; **tògliersi** to get rid of, take off of oneself
tomba *f* tomb
Tommaso *m* Thomas
tonalità *f* tonality
tondetto roundish
tondo round
torinese *from Torino*
tornare to return; **ben tornato** welcome back
Toro *m* Taurus; bull
torre *f* tower
torta *f* tart
toscano Tuscan
tosse *f* cough
totalmente totally
tovagliuolo *m* napkin
tra among, between; (*time*) after the lapse of, in
tràffico *m* traffic
Traiano *m* Trajan
traiano *adj* of Trajan
tram *m* street-car
tramonto *m* sunset
tranquillo tranquil, calm
tràppola *f* trap, snare
trascurare to neglect
trasferirse to move, to change one's address
trasporto *m* transportation
trattarsi di to be a question of
trattorìa *f* restaurant

trazione *f* traction
tre three
trecento three hundred
trédici thirteen
tremendo tremendous
tremila three thousand
treno *m* train
trenta thirty
triste sad
Troia *f* Troy
trono *m* throne
troppo *adj* too much, too many; *adv* too too much
trovare to find; **trovarsi** to be located
trucco *m* trick
tu *2 sg pers pron* you
tufàceo tufa-like, of tufa
tuffarsi to dive
tufo *m* tufa
tùmulo *m* mound
tuo *poss adj* your
tutto *adj* all; *n m* everything

U

uccìdere to kill
udienza *f* audience
uffa! *exclam* what a nuisance! phew!
ufficio *m* office
Uffizi *m pl the Uffizi art gallery in Florence*
ugualmente equally; all the same
ultimamente lately, recently
ùltimo last, latest
umano human
un *indef art* a, an; *num* one
ùndici eleven
ùnico only
unire (II/*isc*) to unite, join
università *f* university
uomo *m* (*pl* **uòmini**) man; **da uomo** for men
uovo *m* (*pl* **le uova** *f*) egg
usare to use
uscire to go out
usign(u)olo *m* nightingale
utensile *m* utensil
uva *f sg* grapes

V

va he, she, it goes; **va bene** O.K., all right

vacanza *f* vacation

vada go

vagone *m* (*railroad*) car; **vagone ristorante** *m* dining car

valigia *f* suitcase

valore *m* value, worth

vanno they go; **vanno per i fatti loro** they go on about their business

vantaggio *m* advantage

vantarsi to boast

variare to vary

varietà *f* variety

vàrio various; *pl* several

vaso *m* vessel

vècchio old

vedere to see

vèdovo *m* widower; **vèdova** widow

veglione *m* all-night ball

vela *f* sail

véndere to sell

véndita *f* sale

venerdì *m* Friday

veneto Venetian; *from Venezia*

Vèneto: Via Vèneto *f* *a street in Rome*

venire to come

venti twenty

venticinque twenty-five

ventina *f* score, group of about twenty

vento *m* wind; **tira vento** the wind blows

veramente truly, really

verde green

vergogna *f* shame

verità *f* truth; **per la verità** to tell the truth

vero true; isn't it so?; **vero e pròprio** real

versamento *m* deposit

Vespasiano *m* Vespasian (*Roman emperor*)

vestìbolo *m* vestibule

vestito dressed

vetrina *f* show-window

vi *2 pl pers pron* you, to you

via *f* street, way; **per via aèrea** by air mail; **per via mare** by ocean mail; **Via Vèneto** *a street in Rome*

via! *exclam* come on!

viaggiare to travel

viaggiatore *m* traveller

viaggio *m* trip; **in viaggio** on the way

vicenda *f* event, happening

viceversa vice-versa, the other way around; on the other hand

vicino *adj* nearby; *adv* near; **vicino a** *prep* near

viene he, she, it comes

villeggiante *m or f* vacationer

vino *m* wine

violento violent

visione *f* vision; **di prima visione** first-run (*of movie-house*)

visitare to visit

vista *f* view

visto *past part* seen

vita *f* life

vìvere to live

vivo alive

vìzio *m* vice

vocale vocal

voce *f* voice; **a voce bassa** in a low voice

vògliono you want, they want

voi *2 pl pers pron* you

volentieri gladly

volere to want, wish; **ci vuole** there is necessary; **cosa vuole?** what do you expect? **voler dire** to mean

volta *f* time

vorrei I'd like

vostro *poss adj* your, yours

votante *m or f* person voting, voter

votare to vote

vuoi you want

vuole he, she, it wants; you want; **vuol dire** you mean

Z

zia *f* aunt

zii *m pl* aunt and uncle

zio *m* uncle

zucchina *f* squash

A

a, an un(o) *m*, una un' *f*

able : to be able potere; **not to be able to wait (until)** non veder l'ora (di)

about: to be about to stare per

above sopra

absolutely assolutamente

accept accettare

accompany accompagnare

according to secondo

account conto *m*; **current account** conto corrente *m*

acquaintance conoscenza *f*

acquainted: be, get acquainted with conóscere, familiarizzarsi con (*e.g. a city*)

act (*in play, movie etc.*) recitare

acting recitazione *f*

activity attività *f*

actor attore *m*

addition: in addition to oltre a

administration amministrazione *f*

administrative amministrativo

admit amméttere

advance: in advance in antìcipo

advantage vantaggio *m*

advise consigliare

Aeneas Enea *m*

aerial aèreo

aesthetic estètico

affirmation affermazione *f*

afraid: to be afraid of temere

after dopo

afternoon pomeriggio *m*

afterwards poi

again di nuovo

against contro

age età *f*

agree èssere d'accordo

agreement accordo *m*; **in agreement** d'accordo

ahead: go ahead! *exclam* avanti !; **straight ahead** sempre dritto

air ària *f*; **pertaining to the air** aèreo; **to put on airs**; darsi delle àrie; **in the open air** all'aperto

alive vivo

all tutto; **after all** in fondo; **(not) at all** affatto; **all the same** ugualmente

all-night ball veglione *m*

allow lasciare, permettere

almost quasi

already già

also anche

although sebbene

always sempre

amaze stupire; **to be amazed** stupirsi, meravigliarsi

American americano

among fra, tra

amuse divertire

amusement divertimento *m*

amusing divertente

analysis: in the last analysis in fondo

ancient antico

and e, ed; **and so forth** e così via

anew di nuovo

anger rabbia *f*

Anna, Ann(e) Anna *f*

answer risposta *f*

Anthony Antònio *m*

antiquity antichità *f*

any: in any case tanto

ape scìmmia *f*

apéritif aperitivo *m*

apostle apòstolo

apparently apparentemente

appear (*seem*) parere

appearance apparenza *f*

applaud applaudire (*optionally* II/*isc*)

appointment appuntamento *m*

approach avvicinarsi

April aprile *m*

aqueduct acquedotto *m*

archaeological archeològico

archaeology archeologìa *f*

architectural architettònico

architecture architettura

arm braccio *m* (*pl* le braccia *f*); (*weapon*) arma *f* (*pl* le armi)

armchair poltrona *f*

aromatic aromàtico

around *adv* intorno; *prep phr* intorno a

arrangement disposizione *f*
arrive arrivare
art arte *f*
article artìcolo *m*
artificially artificialmente
artist artista *m*
as come; **as if** quasi; **as much as** quanto; **to act as** fare da
ascend salire
ask (for) domandare
aspect aspetto *m*
assertion affermazione *f*
assure assicurare
at a, ad; **(not) at all** affatto;
attach attaccare
attack: to attack attacare
attention retta *f*; **to pay attention** dar retta
attitude atteggiamento *m*
attractive carino
attribute: to attribute attribuire (II/*isc*)
audience udienza *f*
August agosto *m*
Augustus Augusto *m*
aunt zia *f*; **aunt and uncle** zii *m. pl*
auto(mobile) automòbile *f*, màcchina *f*; **auto bus** àutobus *m*
autumn autunno *m*
avenue corso *m*
average mèdia *f*
away: to take away tògliere

B

back fondo *m*; **at the back** in fondo
background sfondo *m*
bad: too bad ! *exclam* peccato !; "**in a bad way**" ridotto male
ball: all-night ball veglione *m*
banana banana *f*
bankruptcy fallimento *m*
baptize battezzare *m*
bar: espresso bar bar *m*
baroque barocco *m*
based basato
basilica basìlica *f*
bated: with bated breath con il fiato sospeso

bath bagno *m*; **to take a bath** fare il bagno
baton bacchetta *f*
be èssere; **to be (feel) cold** aver freddo; **to be (feel) hot** aver caldo; **to be cold** (*of weather*) far freddo; **to be hot** (*of weather*) far caldo; **to be present** assìstere
beach attendant bagnino *m*
beans: string beans fagiolini *m*
bear (*animal*) orso *m*
bearer portatore *m*
beat down abbàttere
beautiful bello
beauty bellezza *f*
because perché
become divenire, diventare, farsi; **become lower** abbassarsi
bed letto *m*
beer birra *f*
before (*in time*) *adv* precedentemente; *prep phr* prima di
beg (*request*) pregare
begin cominciare, iniziare
beginning inìzio *m*
behave comportarsi
beheading decapitazione *f*
behind dietro
believe crédere
bell-boy cameriere *m*
bench panchina *f*
beside *adv* accanto; *prep phr* accanto a
best *adj* il migliore; *adv* il meglio
bet: to bet scomméttere
better *adj* migliore; *adv* meglio
between fra, tra
beyond *prep phr* al di là di; **the beyond** (*life after death*) aldilà *m*
big grande, grosso
bill (*banknote*) biglietto *m*; (*statement of sum owed*) conto *m*
black nero
blessèd beato
blond biondo
blouse camicetta *f*
blow: the wind blows tira vento
blue azzurro
boarding-house pensione *f*
boast: to boast vantarsi
boat barca *f*
bomb: to bomb bombardare

book libro *m*; **telephone book** elenco *m*
booklet libretto *m*
bottom fondo *m*
both ... and ... sia ... che ...
bourgeois attitudes borghesismo *m sg*
box-office botteghino *m*
boy ragazzo *m*
bread pane *m*; **what is eaten along with bread** companàtico *m*
break: to break rómpere
breakfast colazione *f*
breath fiato *m*
bride sposa *f*
bridegroom sposo *m*
bridge ponte *m*
brief breve
brilliant brillante
bring portare; **bring back** riportare
broad largo
broth brodo *m*
brother fratello *m*
brother-in-law cognato *m*
brown marrone *invar*
brunet(te) bruno
Brutus Bruto *m*
building edificio *m*; **pertaining to building** edilìzio
burn: to burn scottare; **to get burned** scottarsi
bus (*city*) àutobus *m*; (*suburban or inter-urban*) corriera *f*
business negòzio *m*; **they go on about their business** vanno per i fatti loro
busy occupato
butter burro *m*
buy: to buy comprare
by per; **by the way** a propòsito

C

cabbage càvolo *m*
call: to call chiamare; **to be called** (*named*) chiamarsi; **to call to mind** richiamare
calligraphy calligrafìa *f*
calm calmo, plàcido, tranquillo; **to calm oneself, calm down** calmarsi
campaign campagna *f*

can (**to be able**) potere
candidate candidato *m*
cape promontòrio *m*
capital (*city*) capitale *f*
car (*railroad*) vagone *m*
cares to take care of curare, provvedere (a); **to take care of oneself** riguardarsi
carpet tappeto *m*
carriage carrozza *f*
carry portare
Carso Carso *m*
carve scolpire (II/*isc*)
cash: in cash liquido
cashier's window *or* **desk** cassa *f*
castle castello *m*
cathedral cattedrale *f*
cease cessare, sméttere
celebrated cèlebre
center centro *m*
century sècolo *m*
certain certo, sicuro
certainly certo, certamente, di sicuro
chair sèdia *f*
chance caso *m*; **by (any) chance** per caso
change (*remaining money*) resto *m*; **to change** cambiare
characteristic caratterìstica *f*
charge (*entrust*) incaricare
charity carità *f*
chat chiàcchiera *f*, chiacchierata *f*; **to have a little chat** fare due chiàcchiere; **to chat** chiacchierare
cheap econòmico, a buon mercato
cheerful allegro
cheese formaggio *m*
chemistry chìmica
cheque assegno *m*; **travellers' cheque** assegno viaggiatori *m*
child bambino *m*, bambina *f*
chilly freddoloso
Christ Cristo *m*
Christmas Natale *m*
church chiesa *f*
cigarette sigaretta *f*
cinematograph cinematògrafo *m*
city città *f*
citizen cittadino *m*
civilisation civiltà *f*

civilised civile
class classe *f*
Claudius Clàudio *m*
clean pulito
clear chiaro, lìmpido, sereno
clearly chiaramente
clerk impiegato *m*
close chiùdere
clothing abbigliamento *m*
coffee caffè *m*; **espresso coffee** espresso *m*
cold *n* raffreddore *m*; *adj* freddo; **be (feel) cold** aver freddo; **be cold** (*of weather*) far freddo; **cold-blooded** freddoloso
collect radunare
colonnade colonnato *m*
color colore *m*
colored colorato
column colonna *f*
combat: to combat combàttere
come venire; **come along with** accompagnare; **come near** avvicinarsi; **come on!** *exclam* via!
comedy commèdia *f*
comfortable còmodo
comfortably comodamente
command (*respect*) incùtere
commemorate commemorare
common comune
company compagnìa *f*, società *f*; **insurance company** società di assicurazioni *f*
compartment scompartimento *m*
complain lamentarsi
complete: to complete completare
completely completamente
complex, complicated complesso
compliment complimento *m*
concede concédere
concerned: be concerned (*worry*) preoccuparsi
concert concerto *m*
concierge portiere *m*, portiera *f*
conductor (*of orchestra*) direttore *m*
confess confessare
confession confessione *f*
confirmation conferma *f*
confused confuso
congratulate congratularsi (con)
congratulation congratulazione *f*

connection (*train, bus*) coincidenza *f*
consist consìstere
console: to console oneself consolarsi
constant costante
Constantine Costantino *m*
construct: to construct costruire (II/*isc*)
construction costruzione *f*
continue continuare, proseguire, seguitare
contrast: to contrast contrastare
convenient còmodo
conversation conversazione *f*, chiacchierata *f*, discorso *m*
cook: to cook cucinare
cool fresco; **to cool off** rinfrescare
cordial cordiale
cordially cordialmente
corridor corridoio
cost: to cost costare
costume costume *m*
cotton cotone *m*
cough tosse *f*
counter banco *m*
country (*as opposed to city*) campagna *f*; (*nation*) paese *m*
countryside campagna *f*
couple: married couple sposi *m pl*
courage coraggio; **to lose courage** pèrdersi d'ànimo
courageous: to be courageous farsi coraggio
course corso *m*
cousin cugina *f*, cugino *m*
cover: to cover coprire
cradle: to cradle oneself cullarsi
craze manìa *f*
cream crema *f*; **whipped cream** panna *f*
cross croce *f*
crush (*crowd of people*) calca *f*
cry (*weep*) piàngere
crystal cristallo *m*
cult culto *m*
cultural culturale
cupola cùpola *f*.
current corrente
cushion cuscino
custard: frozen custard semifreddo *m*
cutlet cotoletta *f*; **breaded veal cutlet** cotoletta alla milanese *f*

D

dare: to dare osare
dark scuro, bruno
data dati *m pl*
date (*appointment*) appuntamento *m*
daughter figlia *f*
daughter-in-law nuora *f*
day giorno *m*, giornata *f*
dead morto
dear caro
death morte *f*
début: person making a début debuttante *m or f*
December dicembre *m*
decide decìdere
deck out addobbare
dedicate dedicare
deed fatto *m*
defeat: to defeat sconfìggere
deject abbàttere
delay ritardo *m*
de luxe di lusso
democratic democràtico
demolish demolire (II/*isc*)
demonstrate dimostrare
dentist dentista *m*
depart partire
department reparto *m*
depend dipéndere
deposit depòsito *m*, versamento *m*; to deposit depositare
deputy deputato *m*
descent discesa *f*
describe descrìvere
description descrizione *f*
desire: to desire desiderare
dessert fine pasto *f*
destination destinazione *f*
destroy distrùggere
develop sviluppare
development sviluppo *m*
dialect dialetto *m*
die morire
difference differenza *f*
dining car vagone ristorante *m*
different diverso
difficult diffìcile

dine cenare
dinner cena *f*
director direttore *m*
disagreeable antipàtico
disappoint delùdere
discontented scontento
discourse discorso *m*
discuss discùtere
disembark sbarcare
dish piatto *m*
display mostra *f*; to put oneself on display méttersi in mostra
displease dispiacere
distance distanza *f*
distant lontano
distinguished distinto
dive: to dive tuffarsi
diverse diverso
divide: to divide divìdere
divine divino
do fare; what is to be done il da farsi;
  to do shopping fare delle spese
doctor mèdico *m*; dottore *m*
dog cane *m*
dollar dòllaro *m*
Dolomites Dolomiti *f pl*
dome cùpola *f*
door-keeper portiere *m*; door-keeper's
  wife portiera *f*
dot: (*of time*) on the dot in punto
double dóppio
doubt dùbbio *m*
down: beat down abbàttere; go down
  abbassarsi; down there laggiù
downtown (as *adv*) in centro
dozen dozzina *f*
dream sogno *m*; to dream sognare
dressed vestito
drink bìbita *f*; to drink bere
drop goccia *f*
during durante
duty dovere *m*

E

each ciascuno
ear orécchio *m* (*pl* le orécchia *f*)
earlier *adv* prima

early di buon' ora

earth terra *f*

easy fàcile

eat mangiare; **to eat one's cake and have it too** salvare capre e càvoli

economical econòmico

education educazione *f*

effort sforzo *m*

egg uovo *m* (*pl* le uova *f*)

eight otto; **eight hundred** ottocento; **eight thousand** ottomila

eighteen diciotto

eighth ottavo

eighty ottanta

elect elèggere

election elezione *f*

electoral elettorale

eleven ùndici

eliminate scartare

emperor imperatore *m*

empire impero *m*

employee impiegato *m*, impiegata *f*

empress imperatrice *f*

enchanted incantato

enchanting incantévole

enchantment incanto

encircling walls (*of city*) mura di cinta *f pl*

encore bis *m*

end fine, capo *m*; **to end** terminare

engagement impegno *m*

engineer ingegnere *m*

engineering ingegnerìa *f*

England Inghilterra *f*

English inglese

enjoy godere

enough *adv* abbastanza; **to be enough** bastare; **that's enough!** basta!

enrich arricchire (II/*isc*)

enter entrare (in)

enthusiasm entusiasmo *m*

enthusiast entusiasta *m* or *f*

entrance *f* entrata

entrust incaricare

entry ingresso *m*

environment ambiente *m*

environs dintorni *m pl*

envy: to envy invidiare

epoch època *f*

equally ugualmente

equivalent *adj and n m* equivalente

escape: to escape from sfuggire (*a*)

especially specialmente

espresso coffee espresso *m*

establish stabilire (II/*isc*)

etcetera eccètera

even perfino, persino; **not even** neppure; **perhaps even** magari

evening sera *f*, serata *f*

event vicenda *f*

ever sempre

every ogni; **every so often** ogni tanto

everyone ognuno

everything tutto *m*

evil male *m*

exact esatto

exactly esattamente

exaggerate esagerare

examination esame *m*; **to give an examination to someone** fare un esame a qualcuno

example esempio *m*

excavate scavare

excellent eccellente, òttimo, (*of persons*) bravo

exception eccezione *f*

excursion gita *f*

excuse: to excuse scusare, (**to justify**) giustificare

exist esìstere

expect: what do you expect? cosa vuole?

expedition spedizione *f*

expenditure, expense spesa *f*

expensive caro

explain spiegare

exploit: to exploit sfruttare

explore esplorare

express: to express oneself (*give vent to one's feelings*) sfogarsi

extend estèndere

exterior esterno

extract: to extract ricavare

extraordinary straordinàrio

eye òcchio *m*; **to make eyes at someone** fare l'occhiolino a qualcuno

eyelash ciglio *m* (*pl* le ciglia *f*)

F

façade facciata *f*

facing *prep phr* di fronte a

fact fatto *m*; **in fact** infatti, difatti

fall under (*an influence*) subire (II/*isc*)

familiar: **get familiar** familiarizzarsi

far *adj, adv* lontano; **as far as** fino a(d); **far(ther) out** al largo

farmer contadino *m*

fascinate affascinare

fashion moda *f*

father padre *m*

father-in-law suòcero *m*

favor favore *m*

fear: **to fear** temere

February febbraio *m*

feel sentire, provare; (*with regard to health*) sentirsi

feminine femminile

festival sagra *f*

fever febbre *f*

feverish febbrile

field prato *m*

fifteen quìndici

fifth quinto

fifty cinquanta

fight: **to fight** combàttere

fill, **fill out** riempire; **to fill a tooth** otturare un dente

film (*moving picture*) film *m*; (*used in camera*) pellicola *f*

filter filtro *m*

finally finalmente

find: **to find** trovare

fine bravo

finish: **to finish** finire (II/*isc*), terminare

fire (*in house, etc.*) incèndio; **to set fire to** incendiare

first *adj* primo; *adv* prima; **at first** dapprima

first-run (*said of movie house*) di prima visione

fish pesce *m*

fishing-boat peschereccio *m*

fitting: **to be fitting** convenire

five cinque; **five hundred** cinquecento; **five thousand** cinquemila

fixed fisso

"fixin's" companàtico *m*

flavor sapore *m*

Florence Firenze *f*

Florentine fiorentino

flourish: **to flourish** fiorire (II/*isc*)

flow: **to flow** scórrere

flower fiore *m*

flunk: **to flunk** (*someone*) bocciare

following seguente, successivo

food cibo *m*

foot piede *m*; **on foot** a piedi

for *prep* per; *conj* ché; **for the purpose of** per (*before an infinitive*), da (*before a noun*); **for the most part** per lo più; **for heaven's sake** ! *exclam* per carità !; **for shame** ! *exclam* ohibò !

force: **to force** costringere

foreign èstero, straniero

foreigner straniero *m*

forget dimenticare

fork forchetta *f*

form forma *f*; **to form** formare

fort fortezza *f*

forth: **and so forth** e così via

forthcoming pròssimo

fortunately per fortuna

fortune fortuna *f*

forty quaranta

Forum foro *m*

forward *adv* avanti

found: **to found** fondare

fountain fontana *f*

four quattro; **four hundred** quattrocento; **four thousand** quattromila

fourteen quattórdici

fourth quarto

France Francia *f*

Frances Francesca *f*

free lìbero; **free for nothing** gratis

fresco affresco *m*

fresh fresco

freshman matrìcola (*always f*)

freshness freschezza

Friday venerdì *m*

fried fritto

friend amico *m*, amica *f*

frozen custard semifreddo *m*

fruit frutta *f*

façade

full pieno
fun: to make fun of préndere in giro
function: to function funzionare
functional nature funzionalità *f*
functioning funzionamento *m*
fundamental fondamentale
funny buffo
furnish fornire (II/*isc*)
fuss: to make a fuss fare delle stòrie

G

gallery gallerìa *f*; **top gallery** loggione *m*
game gioco *m*
garden giardino *m*
gather radunare
gender gènere *m*
general generale
generally generalmente
genius gènio *m*
gentleman signore *m*, cavaliere *m*
German tedesco
get (*take*) préndere; (*obtain*) procurare; (*become*) divenire, diventare; (*for passive, use reflexive construction*); **to get up** (*e.g., out of bed*) alzarsi; **to get away** (**from**) sfuggire (a)
gilded dorato
girl ragazza *f*
give dare; **to give back** réndere
glad contento
gladly volentieri
glove guanto *m*
go andare; (*expression of courtesy*) accomodarsi; **go along with** accompagnare; **go around** girare; **go back** (*in time*) risalire; **go down** abbassarsi; **go in** entrare (in); **go out** uscire; **go up** salire
goat capra *f*
god dio *m* (*pl* gli dei)
goddess dea *f*
golly ! *exclam* accipìcchia !, mamma mia !
good buono; **it's a good thing** meno male; **good heavens** ! *exclam* Dio mio !
good-bye addio, arrivederci, (*formal*) arrivederLa; **to say good-bye to someone** salutare qualcuno
gosh ! *exclam* accidèmpoli !

gossip: to gossip pettegolare
Gothic gòtico
government governo *m*
grand-daughter nipote *f*
grand-father nonno *m*
grand-mother nonna *f*
grand-son nipote *m*
grant: to grant concédere
grapes uva *f sg*
grasp: to grasp cògliere
gratis gratis
graze pascolare
great grande
greatest màssimo; **to the greatest extent** al màssimo
greatly grandemente, molto
Greek greco
green verde
greet salutare
greeting saluto *m*, (*well-wishing*) augùrio *m*
Gregory Gregòrio *m*; **Gregory the Great** Gregòrio Magno
grotto grotta *f*
group gruppo *m*, (*knot of people*) cròcchio *m*
grow créscere; **to grow yellow** ingiallire (II/*isc*)
guide guida *f*, cicerone *m*

H

habit abitùdine *f*
hail: to hail grandinare
hair (*single hair*) capello *m sg*, (*hair of head etc., collectively*) capelli *m pl*
half *n* metà *f*; *adj* mezzo; **about half an hour** una mezz'oretta
hall sala *f*
ham prosciutto *m*
hand mano *f*; **on the other hand** invece, viceversa
handkerchief fazzoletto *m*
handwriting calligrafìa *f*
happen accadere, succédere
happening vicenda *f*
happy gioioso
hard (*difficult*) diffìcile
harmful dannoso
harsh aspro

haste fretta *f*

have avere; **have to** dovere

he lùi

head testa *f*

health salute *f*

heap mùcchio *m*

hear sentire

heart: **by heart** a memòria; **to lose heart** pèrdersi d'ànimo

heat caldo *m*

heaven cielo *m*; **for heaven's sake !, good heavens !** *exclam* per carità ! Dio mio !

hello (*during day*) buon giorno, (*in late afternoon and evening*) buona sera, (*on telephone*) pronto; salve (*only to people to whom one would use* tu)

help: **to help** aiutare

Henry Enrico *m*

her *poss adj* suo; *3 sg f disjv pers pron* lèi, *3 sg f conjv dir obj* la, *3 sg f conjv dat* le

here qui; **over here** qua; **here is, here are** ecco; **here it is, done** ecco fatto

herself *3 pers refl disjv pron* sé, *3 pers refl conjv pron* si

hi ciao (*used only to people to whom one would use* tu)

hill collina *f*; **little hill** collinetta *f*

him *3 sg m disjv pers pron* lùi, *3 sg m conjv dir obj* lo, *3 sg m conjv dat* gli

himself *3 pers refl disjv pron* sé, *3 pers refl conjv pron* si

hire nolo *m*; **to hire** nolleggiare

his *poss adj* suo

historian stòrico *m*

historic(al) stòrico

history stòria *f*

hold: **to hold** tenere

holy santo

home casa *f*; **at home, (to) home** a casa

homesickness nostalgìa *f*

honor onore *m*

hope: **to hope** sperare

hors d'œuvres antipasto *m sg*

horse cavallo *m*

hot caldo; **to be** (*feel*) **hot** aver caldo; **to be hot** (*of weather*) far caldo

hotel albergo *m*

hotel-keeper albergatore *m*

hour ora *f*; **an hour or so** un'oretta *f*; **rush hour** ora di punta *f*

house casa *f*

how ? come ?; **how many** quanti *m pl*; quante *f pl.*; **how much** quanto

however però

human umano

humorous spiritoso

hundred cento; **(group of) about a hundred** centinaio *m* (*pl* le centinaia *f*)

hunger fame *f*

hungry: **be hungry** aver fame

hunt caccia *f*; **to hunt** cacciare

hunting: **to go hunting** andare a caccia

hurry fretta *f*; **in a hurry** in fretta

hurt male *m*; **to hurt** far male (a)

husband marito *m*

I

I ìo

ice (*crushed ice with syrup or flavoring*) granita *f*

ice-cream gelato *m*

idea idea *f*, pensiero *m*

ideal ideale

identification identificazione *f*

if se

illuminate illuminare

imagine immaginare, figurarsi

imitation imitazione *f*

immediately sùbito

impatient: **to be impatient (for)** non veder l'ora (di)

importance importanza *f*

important importante; **to be important** importare

imposing imponente

impossible impossìbile

improbable improbàbile

improve one's mind istruirsi

in in; (*time*) fra, tra

indicate indicare

indigestion indigestione *f*

infernal infernale

influence influenza *f*

inform informare

information: **piece of information** informazione *f sg*, notìzia *f sg*; **information** (*collective*) informazioni *f pl*, notìzie *f pl*

innocent innocente
inscription iscrizione *f*
inside *adv, prep* dentro; *prep phr* dentro a
insist insistere
insistent insistente
insistently insistentemente
instant istante *m*
instead invece; **instead of** invece di
instruct istruire (II/*isc*)
insult offesa *f*
insurance assicurazione *f*
intelligent intelligente
interest interesse *m*; **to be interested (in)** interessarsi (di)
interesting interessante
interior interno *adj and n m*
international internazionale
interpret interpretare
interrogation interrogazione *f*
introduction introduzione *f*
inundation inondazione *f*
invigorating rinvigorante
invitation invito *m*
invite: to invite invitare
invent inventare
iron ferro *m*
irregular irregolare
irregularity irregolarità *f*
irritating: how irritating! *exclam* che ràbbia !
it *3 sg conjv dir obj pron* lo *m*, la *f*; *3 sg conj dat pron* gli *m*, le *f*
Italian italiano
Italy Itàlia *f*
its *poss adj* suo
itself *3 pers refl disjv pron* sé, *3 pers refl conjv pron* si

J

jabber: to jabber chiacchierare
jacket giacca *f*
January gennaio *m*
Janus Giano *m*
jewel gioiello *m*
join unire (II/isc)
joke scherzo *m*; **to joke** scherzare
jovial gioviale

July luglio *m*
June giugno *m*
just *adj* giusto; *adv* pròprio, pure
justify giustificare
jutting out over a picco su

K

keep on (*continue*) seguitare
key chiave *f*
kilometer chilòmetro *m*
kind *n* gènere *m*, specie *f*; *adj* (*nice*) gentile
king re *m* (*invar*)
kiosk chiosco *m*
kitchen cucina *f*
knee ginócchio *m* (*pl* le ginócchia *f*)
knife coltello *m*
knight cavaliere *m*
knot (*of people*) cròcchio *m*
know conóscere, sapere (*cf.* Grammar Unit **VI**, §22)

L

lack: to be lacking mancare
lady signora *f*; **young lady** signorina *f*
lamp lume *m*
language lingua *f*
large grande
last (*in a series*) ùltimo, (*most recent*) scorso; **to last** durare
late *adv* tardi, in ritardo: **to be late** far tardi
lately ultimamente
lateral laterale
latest ùltimo
Latin latino *adj and n m*
law legge *f*
lawyer avvocato *m*
leaf foglia *f*
learn imparare
least: at least almeno, per lo meno
leather pelle *f*
leave lasciare, (*depart*) partire; **to leave it up to someone** lasciar fare a qualcuno
lecture conferenza *f*; **to give a lecture** tenere una conferenza

left: to (on) the left   a sinistra
leg   gamba *f*
legend   leggenda *f*
lemon   limone *m*
less   meno
lesson   lezione *f*
let   lasciare
letter   léttera *f*
lie: to lie (*tell a falsehood*) mentire (*optionally* II/*isc*)
life   vita *f*; **life beyond the tomb**   oltretomba *m*
light   luce *f*, lume *m*; **to light up** illuminare; *adj* (*not heavy*) leggèro
like *prep* come; *vb* (*use* piacere, *transforming object of Eng.* like *into subject of* piacere, *and subject of Eng.* like *into indirect object of* piacere: *e.g., gli piace* "he likes")
likeable   simpàtico
liking: to be to someone's liking   andare a gènio a qualcuno
limpid   lìmpido
line   lìnea *f*
lip   labbro *m* (*pl* le labbra *f*)
liquid   lìquido
liquidation   liquidazione *f*
lira   lira *f*
list   lista *f*, elenco *m*; **to list** elencare
listen to   ascoltare
little   pìccolo; **a little**   un po'
live: to live   vìvere
local (train)   accelerato *m*
located: be located   stare, trovarsi
logically   logicamente
long   lungo
look: to look (at)   guardare; **to look out for** provvedere a; **to look out over** dare su
lord   signore *m*
lose   pèrdere
lot: a lot *adj* molto, *adv* molto (*invar*); **to cost a lot**   costare caro
low   basso
lower: become lower   abbassarsi
luxe: de luxe   di lusso
luxury   lusso *m*
lyre   lira *f*

machine   màcchina *f*
magnificent   magnìfico
magnificently   magnificamente
mail: by air mail   per via aèrea; **by ocean mail**   per via mare
main *adj* principale
make   fare; **to make up (lost) time** recuperare
man   uomo *m* (*pl* uòmini); **for men**   da uomo
mania   manìa *f*
manner   maniera *f*, modo *m*; **in this (that) manner**   così
many   molti *m pl*, molte *f. pl*; **how many** quanti *m pl*, quante *f pl*; **many-colored** multicolore
marble   marmo *m*
March   marzo *m*
mark: to mark   segnare
market   mercato *m*
married couple   sposi *m pl*
marry   sposare; **get married**   sposarsi
Martin   Martino *m*
marvel   meraviglia *f*
marvellous   meraviglioso
marvellously   a meraviglia
Mary   Marìa *f*
masculine   maschile
mashed potatoes   puré di patate *m*
masterpiece   capolavoro *m*
match   fiammìfero *m*
matter   cosa *f*; **to matter**   importare
May   maggio *m*
me *i sg disjv obj pers pron* me; *i sg conjv obj* mi
meal   pasto *m*
mean: to mean   voler dire
meaning   significato *m*
means (*esp. of transport*)   mezzo *m*
meanwhile   intanto
mediaeval   medioevale
medicine   medicina *f*
mediocre   mediocre
meet   incontrare; **to meet again** rincontrarsi
meeting   adunanza *f*, (*political*) comìzio *m*
melancholy   malincònico

left

mêlée parapiglia *m* (*invar*)
memory memòria *f*
men's maschile *adj*
mention: don't mention it (*formula of courtesy*) si figuri
menu menù *m*
merry allegro
messenger messaggero *m*
meter metro *m*
middle metà *f*
middle-class (**bourgeois**) **attitudes** borghesismo *m*
midst: in the midst of in mezzo a
Milanese milanese
milch-cow mucca *f*
military militare
milk latte *m*
mind mente *f*; **to call to mind** rievocare
mine (*coal, iron, etc*) miniera *f*
mine *poss adj* mio
mineral minerale
Minerva Minerva *f*
minute minuto *m*
miracle miràcolo *m*
mirror spècchio *m*
misinterpret interpretar male
miss (*young lady*) signorina *f* (*abbrev* Sig.na)
mistake sbaglio *m*; **to make a mistake, be mistaken** sbagliare
mixture misto *m*
model modello *m*
modern moderno
modification modificazione *f*
moment momento *m*
mommy mammina *f*
Monday lunedì *m*
money denaro *m*
monkey scìmmia *f*
monopoly monopòlio *m*
month mese *m*
monument monumento *m*
moon luna *f*
more più; **not ... any more** non ... più; **all the more so because** tanto più che
moreover per di più
morning mattina *f*; **this morning** stamattina
most *adv phr* di più

mother madre *f*, mamma *f*; **little mother** mammina *f*
mother-in-law suòcera *f*
mound tùmulo *m*
mountain montagna *f*, monte *m*; **to (in) the mountains** in montagna
mouth (*of a river*) foce *f*
move: to move muòvere; **to move oneself** muòversi; **to move emotionally** commuòvere; **to move from a previous position** smuòvere
movie-house cìnema *m*
Mr. signore *m* (*abbrev* Sig.)
Mrs. signora *f* (*abbrev* Sig.ra)
much *adj* molto, *adv* molto (*invar*); **how much?** quanto?; **so much** tanto
multicolored multicolore
museum musèo *m*
music mùsica *f*
my *poss adj* mio

N

name nome *m*; **to name** nominare; **to be named** chiamarsi
napkin tovagliuolo *m*
Napoleon Napoleone *m*
narrate raccontare
nasty brutto
national nazionale
naturally naturalmente, logicamente
nature natura *f*
Neapolitan napoletano
near *adj* vicino; *adv* vicino (*invar*); *prep* presso; *prep phr* vicino a
necessary necessàrio; **to be necessary** bisognare, convenire, occórrere, volerci
necktie cravatta *f*
necropolis necròpoli
need bisogno *m*; **to need** aver bisogno di
neglect: to neglect trascurare
nephew nipote *m*
Nero Nerone *m*
never mai
new nuovo
news-dealer giornalaio *m*
newspaper giornale *m*
New Year's Capodanno *m*

next *adj* pròssimo, *adv* accanto; **next to** accanto a

nice (*attractive, pretty*) carino; (*kind*) gentile

niece nipote *f*

night notte *f*

nine nove; **nine hundred** novecento; **nine thousand** novemila

nineteen diciannove; **the nineteenth century** l'Ottocento

ninety novanta

ninth nono

no *interj* no, *adj* nessuno

nobody nessuno

noise rumore *m*

noon mezzogiorno

no-one nessuno

north Nord *m*

nostalgia nostalgìa *f*

not non; **not at all** non ... affatto, non ... mica; **not even** neppure; **not badly** (*sentence answering question about health, etc.*) non c'è male

notable notévole

note biglietto *m*, (*music*) nota *f*

nothing *neg pron* niente, nulla

notice: **to notice** accòrgersi (di), notare

noun sostantivo *m*

novelty novità *f*

November novembre *m*

now adesso, ora

nuisance: **what a nuisance!** *exclam* uffa!

number nùmero *m*

objection obiezione *f*

oblige obbligare

ocean: **by ocean mail** per via mare

Octavian Ottaviano *m*

October ottobre *m*

of di

offend offéndere

offense offesa *f*

office ufficio *m*

often spesso

oh oh

O.K. *adv* bene, *interj* va bene

old vècchio, antico

olive oliva *f*

on su, sopra; **come on!** *exclam* avanti!

one *num* un(o); *indef* (*in indefinite constructions, use reflexive 3 sg, e.g.* si va "one goes"); **the one** *dem pron* quello

only *adj* solo, ùnico; *adv* solo, solamente, soltanto

open aperto; **to open** aprire

opera òpera *f*; **opera star** prima donna *f*

opinion parere *m*

opportunity occasione *f*

opposite *adv phr* di fronte, *prep phr* di fronte a

or o, od

orange arancia *f*

orangeade aranciata *f*

orchestra orchestra *f*; (*floor of theater*) platèa *f*

order òrdine *m*; **to order** ordinare

organise organizzare

organiser organizzatore *m*, organizzatrice *f*

orientation orientamento *m*

original originàrio

ornament ornamento *m*

other altro; **among other things** fra l'altro; **the other way around, on the other hand** viceversa

otherwise altrimenti

out, outside fuori; **to go out** uscire

outward esterno

over there laggiù

overwork: **to overwork** (*someone*) strapazzare

owe dovere

own: **one's own** pròprio; **to be on one's own** (*professionally*) esercitare la professione lìbera

ox bue *m* (*pl* buoi)

P

package: **little package** pacchetto *m*

pain dolore *m*, male *m*

painting (*picture*) dipinto *m*; **pertaining to painting** pittòrico

palace palazzo *m*

Palatine (*hill of ancient Rome*) Palatino *m*

panorama panorama *m*

papal papale

parent genitore *m*

part   parte *f*, brano *m*
participate (in)   partecipare (a)
particularly   particolarmente
party (*group of people*)   comitiva *f*
pass: to pass   passare
passport   passaporto *m*
patience   pazienza *f*
Paul   Pàolo *m*
pay   pagare
payment   pagamento *m*
peace   pace *f*
peach   pesca *f*
peak   picco *m*
pear   pera *f*
peasant   contadino *m*
peculiar (*special*)   particolare
pedant   pedante *m*
people (*folks*)   gente *f* *sg*; (*nation, race*)
   pòpolo *m*
percent   percento
percentage   percentuale *f*
perfect   perfetto
perfection   perfezione *f*
perfectly   perfettamente, alla perfezione
perform   eseguire (II/*isc*)
perhaps   forse; perhaps even   magari
period   perìodo *m*
permit: to permit   perméttere
person   persona *f*
personal   personale
Peter   Pietro *m*
phew ! *exclam* uffa !
photograph   fotografìà *f*; to photograph
   photografare
photographic   fotogràfico
photography   fotografìa *f*
physics   fìsica *f*
physique   fìsico *m*
piano   piano *m*; grand piano   piano a
   coda *m*
pick: to pick   cògliere
picture   quadro *m*
picturesque   pittoresco
piece   pezzo *m*, brano *m*
pillow   cuscino *m*
pin one's hopes (on)   cullarsi (su)
pipe   pipa *f*
pity: what a pity ! *exclam* che peccato !

pizza: little pizza   pizzetta *f*
place   luogo *m*, posto *m*; at ...'s place da
placid   plàcido
plant   pianta *f*
play   gioco *m*; to play (*a game*) giocare,
   (*a musical instrument*) suonare
pleasant   piacévole
please: to please (*give pleasure to*) piacere;
   interj per favore
pleasure   piacere *m*
plural *m*   plurale
poet   poeta *m*
point   punto *m*; to the point of   fino a
pole   polo *m*
political   polìtico
politics   polìtica *f*
poor   pòvero; poor fellow   poveretto *m*
pope   papa *m*
port   porto *m*
possibility   possibilità *f*
possible   possìbile
postage stamp   francobollo *m*
postal   postale
post-card   cartolina (postale)
potato   patata *f*
praise   lode *f*
pray   pregare
precise   preciso
prefer   preferire (II/*isc*)
prejudice   pregiudìzio *m*
preparations   preparativi *m pl*
present: to be present   assìstere
pretty   carino
previously   precedentemente
price   prezzo *m*
primitive   prmitivo
principal   principale
principle   princìpio
prized   pregiato
probable   probàbile
problem   problema *m*
procure   procurare
profession   professione *f*
professor   professore *m*
profit: to profit   approfittare
profundity   profondità *f*
program   programma *m*
prohibitive   proibitivo

promenade passeggio *m*
promise promessa *f*
promontory promontòrio *m*
pronunciation pronuncia *f*
protect protèggere
prove provare
province provincia *f*
provide provvedere
public pùbblico *n m* and *adj*
pull: to pull tirare
pure puro
puree puré
Puritan puritano
purse borsa *f*
put méttere; to put up (*as a guest*) ospitare

Q

quarter quarto *m*
queer originale
question domanda *f*; trick question do-manda a trucco *f*; to ask a question fare una domanda; to be a question of trat-tarsi di
quickly presto
quiet *n* pace *f*

R

railroad ferrovìa *f*; of, pertaining to the railroad ferroviario
rain pioggia *f*; to rain pióvere
raincoat impermeàbile *m*
raise: to raise alzare
rapid ràpido
rapidly in fretta
rather piuttosto
read: to read lèggere
ready pronto
real vero e pròprio
realise réndersi conto (di)
reality realtà *f*
really davvero, pròprio, veramente
reason ragione *f*
recall: to recall (*bring to mind*) rievocare
receipt ricevuta *f*
receive ricévere
recently ultimamente

reception ricevimento *m*
recognise riconóscere
record (*e.g., written document*) ricordo *m*
recount: to recount (*tell*) raccontare
red rosso
reduce ridurre
refreshment rinfresco *m*
refugee sfollato *m*
regard: to regard riguardare
regular regolare
regularly regolarmente
reject: to reject bocciare
relative parente *m* or *f*
religion religione *f*
remain: to remain restare, rimanere, stàrsene
remember ricordare, ricordarsi
Remus Remo *m*
render réndere
rent: to rent noleggiare; to rent out dare a nolo
repeat: to repeat ripétere
replace sostituire
represent rappresentare
representational figurativo
republican repubblicano
request: to request chièdere
research ricerca *f*
resemble somigliare a
reservation (*hotel, etc.*) prenotazione *f*
resolve: to resolve risòlvere
rest riposo *m*; to rest riposare
restaurant ristorante *m*, (*less pretentious*) trattorìa *f*
restoration (*of building*) restaurazione *f*
resuscitate risuscitare
return ritorno *m*; to return (*give back*) rén-dere, (*come or go back*) tornare, ritornare
review (*of book, film, etc.*) recensione *f*; to review (*give a review, e.g. to a film*) fare una recensione di
rid: get rid of tògliersi
right (*hand*) destro, (*accurate, just*) giusto; *adv* pròprio; to (on) the right a destra; to be right aver ragione; right away senz'altro; all right va bene, d'accordo
rise salita *f*; to rise (*go up*) salire
risk rischio *m*

river fiume *m*

road strada *f*; **to take the wrong road** sbagliare strada; **pertaining to roads, of roads** stradale

roasted arrosto *invar*

Robert Roberto *m*

robust robusto

rock roccia *f*

roll (*bread*) panino *m*

Roman romano

Romanesque romànico

Rome Roma *f*

Romulus Ròmolo *m*

room stanza *f*

round tondo; **roundish** tondetto

row (*of seats, etc.*) fila *f*

rowboat pattino *m*

rugged (*of landscape*) aspro

ruin rovina *f*

rush hour ora di punta *f*

rustic campestre

S

sack sacco *m*

sail vela *f*

Saint santo, san *m*, santa *f*

salad insalata *f*

salame salame *m*

sale véndita *f*; **on (cheap) sale** in liquidazione

saleswoman commessa *f*

salon sálone *m*

same: all the same *adv* ugualmente

sand sàbbia *f*

sandwich panino *m*, panino imbottito *m*

Saracen saraceno

sardine sardina *f*

satisfy soddisfare

Saturday sàbato *m*

save (*money, etc.*) risparmiare, (*rescue*) salvare

savings rispàrmio *m*

say dire; **without saying yea or nay** senza dire né tanto né quanto; **to say good-bye to** salutare

scales (*for weighing*) bilancia *f sg*

scarcely appena

scattered sparso

scene scena *f*

scholarship *grant of money*) borsa di stùdio *f*

school scuola *f*

score (*group of twenty*) ventina *f*

sea mare *m*

season stagione *f*

seat (*in theater*) poltrona *f*; (*smaller type of seat*) poltroncina *f*

seated seduto

second *adj* secondo

see: to see vedere; **to see to something** pensare a qualcosa

seek cercare

seem parere, sembrare

seize cògliere

sell: to sell véndere

senator senatore *m*

send mandare, spedire (II/*isc*)

sense senso *m*

sensitivity sensibilità *f*

sentimental sentimentale

sentimentalist sentimentale *m* or *f*

separate: to separate separare

September settembre *m*

sepulchre sepolcro *m*

serious grave, sèrio

serve: to serve servire

session sessione *f*

set: to set fire to incendiare; **to be all set** èssere a posto

seven sette; **seven hundred** settecento; **seven thousand** settemila

seventeen diciassette

seventh sèttimo

seventy settanta

several parecchì (*f pl* parécchie), diversi

sewer fognatura *f*

shadow ombra *f*

shame vergogna *f*; **shame on you! for shame!** *exclam* ohibò!; **what a shame!** che peccato!

sharp (*exactly on time*) in punto

she lei

she-bear orsa *f*

sheep pècora *f*

sheet lenzuòlo *m* (*pl* le lenzuola *f* [*by pairs*], i lenzuoli *m* [*not by pairs*])

ship nave *f*

shoe scarpa *f*

short breve; **in short** insomma

show (*exhibition*) mostra *f*; **to show** dimostrare, indicare

shower doccia *f*

show-window vetrina *f*

shut chiùdere; **shut up** (*be silent*) tacere

sick malato

sickness malanno *m*

sign: to sign firmare

silent silenzioso; **to be silent** tacere

simple sémplice

simply semplicemente

sin peccato *m*

since poiché

sing: to sing cantare

singer cantante *m* or *f*

singing canto *m*

single sìngolo, solo

singular singolare

sir signore *m*

sister sorella *f*; **little sister** sorellina *f*

sister-in-law cognata *f*

sit down accomodarsi

six sei; **six hundred** seicento; **six thousand** seimila

sixteen sédici

sixth sesto

sixty sessanta

size grandezza *f*

ski: to ski sciare

skilled provetto

skin pelle *f*

skirt gonna *f*

sky cielo *m*

slap: big slap schiaffone *m*

sleep: to sleep dormire

sleeping bag sacco a pelo *m*

slip (*sales*) distinta *f*

slender snello

slow lento

small pìccolo

smart (*intelligent*, "*on the ball*") in gamba

smoke: to smoke fumare

snob snob *m*

snow: to snow nevicare

so così; **so-so** così così; **so forth** così via; **so much** tanto

social sociale

society società *f*

sock (*footwear*) calzino *m*

soft *adv* piano

sojourn soggiorno *m*

some *indef adj* alcuni (*f* alcune), qualche (*with singular*) *or use partitive* (Grammar Unit **III**, § 8); *English pronominal use of* **some** *corresponds to the Italian use of* ne *as pro-phrase* (*e.g.*, "I have some" = ne ho)

somebody *indef pronoun* qualcuno

something qualcosa; **something else** altro *m*

son figlio *m*

son-in-law gènero *m*

sonorous sonoro

soon: as soon as appena

soprano soprano *m*

sorry: I'm sorry mi dispiace

sort (*kind*) tipo *m*

soul ànima *f*

speak parlare

special speciale

specialty specialità *f*

species specie *f*

speech discorso *m*

spirit ànimo *m*

spite: in spite of malgrado

splendor splendore *m*

spoil: to spoil sciupare

spoon cucchiaio *m*

sport sport *m*

sporting sportivo

spring (*season*) primavera *f*, (*of water*) sorgente *f*

square (*city plaza*) piazza *f*

squash (*vegetable*) zucchina *f*, (*crush of people*) calca *f*; **to squash** strìngere

squeeze: to squeeze stringere

stair scala *f*

stamp (*postage*) francobollo *m*

stand chiosco *m*; **to stand** (*be located*) stare, (*as opposed to sitting*) stare in piedi, (*suffer, endure*) soffrire, sopportare; **not to be**

able to stand it any longer non fàrcela più

start: to start cominciare, iniziare, méttersi (*a*)

state stato *m*; **the United States** gli Stati Uniti

station stazione *f*

steak bistecca *f*; **grilled steak** bistecca ai ferri

step passo *m*

Stephen Stèfano *m*

still *adv* ancora

stomach stòmaco *m*

stone pietra *f*, (*especially with inscriptions*) làpide *f*

stop fermata *f*; **to stop** (*cease*) sméttere, cessare; **to stop somebody** fermare qualcuno; **to stop oneself** fermarsi; **to stop it** smétterla, farla finita; **to stop up** otturare

store negòzio *m*

storm temporale *m*

straight dritto

strange strano

strawberry fràgola *f*

street via *f*; **sharply descending street** discesa *f*; **sharply rising street** salita *f*

street-car tram *m*

strike: to strike colpire (II/*isc*); **to strike up** (*music, etc.*) attaccare; **to strike in** incùtere

string beans fagiolini *m pl*

strong forte

structure struttura *f*

student studente *m*

study stùdio *m*; **to study** studiare

stupendous stupendo

style stile *m*

substantial sostanzioso

substitute: to substitute sostituire

subterranean sotterràneo

succeed riuscire

such tale

suffer soffrire

suit (*women's clothing*) completo *m*; **bathing suit** costume (da bagno) *m*

suitcase valigia *f*

suited adatto

summer estate *f*

summit cima *f*

sun sole *m*

sun-bath: to take a sun-bath préndere il sole

sundae coppa *f*

Sunday doménica *f*

sunset tramonto *m*

sun-tan tintarella *f*

superb superbo

super-elevation sopraelevazione *f*

superficial superficiale

support: to support (*endure*) sopportare

sure sicuro

surprise sorpresa *f*

surrounding circostante

surroundings (*geographical*) dintorni *m pl*; (*psychological, social, intellectual*) ambient *m sg*

suspect: to suspect sospettare

suspend sospéndere

swear giurare

sweet dolce

sweet-smelling aromàtico

swim: to swim nuotare

symbolise simboleggiare

symphony sinfonìa *f*

system sistema *m*

T

table tàvola *f*, tàvolo *m*

tail coda *f*

take: to take préndere, portare; **taken as a whole** nel complesso

talk: to talk parlare

tanned: to get tanned abbronzarsi

tart torta *f*

taste gusto *m*

tax tassa *f*

taxi tassì *m*

tea té *m*

teach insegnare

teacher professore *m*

telephone telèfono *m*; **to telephone** telefonare

tell raccontare

temple tèmpio *m*
temporarily temporaneamente
ten dieci; (**a group of**) **about ten** diecina *f*; **ten thousand** diecimila
tenor tenore *m*
tent tenda *f*
tenth dècimo
tepid tièpido
terminate terminare
terrace terrazza *f*
terrain terreno *m*
text testo *m*
thanks, thank you grazie *f pl*
that *dem adj, pron* quello; *conj* che; **that is** cioè
the *def art* il, lo, la, l' *sg*; i, gli, le *pl*
them *3 pl disjv obj pron* loro; *3 pl conjv dir obj pron* li *m*, le *f*
themselves *3 pers refl disjv obj pron* sé; *3 pers refl conjv obj pron* si
their *3 sg poss pron* loro (*invar*)
them *3 pl disjv pers pron* loro; *3 pl m conjv dir obj pron* li; *3 pl f conjv dir obj pron* le
then allora
Theodora Teodora *f*
there *adv* lì, là; *pro-phrase* ci; **down there, over there** laggiù; **there is, there are** (*pointing something out*) ecco; **there is** (*telling of something's existence*) c'è; **there are** (*telling of something's existence*) ci sono
they *3 pl disjv pers pron* loro
thing cosa *f*; **it's a good thing** meno male
think pensare
third terzo
thirst sete *f*
thirteen trédici
thirty trenta
this *adj, pron* questo; *pron* esso; **this morning** stamattina
Thomas Tommaso *m*
thought pensiero *m*
thousand mille; (**group of**) **about a thousand** migliaio *m* (*pl* le migliaia *f*)
three tre; **three hundred** trecento; **three thousand** tremila
thrill: to thrill emozionare
throat gola *f*

throne trono *m*
Thursday giovedì *m*
thus così
Tiber Tévere *m*
ticket biglietto *m*; **to get one's ticket** fare il biglietto
ticket-window sportello *m*
tight stretto
tile mattone *m*
time tempo *m*; (*occasion*) volta *f*; (*time of day*) ora *f*; **time of year** stagione *f*; època *f*; **once upon a time** un tempo; **with the passage of time** con l'andar del tempo; **to have a good time** divertirsi; **on time** in oràrio
time-table oràrio *m*
tip (*money given to servant*) mancia *f*
tired stanco; **dead tired** stanco morto
tiresome noioso
to a, ad
tobacco tabacco *m*
tobacconist tabaccaio *m*
today oggi
together insieme; **together with** insieme a(d)
toilet gabinetto *m*
Tom Maso *m*
tomato pomodoro *m* (*pl* i pomodori *or* i pomidoro)
tomb tomba *f*; **life beyond the tomb** oltretomba *m*
Tommy Masuccio *m*
tomorrow domani
tonality tonalità *f*
too (*also*) anche; (*excessively*) *adv* troppo; **too bad !** *exclam* peccato !; **too much** troppo; **too many** troppi *m pl*, troppe *f pl*
tooth dente *m*
top cima *f*; **on top of** in cima a
totally totalmente
town città *f*, paese *m*; **in, to town** in città
track binàrio *m*
traffic tràffico *m*
train treno *m*
Trajan Traiano *m*
tranquil tranquillo
transportation trasporto *m*
travel: to travel viaggiare

traveller viaggiatore *m*; **traveller's cheque** assegno viaggiatori *m*
treasure tesoro *m*
tree àlbero *m*
tremendous tremendo
trick trucco *m*
trolley-bus fìlobus *m*
trouble malanno *m*
troublesome laborioso
Troy Troia *f*
trip viaggio *m*, giro *m*
true vero
truly veramente
truth verità *f*
try: to try cercare, provare, tentare
Tuesday martedì *m*
tufa tufo *m*
tufa-like, of tufa tufàceo
turn giro *m*
Tuscan toscano
twelve dódici
twenty venti; **(group of) about twenty** ventina *f*
twins gemelli *m pl*
two due; **two hundred** duecento; **two thousand** duemila
type tipo *m*

U

Uffizi (*art gallery in Florence*) gli Uffizi *m pl*
ugly brutto
umbrella umbrello *m*
uncle zio *m*; **aunt and uncle** zii *m pl*
uncomfortable scòmodo
undergo subire (II/*isc*)
underground *adj* sotterràneo
understand capire (II/*isc*); **not to understand anything** non capire un bel niente
undertaking impresa *f*
undoubtedly senz'altro
undulation ondulatura *f*
unexpected impensato
unfortunately purtroppo
unite unire (II/*isc*)
United States Stati Uniti *m pl*
university università *f*
unknown sconosciuto

uphill in salita
us *1 pl disjv pers pron* noi; *1 pl conjv pers pron* ci
use: to use usare
usual sòlito; **as usual** al sòlito; **than usual** del sòlito
utensil utensile *m*

V

vacation vacanza *f*
vacationer villeggiante *m*
valuable pregiato
value valore *m*
variety varietà *f*
various vàrio
vary variare
vegetables (*accompanying a meat dish*) contorno *m*
very molto
Vespasian Vespasiano *m*
vessel (*pitcher etc.*) vaso *m*
vestibule vestìbolo *m*
vice vìzio *m*
vice-versa viceversa
view vista *f*
village: little village paesino *m*
violent violento
vision visione *f*
visit: to visit visitare
vocal vocale
voice voce *f*; **in a low voice** a bassa voce, sottovoce
vote: to vote votare
voter votante *m or f*

W

wait: to wait (for) aspettare; **not to be able to wait until** non veder l'ora di
waiter cameriere *m*
walk passeggiata *f*; **to walk** camminare; **to take a little walk** fare quattro passi
wall muro *m* (*pl* le mura *f* [*city walls*], i muri *m* [*house walls*]); (*of a room*) parete *f*; **big wall** muraglione *m*; **encircling walls** (*of a city*) mura di cinta *f pl*

want   volere

war   guerra *f*; **World War** guerra mondiale *f*; **war refugee** sfollato *m*

warehouse   empòrio *m*

warm   caldo

warmly   con calore

warmth   calore *m*

wash: to wash   lavare

water   acqua *f*

wax match   cerino *m*

way (*street, road*) strada *f*, via *f*; (*manner*) maniera *f*; **by the way** a propòsito; **along the way** per la strada; **on the way** in viaggio; **"in a bad way"** (*in bad shape*) ridotto male

we   noi

weapon   arma *f* (*pl* le armi)

Wednesday   mercoledì *m*

week   settimana *f*

weep: to weep   piàngere

weigh   pesare

welcome   benvenuto; **welcome back** ben tornato; **you're welcome** prego

well   bene; **very well** benìssimo; **very well indeed** benone

what *interr pron* che ? cosa ?; *interr pron phr* che cosa ?; *interr adj* che, (*which* ?) quale; **what a ... !** *exclam* che ... !; **what a nuisance !** *exclam* uffa !

when   quando

where   dove

whether   se

which *rel pron* che; *poss, dat* cùi; *interr pron, adj* quale ?

while   mentre

whipped cream   panna *f*

whisper: to whisper   bisbigliare

white   bianco

who, whom *interr pron* chi ?; *rel pron* che; **to whom** *dat rel pron* cùi

whole: taken as a whole, on the whole nel complesso

whose *rel pron* cùi, di cùi; *interr pron* di chi ?

wife   moglie *f*

wind   vento *m*; **the wind is blowing** tira vento

window (*of train*) finestrino *m*; **show-window** vetrina *f*; **ticket-window** sportello *m*

wine   vino *m*

winter   inverno *m*

"wise guy"   spiritoso *m*

wish: to wish   volere

with   con

withdraw   ritirare

without   senza

witty   spiritoso

woman   donna *f*

wonderful   stupendo

wool   lana *f*

word   parola *f*; **in "words of one syllable"** in parole pòvere

work   lavoro *m*, òpera *f*; **to work** lavorare

World War   guerra mondiale *f*

world-wide   mondiale

worry: to worry (*oneself*) preoccuparsi

worse *adj* peggiore, *adv* peggio

worship   culto *m*

worth   valore *m*

write   scrìvere

Y

year   anno *m*

yearning   nostalgìa *f*

yellow   giallo; **to grow yellow** ingiallire

yes   sì; **yes indeed** (*passive assent*) già

yesterday   ieri

yet   ancora

yield: to yield   concèdere

you   2 *sg subj pers pron* tu; 2 *sg disjv obj* te; 2 *sg conjv obj* ti; 2 *pl subj, obj disjv* voi; 2 *pl conjv obj* vi; 3 *sg subj, disjv obj* Lei; 3 *sg conjv dir obj* La; 3 *sg conjv dat* Le; 3 *pl subj, disjv dir obj, poss, dat* Loro; 3 *pl m conjv dir obj* Li; 3 *pl f conjv dir obj* Le

young   gióvane; **young lady** signorina *f*

your *poss adj* tuo 2 *sg*, vostro 2 *pl*, suo 3 *sg*; *poss pron* Loro 3 *pl* (*invar*)

you're welcome   prego

INDEX

Address, formal and informal § 7

Adjectives: comparative § 27; demonstrative § 13; in **-ante -ente,** on verbs § 67; indicating extremes, subjunctive with § 71; irregular § 12; ordinal § 57; possessive § 14; prepositions after § 81; regular § 12; superlative § 27

Adverbs: comparative § 27; in **-mente** § 35; superlative § 27

Agent, complement of § 72

Apocope § 49

Article, definite § 2; in generic meaning § 47; with prepositions § 4

Article, indefinite § 1

Augmentative suffixes § 76

Automatic replacements: in combinations of pro-complements § 23; in compound past of reflexive verbs § 40

Automatic uses of subjunctive § 56, 64

Auxiliaries: in compound past § 29; modal, present of § 11; with reflexive verbs § 40

Causative phrases § 73

Clauses, dependent, transformations of § 65

Collectives on numerals § 58

Commands, subjunctive in § 25

Comparative of adjectives and adverbs § 27

Comparison, term of § 27, 61

Compound past tenses § 29, 54; of reflexive verbs § 40

Conditional tense § 45

Conjugations: First § 9; Second § 15; Third § 16; sample verbs pp. ix-xi

Conjunctions, pre-vocalic forms of § 59

Conjunctive pronouns: direct object § 18; direct + indirect object § 37; indirect object § 18; reflexive § 19

conóscere, use of § 22

Consonants pp. ii-v; "impure" and "pure" § 1

da, present tense with § 32; uses of § 72, 80

Dative: conjunctive pronouns § 18; of person affected § 51

Definite article § 2; in generic meaning § 47; with prepositions § 4

Demonstrative adjectives § 13

Dependent clauses, transformations of § 65

Diminutives § 48

Direct object pronouns § 18

Disjunctive pronouns § 36

ecco with pro-compliments § 52

Elision § 63

Exclamations § 75

Extremes, adjectives indicating, subjunctive with § 71

fare: with impersonal meteorological expressions § 74; with other constructions § 79

Formal address § 7

Future: forms § 31; of probability § 70

il quale as relative pronoun phrase § 55

Imperatives § 24

Imperfect § 38

Impersonal constructions: pro-complements with impersonal **si** § 69; reflexive verbs, impersonal-passive use of § 20

"Impure" consonants § 1

Indefinite article § 1

Indirect object pronouns § 18

Infinitives: first conjugation § 9; second conjugation § 15; third conjugation § 16; verb + preposition + infinitive § 68

Inflection of substantives and verbs pp. vii-xvi

Informal address § 7

Interrogative pronouns § 44

Irregular verbs pp. xi-xvi

Lei in formal address § 7

-mente, adverbs in § 35

Modal auxiliaries, present of § 11

Modal verb phrases § 11; pro-compliments in § 66

Negatives § 46

Nouns: plural (irregular) § 26, 33; plural of masculine nouns in **-a** 34; plural (regular) § 3, 34; with m. sg. in **-o** and f. pl. in **-a** § 34

Numerals: cardinal pp. 11, 19, 49; collectives on § 58; ordinal § 57

Object pronouns: conjunctive § 18; disjunctive § 36

Ordinal numeral adjectives § 57

parere with subjunctive § 77

Participles: past § 28, 39; present § 41

Partitive § 8

Passive § 72; impersonal-passive use of reflexive verbs § 20

Past participle § 28; agreement in compound past with **avere** § 39

Past tenses: compound past § 29, 54, (reflexive of) § 40; imperfect § 38; past absolute § 50; past subjunctive § 64, 78

Pejorative suffixes § 76

Perfect phrases § 29, 54

piacere, use of § 21

Plural of nouns: irregular § 26, 33; regular § 3, 34

Possessives § 14

Prepositions and prepositional phrases § 62; after adjectives § 81; pre-vocalic forms § 59; with definite article § 4; with verbs and dependent infinitives § 68

Present participle § 41

Present: first conjugation § 9; modal auxiliaries § 11; second conjugation § 15; third conjugation § 16; with **da** "since" § 32

Present of individual verbs: **andare** § 17; **avere** § 10; **dare** § 17; **dire** § 17; **èssere** § 5; **fare** § 17; **stare** § 6; **tenere** § 30; **uscire** § 30

Pre-vocalic forms of prepositions and conjunctions § 59

Pro-complements § 23; in modal phrases § 66; with **ecco** § 52

Progressive phrases § 42

Pronouns, interrogative § 44

Pronouns, personal: conjunctive § 18; direct object § 18; disjunctive § 36; indirect object § 18; reflexive § 19

Pronouns, relative § 44; phrases § 55

Pronunciation pp. ii-v

Pro-Phrases § 23

"Pure" Consonants § 1

quale (il) as relative pronoun phrase § 55

Reflexive: compound past of § 40; impersonal-passive use of § 20; pronouns § 19; verb phrases § 19

Relative pronouns § 44; phrases § 55

sapere, use of § 22

sembrare with subjunctive § 77

stare in progressive phrases § 42

Subject pronouns § 36

Subjunctive: automatic uses of § 56, 64; in commands § 25; meaningful uses of § 60, 64; past subjunctive, forms of § 64; present subjunctive, forms of § 53; with adjectives indicating extremes § 71; with **come se** or **quasi** § 78; with **sembrare** and **parere** § 77

Substantive Inflection p. vii

Suffixes: augmentative § 76; diminutive § 48; pejorative § 76

Superlative of adjectives and adverbs § 27

Term of comparison § 27, 61

Transformations of dependent clauses § 65

Verbs: adjectives in **-ante -ente** formel on verbs § 67; causative phrases § 73; commands § 24, 25; **fare,** uses of § 74, 79; irregular pp. xi-xvi; modal auxiliaries § 11; passive phrases § 72; perfect phrases § 29, 40, 54, 72; progressive phrases § 42; reflexive § 19, 20, 40; with preposition and infinitive § 68

Vowels p. ii